Blessed Rage for Order

Blessed Rage for Order

The New Pluralism in Theology

David Tracy

1817

HARPER & ROW, PUBLISHERS, SAN FRANCISCO

Cambridge, New York, Philadelphia
London, Mexico City, São Paulo, Singapore, Sydney

Grateful acknowledgement is made to Alfred A. Knopf, Inc., for permission to quote from "The Idea of Order at Key West," from *The Collected Poems of Wallace Stevens*.

Harper & Row, Publishers, Inc.
10 East 53rd Street
New York, NY 10022

LIBRARY OF CONGRESS CATALOGING IN PUBLICATION DATA

Tracy, David.
    Blessed rage for order.

    Includes index.
    1. Theology—20th century. 2. Religion and language. I. Title.
BT28.T65   230   75–8803
ISBN 0-8164-0277-9
ISBN 0-8164-2202-8 pbk.

Fourth printing

To my mother
Eileen Marie Rossell Tracy Couch

Ramon Fernandez, tell me, if you know,
Why, when the singing ended and we turned
Toward the town, Tell why the glassy lights,
The lights in the fishing boats at anchor there,
As the night descended, tilting in the air,
Mastered the night and portioned out the sea,
Fixing emblazoned zones and fiery poles,
Arranging, deepening, enchanting night.

Oh! Blessed rage for order, pale Ramon,
The maker's rage to order words of the sea,
Words of the fragrant portals, dimly-starred,
And of ourselves and of our origins,
In ghostlier demarcations, keener sounds.

Wallace Stevens, *The Idea of Order at Key West*

Contents

ix

10. *HISTORY, THEORY, AND* PRAXIS

A Word of Thanks in Place of a Preface

In the hope that the first chapter serves to preface the problematic structure of this book, I shall take the liberty of omitting the traditional preface. What I cannot omit, however, is my inadequate thanks to the many colleagues and students whose criticisms and encouragements have impelled this book into print. Among the many who deserve my public thanks, allow me to mention merely the few: my friends, both colleagues and students at The University of Chicago Divinity School, who have endured and helpfully criticized the earlier versions of this book in its various settings, especially Dean Joseph Kitagawa, Brian Gerrish, Langdon Gilkey, James Gustafson, Bernard McGinn, Schubert Ogden, Norman Perrin and Paul Ricoeur; my many colleagues and friends elsewhere who have likewise endured, and also contributed their critical reflections, especially David Burrell, Hugh Corrigan, Mary Gerhart, Joseph Komonchak, Andrew Greeley, Matthew Lamb, Karen Laub-Novak, Michael Novak, and William Warthling. For the hard-pressed labors and always constructive critical suggestions of the editors and their assistants at The Seabury Press, my thanks, especially to Justus George Lawler, Francis Oveis, and John Huckle. Finally to the several institutions which have honored me over the last three years by listening to earlier versions of various sections of this book, my appreciation for their critical reflections, especially to the Catholic University of America, Cathedral College at Douglaston, Harvard Divinity School, Hobart and William Smith Colleges, St. John's University at Collegeville, Niagara Community College, Princeton Theological Seminary, St. Louis University, The Thomas More Lectureship Committee at Yale, and the University of San Francisco.

Chapter three represents a revised version of The Dudleian Lecture at Harvard and chapters two, five, and six, a revised and partial version of the Thomas More lectures at Yale, the Breslin lecture at Douglaston, and the Bellarmine lecture at St. Louis. I hope the revisions from these lectures suggest, even if they do not satisfy, my efforts at attempting the kind of critical collaboration for which this entire book pleads and to which my many critics on those occasions greatly contributed.

My final thanks go to the splendid persons who helped organize, index, and type this work: to Prof. Mary J. Gerhart for the painstaking index, and to Mrs. Rehova Arthur, Ms. Jan Stickney, and my tireless and selfless mother, Mrs. Eileen Couch, for the typing.

I should mention many others as well. But I trust that each of them will know that my gratitude, though inadequate, is real. A final word: I have tried to listen to and, where possible, absorb the many kind and critical remarks of the thinkers listed above. But, at the final moment (as for any one of them), I must assume the full responsibility for my own judgments. I do not imagine that any one of them agrees with every position in this book. Yet I do hope that each will see that, here and there, I have listened and, perhaps, even learned. But that is another story—and this was to be a word of thanks, not a preface.

Chicago, September, 1974

Blessed Rage for Order

Part I

Chapter 1

The Pluralist Context
of Contemporary Theology

INTRODUCTION: Pluralism and Revision

That the present situation in theology is one of an ever-increasing pluralism is by now a truism.[1] That such a pluralist condition enriches the possibilities for theology would seem at least equally clear and true. For a theologian to accept the present pluralism as a state of pure enrichment, of gratuitous and untarnished blessing, is another matter entirely. Certainly, the richness of imagination which these various theologies, these several ways of envisioning the world, offer to the theologian can be counted pure gain. However, can theology afford to relax into that attitude of lazy intellectual "tolerance" with which Marxists and Christians alike have charged our consumer society?[2] Is such a merely pluralist attitude worthy either of a serious intellectual commitment or of the traditional Christian claim to illuminate the meaning and truth of our common humanity?[3]

The present work operates on two principal assumptions. The first assumption insists that the present pluralism of theologies allows each theologian to learn incomparably more about reality by disclosing really different ways of viewing both our common humanity and Christianity. Throughout this book I shall appeal to several theological traditions for their insights into some single or multiple facet of our common situation. In order to assure that such an affirmation of pluralism does not result in that kind of consumer-tolerance familiar to "the unhappy conscience" of the modern pluralist intellectual, or in a common-sense eclecticism that can mask intellectual chaos,[4] I shall employ a second assumption about the present situation. That assumption holds that each theologian must attempt to articulate and defend an explicit method of inquiry, and use that method to interpret the symbols and texts[5] of our common life and of Christianity. More summarily stated, each theologian must take a stand on both the basic formal methodological and material constructive issues which face us all.[6] That stand should be taken as explicitly and as systematically as present resources will allow. Finally, that stand should take a self-consciously revisionist attitude[7] toward the major present alternative models for a contemporary Christian theology.[8] For such reasons, this present work will risk both an interpretation of the presently existing models for theology and an

3

initial defense of a proposed revisionist model which may prove more adequate to the present crisis of theological self-understanding.

Before those principal tasks are attempted, one must first try to understand the basic dimensions of the crises which plague the very attempt to theologize with integrity today. In the rather global terms appropriate to this initial description, I shall first attempt a summary-analysis of the cognitive, ethical, and existential crises which confront any theologian who finds himself or herself personally committed to both the modern experiment and to the Christian vision of human possibilities.[9]

The full dimensions of those crises can only, I fear, be summarily analyzed throughout this entire book. Yet an initial attempt can be made in this chapter by delineating that strange *pathos* which seems to characterize both the crisis of meaning and the struggle for an authentic humanity operative in our contemporary period.[10] For many, perhaps most of those intellectuals who have experienced and analyzed this present Western, indeed global crisis of meaning, Christianity has exactly nothing to offer for its possible resolution. For others, however, Christianity, if critically reinterpreted, still bears a real hope for a meaningful vision upon our common life. A successful articulation of that vision, however, depends upon the individual theologian's ability to experience and to understand both the crisis of meaning of traditional Christianity in the modern "post-Christian" period and the present crisis of traditional modernity in the contemporary "post-modern" world.[11] If this dilemma is experienced, it cannot but become a theologian's preoccupation, "haunting one's dreams like a guilty romance." Authentic theological attempts at revision do not really stem from a too often meretricious desire for "relevance." [12] The reality of the situation is both more simple and more basic: when all is said and done, one finds that he can authentically abandon neither his faith in the modern experiment nor his faith in the God of Jesus Christ.[13] Anyone who experiences at all such a seemingly unenviable condition finds the attempt to theologize pure necessity.[14] For anyone who correctly understands the full dimensions of that experience, neither traditional Christian self-understanding nor recent modern self-understanding nor any combination thereof will suffice to resolve that dual dilemma. Only a basic revision of traditional Christianity and traditional modernity alike would seem to suffice. Before such a revision is attempted, I shall try to outline those distinct but related crises of meaning which both the Christian and the modern traditions have undergone.

THE CRISIS OF THE CHRISTIAN THEOLOGIAN IN THE MODERN WORLD: The Disenchantment with Mystifications

The forces for demystification of the Western religious world-view were set loose by the Enlightenment's demand for freedom from oppressive authorities and freedom for autonomous, critical, rational thought.[15] Such forces were eventually institutionalized when the soon all-encompassing process of secularization took root in the basic vision and the academic institutions of Western intellectuals.[16] Traditional Western Christianity in its major Catholic and Protestant forms[17] soon felt the full force of this demand for rationality; as its most cherished cognitive, ethical, and existential beliefs were examined by the new methods of the now autonomous and soon dominant natural and social sciences, the historical disciplines,[18] the new philosophies, and the new ethical systems. Western Christians, insofar as they too shared that commitment to truth which Christianity and Enlightenment alike preached as the only authentic way of life, soon experienced that demand for wholesale demystification of the Christian religion which issued forth in the experience described by Max Weber with stoic resignation as "the disenchantment of the world." [19] The principal question became whether such methods of rational analysis must simply lay waste the once rich and mythical imagination and style of life of Western Christians.[20] Alternatively, could that mode of rational analysis, itself initially fostered by the basic Christian vision of the world,[21] become the occasion for a process that would both eliminate the merely mystifying components of that vision and yet restore with contemporary integrity Christianity's central vision of God and humanity? [22] The struggle of modern theology has been largely the struggle to see how and in what fashion that latter claim can be upheld. The struggle eventually reached the stage of challenging every important cognitive claim of the Christian tradition, every major ethical stance it traditionally proclaimed, and, at its limit, the most basic understanding of exactly what the fundamental existential faith of Christians really meant.[23] This section will have as its principal task the documentation of some typical instances of that struggle in the cognitive, ethical, and existential realms respectively.[24]

Clearly the most obvious crisis was what the Victorians called the "crisis of belief" but which can now be designated the crisis of cognitive claims.[25] Most Christians now recognize that much of the traditional Christian manner of understanding the cognitive claims made in the Christian scriptures should be rejected by the findings of history and of the natural and human sciences.[26] To continue to uphold a literal interpretation of the Genesis account is simply and irrevocably impossible for anyone who accepts the findings of the modern physical and life sciences. To continue to believe a literalist theory of scriptural inspiration seems no longer an option to anyone who has investigated the results of modern historical study of the scriptures.[27] The list of such cognitive crises could be expanded almost indefinitely. As the principal sections of this book shall argue, the list includes even the traditional Christian cognitive claims for its central symbols of revelation, God, and Christ. Even more basic for modern

Christians than the familiar crisis of knowledge are the ethical and existential crises which that cognitive crisis discloses.

As Van Harvey argues persuasively in *The Historian and the Believer*,[28] the basic clash underlying the claims and counter-claims of traditional Christianity and the modern sciences has been a clash of moralities. The traditional Christian theologian, of whatever tradition, preached and practiced a morality of belief in and obedience to the tradition and a fundamental loyalty to the church-community's beliefs. The modern historian and scientist—whether in the natural or social sciences—preaches and practices an exactly contrary morality. For him, one cannot investigate a cognitive claim with intellectual integrity if one insists simultaneously that the claim is believable because the tradition has believed it. For the new scientific morality, one's fundamental loyalty as an analyst of any and all cognitive claims is solely to those methodological procedures which the particular scientific community of inquiry in question has developed. This "morality of scientific knowledge" insists that each inquirer start with the present methods and knowledge of the field in question, unless one has evidence of the same logical type for rejecting those methods and that knowledge. Many traditional Christians have asserted that this "scientific" moral presupposition is at least as "arbitrary" as their own moral presupposition in favor of traditional belief.[29] Yet the moral dilemma for the Christian is really not so easily resolved. The scientific morality, unlike the traditional Christian one, leaves room *in principle* for the overthrow of present scientific methods, paradigms, and conclusions.[30] The scientific attitude makes only the ethical demand that every progress in knowledge must be made by the advancement of critical evidence for or against the present reigning theories, methods, and paradigms.

The ethical dilemma of the Christian theologian in such a situation is both painful and clear. Traditionally, his fundamental loyalty was to the church-community of which he was a believing member. His second—but real—loyalty was to whatever community of inquiry[31] (usually philosophy) aided him to defend and to reinterpret the tradition's beliefs for his contemporaries. Now all seems changed. The modern theologian ordinarily shares the morality of scientific knowledge of his contemporaries. He recognizes that such a commitment imposes the ethical duty to provide the proper kind of evidence for whatever claim he advances. He recognizes further that the announcement of his own tradition's beliefs does not and cannot constitute such evidence for his fellow community of historical or philosophical inquirers—*or even for himself* as one committed to the morality of autonomous critical inquiry implicit in the canons and methods of the discipline in question. He approves, in fact commits himself to, that ethical model of the autonomous inquirer which the new morality discloses. In several cases, as in the paradigmatic case of Paul Tillich, the modern theologian wishes to challenge the adequacy of that modern ethical model. Still, the challenge will not include a plea for the return to that heteronomous model rejected by the new morality. Rather, that challenge will be made on the same scientific grounds, with the same kind of arguments and evidence advanced. The basic argument will take the form of some new model (a theonomous one for Tillich) which accounts more adequately for our moral experience as authentic inquirers.[32]

In fact, the modern Christian theologian cannot ethically do other than challenge the traditional self-understanding of the theologian.[33] He no longer sees his task as a simple defense of or even as an orthodox[34] reinterpretation of traditional belief. Rather, he finds that his ethical commitment to the morality of scientific knowledge forces him to assume a critical posture towards his own and his tradition's beliefs. He insists, to be sure, that the concept "critical" does not bear a simply negative meaning. But critical does mean a fidelity to open-ended inquiry, a loyalty to defended methodological canons, a willingness to follow the evidence wherever it may lead. Such conclusions may, in fact, negate a particular traditional belief; they may find that the belief simply needs rearticulation for a different cultural setting; they may find that the belief is as true today as it was when first proclaimed. In any and every case, the fundamental ethical commitment of the theologian *qua* theologian remains to that community of scientific inquiry whose province logically includes whatever issue is under investigation.[35]

On the other hand, the Christian theologian's basic loyalty to his church tradition can be formulated as his honest resolve to study that tradition critically and thereby aid its self-understanding. A sociologist of religion, a historian of religion, a philosopher of religion, need not resolve to commit himself to an explicit study of the Christian religion. The Christian theologian, by professional and, thereby, ethical commitment, has resolved to study that tradition's past and present claims to meaning and truth. Ordinarily he will choose to do so because he has committed himself to a Christian self-understanding. Yet, in principle, such commitment need not be the case. In principle, the fundamental loyalty of the theologian *qua* theologian is to that morality of scientific knowledge which he shares with his colleagues, the philosophers, historians, and social scientists. No more than they, can he allow his own—or his tradition's—beliefs to serve as warrants for his arguments.[36] In fact, in all properly theological inquiry, the analysis should be characterized by those same ethical stances of autonomous judgment, critical reflection, and properly skeptical hard-mindedness that characterize analysis in other fields. However, even this brief delineation of the "ethical crisis" of the modern Christian theologian does not do full justice to the dimensions of the actual situation. For those dimensions, one must study the self-understanding of the basic "faith" which is operative for the modern Christian theologian.

In the realms of knowledge and ethical action alike, the contemporary Christian theologian often finds himself on the side of the secular criticism levelled at many of the expressions of traditional Christianity. To be sure, eventually the Enlightenment models for humanity's critical knowledge and ethical action were themselves challenged in favor of a model of contemporary "authenticity." Yet even this factor ordinarily does not lead many contemporary Christian theologians to a simple return to traditional beliefs or loyalties. Instead, this "post-modern" spirit leads to a deeper clarification of the full implications of the formerly "modern" and now "contemporary" secular struggle for authentic and full-scale human liberation. It is true that the classical post-modern critiques of Enlightenment "illusion" expressed in the life-works of such thinkers as Freud, Marx, and Nietzsche called into serious question the naively rationalist claim of the Age of Enlightenment.[37] These "masters of suspicion" forever cast doubt on the belief that the solitary autonomous rational thinker could achieve, much less had already achieved, "enlightenment." What remains constant in the shift from modernity to post-modernity is the fact that such contemporary critiques of modernity deepen the fundamental commitment to those purely secular standards for knowledge and action initiated by the Enlightenment. Indeed the shift from what Lionel Trilling has delineated as the model of modern "sincerity" to the post-modern model of contemporary "authenticity" has only served to clarify that basic commitment.[38] The "authentic" person is committed above all else to the full affirmation of the ultimate significance of our lives in this world.

Such a fundamental commitment can be described as a faith, i.e., as a basic orientation or attitude which determines one's cognitive beliefs and one's individual ethical actions. The most basic expression of such faith, moreover, is probably best described as the faith of secularity: that fundamental attitude which affirms the ultimate significance and final worth of our lives, our thoughts, and actions, here and now, in nature and in history. An explicit and full recognition of this faith as, in fact, *the* common faith shared by secularist and modern Christian is perhaps the most important insight needed to understand the contemporary theological situation in its full dimensions and its real possibilities.[39]

The modern theologian of the kind described above is not merely a theologian intellectually troubled by certain traditional Christian cognitive beliefs, nor even is he just ethically disturbed by the imperatives to obedience or the presumptions for belief which traditional theological practice manifested. Rather, that theologian finds that his basic faith, his fundamental attitude towards reality, is the same faith shared implicitly or explicitly by his secular contemporaries. No more than they, can he allow belief in a "supernatural" realm[40] of ultimate significance or in a supernatural God who seems, in the end, indifferent to the ultimate significance of our actions. Such beliefs do not represent his faith, his basic understanding of existence, his fundamental commitments. Critics outside this theological circle—church leaders and secular thinkers alike—have often commented that such a theologian, if really committed to honesty, should abandon all claims to the title "Christian" as a legitimate self-description. As expressed by Sidney Hook's ironic suggestion that Paul Tillich was really the agnostics' "Trojan horse in the camp of the Christians," [41] the ready judgment (upon such "revisionist" theologians) by either their Christian or their secularist critics is that they are at best muddled and at worst dishonest in their own presumably Christian self-understanding.

As these criticisms suggest, why not simply abandon this strange theological enterprise altogether? Why not put one's talents fully at the disposal of those movements which claim clearly that one's fundamental faith lies in the struggle to render concrete in thought and action the ultimate significance of our lives here and now? Yet what the secularist critics[42] seem to fail utterly to comprehend is the fact that the Christian theologian holds that a proper understanding of the explicitly Christian faith can render intellectually coherent and symbolically powerful that common secular faith which we share.[43] The revisionist theologian's fundamental claim is not that he happens to be Christian or that he personally finds attractive the Christian symbols as imaginative understandings of our common destiny. Rather, his claim is that nothing less than a proper understanding of those central beliefs—in "revelation," in "God," in "Jesus Christ"—can provide an adequate understanding, a correct "reflective inventory," or an existentially appropriate symbolic representation of the fundamental faith of secularity. Indeed such theologians believe that they can provide evidence to fair-minded critics inside and outside Christianity for the meaning and truth of the central Christian symbols.[44] They believe, as we shall see below, that neither supernaturalism nor pure secularism, neither classical theism nor atheism, neither an exclusivist christology nor the rejection of Jesus the Christ can allow us to reflect appropriately or to represent adequately our fundamental faith in the ultimate worthwhileness of our present action.

More specifically, such theologians wish to deny the purely secularist negation of any real ground of meaning outside ourselves which assures us that our faith is not simply illusion. They also intend to negate any essentially positivist "revelational" affirmation of our supposed ability to transcend this faith in this world in favor of some presumably greater, indeed supernatural world. They believe that neither secularism nor supernaturalism can adequately reflect or appropriately ensure our commitment to the final worthwhileness of the struggle for truth and honesty in our inquiry, and for justice and even agapic love in our individual and social practice. In sum, the contemporary Christian theologian is unable to share many of the traditional Christian self-understandings precisely because he believes that such understanding negates the fundamental faith of his life as that very faith is appropriately expressed in the true faith of Christianity itself.

The same theologian cannot share the secularist self-understanding of the secular affirmation of the ultimate worth of our lives in nature and history for precisely the same reason. For that latter understanding, he argues, is inconsistent with the fundamental faith which it reflects.[45] In keeping with both the basic cognitive criteria and ethical attitudes of secularity, the secularist must, to be consistent, heed the charge that his rejections of theism and Christianity are neither coherent in themselves nor able to provide a reflective account of our common experience as involving either explicitly or implicitly an affirmation of the final worthwhileness of existence.[46] That is precisely the claim which the revisionist theologian asks his secularist colleagues to note. As we shall see in the discussions of religion,[47] theism, and christology below, such theologians believe that only a coherent articulation of the reality of the Christian God can provide an adequate reflective account of both the unavoidable presuppositions of our inquiry and our moral activity, and of the basic faith in the final meaningfulness of an authentic life which secularity itself has articulated with such power.

This, in brief outline, is the situation of the modern Christian theologian. He finds himself disenchanted with the mystifications promulgated by too many church officials and the mystifications proclaimed with equal certitude by the secularist self-understanding of the age. He believes he shares the basic Christian faith of the former and the secular faith of the latter. Indeed, he believes that the Christian faith is at heart none other than the most adequate articulation of the basic faith of secularity itself. He also realizes that his understanding of Christianity must take a revisionist form which takes proper account of the cognitive, ethical, and existential crises of much traditional Christian self-understanding. No longer can his secular faith find adequate articulation through the model for rational reflection developed by the Age of Enlightenment. Rather, that model must yield to one which can account for those insights developed since the "liberal" period and simultaneously negate those illusions of liberal secularity which both recent history and recent reflection have brought to light.

THE CRISIS OF THE MODERN SECULAR MIND: The
Disenchantment with Disenchantment

How is one to delineate the post-modern (i.e., post-liberal), secular situation in those cognitive, ethical, and existential realms which we have already seen operative in the modern Christian theological situation? Initially, this change may be more readily apparent in the more significant differences between the "modern" and "post-modern" or "contemporary" models for humanity. The primary model for modernity, paradigmatically expressed in Peter Gay's image of David Hume as a "modern pagan" [48] and in Immanuel Kant's programmatic essay *What is Enlightenment?*, discloses an autonomous and lonely critic who rejects the oppressive tutelage of established authorities and dares to impose methods of rational inquiry upon any and all subject-matters. As "enlightened," this modern intellectual feels not merely free from tradition but morally obliged to develop a rational model for human possibility. As a "modern pagan" the modern intellectual feels free from the oppressive weight of Western Christianity's traditional moral norms. He also feels free to retrieve, in modern form, classical paganism's restrained and rational attitude towards the possibilities of self-fulfillment. Many modern intellectuals, as social analysts, believe that the wholesale application of scientific methods to natural and human reality is the surest way to assure progress and to actualize the responsible and enlightened human being on a societal level.[49] In explicitly theological form, the recently influential analysis of Harvey Cox's *Secular City* or the more radical analysis in Paul van Buren's *The Secular Meaning of the Gospel* evoke the same image, albeit now with Christian overtones, of modernity's model of the rational man finally "come of age." [50]

Such a restrainedly optimistic portrait of the rational man's individual and societal possibilities does not in fact fit the post-modern model of humankind. On the one hand, that model joins modernity in its rejection of a model of self-abnegation and in its demand for full-scale criticism, now ordinarily described by the more radical term "liberation." [51] On the other hand, the contemporary model reveals certain illusions in the modern model.[52] It points out, for instance, that the "modern pagan's" struggle for rational self-fulfillment is no longer an apt ethical model for our actual situation. By and large, the contemporary model can be described as a demand for "self-transcendence" [53]: a radical commitment to the struggle to transcend our present individual and societal states in favor of a continuous examination of those illusions which cloud our real and more limited possibilities for knowledge and action. Indeed, in the examination of the modern human model by those paradigmatic post-modern analysts, Marx, Freud, Nietzsche, and Kierkegaard, the cry of "illusion" is surely the most frequent and the most damaging charge to the Age of Enlightenment. That charge has been expressed in a variety of ways: in Marxian terms, by the bourgeois intellectual's refusal to take note of or to struggle against the economic conditions which allow and enforce his privileges; in Freudian terms, by the disclosure of the subterranean forces of the unconscious which in fact motivate our presumably pure and autonomous conscious rationality; in the charges of Nietzsche and Kierkegaard alike, that our primary task is not the development of a finely tuned autonomous and sincere rationalism, but the far more difficult task of becoming "individuals," of becoming a self who realizes his or her own radical limitations and possibilities and yet struggles to become a human being of self-transcending authenticity.[54]

In all the major expressions of the post-modern spirit, the modern model of the enlightened thinker has been challenged as illusory, indeed—in the words modernity most feared—as mythical.[55] The enlightened thinker is neither as autonomous nor as critical as his pronouncements would suggest. In fact, the autonomous thinker is living out a myth whose destructive innocence has damaged our recent history—perhaps irretrievably—and obscured our actual situation of radical limitation and radical need for self-transcending personal and societal liberation. To be sure, such post-modern insights can become the occasion for a conservative resurgence as typified by the work of Michael Oakeshott or Russell Kirk, and by the anti-scientific and anti-technological aspects of the thought of Martin Heidegger.[56] Such insights can even give rise to cries for the need to return to the realistic Christian image of man exemplified in some expressions of orthodox and neo-orthodox theologies alike.[57] Still, for the most part, the post-modern intellectual does not believe that the recognition of the illusory character of the liberal model of human possibilities should lead to that conservative intellectual failure of nerve which would have us negate the critical forces set in motion by the Enlightenment. Rather, the post-modern intellectual believes that he must remain in fundamental fidelity to the critical exigencies of the liberal period. He further believes that his application of this critique to the liberal self-image itself is the finest expression of his real ethical commitment to the deepest demands of the liberal spirit. That spirit has, I believe, been admirably articulated in recent theology by Bernard Lonergan's formulation of the imperatives operative in a model of self-transcendence: "Be attentive, be intelligent, be rational, be responsible, develop and, if necessary, change." [58] To such imperatives and to the possibilities for authentic self-transcendence which a fidelity to those imperatives promise, the post-modern intellectual is irretrievably committed.

The fulfillment of that commitment can, perhaps, be best witnessed in recent reinterpretations of the significance and limitations of the Age of Enlightenment. Even Peter Gay, the most eloquent defender of the Enlightenment model for humanity, cannot but admit: "They [the *philosophes*] never wholly discarded that final, most stubborn illusion that bedevils realists—the illusion that they were free from illusions. This distorted their perception and gave many of their judgments a certain shallowness." [59] Still other interpreters of the liberal model find the problem far more radical. For Hans-Georg Gadamer, the Enlightenment's wholesale attack upon "tradition" leads to both philosophical folly and human impoverishment.[60] Any philosophical recognition of the actual historicity of our being should alert one to the reality that tradition is never simply eliminated. Rather, its permanent achievements can and must be won, over and over again, by a contemporary commitment to a hermeneutics of restoration. Further, any serious study of the rich Christian and classical images of humanity's actual situation and its real possibilities for existence should allow one to engage in a hermeneutics of retrieval [61] by means of which humanity may enrich its present impoverished lot.

On yet another level, probably the strongest critique of the Enlightenment in recent history comes not from conservative forces but from the radical left. As that radical movement finds expression in the critical social theory of the Frankfurt School, that critique takes on a power unmatched in the more conservative literature.

Perhaps the most telling criticism by the Marxists is that which argues, through a variety of dialectical analyses of both infra-structural and super-structural forms of modern scientific rationality and technocracy, that the reification of reality enforced by modern scientific processes of demystification and rationalization is in fact responsible for some of the oppressive horrors of the twentieth century.[62] More specifically, the Enlightenment's belief in the powers of calculatory, instrumental, formal rationality eliminated the power of negation from both our present conceptual and symbolic languages.[63] In place of true concepts which include both negation and its transformation, one finds merely modern formulae which become too readily the tools of the dominant forces in the society at large. In place of liberating symbols which can include the protest of the oppressed, the memory of their suffering, the demand for the negation of their oppression, and the radical affirmation of the possibilities of personal and societal liberation,[64] one finds instead demystified, reified, impoverished symbols of a conformist development which effectively insure—as they are articulated at the level of mass-culture[65]—the continued domination of the developed powers in modern technological society. In place of such a "one-dimensional" view of human possibilities, we need both the analytic tool of "negative dialectics" and the hermeneutical tool of *mimesis* for a retrieval of the symbolic and conceptual powers which can allow for the negation of present intellectual, linguistic, and societal oppression.[66] We need as well, so Jürgen Habermas, a present member of this tradition, argues, a retrieval of the radically critical and thereby emancipatory power of human rationality itself.[67] Only the latter can assure the negation of present illusions and reifications in a technological society. Only a truly critical rationality can affirm and enforce in *praxis* human liberation on a personal and societal scale.[68]

I shall take note of the theological use of this criticism of liberal modernity in the work of the eschatological theologians later. For the moment, it is important to note only that a radical critique of modernity's basic assumptions about knowledge and action need not take the form of a merely conservative protest. Rather, the more radical and—in my judgment—the more important criticisms of modernity have been these critiques from the left.[69] While maintaining a fundamental fidelity to the critical exigencies initiated by the Enlightenment, they developed methods for critical analysis and for their application to that oppressive reification of our language and our experience which a merely instrumentalist concept of rationality and an illusion-ridden concept of liberal purity of motive and institutions tend to encourage. Modern secularity of this critical variety need not retreat into either those Romantic attacks upon science and technology so prevalent in both conservative and counter-cultural critiques of modernity,[70] or into that mood of stoic resignation which Max Weber's own attitude towards the "disenchantment of the world" exemplified. Instead, such a revisionist attitude can affirm that commitment to critical inquiry constitutive of the morality of scientific inquiry while exposing, negating, and transforming the reification of the human world which a merely Enlightenment attitude encourages and perhaps enforces.

In sum, that fundamental faith in the ultimate worth of our life here and now which constitutes the basic faith common to the committed secular thinker and the committed Christian alike is maintained, clarified, and deepened by the post-modern critics of modernity. One further tenet, which this book shall try to defend, is that a revisionist reinterpretations of Christianity is an adequate critical articulation of, and symbolic representation for, both this secular faith and the basic meaning of the Christian faith itself. Indeed, I think that the more usual alternatives for analyzing this situation—secularism vs. supernaturalism, liberalism vs. conservatism, science vs. poetry, concept vs. symbol, atheism vs. classical theism, religion vs. revelation, special revelation vs. original revelation, an exclusivist christology vs. the man Jesus as "the man for others"—are, one and all, inadequate to the full dimensions of the present secular and Christian situations. What seems needed is a new look at the possibilities of a revisionist theology which will be appropriate to the central meanings of the secular faith we share and to the central meanings represented in the Christian tradition. Such a model for theology, however, can be set forth with clarity only after a prior analysis of the possibilities and limitations of the major reigning models for theologizing in the contemporary situation.

Notes

(1) Amidst the extensive literature here, for some recent examples of this in Roman Catholic theology, cf. Karl Rahner, "Pluralism in Theology and the Oneness of the Church's Profession of Faith," in *The Development of Fundamental Theology*, Concilium 46, ed. Johann Baptist Metz (New York: Paulist, 1969), pp. 103–23; idem "The Historicity of Theology," in *Theological Investigations*, IX (New York: Herder and Herder, 1972), 64–83; Walter Kasper, "Geschichtlichkeit der Dogmen?" *Stimmen de Zeit*, 179 (1967), esp. pp. 414–17; Bernard Lonergan, *Doctrinal Pluralism* (Milwaukee: Marquette University Press, 1971). For a relevant analysis of the modern "secular spirit," including "relativity" and "temporality," cf. Langdon Gilkey, "Cultural Background of the Current Situation," in *Naming the Whirlwind: The Renewal of God-Language* (New York: Bobbs-Merrill, 1969), passim, esp. pp. 48–57.

(2) Cf. Herbert Marcuse's analysis of "Repressive Tolerance" in *A Critique of Pure Tolerance* with Robert Paul Wolff and Barrington Moore, Jr. (Boston: Beacon, 1965).

(3) It may be noted that I do, in fact, assume that Christian self-understanding does involve a universalist claim: a claim clearly implied by all its major doctrines (creation, redemption, God, etc.). Such a historical-systematic assumption, however, is not synonymous with the assumption that the traditional historical understanding of this claim must remain. For the classic modern formulation of this dilemma in Christian self-understanding, cf. Ernst Troeltsch, *Die Absolutheit des Christentums* (Tübingen: J. C. B. Mohr, 1902) and the vast literature emerging from the Troeltsch discussion.

(4) For a penetrating analysis of the difficulties with common-sense eclecticism, cf. Bernard Lonergan, *Insight: A Study of Human Understanding* (London: Longmans, Green & Co., 1957), pp. 416–21.

(5) The present study involves principally an investigation of texts, not events. The category the "Christian fact," however, is clearly meant to include not merely texts but also symbols, rituals, events, witnesses. Although an extension of the hermeneutical theory outlined in chapter four to include more than written texts is needed in order to allow for a full investigation of the "Christian fact," the method is in principle open to such a development. The limitation seems appropriate for the present work insofar as Christianity as a religion of the word clearly involves written texts (the scriptures) as at least its charter document. The limitation remains a limitation insofar as further investigation of historical meaning (events, witnesses, etc.) is clearly needed to interpret the fuller meanings of the "Christian fact"—as Catholic Christians through their insistence upon the centrality of the notion of "tradition" witness. For a clear description of recent Catholic interpretations of tradition as *traditio,* not mere *tradita,* cf. James Mackey, *Modern Theology of Tradition* (New York: Herder and Herder, 1962).

(6) The distinction between "method" and "content" leads to a methodologism only, I believe, when that distinction becomes a separation, i.e., where the search for a method is separated from a search for truth. For the classical modern formulation of this difficulty, cf. Hans-Georg Gadamer, *Wahrheit und Methode: Grundzuge einer philosophischen Hermeneutik* (Tübingen: J. C. B. Mohr, 1965), esp. pp. 1–39.

(7) The term "revisionist," although often identified with inner-Marxist discussions, is perhaps appropriate to describe the post-neo-orthodox and post-liberal attempts of contemporary theologies to revise in a major way all the reigning models for Christian theology outlined in the following chapter.

(8) The present work is an attempt to work out a fundamental theology (i.e., the basic criteria and methods for theological argument). A dogmatic or systematic theology would be a distinct but related enterprise: distinct insofar as, in the manner of H. Richard Niebuhr's "confessional" theology or Ernst Troeltsch's *Glaubenslehre* or Karl Rahner's "dogmatics," dogmatic theology would involve a more intimate relationship to the "community of inquiry" of a particular church tradition; related insofar as the same criteria for meaning, meaningfulness, and truth would be applicable. I hope, in a future work, to be able to address directly this question of a dogmatic theology (and its attendant questions of methods of historical inquiry referred to above in note 5) in the context of my own ecclesial tradition, the Roman Catholic with its host of specific questions (dogma, doctrine, development, magisterium, tradition, sacrament). For the present work, I am content to address the initial (and perhaps still over-ambitious question) of the criteria for a Christian fundamental theology.

(9) An assumption of this entire study may need explicit statement here: the theologian, as an intellectual—and thereby committed to disciplined search for the appr - priate formulation of the value "truth"—finds himself involved in these three levels of crises in a manner that the non-intellectual church member need not be. This assumption is worth noting since I share the cautions which thinkers like Andrew Greeley in *Unsecular Man* (New York: Schocken, 1972), esp. pp. 1–54, make about the religious intellectual's unhappy tendency to generalize for the entire population. But, having said this, the intellectual's (i.e., here the theologian's) problems remain —as can be clearly seen in Greeley's own forthright theology, *The New Agenda* (New York: Doubleday, 1973).

(10) For an excellent description of this phenomenon, cf. Van A. Harvey, "The Alienated Theologian," in Robert A. Evans (ed.), *The Future of Philosophical Theology* (Philadelphia: Westminster, 1971), pp. 85–113.

(11) The terms will be clarified in the following section of this chapter.

(12) The term "relevance" is probably now spent and too emotion-ridden to bear much meaning. Its positive side is perhaps best captured by Whitehead's central notion of "importance" or Gadamer's insistence upon the need for "application" in the hermeneutical process.

(13) Throughout this work, I am employing the familiar distinction between "faith" as a basic orientation and attitude (primal and often non-conceptual) and "belief" as a thematic explication of a particular historical, moral, or cognitive claim involved in a particular "faith" stance.

(14) To repeat, the problematic developed here is principally one for intellectuals. Still, the dilemmas are less clearly but often more painfully present to the somewhat fictional "man-in-the-street" who cannot but sense that something is askew when he tries to reconcile what he was "taught" with what he "experiences." As Bultmann reminds us, anyone who even so much as decides that the "last trumpet" is fictional is caught up, willy-nilly, in the process of demythologization.

(15) For classically contrasting views on the Enlightenment model, cf. Peter Gay, *The Enlightenment: An Interpretation* (New York: Vintage, 1968); and Max Horkheimer and Theodor W. Adorno, *Dialectic of Enlightenment* (New York: Seabury, 1972). The classical formulation of the Enlightenment ideal remains Immanuel Kant, "What is Enlightenment?" in Lewis W. Beck (ed.), *Critique of Practical Reason and Other Writings in Moral Philosophy* (Chicago: University of Chicago Press, 1949), esp. pp. 286–92.

(16) This modified use of Max Weber's insistence upon the institutionalization of secularization could, of course, be expanded to include not only the academic institutions of the intellectuals but also modern media.

(17) Clearly this is the case in Judaism as well; in Eastern Orthodoxy possibly such figures as Nicholas Berdyaev, or even Leo Tolstoy and, more recently, Alexander Solzhenitsyn may be representative of the same kind of situation.

(18) I am here employing Bernard Lonergan's helpful distinction between a human *science* as studying all meaning that is "the repetition of routine in human speech

and action and all that is universal in the genesis, development, breakdown of routines" and history as concerned with the concrete and particular (e.g., the common-sense understanding of another era); cf. Bernard Lonergan, *Method in Theology* (New York: Herder and Herder, 1972), esp. pp. 175–96. Stephen Toulmin's notion of the emergence of modern "disciplines" is also extremely helpful here, cf. Stephen Toulmin, *Human Understanding: Vol. I: The Collective Use and Evolution of Concepts* (Princeton: Princeton University Press, 1972), esp. pp. 145–200 and 364–412.

(19) It continues to seem appropriate to describe Weber's own attitude as "stoic" even if it reached the authentically heroic proportions described by Karl Jaspers in *Max Weber: Politiker, Forscher, Philosoph* (Bremen: Joh. Storm-Verlag, 1946).

(20) The same meanings of "myth" will be analyzed in later chapters. For the present, "mystification" is employed as a pejorative term for the temptation to misuse the powerful forces of mythical imagination.

(21) The Christian doctrine of creation seems especially influential in fostering science in the West—as suggested by the wide discussion of this issue following the "secularity" insistence of the secular theologies of the sixties. For a good survey of the state of the question, cf. Ian Barbour, *Issues in Science and Religion* (Englewood Cliffs, N.J.: Prentice-Hall, 1966), and Ian Barbour (ed.), *Science and Religion* (New York: Harper & Row, 1968).

(22) As the later chapters will argue, the theological "turn to the subject" need not become the occasion to turn theology into anthropology. Indeed the basic argument of the book will be on the need for a "*theological* anthropology."

(23) A contemporary example of how all these factors are involved in a concrete community may be found in the several and diverse questions addressed by the American Catholic theological community in the *Proceedings for the Catholic Theological Society of America* (Yonkers, N.Y.: CTSA, to be published in 1975).

(24) The *ordo cognoscendi* of the dilemmas is the one listed: a clash of cognitive claims between modernity and traditional Christianity manifests a clash of ethical claims (how is one to be faithful to his commitment to the value, truth?) which in turn can manifest a seeming clash of basic attitudes or orientations (the "existential" realm). The *ordo essendi* is the reverse: our basic attitudes orientate us to certain values (e.g., truth or security) and thereby provide the context for our willingness or unwillingness to face disturbing cognitive questions.

(25) The great Victorian Christian thinkers—for example, John Henry Cardinal Newman or Frederick Denison Maurice—were clearly aware of the full dimensions of the crisis. Others tended to regard the crisis in less radical terms—as when a naive "liberal" cannot understand the fierce reactions of an intransigent conservative (or vice versa). Newman, for example, seems to receive as little real understanding from such later liberals as Lytton Strachey in *Eminent Victorians* as he received in his own time from W. G. Ward or Pius IX. For an exceptionally helpful interpretation to the nineteenth-century background, cf. Claude Welch, *Protestant Theology in the Nineteenth Century: Vol. I, 1799–1870* (New Haven: Yale University Press, 1972), esp. pp. 170–292; cf. also T. M. Schoof, *A Survey of Catholic Theology, 1800–1970* (New York: Paulist, 1970).

(26) Cf. Langdon Gilkey, *Religion and the Scientific Future* (New York: Harper & Row, 1970), esp. the examples cited in pp. 3–34 and 137–52.

(27) Cf. James T. Burtchaell, *Catholic Theories of Biblical Inspiration Since 1810* (Cambridge: Cambridge University Press, 1969).

(28) Van A. Harvey, *The Historian and The Believer: The Morality of Historical Knowledge and Christian Belief* (New York: Macmillan, 1966). This entire section is deeply indebted to Harvey's analysis—as his subtitle may serve to manifest.

(29) Ibid., pp. 102–27.

(30) Ibid., esp. pp. 117–18. For a more extended analysis of paradigm-change in science, cf. Thomas Kuhn, *The Structure of Scientific Revolutions* (Chicago: University of Chicago Press, 1962). For a theological application of Kuhn's analysis to Roman Catholic ecclesiology, cf. Thomas H. Sanks, *Authority in the Church: A Study of Changing Paradigms* (Missoula, Montana: AAR Scholars' Press, 1975).

(31) The concept of "community of inquiry" seems especially valuable for formulating the social dimension of the value-choice made, especially as the tradition of Josiah Royce finds more contemporary formulation in the work of John E. Smith (cf. John E. Smith, *Royce's Social Infinite: The Community of Interpretation* [New York: Archon, 1969], esp. pp. 126–75; idem, *Themes in American Philosophy* [New York: Harper & Row, 1970] pp. 109–22), as well as in the work of the late H. Richard Niebuhr and that of several of his former students: for example, James M. Gustafson (cf. *The Church as Moral Decision Maker* [Philadelphia: Pilgrim Press, 1970], esp. pp. 63–97; idem, *Treasure in Earthen Vessels: The Church as a Human Community* [New York: Harper & Row, 1961]; idem, "The University as a Community of Moral Discourse," in *Journal of Religion*, 53 [1973], pp. 397–410) and Van A. Harvey. As mentioned above (n. 8), this tradition seems especially fruitful in the distinct effort of formulating the notion of a dogmatic theology for a particular religious tradition.

(32) Cf. Paul Tillich, *Systematic Theology,* I (Chicago, University of Chicago Press, 1951), e.g., pp. 147–50; idem, "Moralisms and Morality: Theonomous Ethics" in *Theology of Culture*, ed. Robert C. Kimball (New York: Oxford, 1964), pp. 133–46.

(33) For an exemplary summary and defense of this traditional self-understanding, cf. John Connelley, "What is Theology?" *Proceedings for the Catholic Theological Society of America,* 1974, especially for Prof. Connelley's use of the "inner" and "outer" word distinction to reformulate this tradition.

(34) "Orthodox" is used throughout as a purely descriptive term. There is always the danger that "orthodox" theologies can become the "heresy" of "orthodoxy." On the revision of "dogma" in the Roman Catholic context, see Avery Dulles, *The Survival of Dogma* (New York: Image, 1973), esp. pp. 139–212.

(35) Perhaps this commitment is the clearest reason for differentiating the role of believer and his responsibility to a particular church tradition from the role of exegete, historian, sociologist—or theologian. Although the dogmatic theologian's "confessional" role will make this distinction more subtle than that of the fundamental theologian's, in principle, the distinction should stand. For example, to John

Connelley's "What is Theology?" (op. cit.) see "Replies" of Schubert Ogden and David Tracy in that same issue.

(36) Cf. Stephen Toulmin, *The Uses of Argument* (New York: Cambridge University Press, 1958) and the use made of Toulmin's paradigm by Van Harvey in *The Historian and the Believer*, pp. 38–64.

(37) "Rationalist" in the sense that the autonomous consciousness of the thinker could adequately account for any reality by the strict application of the methods of natural science and logic.

(38) Lionel Trilling, *Sincerity and Authenticity* (Cambridge: Harvard University Press, 1972), esp. pp. 1–26, 106–34; cf. also Nathan A. Scott, Jr., *Three American Moralists: Mailer, Bellow, Trilling* (South Bend: University of Notre Dame Press, 1973), pp. 151–217.

(39) Perhaps the classic modern formulation of this insight remains John Dewey's *A Common Faith* (New Haven: Yale University Press, 1971), esp. pp. 1–29, 59–87.

(40) The use of the concept "supernatural" here is the modern sense of religious studies where it is roughly equivalent to "fundamentalism," not in the more restricted medieval sense where it is a strictly theoretical concept for thematizing the Christian religion. For an example of the former use, cf. Yervant Krikorian (ed.), *Naturalism and the Human Spirit* (New York: Columbia University Press, 1944); for the latter, more restricted use of the *theorem* of the supernatural, cf. Bernard Lonergan's discussion in *Grace and Freedom* (New York: Herder and Herder, 1971), p. 16.

(41) Sidney Hook, "The Atheism of Paul Tillich" in *Religious Experience and Truth: A Symposium*, ed. Sidney Hook (New York: New York University Press, 1961), p. 63.

(42) For a succinct formulation of the secularity-secularism distinction, cf. Schubert M. Ogden, *The Reality of God* (New York: Harper & Row, 1964), pp. 6–20. For a penetrating analysis of the characteristics of secularity, cf. Langdon Gilkey, *Naming the Whirlwind: The Renewal of God-Language*, pp. 3–31.

(43) For the criteria implied by this, cf. the discussion in chapter four; a recent example of the seeming secularist inability to articulate a powerful symbol-system may be found in Robert Heilbroner's analytically impressive but symbolically weak formulation of the Prometheus and Atlas myths for our contemporary crisis in his *An Inquiry into the Human Prospect* (New York: W. W. Norton, 1974), pp. 127–44.

(44) Furthermore, this should in principle be possible without simply charging "reductionism" to the critic of Christianity in the manner correctly criticized by Kai Nielsen in "Some Meta-Theological Remarks about Reductionism," in *Journal of the American Academy of Religion*, XLII (1974), 336–39.

(45) For a formulation of this position in terms of the symbolic inadequacy of secularism, cf. Langdon Gilkey, *Naming the Whirlwind*, esp. pp. 147–78; for the symbolic adequacy of God-language, ibid., esp. pp. 305–415.

(46) Cf. Schubert M. Ogden, *The Reality of God*, pp. 15–20, 40–43. For a survey and

analysis of the secularist critique in the Anglo-Saxon analytical tradition, cf. Rae-burne S. Heimbeck, *Theology and Meaning: A Critique of Metatheological Skepticism* (Stanford: Stanford University Press, 1969).

(47) The discussions of "religion" are often under the theological rubric of the doctrine of "revelation" as in the work of Karl Rahner on "transcendental" and "categorial" revelation; cf. Karl Rahner and Joseph Ratzinger, *Revelation and Tradition* (New York: Herder and Herder, 1966), pp. 9–25.

(48) Peter Gay, *The Enlightenment*, pp. 64–7.

(49) One example in our own period is B. F. Skinner's prescription of a practice of scientific behaviorism along with a muted Utopianism. Cf. B. F. Skinner, *Walden Two* (New York: Macmillan, 1948) for the muted Utopian vision; and B. F. Skinner, *Beyond Freedom and Dignity* (New York: Vintage, 1971) for the scientific vision.

(50) Harvey Cox, *The Secular City* (New York: Macmillan, 1965); Paul van Buren, *The Secular Meaning of the Gospel* (New York: Macmillan, 1963).

(51) For example, Latin American theologians, feminist theologians, or the Black theologians in North America seem entirely correct in rejecting the symbols of "development" for symbols of "liberation."

(52) For an analysis of "illusion" as distinct from "error," cf. Paul Ricoeur, "The Atheism of Freudian Psychoanalysis," in *Is God Dead?*, Concilium Vol. 16 (New York: Paulist, 1966), esp. pp. 59–62.

(53) For example, Bernard Lonergan's transformation of the Aristotelian ethical tradition into the model of "self-transcendence," cf. *Method in Theology*, pp. 36–40, 104–5. The chief alternative models seem to be either "self-abnegation" or "self-fulfillment."

(54) On the latter, cf. Karl Jaspers, *The Way to Wisdom* (New Haven: Yale University Press, 1954), p. 138.

(55) The "fear" seems proper to an "illusion" as distinct from an "error" (cf. above n. 52)—since modernity was under the illusion that myth could only have a purely negative meaning.

(56) Cf. Michael Oakeshott, *Rationalism in Politics and Other Essays* (London, 1962); William F. Buckley, Jr. (ed.), *Did You Ever See a Dream Walking? American Conservative Thought in the Twentieth Century* (New York: Bobbs-Merrill, 1970). Gibson Winter's recent reinterpretation of Heidegger's position as providing a new *ethos* may meet this familiar criticism of Heidegger by Marcuse, Adorno, Habermas, et al.

(57) Most powerfully in Reinhold Niebuhr's *The Nature and Destiny of Man*, I and II (New York: Scribner's, 1941–43).

(58) Bernard Lonergan, *Method in Theology*, pp. 53–55, 231–32.

(59) Peter Gay, *The Enlightenment*, p. 27.

(60) Hans-Georg Gadamer, *Wahrheit und Methode*, pp. 250–75.

(61) As occurs, for example, in Karl Rahner's use of the Heidegerrian notion of "retrieval" to retrieve the contemporary meanings of the Roman Catholic doctrinal tradition.

(62) Cf. Martin Jay, *The Dialectical Imagination: A History of the Frankfurt School and The Institute of Social Research, 1923–1950* (Boston: Little, Brown, 1973), for a history of the Frankfurt School up to but not including Jürgen Habermas.

(63) Cf. Max Horkheimer and Theodor W. Adorno, *Dialectic of Enlightenment,* esp. pp. 29–42.

(64) Ibid., pp. 120–68; for a theological use of this dialectical insight, cf. Johann Baptist Metz, "The Future *Ex Memoria Passionis,*" in *Hope and the Future of Man,* ed. Ewert H. Cousins (Philadelphia: Fortress, 1972), pp. 117–31.

(65) Cf. Herbert Marcuse, *One-Dimensional Man* (Boston: Beacon, 1964), esp. 1–199. Note also how easily many authentic witnesses and visions can be co-opted for mass distribution in the complaint of Saul Bellow's Herzog that the visions of genius become the canned goods of the intellectuals.

(66) Cf. Herbert Marcuse, *Eros and Civilization* (Boston: Beacon, 1955), esp. pp. 211–13; cf. also Jürgen Habermas, *Erkenntnis und Interesse* (Frankfurt: Suhrkamp Verlag, 1968), esp. pp. 262–74.

(67) Cf. Jürgen Habermas, ibid., passim; and idem, *Theory and Practice* (Boston: Beacon, 1971), pp. 195–283; Albrecht Wellmer, *Critical Theory of Society* (New York: Herder and Herder, 1971), pp. 9–65 and 121–39; and Trent Schroyer's own critical development of the Habermas mode of analysis in *The Critique of Domination: The Origins and Development of Critical Theory* (New York: Braziller, 1973), esp. pp. 132–74.

(68) Cf. chapter ten of this work for a fuller study of *praxis.*

(69) Such criticisms are not limited to Marxist writings; indeed the largely non-Marxist left ("old" and "new") in the United States in such journals as *Commonweal, Christian Century, Commentary, The New York Review of Books,* and *Daedalus* often include similar criticisms.

(70) Cf. Theodore Roszak's insightful works, *The Making of a Counter Culture* (New York: Doubleday, 1969), and *Where the Wasteland Ends* (New York: Doubleday, 1972). On the debit side of the counter-culture, cf. such happily short-lived works as Charles A. Reich's paean of praise to "consciousness III," in *The Greening of America* (New York: Random House, 1970).

Chapter 2

Five Basic Models in Contemporary Theology

INTRODUCTION: The Need for Models

A widely accepted dictum in contemporary theology is the need to develop certain basic models or types for understanding the specific task of the contemporary theologian.[1] The reemergence of interest in types and models is prompted by several factors. Given the *de facto* existence of different sets of criteria, different uses of evidence, and varying employments of the social, historical, hermeneutical, and philosophical disciplines within theologies,[2] the more general cultural factors outlined in the prior chapter create an even more complex situation. In such a situation, it becomes imperative for a theologian to set forth his own model for theological judgment and to compare that model critically with other existing models. The second factor encouraging interest in the discussion of models is the continuing clarification of basic theological positions afforded by more recent forms of linguistic analysis. The work of Ian Ramsey, Frederick Ferré, and Max Black are illustrative of the linguist's ability to make such basic distinctions as that between "picture (or scale) models" and "disclosure (or analogue) models."[3] Such a distinction allows one to affirm that theological models do not purport to provide exact pictures of the realities they disclose (picture models). Rather, theological models serve to disclose or re-present the realities which they interpret (disclosure models). Theological disclosure models like the religious symbols upon which they reflect,[4] in Reinhold Niebuhr's famous phrase, should be taken seriously but not literally. Theologies do not—or should not—claim to provide pictures of the realities they describe—God, humanity, and world; they can be shown to disclose such realities with varying degrees of adequacy.

This chapter will try to take this familiar discussion of models a step further by specifying the two realities (viz., the self and the object)[5] which are referred to in the five major theological models of our present situation: the orthodox, liberal, neo-orthodox, radical, and revisionist models.[6] The major task of this chapter, therefore, is to determine with some exactitude the self- or subject-referent and the object-referent of each major theological option. The task in successive chapters will be to spell out the basic contours of the revisionist model as it promises to be more adequate for the contemporary theological situation.

A few further summary observations on the present use of models may be in order. The basic need for the development of models is probably best expressed by Paul Tillich when he states that, in matters of historical description, contemporary theologians cannot be content with the usual alternatives of either trying to say everything or of saying nothing at all.[7] If we wish to locate our own enterprise historically, we must try to develop certain characteristic ideal types or models for interpreting the basic factors present in concrete historical realities. Such models or types do not even attempt the empirical historical claims of Anders Nygren's "basic motifs." [8] Technically, disclosure models do not provide an exact description of particular historical phenomena. They do provide intelligible, interlocking sets of basic terms and relations[9] that aid us to understand the point of view expressed in particular historical positions. To express my own hypothesis, the most basic of such terms and relations is, in fact, those references to the self of the theologian and to the objects within that self's horizon which any given model discloses. If we can legitimately label theological models as "disclosure models" in the manner of Ramsey and Ferré, then we can also find a way to explicate the realities of self and object which each theological model discloses.

Before testing that proposal by employing it to determine the self and the object referents disclosed in five major contemporary theological models, one further observation is needed. We must know what general characteristics will be shared by· all models which we call "contemporary Christian theological" positions. Any contemporary Christian theological position will consider itself obliged to interpret two basic phenomena: the Christian tradition and contemporary understandings of human existence.[10] At the same time, the most helpful way to understand how either of these phenomena is interpreted by any given model is the following: one may specify what role each position gives to the apparent cognitive, ethical, and existential clashes analyzed above—for example, the clash between the traditional Christian commitment to such values as obedience to the tradition (however understood) over against such typical modern commitments as loyalty to one's own autonomous, critical judgments.[11] As the first chapter argued, precisely such clashes provide the most basic context for all modern and contemporary theologies. More exactly, it may prove helpful to try to pinpoint the exact understandings each model has of the theological self and of the object of theological discourse in the context or horizon of that all-pervasive clash of beliefs, values, and faiths.

Treating the five models chosen for investigation in the chronological sequence of their emergence, I will now begin to test my hypothesis with a study of the orthodox model.

ORTHODOX THEOLOGY: **Believers and Beliefs**

Throughout my interpretation, I assume that each theological model will, in some way, attempt to interpret the Christian tradition in the context of modernity; further, that a specification of the disclosure model employed by each basic theological position will allow one to explicate the self-referent and the object-referent of that position with some exactitude. For these reasons, the discussion of each model will begin with a brief description of the general attitude towards both modernity and Christianity which that model presupposes. Each analysis shall then turn to the task of specifying the referents disclosed by that model.

In an orthodox theological model, the claims of modernity are not understood to have any inner-theological relevance. Rather, the theologian's task as theologian is to express an adequate understanding of the beliefs of his particular church tradition.[12] Orthodox theologians do not seem impressed by the counter-claims of modern scientific, historical, or philosophical scholarship made to the traditional Christian faith's understanding of reality. In fact, such theologians hold that a firm commitment to the perennial truths of traditional Christianity is the best bulwark against the onslaughts of modern criticism. As is the case with all five models, the orthodox one admits to a wide spectrum of specific theological options. Indeed, the orthodox spectrum is at least as wide as the correlative spectrum of various church traditions—stretching from essentially fundamentalist positions through most theologies labelled "biblical" to various systematic understandings of the several church traditions.[13]

In principle, what does this orthodox theological model show about the subject-theologian and about the object which the theologian investigates? It seems reasonably clear that the self-referent of the orthodox theologian is to a believer in a specific church tradition; the object-referent is to a (usually systematic) understanding of those beliefs. A classical and sophisticated formulation of the orthodox model for theological reflection like the description of the task of theology provided in the First Vatican Council [14] provides a case in point. As careful interpreters of that document have noted, the position of Vatican I on theology is highly nuanced. For Vatican I, the aim of theology is not "proof" of mysteries of the Catholic faith, but an "understanding" of those mysteries. That understanding is best achieved by following the classical medieval model. More exactly, theology attempts a partial, incomplete, analogous, but real understanding of the "mysteries" of the Catholic faith. Theology may best perform this task by employing the following specific model: (1) find analogies in nature for these beliefs; (2) use these analogies to provide a systematic understanding of the interconnection of major mysteries of faith (Christ, Grace, Trinity); (3) try to relate that analogous understanding to the final end of man (Beatific Vision).[15]

One must admit that the Vatican I model for theology fits the structure of the general orthodox model described above. The subject-referent of this model manifests that the theologian precisely *qua theologian* is a believer in the Roman Catholic tradition.[16] The object-referent, in turn, manifests an "analogous" understanding of the "beliefs" of that tradition. The orthodox theologian's task is not to prove those beliefs ("rationalism and semi-ration-alism"). Nor is that task simply to state those beliefs ("fideism").[17] Rather his task becomes the distinct need to provide an analogous and systematic understanding of the Catholic beliefs (dogmatic theology), and a reasoned defense (not proof) of those beliefs (apologetic or fundamental theology). In either case, the cognitive claims of other modern disciplines and the value claims of the wider culture do not enter into the inner-theological circle ex-cept to suggest analogies for systematic reflection or to aid argumentation for strictly apologetic reflection.[18]

The major strength of the orthodox theologian is precisely his ability to develop sophisticated models for providing systematic understanding of the basic beliefs of his church community. His major weakness, I suggest, lies in his inability to make intrinsic (i.e., inner-theological) use of the other schol-arly disciplines. More pointedly perhaps, his weakness lies in his theological inability to come to terms with the cognitive, ethical, and existential coun-ter-claims of modernity. This weakness is directly dependent upon the pres-ence of a relatively narrow self-referent (the explicit believer) and of an ob-ject-referent of parallel narrowness (an understanding of the beliefs and values of his own church tradition). To understand how that narrowness might be corrected, one must turn to the second model for theological reflection, the liberal.

LIBERAL THEOLOGY: Modern Secularity and Christian Belief

With the emergence of liberal and modernist Christian theologies,[19] we find the explicit commitment of the Christian theologian to the basic cogni-tive claims and ethical values of the modern secular period. To be sure, this challenge is provoked by the wide application of distinctly new scholarly disciplines to the cognitive and historical claims of Christianity. From the new philosophies, the new natural sciences, and especially from the new his-torical disciplines, Christian theologians in every church tradition found major and minor theological claims severely challenged. Yet it is not the cognitive challenge alone which occasioned the deepest crisis for the liberal and modernist Christian theologians. Rather, the liberal theologian's ethical and existential commitment to that secular faith constitutive of the critical drive present in all modern science is at the heart of the liberal enterprise.[20] The liberal and modernist theologian accepts the distinctively modern commitment to the values of free and open inquiry, autonomous judgment, critical investigation of all claims to scientific, historical, philosophical, and religious truth.[21] The liberal theologian finds himself committed not marginally but fundamentally to the values of the modern experiment. He cannot but find himself open to the challenge which those values, when applied by modern cognitive disciplines, pose for the classical claims of traditional Christianity to truth and to value.

At the same time, the liberal theologian remains committed to the cognitive claims and the fundamental values of the Christian vision.[22] But how can he responsibly maintain both commitments? In extreme cases—as in Ludwig Feuerbach—one of the commitments will be abandoned. In most cases, however, the enterprise of liberal Christian theology will be the attempt to show how a proper reinterpretation of modernity's most basic value commitments and a proper reinterpretation of Christianity's historic claims to truth and value can be—indeed must be—reconciled.[23] The genius of the liberal and modernist theologians, I believe, was precisely their frank and full admission of this challenge and their willingness to reformulate the very task of Christian theology in accordance with it.

The spectrum of concrete historical options for liberal theologies is almost as wide as the spectrum of specific orthodox theologies. From the great figures of German and Anglo-American Protestant liberalism through the Catholic modernists, there were those in every church tradition who attempted to rethink and reformulate their tradition in accordance with the values and cognitive claims of modern thought. From the philosophical interests of Hegel, Schleiermacher, or Blondel, through the ethical interests of Ritschl or Wieman, to the historical interests of Harnack, Troeltsch, or Loisy, the same pattern emerges: the need to rethink the fundamental vision and values of traditional Christianity in harmony with the fundamental vision and values of modernity.

What of the referents to self and to object of this theological model? The liberal's self-referent is principally to the subject-theologian's own modern consciousness as committed to the basic values of modernity, especially the value of insisting upon a critical investigation of all claims to meaning and truth, religious or otherwise. The object-referent is principally to the Christian tradition (usually the tradition of one's own church) [24] as reformulated in accordance with such modern commitments and critiques.

The clearest example—indeed, the still towering paradigm—for this liberal model remains Friedrich Schleiermacher.[25] Schleiermacher's great achievement—ranging from the *Speeches* through his systematic theology, *The Christian Faith*—is largely constituted by his consistent commitment to working out a new model for Christian theology. Such a model would allow—in fact, demand—that the Christian theologian be responsible to both the community of modern philosophic, scientific, and historical discourse and to that community of religious discourse called the Christian church.[26] In Schleiermacher's mind, the model for a responsible, modern Christian theology could no longer be the orthodox model of "dogmatics." Rather, in his famous phrase, the theses of faith must now become the "hypotheses of the theologian." This dictum, in turn, can be refined to develop a whole new model for theology—the model of *Glaubenslehre*.[27]

By now, it is well-nigh universally admitted that the liberals and modernists were not fully successful in the completion of the task they initiated.[28] Their chief strength and their legacy are that they set up the proper post-orthodox model for contemporary theological reflection. How that formal ideal might be maintained without a continuance of the inadequacies of the specific material conclusions of the liberals and modernists remains, I believe, the major task of the contemporary post-liberal period in theology.

NEO-ORTHODOX THEOLOGY: Radical Contemporary Christian Faith and the God of Jesus Christ

In the context of the prior discussion of the liberal task, it seems fair to state that even the neo-orthodox critics of liberalism and modernism fundamentally share the liberal and not the orthodox understanding of the task of theology. There seems every good reason to agree with the judgment of Wilhelm Pauck that neo-orthodoxy is not really a radically new alternative model for theology, but rather is a moment—to be sure, a critical one—in the larger liberal theological tradition. Pauck is, I believe, exactly right when he states: "Orthodox theologies give rise to more orthodoxies; liberal theologies give rise to neo-orthodoxies." [29]

So much is this the case that even *the* neo-orthodox theologian, Karl Barth (at least the Barth of *Romans*),[30] however critical he may be of his liberal predecessors, in a major sense continues the liberal tradition. Indeed, the neo-orthodox theologians can be interpreted as the theological expression of that same role of both acceptance and negation of liberal modernity which Marx, Freud, and Nietzsche played in the wider secular culture. No more than their post-modern secular contemporaries were the principal neo-orthodox theologians (Barth, Brunner, Bultmann, Tillich, the Niebuhrs) willing to accept either orthodoxy or liberalism as adequate to contemporary needs.[31] Not a lack of regard for the theological relevance of cultural analysis (as with the orthodox), but a different, a post-modern cultural analysis impelled the early Barth to challenge his liberal forebears.[32] The fact is that the neo-orthodox theologians (here Barth joins Bultmann, Brunner, Tillich, and the Niebuhrs) shared the repugnance of the post-war cultural period for the evolutionary optimism and for the now oppressive modernist model of autonomous man's possibilities widespread in the late nineteenth- and early twentieth-century liberal periods.[33] On this interpretation, the criticism which neo-orthodoxy made against liberalism and modernism was not a simple rejection of the liberal enterprise. Rather, neo-orthodoxy was a continuation of that enterprise by means of a two-pronged critique: on the first front, the neo-orthodox insisted that the liberal analysis of the human situation was able to account at best for human finitude and possibility, but was utterly unable to account for those negative elements of tragedy, of terror, indeed, of sin in human existence.[34] On a second front, the neo-orthodox insisted that the liberal reinterpretation of Christianity (especially its reinterpretation of the event of Jesus Christ) was a failure. The central belief of the Christian tradition—that justification comes only from grace through faith in God's manifestation of self in the event of Jesus Christ[35]—was, in the judgment of the neo-orthodox, nowhere adequately explicated in the liberal analysis of the modern religious consciousness.

The response of the neo-orthodox theologians to these weaknesses of their liberal forebears seems signally clear. Fundamentally, they argued that only an explicit recognition of the unique gift of faith in the Word of God could provide an adequate foundation for a truly Christian theology. Here, it is true, the neo-orthodox theologian joins the orthodox in insisting upon the theologian's own faith as an existential condition of the possibility of theology. Yet it is also noteworthy that the neo-orthodox theologian's faith, unlike the orthodox's, is radically experiential and claims, in effect, like the liberal's, to illuminate all human existence.[36] So, like his post-modern secular counterpart, the neo-orthodox demands a deeper recognition of the intrinsically dialectical character of all human experience which the more sanguine liberal tended to discount.[37] Correlatively, the neo-orthodox continues to insist that the experience of Christian faith shows the radically dialectical and experiential relationship now available to every human being who, in experiencing contemporary estrangement, may also be open to experience the justifying, salvific power of this faith in the Christian God.[38]

This understanding of the neo-orthodox model for theology, therefore, is one which directly relates that theological alternative to its parent, classical liberalism. Such an interpretation may prove not only more faithful to the actual performance of neo-orthodoxy, but also may allow the permanent achievements of that tradition to continue into the more complex present theological moment. We can begin to summarize those achievements by recognizing that the neo-orthodox, by their profound analyses of the negative elements in the human situation (death, guilt, tragedy, sin), allow a more dialectical, a more contemporary, and, most importantly, a more accurate[39] understanding of the actual human condition than did most of their liberal and modernist forebears. Furthermore, the frequent neo-orthodox insistence on both the infinitely qualitative distinction between God and humanity and on the irrevocably dialectical character of the relationship of God and world serves to assure a firm grasp of an element of radical mystery, which anyone hoping to understand the Christian God should at some point recognize.[40] In addition, the neo-orthodox retrieval of the christocentric character of New Testament faith had at least one positive effect.[41] That demand forced any Christian theologian claiming a fundamental continuity between his own theology and the original Christian witness to explicate that christological claim in a more adequate manner than liberal and modernist discussions of symbol, of history, and of religious consciousness were able to manage. Finally, the neo-orthodox reformulation of the liberal task widened and deepened the understanding of the theological task itself as involving not only "criteria of adequacy" to human experience but also "criteria of appropriateness" to the central meanings of the Christian tradition.[42] In fact, perhaps the most enduring achievement of neo-orthodoxy was its ability to allow for a more adequate formulation of the intrinsically hermeneutical aspect of the contemporary theological task.[43] One need not hold that the neo-orthodox theologies really resolved the liberal dilemma. Yet the neo-orthodox recognized that the discipline of contemporary Christian theology had to come to terms with the post-modern understanding of liberal illusions and had to develop more adequate hermeneutical tools to disclose the profoundly transformative meanings of the central Christian symbols.[44] Still, the neo-orthodox seemed to have bought these gains at a great price—viz., at the price of not analyzing with critical and deliberate hardmindedness the central revelational, theistic, and christological doctrines of the Christian tradition.[45]

It seemed to them sufficient that such symbols had real existential impact upon the contemporary situation of alienation. The rest could be left to "paradox" or "mystery" or "scandal." [46] Yet when the "rest" often included the critical questions of whether those symbols, however existentially meaningful, could really stand up to critical analysis of their coherence and their truth, it became inevitable that the neo-orthodox hegemony must and did fall.[47] Eventually, some critics, secular and Christian, had to ask the question which the neo-orthodox theologian seemed unable to answer: however paradoxical Christian faith may be, is that paradox adequately represented by concepts and symbols which are neither internally coherent nor capable of withstanding a critical experiential analysis of their truth.[48] The liberals and modernists may not have been able to solve the problem which secular modernity posed for Christian self-understanding; but the neo-orthodox seemed unwilling at some inevitable final moment to follow to a truly critical conclusion the task which they themselves initiated.

In terms of the "disclosure model" approach to this analysis, one may explicate the subject-referent and the object-referent of the neo-orthodox model in the following manner. The subject-referent of the neo-orthodox theologian is not really the "believer" as for the orthodox, but rather the more radical model of the human being of authentic Christian faith.[49] More exactly, the self-reality for the neo-orthodox is not some set of beliefs of the traditional believer but the basic existential attitudes of Christian faith, trust, and agapic love.[50] This subject-referent of the neo-orthodox theologian can also be said to include elements of an authentic post-modern contemporary consciousness as distinct from the modern (or Enlightenment) consciousness of the liberal. Negatively, the neo-orthodox theologian is familiar with the collapse of Enlightenment optimism. Positively, he is fully committed to explicating what he ordinarily calls the dialectical character of our human existence. In other words, the neo-orthodox theologian shares the critical attitude towards the illusions of the liberal and secular consciousness present in such paradigmatic figures as Marx, Freud, and Nietzsche. As much as did these latter secular thinkers, the neo-orthodox theologians produced penetrating analyses of the illusions and naiveté of the liberal or Enlightenment attitude. As Lionel Trilling might add, the great neo-orthodox theologians wanted to move away from a subjective base of modern or liberal "sincerity" to a subjective base of contemporary —illusionless—Christian "authenticity." Indeed, much of the power and attractiveness of the neo-orthodox position—especially as represented by Reinhold Niebuhr's model of authentic self-transcendence—comes from this highly contemporary, this surely more realistic experiential base.[51]

In terms of the object-referent of the neo-orthodox model, the dialectical character of the subject's experience allows the object of that faith-experience to be described in similarly dialectical terms: often as the wholly other God of Jesus Christ.[52] To be sure, in the major Protestant proponents of neo-orthodox theology, this object-referent will be formulated in terms of neo-Reformation themes like God's Word operative in human existence as unexpected, unmerited, justifying Event.[53] But the use of the model "neo-orthodoxy" should in fact be expanded to include not only the obvious giants of neo-Reformation theology but also those Catholic theologies of contemporary retrieval called neo-Thomism and contemporary Catholic sacramental (or incarnational) theologies.[54] In such Roman Catholic proponents of a fundamentally neo-orthodox position as Karl Rahner, this object-referent (for Rahner "the Radically Mysterious God") will be formulated in terms proper to a systematic rearticulation of the major dogmatic and theological moments of the Catholic tradition.[55]

Moreover, it would seem that the liberal vs. neo-orthodox clash continues to dominate much of contemporary Christian theology. As we shall see in a later chapter, the eschatological theologians (with some exceptions) do not substantially differ from the model of neo-orthodoxy. Moltmann, Braaten, Gutierrez, Alves, et al. also employ basically the same self-referents and object-referents of their more existentialist and sometimes individualist predecessors.[56] Alternatively, several contemporary theologians of culture do not significantly differ from the classical liberal or modernist position in their ever more fruitful, if not methodologically more adequate, search for symbolic expressions of contemporary religious experience.[57] To be sure, both these major positions do represent substantial developments upon individual questions over their liberal and neo-orthodox predecessors. But that they represent any substantial development on the the basic problematic of a fully adequate model for theology itself remains an open question.

RADICAL THEOLOGY: Secular Affirmation and Theistic Negation

In more recent history we have seen the development of the radical theology model employed by certain theologians—of whom the "death of God" theologians remain the primary instance.[58] Fundamentally, the radical theologians are clearly informed by the liberal and neo-orthodox models for theology. With equal clarity, their consciousness is best described as contemporary rather than modern. The crucial step they take seems to be the application of the dialectical method of contemporary and neo-orthodox consciousness to the Christian tradition itself.[59] More exactly, the central difficulty of Christianity for the radical theologian is that the God of the neo-orthodox, the liberal, and the orthodox theologians alienates the authentic conscience of the illusionless and liberated contemporary human being.[60] A conscience commited to the struggle for human liberation cannot really affirm a radical faith in and dependence upon the God of orthodox or liberal or neo-orthodox Christianity. To be sure, the articulation of this contemporary consciousness may differ as widely as does Paul van Buren's linguistic analysis of radical secularism from William Hamilton's more autobiographical remarks or from Thomas J. J. Altizer's neo-Hegelian and neo-Blakean expression. Yet the same rallying cry unites these diverse figures: this Wholly Other God must die in order that the authentically liberated human being may live.

Again in terms of our disclosure model approach, the following referents seem clear. The self referred to by the radical model for theology is a subject committed to post-modern, contemporary, secular intellectual and moral values. The object-referent of the radical model for Christian theology is now a familiar one: an explicit reformulation of traditional Christianity which negates the central belief of that tradition in God. This negation is usually paired with an equally important affirmation: an affirmation of Jesus either as the paradigm of a life lived for others or as the decisive incarnational manifestation of a liberated humanity.[61] Fundamentally opposed to the God of traditional or liberal or neo-orthodox theologies, the radical argues that the Christian God cannot but alienate human beings from one another, from the world, and from their authentic selves. The central assertion of traditional Christianity which must be maintained is the Christian affirmation of a life which, in its commitment to liberation and to others, may serve to humanize the world: a life like that made present—perhaps even "contagious"—[62] in Jesus of Nazareth and in the liberating event of the death of God in the contemporary world.

The strength of the radical theological model, in my view, is its ability to pinpoint the question which any thinking human being committed to the authentic values of contemporary secularity and to the Christian vision of life's possibilities must face: the question of the traditional understanding of the Christian God.[63] The corresponding weakness of the radical position is by now apparent: can one really continue the enterprise of Christian theology if there is no meaningful way to affirm the reality of God.

THE REVISIONIST MODEL: A Critical Correlation

The reasons for the label "revisionist" are both historical and systematic. Historically, it seems clear that classical liberalisms, classical orthodoxies, various kinds of neo-orthodoxy, and various radical alternatives are now legitimately judged inadequate models for the present theological task. At the same time, the model called "revisionist" might be said to be an accurate label for at least some major contemporary theologies. Although some process theologians are the most obvious example of this position, still many other positions—for example, such Roman Catholic thinkers as Leslie Dewart, Gregory Baum, or Michael Novak, or such Protestant thinkers as Langdon Gilkey, Van Harvey, or Gordon Kaufman[64]—seem to fit the same general model. The principal reasons for the label "revisionist," however, are systematic ones. With the relative strengths and limitations of liberalism, orthodoxy, neo-orthodoxy, and radical theologies in mind, the revisionist theologian is committed to continuing the critical task of the classical liberals and modernists in a genuinely post-liberal situation. By that commitment, the revisionist will also try to rectify earlier theological limitations both in the light of the new resources made available by further historical, philosophical, and social scientific research and reflection and in the light of the legitimate concerns and accomplishments of the later neo-orthodox and radical theological alternatives.[65] In short, the revisionist theologian is committed to what seems clearly to be the central task of contemporary Christian theology: the dramatic confrontation, the mutual illuminations and corrections, the possible basic reconciliation[66] between the principal values, cognitive claims, and existential faiths of both a reinterpreted post-modern consciousness and a reinterpreted Christianity. The revisionist theologian is encouraged in this enterprise by certain historical judgments: that even neo-orthodoxy is best understood as a self-critical moment in the history of liberalism; and, in the opinion of B. M. G. Reardon, that various orthodox theologies are properly understood not as the mere self-expression of a faith community, but rather as self-expressions deeply influenced by the orthodox reactions to the challenge of liberalism.[67] He is further encouraged by the recognition of and commitment to both that critique of modern liberalism present in contemporary secular thought[68] and that radical secular affirmation of our common human faith in the worth-whileness of our struggle for liberation. The revisionist Christian theologian joins his secular colleague in refusing to allow the fact of his own existential disenchantment with the reifying and oppressive results of Enlightenment disenchantment to become the occasion for a return to mystification, Christian or otherwise.[69] Rather he believes that only a radical continuation of critical theory, symbolic reinterpretation, and responsible social and personal *praxis* can provide the hope for a fundamental revision of both the modern and the traditional Christian self-understandings. Revisionist theology, then, is intrinsically indebted to and derived from the formulations of the liberal task in theology classically formulated in the nineteenth century. It is post-liberal in the straightforward sense that it recognizes and attempts to articulate not a new ideal for the theological task, but new methodological and substantive resources for fulfilling that ideal.[70]

Included among such resources would be the development of certain ideal types and models which would be faithful to the historical phenomena of alternative models[71] and would make the authentic achievements of those models more readily available to the contemporary problematic. Hence, the contemporary systematic theologian of the type described above—precisely because of the nature of his understanding of the systematic task—recognizes the ever more urgent need to try to retrieve both the liberal enterprise of the nineteenth century and the liberal, neo-orthodox, and radical enterprises of this century. The post-liberal theologian cannot simply "return to liberalism" and bypass either neo-orthodoxy or radical theology. Those positions were not mere "fads," but authentically self-critical moments in the larger enterprise of reconstructing an adequate model for contemporary Christian theology. It is not a surprise, perhaps, that many contemporary theologians are once again finding Schleiermacher, Ritschl, Newman, F. D. Maurice, Reinhold Niebuhr, Paul Tillich, Karl Rahner, et al. centrally important for their present reflection. However, what continues to be needed is some method of interpretation that can make their permanent achievements more readily available for present reflection. As one suggestion along that line, this chapter has risked an analysis of the major models for theology and has tried to articulate certain definable self-referents and object-referents in each model.

For the revisionist model for theology, the self-referent is a subject committed at once to a contemporary revisionist notion of the beliefs, values, and faith of an authentic secularity and to a revisionist understanding of the beliefs, values, and faith of an authentic Christianity. Precisely that dual commitment, it seems, provides every good reason for challenging both the more usual self-understanding of secularity (viz., a non-theistic and anti-Christian secularism) [72] and the more usual self-understanding of Christianity (viz., as an anti-secular, religious supernaturalism).[73] For the post-liberal theologian, both secularity and traditional Christianity should be challenged in accordance with publicly available criteria for meaning, meaningfulness, and truth.

The object-referent of the revisionist model can perhaps be best described as a critical reformulation of both the meanings manifested by our common human experience and the meanings manifested by an interpretation of the central motifs of the Christian tradition. More exactly, the revisionist model for Christian theology ordinarily bears some such formulation as the following: contemporary Christian theology is best understood as philosophical reflection upon the meanings present in common human experience and the meanings present in the Christian tradition.[74] The major burden of the remainder of this book will be the attempt to clarify the exact meaning and the possibilities of just such a revisionist model for our common theological task.

Notes

(1) The literature on "ideal types" from Max Weber and on "models" from the analytical tradition is vast. For a *locus classicus* in Weber, cf. Max Weber, *The Protestant Ethic and The Spirit of Capitalism* (New York: Scribners, 1958), pp. 13–31. On models, cf. Max Black, *Models and Metaphors* (Ithaca: Cornell University Press, 1962); Frederick Ferré, *Language, Logic and God* (New York: Harper & Row, 1961); idem, "Metaphors, Models, and Religion," *Soundings*, No. 51, pp. 377–45; Ian Ramsey, *Christian Discourse* (London: Oxford University Press, 1956); idem, *Models and Mystery* (London: Oxford University Press, 1964); idem, *Religious Language: An Empirical Placing of Theological Phrases* (New York: Macmillan, 1967); idem (ed.), *Words About God* (London: SCM Press, 1971). It might be noted that, although later chapters of this work will make more extensive use of the work of Ferré and Ramsey, this chapter is limited to employing Ramsey's notion of theological models as "disclosure," not "picture" models. The basic notion of model or ideal type employed in this chapter is Bernard Lonergan's more general notion, viz., "Models, then, stand to the human sciences, to philosophies, to theologies, much as mathematics stands to the natural sciences. For models purport to be, not descriptions of reality, not hypotheses about reality, but simply interlocking sets of terms and relations" (*Method in Theology* [New York: Herder and Herder, 1972], pp. 284–5). I am developing Lonergan's notion of model here by uniting it to his allied notion of horizon or intentionality analysis: in short, the chapter attempts to develop each "model" in accordance with the "subject and object poles" of any given theological "horizon." On the latter notion in Lonergan, cf. David Tracy, *The Achievement of Bernard Lonergan* (New York: Herder and Herder, 1970), pp. 1–22. I am not attempting here to relate this discussion to the more technical linguistic discussion of models in Black, Hesse, and others. Indeed, in terms of that analysis, the present chapter is an exercise in "types" not "models." For a summary of the former analysis, cf. Ian Barbour, *Myths, Models and Paradigms: A Comparative Study in Science and Religion* (New York: Harper & Row, 1974), pp. 29–92.

(2) This can be more briefly formulated as the differing theological uses of argument in the sense of Stephen Toulmin's helpful clarifications on the structure of argument, cf. Stephen Toulmin, *The Uses of Argument* (New York: Cambridge University Press, 1958).

(3) For the basic distinctions, cf. Max Black, *Models and Metaphors*, pp. 219–43; Ian Ramsey, *Models and Mystery*, pp. 1–21.

(4) It might be noted that, unlike Ramsey and Ferré, I restrict the use of models to theological as distinct from religious discourse. For a similar judgment, cf. Robert M. Scharlemann, "Theological Models and Their Construction," *Journal of Religion*, 53 (1973), 68.

(5) Cf. references in Lonergan's work in n. 1 above. It might also be noted that I refer here to Lonergan's notion of "models" in "dialectics," not to his more fundamental position on method itself as a model, but more than a model; on the latter, cf. *Method in Theology*, p. xii.

(6) The reasons for the choice "revisionist" over the earlier label "neo-liberal" are cited in chapter one, n. 7. The other titles seem obvious and non-controversial as self-descriptive of the positions.

(7) Cf. Paul Tillich, *Systematic Theology*, I (Chicago: University of Chicago Press, 1951), 218–35.

(8) For a concise summary of Nygren's complex and sophisticated notion of "motif-research," cf. Anders Nygren, *Meaning and Method* (Philadelphia: Fortress, 1972), pp. 351–790. For Nygren's own use, cf. his *Agape and Eros* (New York: Harper & Row, 1969). For a classical systematic use of motif-research, cf. Gustaf Aulen, *The Faith of the Christian Church* (Philadelphia: Fortress Press, 1960). The brief comment in the text does not pretend to do justice to the complex and fruitful reality of motif-research undertaken by Nygren and his many colleagues. Indeed, in a later work on dogmatic theology, I hope to be able to employ this important tradition in a more positive way. In the present work, the interest in Nygren's work is largely restricted to a critical appraisal of his earlier "scientific philosophy of religion" (cf. chapter seven), and to the suggestion that the present exercise in "model" development does not attempt to develop basic motifs in the manner of Nygren and Aulen.

(9) Bernard Lonergan, *Method in Theology*, pp. 284–5.

(10) Whether articulated in this manner or not, even orthodox theologies, as historical research makes clear, were never "purely" Christian but always also involved contemporary understandings.

(11) The tradition of Josiah Royce in terms of its insistence on the value "loyalty" to particular "communities of interpretation" is particularly relevant here; for references, cf. chapter one, n. 31. For Royce himself, cf. esp. *The Problem of Christianity* (Chicago: University of Chicago Press, 1968), esp. pp. 75–99, 297–343.

(12) The phrase "inner-theological" suggests that all norms for theological statements are to be found in the "authorities" affirmed by the particular church community, not by "outside" communities of inquiry.

(13) The range of "orthodox" positions can, therefore, include not merely "Denziger-theologies" but also such sophisticated biblical theologies as the "salvation-history" approaches of Oscar Cullmann and others. "Dogmatic" as distinct from

"fundamental" theologies will often be "orthodox." But if fundamental theologies are allowed to operate *as fundamental* the later "dogmatics" will also need reformulation—for example, into a *Glaubenslehre*.

(14) For an interpretation of Vatican I here, cf. Bernard Lonergan, *Method in Theology*, pp. 320–6.

(15) For an excellent example of the proper understanding and application of this orthodox model in the Roman Catholic tradition, cf. Bernard Lonergan, *Divinarum Personarum* (Rome: Gregorian University Press, 1959), esp. pp. 7–68.

(16) Note the meaning of *"fides"* in Vatican I, for example, as "belief" not "faith," cf. Bernard Lonergan's use of H. J. Pottmeyer's work in "Faith and Beliefs," *Second Collection* (Philadelphia: Westminster, 1975). The present work holds that the Christian theologian *qua* theologian need not be an explicit believer. What he needs is some adequate pre-understanding of the subject-matter (religion)—a pre-understanding basically present to anyone able to ask the fundamental questions of human existence articulated in religious and theological speech. Such an understanding also assumes that a *Sach-Kritik* of traditional answers is possible for the theologian *qua* theologian. For a discussion of this important issue, cf. John Connelley, "What Is Theology?" and "Replies" (by Schubert M. Ogden and David Tracy) in *Proceedings for the Catholic Theological Society of America*, 1974.

(17) Once removed from their nineteenth-century context, these familiar typologies can still, I believe, be operative as models to avoid even for the revisionist theologian whose final position is neither "fideism" nor "rationalism." For the nineteenth-century typologies, cf. Bernard Lonergan, *Method in Theology*, p. 324.

(18) This was the *in principle* claim. In fact, of course, matters worked differently. For an analysis, cf. Walter Kasper, "Geschichtlichkeit der Dogmen?" *Stimmen der Zeit*, 179 (1967), 401–16.

(19) In general terms, "liberal" refers to Protestant theologians; "modernist" to Catholic theologians. For the Roman Catholic context, cf. Edgar Hocedez, *Histoire de la théologie au XIX siècle, Museum Lessianum–Section Théologique*, no. 43, 3 vols. (Brussells: Edeticus Universelle, S.A., 1947–52); Émile Poulat, *Histoire, dogme et critique dans la crise moderniste* (Tournai: Castermann, 1962); Alec R. Vidler, *The Modernist Movement in the Roman Church* (Cambridge: Cambridge University Press, 1934); Bernhard Welte, "Zur Strukturwandel der Katholischen Theologie in 19. Zahrhundert," in *Auf der Spur des Ewigen* (Freiburg: Herder Verlag, 1965), pp. 380–408. For American Protestant liberal theology, cf. Kenneth Cauthen, *The Impact of American Theological Liberalism* (New York: Harper & Row, 1962).

(20) Cf. Langdon Gilkey, *Religion and the Scientific Future* (New York: Harper & Row, 1970), pp. 35–65.

(21) This is clearly the case, for example, in F. C. Baur; more ambiguously, but also present in a Catholic modernist like Alfred Loisy.

(22) A clear example of this commitment, often misunderstood by both conservative and secularist critics, is the work of Henry Nelson Wieman in *The Source of Human Good* (Carbondale, Ill.: Southern Illinois University Press, 1946).

(23) This is especially true, of course, of the "mediation theologies" but is also true of such "critical orthodoxies" as those of Frederick Denison Maurice or Horace Bushnell. For a refinement and application of these typologies, cf. Claude Welch, *Protestant Thought in the Nineteenth Century: Vol. I, 1799–1870* (New Haven: Yale University Press, 1972), esp. pp. 147–292.

(24) This commitment to a particular church tradition seems clearly operative in most liberals and modernists. Two exceptions seem to be Ernst Troeltsch (where a more "Catholic" notion of "tradition" is united to his own Reformed heritage) and F. D. Maurice (with his Anglo-Catholic sense of historical tradition and his Protestant sense of ongoing reformation). Indeed, in the present ecumenical atmosphere, both Troeltsch and Maurice, along with Paul Tillich's insistence upon the need for both Protestant principle and Catholic substance, should, I believe, be contemporaneously "retrieved" as suggesting genuinely ecumenical models for a Christian dogmatics.

(25) Cf. esp., Friedrich Schleiermacher, *The Christian Faith* (Edinburgh: T. & T. Clark, 1928); idem, *Brief Outline of the Study of Theology* (Philadelphia: Westminster, 1966); also, *Schleiermacher as Contemporary*, ed. Robert Funk, *Journal for Theology and the Church*, vol. 7 (New York: Herder and Herder, 1970); Richard R. Niebuhr, *Schleiermacher on Christ and Religion* (New York: Harper & Row, 1964); for a bibliography of Schleiermacher's works and the secondary literature from 1800–1964, cf. Terrence N. Tice, *Schleiermacher Bibliography* (Princeton: Princeton University Press, 1966).

(26) Cf. chapter one, n. 31 for references here.

(27) For an excellent analysis of how Schleiermacher's model of *Glaubenslehre* is reformulated and refined by Ernst Troeltsch, cf. B. A. Gerrish's study of Troeltsch's notion of *Glaubenslehre*, to appear in *Ernst Troeltsch and the Future of Religion*, ed. John Powell Clayton, to be published by Cambridge University Press in 1976. Precisely a model in that mode is what, in my judgment, is needed for a "systematic" as distinct from a fundamental theology.

(28) Note, for example, Wilhelm Pauck's attempt to mediate certain authentic Barthian insights to the liberal theological tradition in Wilhelm Pauck, *Karl Barth: Prophet of a New Christianity?* (New York: Harper, 1931).

(29) A quoted oral comment from a lecture by Wilhelm Pauck. The same general insistence may be found in Pauck's work on Barth cited above or in his interpretations of the continuing importance of Harnack and Troeltsch; cf. Wilhelm Pauck, *Harnack and Troeltsch: Two Historical Theologians* (New York: Oxford University Press, 1968), esp. pp. 43–5 on Troeltsch's influence on the Niebuhrs and on Paul Tillich.

(30) Cf. that still extraordinary Barthian thunderbolt, *The Epistle to the Romans* (London: Oxford University Press, 1972), for what is probably still the classical neo-orthodox statement. The Barth of the *Dogmatics* might be described as moving (sometimes within a single section) between his own earlier neo-orthodox and his later sometimes orthodox model. For a critique of Barth from the "orthodox model" side, cf. G. C. Berkouwer, *The Triumph of Grace in the Theology of Karl Barth* (Grand Rapids: Eerdmans, 1956).

(31) Indeed, the neo-orthodox theologians made the same charge of "illusion" not just "error" to their liberal predecessors as Marx, Nietzsche, and Freud made to their Enlightenment predecessors (cf. chapter one, n. 52 for references). Perhaps the outstanding example of this charge may be found in Reinhold Niebuhr's critique of political and religious liberalism; cf. Reinhold Niebuhr, *Moral Man and Immoral Society* (New York: Scribners, 1932); idem, *Reflections on the End of an Era* (New York: Scribners, 1936).

(32) Cf. Karl Barth, *The Epistle to the Romans*, esp. "The Preface to the Second Edition," pp. 2–15.

(33) Note Tillich's consistent attempts to move beyond both "autonomy" and "heteronomy" to "theonomy." For an example (on the doctrine of revelation), cf. Paul Tillich, *Systematic Theology*, I, 147–50, 155–63.

(34) Cf. especially Reinhold Niebuhr, *The Nature and Destiny of Man*, I (New York: Scribner, 1964), esp. 178–241; Paul Tillich, *Systematic Theology*, II, 44–78. Note also how a neo-orthodox document like Anders Nygren's *Agape and Eros* can relate its agapic Christian theme to the "transvaluation of all values" motif of Nietzsche against modernity; cf. *Agape and Eros*, p. 28.

(35) This formulation is representative, of course, of the neo-Reformation theologians. A Catholic formulation of a neo-orthodox kind, as suggested below, may be found in thinkers like Maurice Blondel and Karl Rahner: for example, cf. Rahner's retrieval of the Catholic sense of symbol in *Theological Investigations,* IV (Baltimore: Helicon Press, 1966), 221–52.

(36) Note that for the neo-orthodox (like the liberal) "faith" rather than "beliefs" is the central factor demanding theological explication.

(37) Despite its varying meanings, the shared sense of "dialectical" includes an incisive account of "negations" in experience and in thought and, ordinarily, an account of the originality of a Christian negation of those negations (e.g., through agapic love). For texts illustrative of how such a dialectical view of life is pervasive in neo-orthodox theology, cf. James M. Robinson (ed.), *The Beginning of Dialectic Theology* (Richmond: Knox, 1968).

(38) For example, cf. Rudolf Bultmann, *Existence and Faith*, trans. Schubert Ogden, (New York: World Publishing Co.), pp. 25–39.

(39) In chapter four, the criteria of "relative adequacy" by means of which such a claim may be upheld are articulated; a partial fulfillment of that claim may be found in chapter nine in the section on the "fact of evil."

(40) The "at some point" must remain vague here. The later chapters' development of the notion "limit-language" will allow for a partial specification of "at what point." Perhaps a cryptic comment may be allowed me here: the interpreter of theological texts should be wary when Catholic theologians announce that they have shown "where the mystery lies," or when Protestant theologians announce that such is the "paradox" or "scandal" of faith. Perhaps—but it may be that the theology is breaking down, not that the religious reality of the "mystery" or "scandal" is breaking through.

(41) For further clarification of the negative and positive aspects of the neo-ortho-dox insistence upon "christocentrism," cf. the discussion in chapter nine on "ex-clusivist" and "inclusivist" christologies.

(42) The articulation of the criteria may be found in Schubert M. Ogden, "The Task of Theology," *Journal of Religion* 52 (1972), 22–40, esp. 25–27, 30–34. They are expli-cated in this work in the following two chapters. It seems to me a legitimate exten-sion of Ogden's argument to suggest that the neo-orthodox theologians refined not only certain contents for Christian theology but also the "criteria of appropriate-ness" for any Christian theology.

(43) For a post-neo-orthodox formulation of this insight, cf. Ray Hart, *Unfinished Man and the Imagination* (New York: Herder and Herder, 1968), esp. pp. 21–109.

(44) The "transformation-model" seems to be one major key to the relative ade-quacy of a particular symbol system to disclose meaningfulness. Recall, for exam-ple, the responsibility model of H. Richard Niebuhr in *The Responsible Self* (New York: Harper & Row, 1963); or Bernard Lonergan's transformation-models of "conversions" and "self-transcendence" in *Method in Theology*, esp. pp. 235–37 and 267–71. The uses of psychological transformation-models can be witnessed, for ex-ample, in the recent use of Jung by several Catholic theologians, or in Sam Keen, *Apology for Wonder* (New York: Harper & Row, 1969). For an extensive analysis of pertinent transformation-models, cf. Don Browning, *Generative Man* (Philadelphia: Westminster, 1974).

(45) This comment seems especially appropriate to the Barth of the *Dogmatics*, al-though most of the other neo-orthodox theologians maintain a similar commitment at some point. Recall, for example, the "left-wing" critiques of Bultmann from this viewpoint, e.g., Schubert M. Ogden, *Christ Without Myth* (New York: Harper & Row, 1961), pp. 105–26.

(46) Although one may share the respect for the insistence behind these concepts one may also share the reluctance to use them as often or perhaps as easily as the neo-orthodox were tempted to do. For a critique in that direction, cf. Ronald W. Hepburn, *Christianity and Paradox* (London: Watts, 1958), esp. pp. 62–90 (on Barth), or pp. 26–59 (on Buber and Brunner).

(47) Compare, for example, Langdon Gilkey's earlier neo-orthodox work *Maker of Heaven and Earth* (Garden City, N.Y.: Doubleday, 1959) with his later post-neo-or-thodox *Naming the Whirlwind: The Renewal of God-Language* (New York: Bobbs-Merrill, 1970).

(48) This point can be made by such different critics of religious language as Kai Nielsen, for example, in *Contemporary Critiques of Religion* (New York: Herder and Herder, 1971), or Charles Hartshorne in "Philosophical and Religious Uses of 'God' " in *A Natural Theology for Our Time* (La Salle, Ill.: Open Court, 1967).

(49) Note that the basis is "faith" not "beliefs"; note also that the reigning models are: first, "self-transcendence," neither "self-fulfillment" nor "self-abnegation"; sec-ond, "authenticity," not liberal "sincerity."

(50) Cf., for example, Nygren's insistence in *Agape and Eros*, esp. pp. 722–39; a Catholic formulation of this basic attitudinal orientation may be found in Bernard

Lonergan's notion of "being-in-love-in-an-unrestricted fashion" in *Method in Theology*, pp. 105–112.

(51) Cf. *The Nature and Destiny of Man*, I, 93–123, 123–50.

(52) The insistence upon the "infinitely qualitative distinction" between God and humanity is especially true of Barth's earliest writings when the influence of Kierkegaard is still paramount, cf. *The Epistle to the Romans*, p. 10: ". . . if I have a system, it is limited to a recognition of what Kierkegaard called the 'infinite qualitative distinction' between time and eternity, and to my regarding this as possessing negative as well as positive significance: God is in heaven, and thou art on earth."

(53) Event in the German sense of *Ereignis*; perhaps the American English "happening" communicates something of the force of the original better than our more ordinary *(historisch)* "event."

(54) One of the real strengths of these theologies is that behind all the major neo-orthodox theologies, Protestant and Catholic, there lie major works of historical research and historical-theological retrieval: e.g., the major Luther and Calvin revivals among Protestants; the major Thomist and patristic revivals among Catholics. The latter, for example, issued forth into the French and German Catholic theologies of sacramental, liturgical, and patristic *ressourcement* of Henri de Lubac, Yves Congar, Jean Daniélou, and Hans Urs von Balthasar which became, at Vatican II, universal Catholic *aggorniamento*. After the collapse of modernism, moreover, and the difficulties of *la nouvelle théologie* in the 1930's and 1940's, Catholic theologians could take advantage of both the work of such great medieval historians as Gilson, Chenu, Lottin, and Grabmann, and the pioneering work into modern forms of philosophical thought by J. Maréchal and J. Rousselot to issue forth into that special kind of Catholic theological neo-orthodoxy, neo-Thomism, as manifested in the early works of such signal Catholic theologians as Bernard Lonergan, Karl Rahner, and Edward Schillebeeckx. For examples of the latter, cf. especially Karl Rahner, *Spirit in the World* (New York: Herder and Herder, 1968); Bernard Lonergan, *Verbum: Word and Idea in Aquinas* (South Bend: University of Notre Dame Press, 1968); Edward Schillebeeckx, *Marriage: Secular Reality and Saving Mystery*, 2 vols. (London: Sheed and Ward, 1965). For a readable account of these developments, cf. T. M. Schoof, *A Survey of Catholic Theology, 1800–1970*, and Helen James John, *The Thomist Spectrum* (New York: Fordham University Press, 1966). For still clearer examples, cf. the earlier articles in Lonergan's *Collection* (New York: Herder and Herder, 1965); the early volumes of Rahner's *Theological Investigations*, I–III (Baltimore: Helicon, 1961–5); and the early volumes of Schillebeeckx's *Theological Soundings* (New York: Sheed and Ward, 1967).

(55) Cf. Karl Rahner, "The Concept of Mystery in Catholic Theology," in *Theological Investigations*, IV, or the articles of Rahner on christology cited in chapter nine.

(56) For references and discussion, cf. the analysis of the theologies of *praxis* in chapter ten. A critique of the "individualism" present in classical-modern Catholic philosophical theologies may be found in Johann Baptist Metz, *Theology of the World* (New York: Herder and Herder, 1969), pp. 81–101; and of the individualism of existentialist theologians in Jürgen Moltmann, *Theology of Hope* (New York: Harper & Row, 1967), esp. pp. 42–58. It might also be noted that the theologies of Wolfhart Pannenberg and Johann Baptist Metz (and, less clearly, Juan-Luis Segundo) seem closer, in varying ways, to the revisionist model for theological reflec-

tion. On the other hand, the revelational theology of James Cone seems clearly dominated by its originally neo-orthodox (Barthian) origins for its general model for theology in spite of its otherwise radical outlook; cf. James Cone, *Black Theology and Black Power* (New York: Seabury, 1969).

(57) Examples here would include the works of theological-cultural analysis of John Dunne: for example, *A Search for God in Time and Memory* (New York: Macmillan, 1965); and Gabriel Moran's *The Present Revelation* (New York: Seabury, 1973).

(58) Although many seem tempted to dismiss the "death of God" controversy as merely another fad or act of desperation from the sixties in America, this judgment seems to me to miss the profound and enduring consequences of that important period. The crucial documents remain: Thomas Altizer and William Hamilton, *Radical Theology and the Death of God* (Indianapolis: Bobbs-Merrill, 1966); Paul van Buren, *The Secular Meaning of the Gospel* (New York: Macmillan, 1963); Richard L. Rubenstein, Jr., *After Auschwitz* (Indianapolis: Bobbs-Merrill, 1966); Thomas J. J. Altizer, *The Gospel of Christian Atheism* (Philadelphia: Westminster, 1966). The most radical and most theological of these varying thinkers is Thomas J. J. Altizer. For an extended study of his important thought, cf. *The Theology of Altizer: Critique and Response*, ed. by John B. Cobb, Jr. (Philadelphia: Westminster Press, 1970). For a criticism of these thinkers, cf. Langdon Gilkey, *Naming the Whirlwind*, pp. 107–47.

(59) This is especially true of the radically dialectical position developed by Altizer, for example, *The Gospel of Christian Atheism*, p. 103.
(60) For example, cf. the statements in Thomas J. J. Altizer and William Hamilton, *Radical Theology and the Death of God*, pp. 102–4.

(61) Thus does the christocentrism of the earlier neo-orthodox period survive, having undergone a sea-change, in van Buren, *The Secular Meaning of the Gospel*, esp. pp. 157–73; and Altizer's radical incarnationalism, e.g., *The Gospel of Christian Atheism*, esp. pp. 89–95.

(62) Cf. Paul van Buren, *The Secular Meaning of the Gospel*, p. 155.

(63) This issue will be treated at length in chapters seven and eight.

(64) Inter alia, cf. Leslie Dewart, *The Future of Belief* (New York: Herder and Herder, 1966); Gregory Baum, *Man Becoming: God in Secular Experience* (New York: Herder and Herder, 1970); Michael Novak, *Belief and Unbelief* (New York: Macmillan, 1965); idem, *Ascent of the Mountain, Flight of the Dove: An Invitation to Religious Studies* (New York: Harper & Row, 1971); Andrew Greeley, *The New Agenda* (New York: Doubleday, 1973); Langdon Gilkey, *Naming the Whirlwind*; idem, *Religion and the Scientific Future*; Van A. Harvey, *The Historian and the Believer* (New York: Macmillan, 1966); Gordon E. Kaufman, *God the Problem* (Cambridge: Harvard University Press, 1972). As this partial list alone may serve to reveal, the spectrum of theologians employing a "revisionist model" is as wide as those employing any other model.

(65) The success or failure of such an enterprise, I believe, lies in its ability to be faithful to the permanent achievements of each of the earlier models, not to bypass any one of them: for example, by a simple return to the liberal model via some new kind of "neo-liberalism."

(66) The adjective "possible" is important here: as the present exercise in fundamental theology will state in initial terms and as a full-fledged dogmatics would articulate at length, there is often need for "dramatic confrontations" between an authentic Christian view (e.g., on agapic love) and an authentic secular view (e.g., on Utopianism). This remains the case even if a Christian view can genuinely provide not merely a negation, but something like an *Aufhebung* of the secular (as is argued by proponents of the "caritas" synthesis). A Christian dogmatics would need to articulate all those dialectical possibilities. The present work is concerned only to articulate criteria for fundamental theology and their initial application to the questions of religion, theism, and christology.

(67) Cf. B. M. G. Reardon, *Religious Thought in the Nineteenth Century* (New York: Cambridge University Press, 1966), esp. pp. 26–33.

(68) A recent example of this may be found in Robert Heilbroner, *An Inquiry Into the Human Prospect* (New York: W. W. Norton, 1974).

(69) The Bossuets of any given age seem especially prone to this kind of call. One cannot but be suspicious that the rhetorical cries of pain from such contemporary prophets of "orthodoxy" as Billy Graham or Daniel Lyons, S.J., may, however unselfconsciously, be pleas for what amounts to a return to mystification.

(70) For a persuasive analysis of the "post-liberal" period of theology, cf. Bernard Meland, *The Realities of Faith: The Revolution in Cultural Forms* (New York: Oxford University Press, 1962), esp. pp. 109–70.

(71) Again, with the proviso of providing not empirical generalizations but basic terms and relations to aid specific analysis.

(72) "Anti-Christian" should here be understood to be the ideological position which maintains that any self-consciously Christian stance must be obscurantist and/or oppressive.

(73) This phenomenon is familiar enough to any reader of the fundamentalist religious press in this country; as a single example, the conservative Roman Catholic journal *The Wanderer* seems to specialize in this kind of supernaturalism.

(74) The word "tradition" covers the same ground as the expression "the Christian fact"; tradition should be understood, moreover, in the sense of *traditio* not merely of *tradita*.

Chapter 3

A Revisionist Model for Contemporary Theology

In its briefest expression, the revisionist model holds that a contemporary fundamental Christian theology can best be described as philosophical reflection upon the meanings present in common human experience and language, and upon the meanings present in the Christian fact.[1] To explain and to defend this model for the task of theology, five theses will be proposed which are intended to explicate the principal meanings involved in this model for the task of theology. The structure of the present argument is best grasped by an understanding of the interrelationships of the theses themselves. The first thesis defends the proposition that there are two sources for theology, common human experience and language, and Christian texts. The second thesis argues for the necessity of correlating the results of the investigations of these two sources. The third and fourth theses attempt to specify the most helpful methods of investigation employed for studying these two sources. The fifth and final thesis further specifies the final mode of critical correlation of these investigations as an explicitly metaphysical or transcendental one. At the time of the discussion of this final thesis, one should be able to provide a summary of the meaning and truth-value of the present model proposed for theology, viz., philosophical reflection upon common human experience and language, and upon Christian texts. There are, of course, thorny problems and several alternative views possible not only for the model as a whole, but for each "thesis" in the model. I hope that the lengthier discussions of the later chapters may serve to clarify why those alternative views have not been followed—or perhaps should have been followed.

First Thesis: *The Two Principal Sources for Theology Are Christian Texts and Common Human Experience and Language.*

This thesis seems the least problematic of the five proposed. For it seems obvious that any enterprise called Christian theology will attempt to show the appropriateness of its chosen categories to the meanings of the major expressions and texts of the Christian tradition.[2] This source of the theological task is variously labelled: "the message" as with Paul Tillich, the "ker-ygma" as with Rudolf Bultmann, the "Christian witness of faith" as with Schubert Ogden, the "tradition" as with most contemporary Catholic theologians.[3] Whatever title is chosen, the recognition of the need for the Christian theologian to show just how and why his conclusions are appropriate to the Christian tradition remains as obvious in its demand as it proves to be difficult in its execution.[4] A subsidiary but not unimportant corollary of this demand is that the scriptures remain the fundamental although not exclusive expression of that Christian faith.[5] Hence a principal task of the theologian will be to find appropriate interpretations of the major motifs[6] of the scriptures and of the relationship of those interpretations to the confessional, doctrinal, symbolic, theological, and *praxis* expressions of the various Christian traditions. Except for those few theologians who would maintain that theology is without remainder a philosophical reflection upon our contemporary experience and language, this commitment to determining the ability of contemporary formulations to state the meanings of Christian texts remains an obvious, albeit difficult task.

Even from the limited perspective of this understanding of the nature of a theologian's responsibility to the tradition, it would also seem that the task of theology involves an attempt to show the adequacy of the major Christian theological categories for all human experience. In fact, insofar as the scriptures claim that the Christian self-understanding does, in fact, express an understanding of authentic human existence as such, the Christian theologian is impelled to test precisely that universalist claim. He will ordinarily do so by developing criteria that generically can be labelled "criteria of adequacy" to common human experience.[7] Whether this source of theological reflection be called the "situation" as with Paul Tillich, the "contemporary scientific world view" as with Rudolf Bultmann, the contemporary phenomenon of a full-fledged "historical consciousness" as with Bernard Lonergan, or "common human experience" as here, again the task seems a fully necessary one. However, this demand is not forced upon the Christian theologian only by his commitment to the authentic aspects of modernity, much less by a search for contemporary relevance. Rather that task is primarily demanded for inner theological reasons. Rudolf Bultmann, for one, clarifies these reasons by his firm insistence that demythologizing is demanded not only by the contemporary world-view but also by the universalist, existential assumptions of the New Testament self-understanding itself.[8]

This commitment to determine methods and criteria which can show the adequacy of Christian self-understanding for all human experience is a task demanded by the very logic of the Christian affirmations; more precisely, by the Christian claim to provide the authentic way to understand our common human existence. This insight *theologically* disallows any attempt to force a strictly traditional inner-theological understanding of the sources of theological reflection. Whether that inner theological self-understanding be explicated through any of the forms of theological orthodoxy or through the kind of neo-orthodoxy represented by Karl Barth in the *Church Dogmatics* is a relatively minor matter.[9] The major insight remains the insistence present in theological reflection at least since Schleiermacher: the task of a Christian theology intrinsically involves a commitment to investigate critically both the Christian faith in its several expressions and contemporary experience in its several cultural expressions. In this important sense one may continue to find Schleiermacher's slogan for the task of theology still accurate: "The theses of faith must become the hypotheses of the theologian." [10]

Second Thesis: *The Theological Task Will Involve a Critical Correlation of the Results of the Investigations of the Two Sources of Theology.*

Given the fact of two sources needing investigation, some way of correlating the results of these investigations must be developed. The full dimensions of this task of correlation cannot, of course, be developed until the methods of investigation analyzed in the next two theses are clarified. For the moment, however, it is sufficient to clarify the need for some method of correlation. Perhaps the clearest way to clarify the meaning of this thesis will be to compare the method of correlation proposed here with the best known method of correlation in contemporary theology, Paul Tillich's. This "clarification through contrast" procedure[11] is here a useful one since so many contemporary theologians are justly indebted to Tillich for formulating the task of theology in terms of the general model of a method of correlation.

There are, it is true, some significant differences between the Tillichian notions of "situation" and "message" and the present articulation of the two sources of theology as "common human experience" and "Christian texts." [12] Still, the twofold nature of the theologian's commitment implied by these expressions, as well as the recognition that such a commitment logically involves the need for some kind of correlation, is a shared position. Moreover, one may continue to find Tillich's articulation of the ideal for contemporary theology to be fundamentally sound. As Tillich expresses it in volume I of the *Systematics*, the ideal contemporary theological position would provide an *Aufhebung* of both liberalism and neo-orthodoxy. As Tillich expresses the same ideal in his introduction to volume II, the theologian must attempt to move beyond both classical "supernaturalism" and secular "naturalism" by developing some form of "self-transcending naturalism." [13]

In sum, Paul Tillich's position continues to seem peculiarly helpful: for his expression of the proper ideal of contemporary theology; for his insistence that only an investigation of both "situation" and "message" can hope to fulfill this ideal; and for his articulation of the need for some general model of correlation as the proper response to this need.

However, many critics find Tillich's own formulation of how the method of correlation actually functions neither intrinsically convincing nor consistent with the task of theology which he himself articulates. The fact is that Tillich's method does not call for a critical correlation of the results of one's investigations of the "situation" and the "message." [14] Rather, his method affirms the need for a correlation of the "questions" expressed in the "situation" with the "answers" provided by the Christian "message." Such a correlation, in fact, is one between "questions" from one source and "answers" from the other. Even on the limited basis of the position defended in the first thesis, one cannot but find unacceptable this formulation of the theological task of correlation. For if the "situation" is to be taken with full seriousness, then its answers to its own questions must also be investigated critically. Tillich's method cannot really allow this. A classic example of this difficulty can be found in Tillich's famous dictum, "Existentialism is the good luck of Christian theology." [15] We are all indebted to Tillich's brilliant reinterpretation pointing out the heavy debt which existentialist analyses of man's estranged situation owe to classical Christian anthropology. Yet no one (not even a Christian theologian!) can decide that only *the questions* articulated by a particular form of contemporary thought are of real theological interest. [16]

Correlatively, from the viewpoint of the Christian message itself, the very claim to have an answer applicable to any human situation demands logically that a critical comparison of the Christian "answer" with all other "answers" be initiated. To return to the existentialist example, why do we not find in Tillich a critical investigation of the claims that either Jean Paul Sartre's or Karl Jaspers' philosophies of existence provide a better "answer" to the question of human estrangement than the Christian "answer" does?

In summary, a commitment to two sources for theology does imply the need to formulate a method capable of correlating the principal questions and answers of each source. Yet Tillich's method of correlation is crucially inadequate. Tillich's implicit commitment to two sources and his explicit insistence upon a theological ideal which transcends both naturalism and supernaturalism could be successfully executed only by a method which develops critical criteria for correlating the questions and the answers found in both the "situation" and the "message." Any method which attempts less than that cannot really be called a method of correlation. Tillich's method does not actually correlate; it juxtaposes questions from the "situation" with answers from the "message." Insofar as this critique is true, the contemporary theologian can accept Tillich's articulation of the need for a method of correlation, but he cannot accept Tillich's own model for theology as one which actually correlates.

Third Thesis: *The Principal Method of Investigation of the Source "Common Human Experience and Language" Can Be Described as a Phenomenology of the "Religious Dimension" Present in Everyday and Scientific Experience and Language.*

The principal intention of this thesis is to clarify the method needed to investigate the first source of theology. It should be emphasized at once, however, that the present thesis does not involve a determination of the truth-value of the meanings uncovered. Rather this thesis merely attempts to analyze what method will best allow those meanings to be explicated as accurately as possible.[17]

A widely accepted dictum of contemporary theological thought holds that all theological statements involve an existential dimension, indeed a dimension which includes a claim to universal existential relevance.[18] On that basis it seems fair to conclude that the theologian is obliged to explicate how and why the existential meanings proper to Christian self-understanding are present in common human experience. As long as one's understanding of the concept experience is not confined to Humean sense-data but involves a recognition of the pre-reflective, pre-conceptual, pre-thematic realm of the everyday, then the task of theology in this moment of its enterprise seems clear.[19] That task is the need to explicate a pre-conceptual dimension to our common shared experience that can legitimately be described as religious. Historically, that task is best represented by the liberal theological tradition's search for a method capable of explicating an ultimate or final horizon of meaning to our common everyday life and language, and to our scientific and ethical reflection which can properly be described as both ultimate and religious.[20]

One way of formulating this task is to suggest that contemporary phenomenological method is the method best suited for it. The reasons for the choice of the title "phenomenology" at this point are basically twofold. First, several major figures in the phenomenological tradition from Max Scheler through the recent work of Langdon Gilkey have demonstrated the effectiveness of phenomenological reflection in explicating that final or ultimate horizon precisely *as a religious one*.[21] Second, the history of phenomenological reflection on the nature of the method itself has developed ever more sophisticated ways to formulate the full dimensions of any phenomenological investigation. Indeed, phenomenological method has undergone several important transformations from the earlier "eidetic" formulations of Husserl and the Göttingen circle through the existential phenomenology of Sartre, Merleau-Ponty, Scheler, and the early Heidegger to the hermeneutic phenomenology of Gadamer, the later Heidegger, and Paul Ricoeur.[22] Each of these redefinitions of the nature of phenomenology has been impelled by the inability of an earlier method to explicate the full dimensions of the phenomena uncovered by earlier reflection. If the most recent formulations of phenomenology's task (the hermeneutic) be sound, then it seems reasonable to suggest that theologians might employ such a method to analyze those symbols and gestures present to our everyday life and language that may legitimately manifest a religious dimension to our lives.

To be sure, the present position does not argue that only phenomenological method can succeed in this analysis. It does argue that a recognition of the real possibilities of that method promises a new surety to the several attempts to explicate the religious dimension of our common experience and language. As one example of phenomenology's relative adequacy for theology's task, consider the crucial question of the linguistic and symbolic character of our experience. On that question, it seems clear that so-called "hermeneutic phenomenology" is far better prepared than either the "reformed subjectivist principle" of the Whiteheadians or the earlier "critical phenomenology" of Paul Tillich[23] to explicate the linguistic (usually symbolic) character of everyday experience; this holds as well for the properly linguistic and symbolic dimensions of the final and ultimate horizon of that world as religious. Not a plea for exclusive rights, the argument for phenomenology takes the form of suggesting its relative adequacy for uncovering the full dimensions of the common task.

Thus far in this third thesis the emphasis has been upon the kind of method needed for this common theological task. Hopefully, such an emphasis does not obscure the nature of the task itself: the continued search in most contemporary theology for an adequate expression of the religious dimension of our common experience and language.[24] To repeat, that task seems demanded both by the universalist claim of Christian self-understanding and by the otherwise inexplicable character of our shared experience itself.

In fact, so complex does this aspect of theology's contemporary task become that only a phenomenology in continued conversation with those human sciences which investigate the religious dimension in human existence, and in conversation with other philosophical methods can really hope to succeed.[25] As an example of such collaboration, it may prove helpful to close this thesis with mention of a few conversation partners available at the moment. The work of Paul Tillich on this question (viz., his analysis of the religious "ultimate concern" involved in the human "situation") has, in fact, been continued and refined by the work of such diverse interpreters of Tillich as Langdon Gilkey, Tom Driver, Nathan Scott, and David Kelsey.[26] The work of Bernard Lonergan on the religious dimension in human cognition and action is presently being advanced both by Lonergan himself, in his more recent work, and by Lonergan interpreters such as John Dunne, David Burrell, and Michael Novak.[27] Enterprises like these are, I believe, central to any serious contemporary attempt at fundamental theology.

Fourth Thesis: *The Principal Method of Investigation of the Source "The Christian Tradition" Can Be Described as an Historical and Hermeneutical Investigation of Classical Christian Texts.*

This thesis begins with a truism: if the Christian theologian must articulate the meanings of the phenomenon variously called the "Christian fact," "witness," "message," or "tradition," then he is obliged to enter into the discussion of the nature of the disciplines of history and hermeneutics. This thesis does not pretend to resolve the many problems encompassed by historical and hermeneutical knowledge.[28] Rather, it attempts only to outline the particular understandings of the historical and hermeneutical methods that may prove helpful for this aspect of the theological task.

The theological *need* for history and hermeneutics concerns us first. If the phenomenon labelled the "Christian fact" includes the significant gestures, symbols, and actions of the various Christian traditions, then the theologian must learn those historical methods capable of determining exactly what facts can be affirmed as probable. For the present investigation of texts, he must also learn historical methods in order to allow for the historical reconstruction of the basic texts of Christian self-understanding. On that historical basis of reconstruction, the theologian must then find a hermeneutic method capable of discerning *at least* the central meanings of the principal textual expressions of Christianity (viz., the scriptural). The general need for historical method articulated here is a modest one. It does not imply that the theologian employ a specific category like "salvation-history" as a useful theological one. The call for historical method does imply that the theologian as historian pay heed to those historical reconstructions of Christian events and texts which modern historical scholarship has made available. The argument for historical method implied by the first three theses, then, is a limited but important aspect of the theologian's larger task. If one were to define Christian theology as simply a philosophy of religion, then historical method need not be employed.[29] But if Christian theology is adequately defined only as a philosophical reflection upon both common human experience and language and upon Christian texts, then a historical reconstruction of the central texts of that tradition is imperative.

Perhaps the exact nature of the historical task of the theologian might best be understood by recalling a familiar instance of its exercise. That instance is the common Christian affirmation "Jesus of Nazareth is the Christ." That exercise is the attempt to determine what historical and hermeneutical methods can best aid the contemporary theologian to understand what Christians have actually meant by this familiar affirmation.[30] Rather than spelling out at length an understanding of historical and hermeneutic methods, in the remainder of this thesis I shall risk the belief that these crucial theological tasks are best grasped by examining their emergence in a specific theological problem. That problem is the primary existential meanings of christological texts.

The first questions to be addressed to the affirmation that "Jesus is the Christ" are ordinarily historical ones. The historian does want to know what conclusions historical inquiry can reach about the person Jesus of Nazareth and about the belief of the Christian community that Jesus was the Christ. On these historical questions it seems fair to state that, short of a position like J. M. Allegro's at least,[31] the accumulation of historical evidence on the existence of Jesus of Nazareth seems secure, even if the range of interpretations of his significance is wide indeed. Yet whatever interpretation of the "historical Jesus" is accepted as most probable by various historians through old and new "quests," [32] the principal factor demanding *theological* clarification is the religious existential meanings expressed in the New Testament christological texts as those texts are reconstructed by contemporary historical scholarship.

If the historian can reconstruct the texts in question,[33] then the next problem becomes the need to discover what discipline will allow one to determine the meanings of those metaphors, symbols, and "images" used in the New Testament texts to express the religious significance of the proclamation that Jesus of Nazareth is the Christ.[34] Much of the language of the New Testament texts is metaphorical, symbolic, and parabolic as distinct from conceptual; the principal meaning expressed by the texts is one which manifests or represents what can be properly labelled a religious meaning, a religious way of being-in-the-world. These two factors can be discerned by various combinations of historical and linguistic methods.[35] Yet to determine with greater exactness the full meaning of the "images" demands a more explicit formulation of the hermeneutic, as distinct from the historical task. The present discussion of that hermeneutical task does not pretend to provide an exhaustive analysis. Indeed, the history of reflection on the nature of that notoriously complex discipline makes one justifiably wary of any exhaustive claims.[36] For the moment, I will simply advance certain contemporary refinements of the hermeneutic tradition which seem applicable to the problem of discerning the meanings embedded in any written text—and only such developments in recent hermeneutic theory which seem particularly apt for illustrating the nature of the theologian's hermeneutic commitment.

The first development with which we are concerned is the process of linguistic "distanciation" expressed, for example, in the character of written as distinct from spoken language.[37] Summarily stated, this recent development in contemporary linguistic and hermeneutic theory allows the prospective interpreter to understand that a written text, precisely as written, is distanced both from the original intention of the author and from its original reception by its first addressees. If this be correct, the hermeneutic circle as it is ordinarily formulated by theologians needs reformulation. For the task of interpretation is not best understood in terms of the interpreter's own subjectivity attempting to grasp the subjectivity either of the author's intentions or of the original addressee's reception of its meaning.[38] Neither should the interpreter, as his principal concern, attempt to uncover the subjectivity of the historical person (here, Jesus of Nazareth) described in certain images and symbols (e.g., "Son of Man," "the Christ," "Prophet") which seemed especially germane for representing the existential significance of this person.[39] If this be the case, it does not seem to be of major theological import to engage in old and new quests for the historical Jesus as something distinct from finding a hermeneutic method capable of explicating the meanings of those christological texts referring both to Jesus and to a certain Christian mode-of-being-in-the-world.

A second major development in contemporary hermeneutic and linguistic theory should allow one to approach that latter task with greater surety. That development is the insistence that the contemporary interpreter must distinguish clearly between the "sense" and the "referents" of the text and hence between the methods needed to explicate each.[40] The "sense" of the text means the internal structure and meaning of the text as that structure can be determined through the ordinary methods of semantic and literary-critical inquiries. The "referents" of the text do not pertain to the meaning "behind" the text (e.g., the author's *real* intention or the social-cultural situation of the text). Rather, to shift metaphors, "referent" basically manifests the meaning "in front of" the text, i.e., that way of perceiving reality, that mode of being-in-the-world which the text opens up for the intelligent reader.[41]

Although this understanding of "referent" is not divorced from either prior historical or semantic investigations, still "referent" here is clearly distinct from those prior factors. Further, the referents of the text, on this understanding, are *the* factors demanding a properly hermeneutical as distinct from either an historical or a semantic exercise.[42] To show why this understanding of the hermeneutic task of the theologian seems sound, one can concretize the discussion by applying it to the task of understanding the existential referent of the New Testament affirmation that "Jesus is the Christ." At least four related methods are needed for this task: the historical method, semantics, literary-critical methods, and, finally, the explicitly hermeneutical.

First, the historian, by a full application of his methods of historical inquiry, can reconstruct the christological texts, i.e., both those texts of Jesus and about Jesus. Semantics can then help the interpreter to determine the linguistic structure of the images and symbols involved in the text; with literary-critical methods, the interpreter can determine the particular character of the literary genres by means of which the images, metaphors, and symbols are structured, codified, and transformed.[43] Still the meaning of major import *to the theologian*[44] remains a concern that can be formulated by a question like the following: what is the mode-of-being-in-the-world *referred to* by the text? [45] That question is not really answered until an explicitly hermeneutic enterprise is advanced. On this understanding, hermeneutics is the discipline capable of explicating *the referent* as distinct from either the sense of the text or the historical reconstruction of the text.

To continue this reflection upon the christological example, let us suppose that a prospective interpreter of the New Testament christological texts found a degree of high probability in Herbert Braun's dictum that in the New Testament the christologies are the variable while a theological anthropology (the understanding of humanity as existing in the presence of a gracious God) is the constant.[46] In one's search for the theological anthropology referred to by the christological texts, one would be engaged in the explicitly hermeneutical (as distinct from historical, semantic, or literary-critical) task of explicating that mode-of-being-in-the-world, that way of looking at reality which the texts express (a religious, Christian way of being-in-the-world). It seems fair to state that this understanding of hermeneutics could then show that the referent of the christological texts is properly described as a theological anthropology. In short, that referent is the specifically religious mode of being-in-the-world characterized by Braun in the statement that the existential meaning of the christological texts is that one can now live as though in the presence of a gracious God.[47]

Such a determination of a religious referent would, in fact, complete the explicitly hermeneutic task of the theologian.[48] The further question of the truth-status of the referent explicated by hermeneutics remains. For that question, a distinct mode of reflection is needed. Even if his hermeneutic enterprise were successful, the theologian must still face the further task of correlating the results of his hermeneutic reflections with the results of his reflections upon contemporary experience and language. To achieve this correlation he must ask what further reflective discipline will allow him to determine whether his earlier conclusions can legitimately be described not only as accurate meanings but also as true. It will be the purpose of the fifth and final thesis to articulate one understanding of what discipline can undertake this.

Fifth Thesis: *To Determine the Truth-Status of the Results of One's Investigations into the Meaning of Both Common Human Experience and Christian Texts the Theologian Should Employ an Explicitly Transcendental or Metaphysical Mode of Reflection.*

This final thesis on the task of fundamental theology is probably the least commonly accepted position of those argued for thus far. For that reason, I will concern myself here with the attempt to show only the need for and the basic nature of the metaphysical reflection involved in the task of theology.

The word "need" is used advisedly since the proposed argument for metaphysical inquiry is not posed as one alternative way of doing theology.[49] Rather the present claim is that, if the argument of the first four theses is sound, then one cannot but recognize an exigence for metaphysical or transcendental reflection. Indeed, by recalling the conclusions of these earlier theses we should also be able to show the need for the metaphysical reflection suggested here. Summarily stated, the argument has had the following structure: there are two sources for theology (common human experience and language, and Christian texts); those two sources are to be investigated by a hermeneutic phenomenology of the religious dimension in common human experience and language and by historical and hermeneutical investigations of the meanings referred to by Christian texts; the results of these investigations should be correlated to determine their significant similarities and differences and their truth-value.[50] The kind of correlation needed depends, of course, primarily upon the nature of the phenomena manifested in the prior investigation of the two sources. Thus far, the argument has been principally for the formal methods of investigation needed as distinct from the material conclusions reached by such methods. Yet in order to show the need for metaphysical inquiry it will be necessary to advance the earlier discussion by suggesting what conclusions may be reached by contemporary investigations of the type outlined above.

In the case of a phenomenology of ordinary experience and language, several contemporary thinkers have tried to show how a religious dimension is present to our cognitive, moral, and everyday experience and language. Chapter five of this book will treat some of those analyses. At the moment it will be possible only to mention rather than to demonstrate a few widely known examples of such reflection.[51] As a first example, let us recall the existentialist analysis of the manifestation of No-thing (i.e., no object in the world alongside other objects) in an analysis of the phenomenon of anxiety as distinct from the phenomenon of fear. That analysis has provided an occasion not only to show the meaning and possibility of metaphysics (as for Heidegger), but also to show the meaning and possibility of a "negative" entry point to a final, ultimate, and properly religious horizon to our everyday lives.[52] As a second example, the process philosopher's analysis of the phenomenon of that fundamental confidence or trust in existence continually re-presented in the self-conscious faith of our everyday, our scientific, and our moral activities has also provided a way of rendering meaningful the basic "faith" operative in our secular lives.[53] As a third example, Paul Tillich's analysis of the inevitable presence of an ultimate (as distinct from a finite) concern in all human activity (however "demonic" the forms of such ultimacy may become) has rendered intelligible the ontological status of an authentically religious dimension.[54] As a final example, Bernard Lonergan's analysis of the "formally unconditioned" factor presupposed by scientific and moral inquiry as well as his more recent analysis of explicitly religious experience as "a being-in-love-*without-qualification*" manifests a similar explication of the kinds of meanings present in either the implicitly religious dimensions of our secular lives or the explicitly religious language of the Christian tradition.[55]

Moreover, in an intellectual context where a religious dimension to everyday experience and language has been rendered intelligible, the question of God can be formulated anew as the question of the necessary referent (or object) of such a religious or "basic faith" dimension.[56] This theistic question, to be sure, involves further and extensive reflection insofar as it is the case that even some explicitly religious persons (e.g., some Buddhist and lately some Christian theologians) are also non-theistic. However, the theistic question itself seems both logically unavoidable and, as chapter eight will argue, capable of receiving a positive answer once an authentically religious dimension is admitted and explicated.[57]

Correlatively, if one accepts the notion of "referent" articulated in the previous thesis, then religious and theistic meanings can also emerge from properly hermeneutical investigations of Christian texts. From the viewpoint of historical investigation, a secure conclusion would seem to be that whatever else Christianity has been it has also been (and ordinarily understood itself to be) a theistic religion.[58] From the viewpoint of the kind of hermeneutic enterprise suggested above, *the* referent of the classical texts of the Christian tradition can be described as a religious way of being-in-the-world which understands itself in explicitly theistic terms. It is true, of course, that the further specifications of that Christian way of being-in-the-world can be and will continue to be variously described. An interpreter might hold, for example, that Herbert Braun's description of that specification as "humanity living before a gracious God" is the primary Christian self-understanding. Yet whether one accepts Braun's description or some other religious and theistic anthropology as the principal existential referent of Christian texts, any further specifications will not really call into question the basic religious and theistic referents which the theologian seeks.[59]

If the interpretation of both contemporary experience and language and of Christian texts could legitimately reach such similar conclusions, then the first moment of critical correlation—the comparative moment—would be accomplished. For the results of one's investigations into both major sources of theology would conclude to an identical insight: the fundamentally religious and theistic self-understanding presupposed by common human experience and language and explicitly referred to in representative Christian texts. But even this moment of correlation does not complete the theological task. Comparative analysis may allow one to know the basic religious referents of Christian texts and the fundamental meaningfulness of religious and theistic categories for common experience and language.[60]

Such analysis does not of and by itself resolve the question of the truth-status of such meanings.

For that we must ask what reflective discipline can adequately investigate the truth-claims of the religious and theistic meanings manifested by the prior investigations. The exact nature of that discipline is admittedly difficult to determine.[61] However, certain characteristics of the discipline needed seem clear. First, the discipline will have to be a reflective one capable of articulating *conceptual* and not merely *symbolic* categories. Otherwise, the theologian can never be sure that he has avoided either incoherence or vagueness in determining the cognitive character of religious and theistic claims. Second, the discipline must be able to explicate its criteria for precisely those cognitive claims. It seems fair to affirm that such criteria will involve at least such widely accepted criteria as the following: there must be a necessary and a sufficient ground in our common experience for such claims; any such claims must have a coherence both internally and with other essential categories of our knowledge and belief.[62]

If such criteria are in fact the criteria widely accepted for any cognitive claims, it becomes imperative for the theologian to specify how such criteria might function in theology since theology too makes cognitive claims about the nature of experience. Yet the dimension of meaning in question for theology (the religious) is not simply a meaning coordinate with other meanings like the scientific, the aesthetic, or the ethical. Rather the religious dimension precisely as such can be phenomenologically described as an ultimate or grounding dimension or horizon to all meaningful human activities.[63] The reflective discipline needed to decide upon the cognitive claims of religion and theism will itself have to be able to account not merely for some particular dimension of experience but for *all experience* as such.[64] Indeed, precisely this latter insight is required to show why the theologian cannot resolve the religious and theistic cognitive claims of theology by any ordinary criteria of verification or falsification. Rather the very nature of the cognitive claim involved in religious and theistic statements demands a metaphysical or transcendental mediation. As Antony Flew quite properly insists, an investigation of the cognitive claims of religion and theism demands that one seek to answer two fundamental questions: (1) the ground in our common experience for having any notions of religion and God at all; (2) how these notions may be conceptually explicated to avoid both vagueness and incoherence.[65] But as it has been argued that Antony Flew fails to see, only a reflective discipline capable of explicating criteria for the "conditions of the possibility" of all experience could really resolve the question of the meaning and truth of authentically religious and theistic claims.

One clear way of articulating the nature of the reflective discipline capable of such inquiry is to describe it as "transcendental" in its modern formulation or "metaphysical" in its more traditional expression.[66] As transcendental, such reflection attempts the explicit mediation of the basic presuppositions (or "beliefs") that are the conditions of the possibility of our existing or understanding at all. Metaphysical reflection means essentially the same thing: the philosophical validation of the concepts "religion" and "God" as necessarily affirmed or necessarily denied by all our basic beliefs and understanding. We seem to be unavoidably led to the conclusion that the task of fundamental theology can only be successfully resolved when the theologian fully and frankly develops an explicitly metaphysical study of the cognitive claims of religion and theism as an integral moment in his larger task.

For a variety of reasons such a position is unacceptable to many, probably even most contemporary theologians.[67] However, one hopes that the argument of the fifth thesis may be critically investigated in the context of its relationship to the first four theses. If it is correct to state that the task of theology demands that the theologian first uncover the religious and theistic meanings in both our common human experience and language and in explicitly Christian texts, then I find it impossible not to affirm the need for metaphysical or transcendental reflection to investigate the cognitive claims of those religious and theistic meanings.[68]

In outline form, I have tried to present the principal elements in the revisionist model of a contemporary fundamental theology. Whether that model can be successfully employed is, of course, another and more difficult question. However, one may continue to take heart from the fact that others who have a similar understanding of the basic elements involved in the task of theology will continue to advance these collaborative efforts which may lead to its resolution. But before articulating such efforts in Part II of this work, we shall need to analyze with greater precision the nature of the modes of analysis and interpretation employed upon the two sources of theological reflection.

Notes

(1) The task outlined here is a fundamental theology insofar as it attempts to articulate the criteria and evidence for theological argument. It is a task that can be distinguished from dogmatic theology proper, historical theology, and practical theology. For distinct though related articulations of this enterprise, recall Karl Rahner's notion of a "formal-fundamental theology" and Bernard Lonergan's notion of a "foundational" theology. It should be noted that this chapter is a revised version of my essay in the *Journal of Religion* 54 (1974), 13–34.

(2) The concept "tradition" in Catholic theology since the work of Newman and of Maurice Blondel is one that can no longer be interpreted in the narrow and relatively static categories of neo-Scholasticism. Note also that the present analysis is limited to texts; cf. chapter one, n. 5, on the reasons for this present self-limitation.

(3) I have chosen the concept "Christian fact" as expressive of this aspect of the theologian's task since this concept does not imply (as do "message" or "kerygma" or "tradition") that the fundamental theologian need be a believing member of the Christian community.

(4) I am largely indebted here to Schubert Odgen's articulation of the need for the theologian to develop "criteria of appropriateness" as well as "criteria of adequacy" to common human experience. I find these formulations helpful as succinct expressions of the twofold demand upon what I call the "fundamental theologian." See Schubert M. Ogden, "What Is Theology?" *Journal of Religion* 52 (1972), 22–40, esp. 25–27, 30–34.

(5) This insistence is ordinarily formulated under the question of scripture as the *norma normans non normata*. For a nuanced Catholic articulation of this principle, see Karl Lehmann and Karl Rahner, *Kerygma and Dogma* (New York: Herder and Herder, 1969).

(6) For the concept "motif-research," see Anders Nygren, *Meaning and Method in Philosophy and Theology: Prolegomena to a Scientific Study of Religion*, trans. P. S. Watson (Philadelphia: Fortress Press, 1972), pp. 351–78.

(7) See n. 4 above.

(8) Inter alia, see Rudolf Bultmann, "New Testament and Mythology" in *Kerygma and Myth: A Theological Debate*, ed. Hans Werner Bartsch, trans. Reginald H. Fuller (New York: Harper & Row, 1953), esp. pp. 10–16.

(9) This is not meant to suggest that there are not significant differences between "orthodoxy" and "neo-orthodoxy"; cf. chapter two for discussion.

(10) It might be noted that this famous formulation implies both "criteria of appropriateness" (the *theses of faith*) and "criteria of adequacy" (the *hypotheses of the theologian*).

(11) The phrase is Bernard Lonergan's. Examples of Lonergan's own practice of this procedure may be found in his book *Insight: A Study of Human Understanding* (London: Longmans, Green, 1958), pp. 401–31.

(12) The major difference is that, for Tillich, "experience" is not a "source" for systematic theology but a "medium"; see Paul Tillich, *Systematic Theology*, I (Chicago: University of Chicago Press, 1951), 40–47 (afterwards cited as Tillich, *ST*). Since I do not find that this insistence of Tillich's is consistent with his further position that "the material presented by the history of religion and culture" is a "source" of systematic theology (p. 38), I have taken the liberty of not employing Tillich's distinction between "medium" and "source" in the main body of this text.

(13) See Tillich, *ST*, I, 3–11, and II, 5–10.

(14) I admit the possibility that, if Tillich had argued that the "questions" of both the "situation" and the "message" are of the logical type of fundamental philosophical questions whose very explication is a "self-answering" one, he would not be open to this charge. Yet Tillich, in his articulation of the relationships between phi-

losophy and theology (*ST*, I, 18–28), does not argue in that manner. Nor does his actual use of the method of correlation throughout the *Systematics* suggest that such a "critical" reformulation is what he actually meant.

(15) Tillich, *ST*, II, 27.

(16) Again, such an argument would be convincing only if it were also argued that the "questions" under study were the "self-answering" questions involved in fundamental philosophical reflection. For an example of such an argument, see Schubert M. Ogden, "The Task of Philosophical Theology," in *The Future of Philosophical Theology*, ed. Robert A. Evans (Philadelphia: Westminster Press, 1971), pp. 59–65.

(17) This implies, of course, a legitimacy to the frequent analytic distinction between "meaning" and "truth": see Raeburne S. Heimbeck, *Theology and Meaning* (Stanford: Stanford University Press, 1969), esp. pp. 15–46; and James A. Martin, Jr., *The New Dialogue between Philosophy and Theology* (New York: Seabury Press, 1966). Whether this distinction can hold for the properly metaphysical questions of religion and theism will be one of the concerns of the fifth thesis in the text and of chapter seven.

(18) This does not necessarily imply that theological statements have *only* an existential referent. Indeed, they also refer to God and they *may* also refer to the nonhuman world. In all cases, however, they continue to refer to the *self.*

(19) For a clear example of the Anglo-American philosophical tradition's critique of the Humean concept of experience, see John E. Smith, *Experience and God* (New York: Oxford University Press, 1968), esp. pp. 21–46; for an equally clear presentation of a phenomenological discussion of the issue of the "everyday" and the "preconceptual," see Dreyfus-Todes, "The Three Worlds of Merleau-Ponty," *Philosophy and Phenomenological Research* 22:559–65.

(20) I refer, of course, to the tradition of theological reflection since Schleiermacher's originating attempt to fulfill this goal. Insofar as any theological position makes the same attempt it may legitimately be considered as possessing a "liberal" emphasis. For a contemporary example, see Richard R. Niebuhr, *Experiential Religion: A Theology of Power and Suffering* (New York: Harper & Row, 1972).

(21) For example: Max Scheler, *The Eternal in Man* (New York: Harper, 1960); Louis Dupré, *The Other Dimension: A Search for the Meaning of Religious Attitudes* (New York: Doubleday, 1972); Langdon Gilkey, *Naming the Whirlwind: The Renewal of God-Language* (Indianapolis: Bobbs-Merrill, 1969).

(22) For the earlier developments of phenomenology, see Herbert Spiegelberg, *The Phenomenological Movement*, 2 vols. (The Hague: Nijhoff, 1969); for the more recent hermeneutic development, see Paul Ricoeur, "New Developments in Phenomenology in France: The Phenomenology of Language," *Social Research* 34 (Spring 1967), 1–30; idem, "From Existentialism to the Philosophy of Language," *Criterion* 10 (Spring 1971), 14–18; Hans-Georg Gadamer, *Wahrheit und Methode* (Tübingen: J. C. B. Mohr, 1965), esp. pp. 240–50, 361–404; Don Ihde, *Hermeneutic Phenomenology: The Philosophy of Paul Ricoeur* (Evanston, Ill.: Northwestern University Press, 1971), esp. pp. 3–26, 167–83.

(23) For Tillich's notion of a "critical phenomenology," see *ST*, I, 106–8. Actually, the "critical" element for Tillich enters through a theological formulation of the Christian message (here from "final revelation").

(24) The phrase "religious dimension" or "horizon" is used throughout this text in preference to the concept "religious experience" in order to indicate that "religion" is not another human activity coordinate with such activities as art, morality, and science, but is rather a dimension of or horizon to *all* human activities. Chapters five and six will study the concepts "religious dimension of our common experience" and "explicit religious experience" in terms of the notion of "limit."

(25) In fact, as the work of Alfred Schutz alone suggests, phenomenology has been in such conversation with the sciences since its inception. As it remains today, for example, in the "conversation" of Paul Ricoeur with contemporary linguistics and literary criticism.

(26) This is not meant to imply that the work of these theologians is merely an application of Tillich's method to other areas. For example, both Scott and Gilkey have considerably reformulated Tillich's method in directions not dissimilar from those suggested here. See Gilkey, *Naming the Whirlwind*, esp. pp. 306–307, for an example of Gilkey's "ontic" reformulation of Tillich's ontological concern; or Nathan Scott, *The Wild Prayer of Longing: Poetry and the Sacred* (New Haven, Conn.: Yale University Press, 1971), esp. pp. 43–76, for an illustration of how Tillich's basic vision can be continued while still becoming transformed.

(27) Lonergan's own work may be found in *Method in Theology* (New York: Herder and Herder, 1972); see also, inter alia, John Dunne, *A Search for God in Time and Memory* (New York: Macmillan, 1965); Michael Novak, *Ascent of the Mountain, Flight of the Dove: An Invitation to Religious Studies* (New York: Harper & Row, 1971).

(28) For two helpful analyses of what problems historical method and hermeneutical method respectively pose for Christian theology, see Van Harvey, *The Historian and the Believer* (New York: Macmillan, 1965); Robert W. Funk, *Language, Hermeneutic and the Word of God* (New York: Harper & Row, 1966).

(29) There would, of course, remain a historical dimension to philosophy of religion but it would not involve determining the meanings and truth-status of the historical components of the "Christian fact."

(30) Insofar as this aspect of the task of "fundamental theology" successfully completes this task, it is coterminous with the primary role of "historical theology."

(31) See J. M. Allegro, *The Sacred Mushroom and the Cross* (New York: Doubleday, 1970).

(32) For this discussion, see James M. Robinson, *A New Quest of the Historical Jesus* (Naperville, Ill.: Alec R. Allenson, 1959).

(33) For example, in the manner that Joachim Jeremias employs historical method to reconstruct the texts of the parables: cf. Joachim Jeremias, *The Parables of Jesus* (New York: Scribner, 1962). It should be noted again that the interest here is

confined to the question of interpreting written texts. The category the "Christian fact" encompasses not only texts but events, symbols, witnesses, images, rituals, etc. In more traditional theological language, the "Christian fact" includes not only the Protestant emphasis on scripture but also the Catholic insistence upon tradition. As mentioned in chapter one, I hope in a future work to address these further aspects of the question. The present enterprise, if successful, can at least initiate that process of interpretation by providing an account of the interpretation rules for the written texts which all Christians recognize as their charter document.

(34) A clarification of these terms may be found in chapter six. For the moment, the following observations may suffice: metaphors refer to linguistic phenomena; images to non-linguistic; symbols to certain permanent and prevailing metaphors and images; myths to the narrative extension of symbols. The usage here reflects that of Paul Ricoeur outlined in chapter six.

(35) As in Van Harvey's own concluding chapter in *The Historian and the Believer*, pp. 246–93.

(36) For a summary history of same, see Richard Palmer, *Hermeneutics: Interpretation Theory in Schleiermacher, Dilthey, Heidegger and Gadamer* (Evanston, Ill.: Northwestern University Press, 1969). Even in the case of Paul Ricoeur, the term "hermeneutics" has at least two meanings: (1) a general theory of interpretation; (2) the explication of the "referent" of a written text as distinct from the "sense" of the text. Throughout this chapter I am employing the word in this second sense.

(37) I am indebted throughout this section to the recent work of Paul Ricoeur; see, especially, his as yet unpublished text "Interpretation Theory" (presented to a colloquium of the faculty at the University of Chicago Divinity School, May 1971). I have stated my own understanding of some of the possibilities and limitations of Ricoeur's theory for theology in a paper (unpublished) at the same colloquium entitled "Paul Ricoeur's Long Route to Ontology: An Attempt to Interpret His Interpretation Theory." The question of "distanciation," although present in a clear form in written texts, is not limited to written texts. The key to the process itself is the production of different modes of discourse as a work: Cf. Paul Ricoeur, "Philosophy and Religious Language," in *Journal of Religion* 54 (1974), esp. pp. 73–5, 78–9.

(38) The following chapter will expand upon and clarify these presently too brief remarks.

(39) Insofar as this hermeneutic rule is correct, it reinforces the search in contemporary christology for a distinction between fact as actualization (here, the fact of Jesus' own actualization) and fact as re-presentation (here, the affirmation that the history of Jesus of Nazareth is the decisive factual re-presentation of God's relationship to man). For two examples of a similar distinction, see Harvey, *The Historian and the Believer*, pp. 281–89; Schubert M. Ogden, *Christ Without Myth* (New York: Harper & Row, 1961), pp. 161–64; and the discussion in chapter nine.

(40) See Ricoeur, "Interpretation Theory," pp. 12–19.

(41) Ibid., pp. 6–8, 18–19, 22–23. In my judgment, a major theological advantage of this linkage of the hermeneutic task to the concept "referent" is that it distinguishes the role of "decision" as a further question. The emphasis on "decision" in herme-

neutics may be found in existentialist hermeneutics, especially, for theology, in the Bultmannian tradition. In more traditional vocabulary, Ricoeur's theory makes the role of hermeneutics an aesthetic rather than an ethical one. This hermeneutical understanding also clarifies the important but limited role of hermeneutics for theology, thus avoiding the difficulty of employing "hermeneutics" to resolve every theological problem.

(42) Ibid., pp. 16–19, on the "new dialectic between comprehension and explanation."

(43) For an explicit example, see inter alia, Dan O. Via, *The Parables: Their Literary and Existential Dimension* (Philadelphia: Fortress Press, 1967). Cf. discussion of "parables" in chapter six.

(44) The assumption here remains the one articulated earlier, viz., that the theologian *qua* theologian is committed to explicating the meaning and truth of the answers provided by the text to the "fundamental questions" of human existence.

(45) For a defense of the position that the question formulated in the text is not merely a result of this theory of hermeneutics but is implied by the more general position that all theological statements are existential, see the earlier discussion on thesis three of this chapter.

(46) See Herbert Braun, "Der Sinn der neutestamentlichen Christologie," *Gesammelte Studien zum Neuen Testament und seiner Umwelt* (Tübingen: J. C. B. Mohr, 1962), pp. 243–82.

(47) This rephrasing of the religious referent is dependent on the work of Herbert Braun referred to above.

(48) More exactly, such an understanding of hermeneutics would not complete the task of "appropriation" as Ricoeur defines that need in "Interpretation Theory," pp. 22–23. That task, in my judgment, demands further extra-hermeneutical criteria—as I argue in the fifth thesis of this text, and as I suggest in relationship to Ricoeur's own position in my "Paul Ricoeur's Ontology," pp. 7–18.

(49) It might be noted that, insofar as the "meanings" uncovered by the earlier investigations are authentically religious and theistic ones, then their phenomenological and hermeneutic manifestation is also a manifestation of their truth-status. Yet, this insight is clearly affirmed, I believe, only when the metaphysical character of these phenomena as manifesting "self-answering fundamental questions" is explicitly (i.e., transcendentally) formulated. Hence, the reason for the fifth thesis is actually more one of making explicit what is already present than it is a really new concern. But such is the character of all metaphysical and transcendental reflection: metaphysics mediates the most basic and, hence, most obvious presuppositions of all our thinking and living. Some of the objections against the use of metaphysics in theology can be seen by reading several of the comments recorded in the summary of the discussion in Donald M. Mathers, "Dialogue on the Future of Philosophical Theology: A Report," in *The Future of Philosophical Theology*, pp. 169–89. For a fuller discussion, cf. chapter seven.

(50) It might be noted that, as chapters five and six will argue, an interpretation of

the limit-language present in the limit-situations of our everyday experience implies a need for the limit-language of explicit religious experience. Alternatively, the latter needs the locus of limit-situations and limit-questions for its existential meaning. The whole forms a hermeneutical circle informed by the self-answering fundamental questions of theology whose formulation and whose answers take on a properly religious-as-limit character: cf. the fuller discussions in chapters five and six.

(51) It is important to note that the present chapter does not attempt to demonstrate these conclusions but simply to recall certain familiar claims to such demonstration.

(52) For the briefest presentation of Heidegger's analysis, see his *Introduction to Metaphysics* (New Haven: Yale University Press, 1959). This is not to claim, of course, that Heidegger himself, given his strictures against the "onto-theo-logical" status of metaphysical talk on God, would wish to affirm this use of his analysis.

(53) See Schubert M. Ogden, *The Reality of God* (New York: Harper & Row, 1963), esp. pp. 21–43.

(54) Inter alia, see Tillich, *ST*, I, 11–15, for perhaps the clearest formal exposition of this famous Tillichian motif. For a more popular and wide-ranging presentation, see D. Mackenzie Brown, *Ultimate Concern: Tillich in Dialogue* (New York: Harper, 1965), esp. pp. 1–19.

(55) On the first factor, see Bernard Lonergan, *Insight*, pp. 634–87. The latter discussion on religion by Lonergan may be found in his *Method in Theology*, esp. pp. 101–25.

(56) A similar judgment is advanced by Smith, *Experience and God*, pp. 46–68. An important constructive summary on the problem of God may be found in Gordon D. Kaufman, *God the Problem* (Cambridge: Harvard University Press, 1972).

(57) See the discussion of Charles Hartshorne's position in chapter eight.

(58) This is intended as a purely historical observation. In principle, the theistic self-understanding of Christianity may be as time-bound and indeed erroneous as other of its once-cherished beliefs.

(59) Perhaps the most helpful discussion for clarifying this question is that among New Testament scholars (Ernst Käsemann, Herbert Braun, James Robinson, Raymond Brown, et al.) on the need for a "canon within the canons" for clarifying the central New Testament meanings.

(60) The categories "meaning," "meaningfulness," and "truth" will be clarified in the next chapter and applied throughout Part II of this work.

(61) This is factually true at least insofar as "metaphysics," until fairly recently, has been a highly suspect source for contemporary thought. See the history outlined in James Richmond, *Theology and Metaphysics* (New York: Schocken Books, 1971), esp. pp. 1–49.

(62) For an example of a recent exchange on these issues, cf. Antony Flew, "Theol-

ogy and Falsification in Retrospect," and Schubert M. Ogden, "Reply," both to be published in *Theology and Verification*, ed. Malcolm L. Diamond and Thomas Litzenburg, Jr. (Indianapolis: Bobbs-Merrill, 1975).

(63) The analyses of Paul Tillich, the process philsophers, or Bernard Lonergan referred to in the text may be employed as familiar examples of this kind of argument for the ontological character of religious meaning as ultimate. For an "ontic" analysis of the same, see Gilkey, *Naming the Whirlwind.*

(64) This insight can be formulated in more explicitly transcendental terms as follows: if transcendental reflection does mediate the conditions of the possibility of experience as such, there is no "special" particular experience or set of experiences that one can appeal to for "verifying" or "falsifying" that mediation.

(65) I take these general criteria as well-nigh universally acceptable. The basic formulation itself may be found in Antony Flew, *God and Philosophy* (New York: Harcourt, Brace and World, 1966), pp. 27–29.

(66) In other words, although I hold that the "transcendental" formulation assures a critical grounding to metaphysics, I am not opposed to any post-critical formulation of metaphysics. The difference between the two formulations is a difference of degree of adequacy to the task not a difference of kind. For an example of arguments of degree of adequacy, cf. John C. Robertson, "Rahner and Ogden: Man's Knowledge of God," *Harvard Theological Review* 63 (1970), 377–407; idem, "Tillich's Two Types and the Transcendental Method," in *Philosophy and Religion: 1971,* ed. David Griffin (Chambersburg, Pa.: American Academy of Religion, 1971), pp. 48–57.

(67) The major reason is probably that a full sense of historical consciousness has rendered the claims of metaphysics doubtful to many contemporary thinkers. For two helpful (and distinct) analyses of this difficulty, see Gordon D. Kaufman, *Relativism, Knowledge and Faith* (Chicago: University of Chicago Press, 1960); and Emil L. Fackenheim, *Metaphysics and Historicity* (Milwaukee: Marquette University Press, 1961).

(68) Note that the claim for the use of metaphysics is limited to an investigation of cognitive claims. For other "uses," the category "meaningfulness" and criteria of relative adequacy to experience need development (cf. the discussions in chapters four and nine on the latter).

Chapter 4

The Search for Adequate Criteria and Modes of Analysis

To describe the enterprise of fundamental theology as philosophical reflection upon the meanings present in our common human experience and the meanings present in the Christian fact obviously implies that there are two main "sources" of fundamental theological reflection. What the main kinds of criteria and the principal modes of analysis applicable to those two sources are is the task of the present chapter. As a beginning, the ways one may analyze the meanings of common human experience and language will be described. Then the general theory of interpretation informing the analysis of Christian texts will be set out in greater detail. Finally, indications of the kind of critical correlation applicable for fundamental theology will be summarized.

COMMON HUMAN EXPERIENCE AND LANGUAGE:
Modes of Analysis

To claim that one can engage in philosophical reflection upon our common human experience and language is also to claim that one can render more precise the variety of meanings which such a cover-phrase may involve. At least the following questions must be clarified: What is meant by common human experience? What, more exactly, is meant by "philosophical reflection"? How does the latter relate to more familiar modes of analysis of the meaning of human experience? What, finally, is meant by "criteria of adequacy" to experience?

In one sense, of course, we all know what is meant when a speaker appeals to our "experience." Surely, the speaker believes that I can personally validate his claims by recalling my own experience*s*: the various reports of my five senses or even my basic feelings, attitudes, moods or bodily expressions. If the former, "sensationalist" notion is alone involved, then clearly I may verify the claim in the straightforward manner of scientific experiment. If the latter and less obvious appeal to feeling, mood, or "non-sensuous experience," is involved I may validate the claim by something like a "consciousness-raising" exercise that frees me to be attentive to my experience as a self, moving, feeling, attending, sensing, etc.[1]

In some cases, as when a social scientist asks one to note the recurring meanings operative in particular social situations, the appeal to "experience" is an appeal to data, i.e., basically to an experimental report of my five senses. If I can show (for example, through statistical method) that what was claimed to be a recurring factor in human society is, in fact, a random difference, I have effectively falsified the prior straightforward claim to experience. Often only this kind of empirical scientific "verificationist" or philosophical "sensationalist" model is allowed to count as an "empirical" claim.[2]

In fact, however, only a narrow model of social science and an equally limiting philosophical model of "experience" confine themselves to that understanding of an empirical (actually empiricist) claim. On common sense terms alone, most human beings effectively, and sometimes reflectively, realize that an appeal to experience is not always an appeal to what I can see, taste, touch, smell, or hear; much less to what I can scientifically verify through controlled experiment. If I am asked, for example, for my reaction to a friend's actions in a particular situation, I am requested to state how, as a human being, I felt about the actions of this human being in this concrete setting. Questions requesting an eye-witness account are more readily answerable than those other, more troubling and profound experiential questions of tone, of mood, of feeling: questions that ask me, in effect, to evaluate the humanity of a friend's action. What values are hereby apprehended? What understandings of the human situation are hereby disclosed?

Upon reflection most of us would agree that this experience of the self as a self is more difficult to attend to than the reports of our five senses. Yet, somehow that experience—technically, our "non-sensuous experience of the self"—is both prior to our interpretation of our sense-knowledge and more important as source for the more fundamental questions of the meaning of our human experience as human selves. Most of us would also agree that this experience of the self-as-a-self demands the most sophisticated reflective analysis available. We do not want only to feel values and disvalues.[3] We want intelligently to understand, reflectively to judge, and deliberately to evaluate the various ethical theories of the self-as-good.[4] We are not content simply to feel depressed. We want to understand, to know, and to evaluate what factors (nutritional, biological, psychological, cultural, etc.) at what level of intensity (malnutrition, caffeine-addiction, neurosis, psychosis, social dislocation, etc.) are actually involved in this present experience.

Appeals to experience are of various sorts. For example, when in the presence of our closest friends, when experiencing some particularly incisive cultural expression, when reading a first-rate historical analysis, we find that the final appeal to our experience is an appeal not so much to what we may verify through our senses as to what we may validate as meaningful to the experience of the self as an authentic self, to what phenomenologists call our "lived experience." [5] At such moments, we seek aid for understanding, for raising to explicit consciousness—in a word, for mediating—the immediacy of that experience by our own powers of intelligent and critical introspection.[6] When wise we may also turn to such trustworthy modes of mediation as friends, or psychoanalysts, artists, trusted cultural analysts, finely-attuned historians, social and natural scientists, philosophers and theologians. In the most important questions of our lives, we turn not merely to the reports of our five senses or even to controlled experiments.[7] Rather we turn to that community of interpretation where the value of the self as a self is reverenced and where modes of raising that experience to conscious awareness are developed.[8]

In the merely common-sense terms appropriate to the analysis thus far, an appeal to experience may involve either an appeal to the hard data of sense-experience or to the more elusive but somehow more primordial and more important immediacy of the self's non-sensuous experience of the self as the latter is expressed in feeling, mood, tone, bodily awareness and is mediated by various kinds of consciousness-raising.[9] When we state that an appeal to experience is meaningful, we often mean no more and no less than the fact that the appeal "resonates" to our own immediate experience as a self. We also ordinarily attempt to understand, judge, and evaluate that immediacy by such modes of critical mediation as cultural and historical analysis, human scientific analysis, philosophical and theological analysis. In the broadest sense of the term "phenomenological," all these modes of reflective analysis are phenomenological analyses insofar as they mediate the meaning of my experience as a self-in-a-world. More exactly, such analyses mediate the immediacy of our lived experience through some particular image, symbol, metaphor, myth, or concept. Throughout, we shall employ the word "meaningful" to refer to that intrinsic relationship between a mediating symbol, image, metaphor, myth, or concept and the immediate lived experience of the self.[10]

How such "meaningful" symbols may also be called "true" can be clarified only after certain other factors are determined. What, as a first example, is the meaning of the category "philosophical reflection" upon experience as that philosophical reflection is said to involve two principal moments: the phenomenological moment and the transcendental moment.[11] On historical grounds alone, it seems fair to state that the task of contemporary (i.e., post-critical) philosophy can continue to be described as a phenomenological-transcendental one.[12] That task is both intrinsically problematic and intrinsically in continuity with the task of classical philosophy. Since the emergence of historical consciousness, Christian theologians are well aware that their discipline now has a variously interpreted "problematic" status. They are also aware, if not wary, of the seemingly similar problematic stance of theology's classical conversation partner, philosophy. Yet the parallels between the two disciplines are not really exact on this issue. However problematic classical philosophy's claim to be able to explicate the basic and ultimate presuppositions of reality may have been rendered by the arrival of historical consciousness, still another interpretation may be provided to that dilemma. That interpretation is familiar, but well worthy of reflection by contemporary theologians: the crisis of philosophy in the modern and contemporary periods has involved not a rejection of classical philosophy's task and aim but rather a *purification, delimitation, and clarification of that aim.* For philosophy—at least among the great classical philosophers as distinct from their "schools"—has always recognized itself as "problematic." When one states—as Aristotle, for example, does—that the "first principles" of philosophy cannot strictly be proved but can be indirectly validated (through the self-contradiction which their denial involves), then one has a rather exact grasp of the meaning of a properly "problematic" discipline. For that reason, a more accurate description of most of the major critical and post-critical philosophical movements does not concentrate simply upon their frequent distrust of classical "systems" but rather recognizes their more disciplined understanding of philosophy's traditionally problematic status.

If true, this historical reflection allows for a better grasp of the meaning of "problematic" in relationship to philosophy by an investigation of the two "moments" said to comprise "philosophical reflection," the phenomenological and the transcendental. One description of the task of classical philosophy is to state that its fundamental aim was explication of the ground, the basis, the fundament of every phenomenon which appears to human consciousness. As such, philosophy must investigate every subject, every discipline, every method, every phenomenon—every "being," if one wills—with a view towards the basic and fundamental presuppositions of that and every phenomenon. In that sense, philosophy has always been transcendental in its self-understanding, precisely as a rising-above (to use one metaphor) or a going-beneath (to use another) any phenomenon to discover the most basic presuppositions or (more critically formulated) "conditions of possibility" of that phenomenon.[13]

The peculiarly modern formulation of this transcendental task of philosophy—the formulation familiar to all since Kant—may be viewed as a clarification, not elimination of the classical transcendental task. Indeed, the clarification involved is the uniquely transcendental one: an explicit recognition that what one is reflecting upon is never merely "given" for human consciousness. Rather every object—every phenomenon—has *a priori* conditions. Certain of such conditions are basic and universal for all human knowing and experience insofar as those conditions are conditions of possibility, i.e., they are so constitutive of any performance of cognition or experience that they can be reductively exhibited from it.[14] Finally, the peculiarity of several major post-Kantian philosophies does not really deny this transcendental task. Rather these post-critical positions argue that the task can be executed adequately only when the Kantian exclusive attention to the centrality of "understanding" or "reason" is replaced. Instead, there must be an insistence upon the centrality and comprehensiveness of the originating lived "experience" itself over its clear, distinct—and derivative —expressions in human "understanding." [15]

In either philosophy's modern (critical) or its contemporary (post-critical) moments, therefore, the transcendental task of philosophy is both recognized and refined. Both the modern and contemporary reformulations of the philosophical task continue to involve themselves in the central aim of classical metaphysics: what are the basic *a priori* conditions of all human living and thinking? That task alone is properly transcendental—or, if one prefers, metaphysical. The accomplishment of that task will always remain "problematic" in the exact sense that it can no more be indubitably "proved" than it can be avoided by any serious philosophical thinking. In the familiar dilemma posed by Aristotle to the skeptics, the choice is not really between metaphysics or no metaphysics; the only real choice is between a self-conscious and explicit metaphysics or an unconscious yet operative one.

Earlier in this chapter, we saw some initial "broad" meanings of the term "phenomenological." A more technical meaning is now needed. A balanced description of the task of classical philosophy also suggests that it was concerned to analyze any phenomenon (in the basic sense of that which appears to human consciousness) as exactly, as carefully, as explanatorily as possible.[16] It may be true that the phenomenological method developed by Husserl may be a more exact, and surely a more exacting way to perform this task.[17] Still the task itself remains as classical as it is obvious. The reformulations of this task involved in the phenomenological movement may be viewed as a series of clarifications of the means for the difficult and intricate analysis of phenomena involved in all such authentic philosophical investigation.[18] The heightening of such phenomenological self-awareness, moreover, may reach the point where a reflective and explicit raising of the problematic status of phenomenological reflection itself may emerge. Then—as in Husserl or Heidegger—the phenomenologist finds not only phenomena but also an occasion to reformulate and, if need be, retrieve the transcendental question itself.[19] Indeed, unless one is content with phenomenological investigation alone, he is led by the logic of the inquiry itself to ask the question of the basic ground or presuppositions of every and all phenomena or any and all phenomenological reflection. In that sense, both philosophical "moments" (the phenomenological and the transcendental) are two intrinsically linked moments in a single methodological task for any philosopher who wishes to determine the basic and grounding presuppositions of any given phenomenon.

Is this brief apologia for the use of the terms "transcendental" and "phenomenological" as more precise explications of the classical problematic status of the discipline called philosophy really helpful for understanding the presently problematic status of the discipline fundamental theology? I contend that it is: it may well be true that philosophy has always struggled within a hermeneutic circle that was self-consciously problematic, but so now does contemporary theology. Indeed my contention is that both disciplines in their contemporary self-understanding live basically within the same hermeneutic circle. Both disciplines must be involved in "philosophical reflection upon our common human experience and language" in a manner that might be said to include two moments: a phenomenological moment to disclose the meaning and meaningfulness of that experience and a transcendental moment to disclose the true conditions of the possibility of that experience.

Thus far, we have contended that the phrase "philosophical reflection upon our common human experience and language" may be rendered more precise by clarifying four factors. First, "experience" should not be confined to sense-experience alone but should include that immediate experience of the self-as-self which can be reflectively mediated through such disciplines as art, history, cultural analysis, human scientific analysis, and philosophical analysis. Second, all these modes of analysis can be generically labelled "phenomenological" in the broad sense of mediating the relationship of particular expressions, either linguistic (e.g., metaphors or concepts) or non-linguistic (e.g., images) to our immediate lived experience.[20] Third, whenever and however such mediation occurs, the particular symbol, image, metaphor, myth, or concept is rendered *meaningful* to various degrees of adequacy dependent upon its disclosive power for our lived experience. Fourth, the phrase "philosophical reflection" can be further refined to mean explicitly philosophical reflection upon either language or experience. Such reflection may be more technically described as a phenomenological-transcendental method comprised of two distinct but integral moments of the single task of philosophical reflection.

Such reflection, moreover, may clarify more than the philosophical status of the "meaningful" expressions manifested by earlier non-philosophical analyses; it may also clarify the exact philosophical meaning of the symbol, concept, image, metaphor, or myth, and the experience each discloses. Thus the analyst may wish to determine the exact logical status of a particular language and experience.[21] This latter task is especially crucial in any philosophical investigation of religious experience and language. If, for example, the logical status of that experience and language bears the logical note of a limit-language and a limit-experience, philosophy must explicate that. In short, many kinds of experience and language (e.g., aesthetic, ethical, political, economic, and religious) may be "meaningful" in the sense of genuinely disclosive of our authentic lived experience. But any meaningful experience and language bears the note of a *religious meaning*, we shall argue, only when its logical limit-character is also disclosed by explicit philosophical analysis.[22] Let us suppose, for example, that by means of a number of cultural analyses one could legitimately argue that certain rituals in American cultural life (e.g., presidential inauguration addresses, Fourth of July celebrations, or the Thanksgiving holiday) were clearly meaningful in the sense of disclosing a direct relationship between either a text (a presidential inauguration address) or an event (a presidential inauguration ceremony) and the lived-experience of the American people. Suppose, further, that cultural-historical analysts like Robert Bellah, Martin Marty, or Michael Novak argued that such events and texts were not only meaningful in a general cultural sense but in fact bore a genuinely religious meaning (as the American "civil religion").[23] In the terms of the present discussion, philosophical reflection would aid those analyses by determining whether these events and texts bore a limit-character which would *logically* allow the analyst to apply the meaning "religious" to them.

A second example of the kind of aid which explicitly philosophical reflection many bring to bear upon an analysis of religious meaning and meaningfulness should be cited here: the criterion of "internal coherence." [24] On the presupposition that the analyst chooses to articulate the meanings discovered in explicitly conceptual language, the philosophical criterion of "internal coherence" is obviously relevant. As chapters seven and eight will argue on the question of the conceptual understanding of the Christian God, this criterion is crucial for philosophical and theological self-understanding. Many metaphors, symbols, images, myths, or even concepts are meaningful in the initial sense of disclosive of our lived experience. Yet some of these, once conceptually formulated, do not pass the legitimate philosophical test of internal coherence. This may not be a major difficulty for anyone who claims only that the symbol or concept under study has a purely non-cognitive (e.g., attitudinal) use. Once the further claim is made that a particular symbol or concept (e.g., God) also has a cognitive use (e.g., God as the "one necessary existent in reality"), then the earlier criterion of "meaningfulness" no longer suffices. Rather one must also apply the criterion of internal coherence at least for those cognitive claims implied by the symbol or concept (e.g., Can one coherently maintain that this God is really affected by human actions? Can one coherently maintain both that this God is really "omnipotent" and "omniscient" and that human beings are really free? [25]).

Thus far I have suggested the need for two criteria: "meaningfulness" as disclosive of our actual experience and meaning-as-internal-coherence as applicable to any cognitive claims. Even these two criteria combined will not suffice philosophically. In the case of cognitive claims, we want to know not only whether they are meaningful and coherent, but also whether they are "true." To respond to that last and most demanding question, one final set of philosophical criteria are demanded: criteria of "adequacy to experience." To understand how those criteria may operate in relationship to religious language and experience, a review of the prior discussion may clarify in a more technical way the exact kind of philosophical reflection needed. More specifically, let us return to the phrase "philosophical reflection upon common human experience and language" in order to attempt one final summary-clarification of what is meant by the transcendental moment of such "philosophical reflection" [26] and what is meant by "adequacy to experience" when assumed under that philosophical rubric.

The following observations may serve to clarify such "criteria of adequacy" until the more extensive analysis of the role of metaphysical or transcendental reflection for theology is undertaken in chapter seven. First, the primary "experience" which phenomenological reflection undertakes to disclose or mediate is the immediate experience of the self-as-a-self, embodied, feeling, moving, understanding, deliberating, valuing, judging, deciding. Second, a "transcendental" or metaphysical reflection upon that phenomenologically mediated experience is not an attempt to disclose new experiences but to ask the explicit cognitive question of the conditions for the possibility of the primordial experience of the self. Third, as this chapter has merely indicated but as the next four chapters shall study at some length, *if*, in fact, the limit-character of religious experience is of such nature that it includes as its self-referent a final dimension or horizon to all the experience of the self (religion) and as its objective referent in reality an experienced necessary existent (God), then it follows that explicitly transcendental or metaphysical reflection is needed to explicate or mediate the truth-as-adequacy-to-experience of those central metaphysical claims.[27] Only a restriction of "experience" to sense-experiences will eliminate the need for the kind of philosophical reflection upon the experience of the self described above as phenomenological-transcendental. Only an unwarranted restriction of all investigation to the earlier criterion of "meaningfulness" will eliminate the need to employ such explicitly philosophical criteria as internal coherence for "meaning" or transcendental criteria for "truth" as "adequacy to experience." The analyses of "common human experience and language," therefore, should include philosophical reflection of the phenomenological-transcendental type and should thereby demand the application of all three sets of criteria: "meaningfulness," "meaning," and "truth." A particular experience or language is "meaningful" when it discloses an authentic dimension of our experiences as selves. It has "meaning" when its cognitive claims can be expressed conceptually with internal coherence. It is "true" when transcendental or metaphysical analysis shows its "adequacy to experience" by explicating how a particular concept (e.g., time, space, self, or God) functions as a fundamental "belief" or "condition of possibility" of all our experience.

CHRISTIAN TEXTS: **The Possibility of Their Interpretation**

The Need for Criteria of Appropriateness

The first section attempted to spell out the "criteria of adequacy" to human experience implied by the revisionist model for theology. This section will explicate the particular theory of interpretation informing the formulation of "criteria of appropriateness" in that model. The burden of the section will be to investigate the main outlines of that somewhat complex theory of interpretation. Prior to that central concern, however, it may prove helpful to reflect upon the more general concern of why "criteria of appropriateness"—and thereby a theory of interpretation—is needed at all. The easiest entry into that question is to ask oneself how a fundamental Christian theology differs from a philosophy of religion.

It seems reasonable to state that the major specific difference of the theological as distinct from philosophical investigation of Christian language is the Christian theologian's responsibility to show how his or her present categories are appropriate understandings of the Christian understanding of existence.[28] If this responsibility is not addressed, then Christian theology becomes without remainder a philosophy of religion. Comforting though that thought may be to all those justifiably wary of the hazards of hermeneutics and history, a purely contemporary philosophy of religion is not a fundamental theology in either the traditional or even revisionist sense of the term. The theologian's task is neither to invent a new religion nor to leave his interpreters the task of determining the appropriateness of his categories to the Christian tradition. Rather the theologian must himself assume this responsibility. In this connection, it might be noted that this position is by no means confined to traditional theologians. In fact, the radical theologians—Paul van Buren, William Hamilton, and Thomas J. J. Altizer —all maintain that their categories are not merely appropriate to but radically demanded by the Christian gospel.[29] Altizer, for example, maintains that only the Christian can celebrate "the death of God." The responsibility for the Christian theologian to show the appropriateness of his categories to the Christian tradition is a responsibility shared by all Christian theologians, orthodox or neo-orthodox, liberal, revisionist, or radical. How might that responsibility be fulfilled?

In determining "criteria of appropriateness," the phrase "the Christian fact" must first be clarified. This category refers to the meanings involved either explicitly or implicitly in the significant texts, actions, gestures, and symbols of the entire Christian tradition.[30] More specifically, the primary although not exclusive expression of the Christian fact may be found in texts, more explicitly the texts of the Christian scriptures. Insofar as most

Christian theologians, whether Catholic, Protestant, or Orthodox, accept the scriptures as the *"norma normans non normata"* of Christian self-understanding, it makes sense to limit the investigation to a single though major point: how can the theologian best interpret the texts of the New Testament. By confining the present discussion to the question of these written scriptural texts, one need not imply that only these texts comprise the Christian fact. Whatever be the importance of the later confessional, doctrinal, and theological statements of the several Christian traditions and however revealing the later actions and gestures of various Christian witnesses may be (for example, Augustine, Aquinas, Luther, Calvin, Pascal, Newman, Kierkegaard, et al.), still the primary responsibility of the theologian is to show the appropriateness of his own categories (and, by implication, the categories of the later tradition) to the meanings expressed in that collection of texts called the Hebrew and Christian scriptures. In that case, it becomes imperative for the theologian to seek an adequate method of interpretation for texts.

Interpretation Theory[31]

It would seem a fair generalization on the central problematic of contemporary theology that the phenomenon of historical consciousness is the primary factor behind both the central achievements and the crucial difficulties for Christian theology from Troeltsch through Bultmann and, more recently, Bernard Lonergan.[32] It is difficult to see why there would be any remaining hesitancy in affirming that precisely a recognition of the historical context of all religious texts and the allied recognition of the historical distance of all such contexts from the contemporary interpreter have been the two principal factors forcing the problematic of interpretation to the very center of theological attention. Very few theologians remain to defend a traditional theological reliance upon "proof-texts" shorn of their historical context. The interpretative procedures of Aquinas, Calvin, Luther, or even, in several cases at least, of Karl Barth or Karl Rahner now strike most theologians as not sufficiently historically conscious for the task of adequate interpretation.[33]

Yet even if historical consciousness has forced the problem of the contemporary interpretation of the meaning of the Christian faith, several critics are no longer convinced that the usual way in which that consciousness informs the problem of interpretation is an altogether accurate one.[34] So largely influential has the phenomenon of historical consciousness been for contemporary theologians that such consciousness has effectively determined the nature of the task of theological interpretation in too psychological a direction. Such a determination is perhaps best understood by recalling the widely-shared understanding of the "hermeneutic circle" present in theology since Schleiermacher and Dilthey through Bultmann, Ebeling, Fuchs, et al.

Summarily stated, the category "hermeneutic circle" articulates the task of interpretation to be the effort of one subjective consciousness (the interpreter) to understand another consciousness (the author). This understanding of the hermeneutic task is not merely informed by historical consciousness. In fact it is fully determined by the psychologizing tendencies of that consciousness. What is the contemporary interpreter attempting to do in this understanding of the hermeneutical task? [35] He is, it would seem, attempting to give the meaning of the text in one of the following manners: either by determining the author's original intention (for example, through redaction criticism); or by determining the original discourse situation (for example, Dodd and Jeremias on understanding the parables by finding the situation in the life of Jesus or of the primitive Christian community which the parables address); or by explicating the first historical addressee of that text (for example, social-cultural analyses of the communities at Corinth who received the Pauline letters). Even on the limited basis of the prior remarks on historical consciousness, it should be clear that no hesitancy should be made in applauding all these enterprises as legitimate and fruitful ones. However, there do seem to be good reasons to suggest that one should be reluctant to state that any one of these historical analyses—or even the sum total of all of them—would actually give the theological meaning of the text.

This reluctance to agree with what remains the majority opinion in contemporary theology on the nature of the task of interpretation is best understood by appealing to certain recent developments in linguistic and hermeneutic theory—developments which seem to recent interpreters both correct in theory and important in fact for the interpreter of the meaning of Christian texts. I will not pretend here to provide an exhaustive study of the complex terrain of contemporary interpretation theory. Rather I shall signalize certain major recent developments in that theory which seem both corrective of the earlier psychological formulations of "Romanticist" hermeneutics and of considerable importance for the formulation of the present fundamental theological task of the interpretation of the meaning of Christian texts.

The first development in contemporary hermeneutics concerns the understanding of the terms "event" and "meaning" in discourse.[36] Contemporary hermeneutic theory has often signalized the concept "speech-event" as the central category informing the work of interpretation. Insofar as this concept refers to the moment of actualization of any language system into discourse it would seem to be a correct emphasis. Contemporary linguistic theory does continue to distinguish the temporal, personal, communicative, and referential speech-event of discourse ("*parole*"—"performance") from the atemporal, non-personal, non-communicative, and extra-linguistic referential category of language as a system of signs ("*langue*-system"). On the other hand, insofar as the concept "speech-event" becomes the "meaning" to be interpreted, these recent critics argue that the hermeneutic enterprise begins to go astray.

It is one thing to maintain that all discourse as language actualizes itself in a speech-event *(parole)*. It is quite another matter to assume that this "speech-event" is *the* meaning of the text. For example, written language, especially language codified in literary genres, is an intending (a *meinen*), *because* it suppresses the original speech-event in order to fix and retain the meaning intended. This insight can be recognized in its initial stages by reflection upon both the production of discourse by means of "modes of discourse" in oral language and the presence of certain important differences between written and spoken language. Since the latter example of written language lends itself to a clearer and less controversial formulation of the issue, we shall examine it as a test-case of the more general hypothesis. What we write is the meaning, the *noema* of our speech-events, not the event itself. Once I write, it is my text alone which bears the meaning; not my intention in writing it; not my original audience's reaction to it.

Furthermore, the meaning is not grasped simply by understanding the original dialogical situation of the text. Rather that meaning refers to a "world," a certain mode-of-being which precisely as "fixed" or codified by means of the particular literary genre employed in the text is also noematic or ideal. The meaning or intention of the text is now available not merely to the original conversation partner (who may or may not have properly understood it) but rather to anyone who can read. In this theory of interpretation, the concept of meaning is the Husserlian one adapted by Paul Ricoeur: meaning is neither a psychic nor a physical event but is *ideal* or *noematic*. As ideal and as fixed in written texts or in oral modes of discourse,[37] the meaning undergoes a process of distanciation from the author's intention, from the original dialogue situation, and from its first audience. At the same time, the meaning is now available in these texts for any intelligent interpreter to understand upon reading them. The interpreter's task, therefore, is *not* to psychologize the meaning by identifying it with the speech-event of the original author's intention. Rather his task becomes the distinct one of finding methods capable of explicating the meaning of the text itself. For a more technical summary of this first development in interpretation theory, recall the major dictum of contemporary linguistics which informs this approach : "Just as language in actualizing itself in discourse goes beyond itself in the speech-event, so speech in entering into the process of comprehension goes beyond itself in the meaning." [38]

The second important development in contemporary hermeneutic theory may be labelled (as it is by Paul Ricoeur) the reformulation of the "dialectic of explanation and understanding." [39] This development is, in fact, directly dependent upon the first development outlined above. Insofar as the author's own intention is surpassed by the meaning codified in the text, or codified in the production of oral discourse by a particular mode of discourse, then an understanding of the text demands a semantical as distinct from a psychological method of interpretation. To reformulate this insight in the terms of the hermeneutical tradition, the famous dichotomy of Dilthey between "explanation" *(Erklären)* and "understanding" *(Verstehen)* should be abandoned in favor of a method of interpretation which will relate the semantical and literary-critical explanation of the "sense" of the text with the properly hermeneutical understanding of the "referents" of the text.

The remainder of this section will attempt to explicate the several meanings involved in that distinction. A negative clarification may prove initially helpful: this theory of interpretation denies that the meaning of a text is to be achieved by a psychological process of "empathy" or "divination" of the author's intention. Indeed, the present understanding of the task of interpretation insists that the meaning of the text is fixed in the text as ideal and not as a psychic event of the author. The author remains present but now as that author's vision is referred to by the text itself, not as that vision can be determined by historical and social-scientific analyses of the author's psychological, biographical, cultural, and sociological situations. In more technical terms, the author of interest for the interpreter of the text's meanings is not the author as reconstructed, for example, by psycho-historical methods. Rather the particular vision of the author on reality becomes the self-referent of the text itself. In the more familiar terms of contemporary American literary criticism, the "author" for this theory of interpretation becomes what Wayne Booth has named the "implied author": that personal vision of the world codified in or referred to by the *oeuvre* of any particular author.[40] In interpreting texts one may employ those non-psychological methods which can explicate the "meaning" of the text. Such methods are needed to determine the "explanation" of the "sense" of the text. At that point, the task of "understanding" as distinct from "explanation" can be specified as the task of understanding the extra-linguistic "referents" of the text.

Certain familiar questions should allow us to explain these initially obscure meanings more clearly. What is meant by the explanation of the sense of a text? The sense or the meaning of the text is the ideal object which is intended. As ideal, this meaning is purely immanent. The words do not refer to an extra-linguistic reality but rather to other words. The immanent sense of the text can be determined through the ordinary methods of semantical and literary-critical explanation. These latter methods, of course, are not inventions by contemporary exponents of this theory of interpretation. In fact, the European structuralist school of Lévi-Strauss and the American literary-critical school of the "New Criticism" have long insisted that their non-psychological approach to the semantical and literary structure of texts is a correct approach to the meaning of the text itself. Insofar as the present understanding of hermeneutics also focuses on the meaning of the text as a non-psychological reality, it too can encourage and attempt to incorporate the results of the explanation of texts through explicitly semantical and structuralist methods.[41]

In the case of Christian texts, this task of explanation is probably best understood by recalling certain New Testament scholars who incorporate these methods. As one example, the discussion of the meaning of the New Testament parables has moved in basically the following stages.[42] Throughout the history of Christian theology, the temptation to allegorize the parables (the medieval "four senses" of scripture being one way) has been the predominant tradition of interpretation for the parables. This temptation was probably forever laid to rest in the latter part of the last century by the work of Jülicher who refuted all allegorizations of the parables in favor of determining the basic moral point of each parable. Jülicher's own efforts were later called into question by the further emergence of historical consciousness as represented by the work of C. H. Dodd and Joachim Jeremias. Both these scholars attempted to provide *the* meaning of each parable by determining through exegesis and historical criticism the life-situation of either Jesus or the community to which or from which the parable spoke. Until fairly recently, in fact, this *Sitz-im-Leben* approach to the question of the meaning of the parables seemed the correct one to most scripture scholars. Yet on the understanding of the task of interpretation explicated above, this historical interpretation of a parable's meaning is radically inadequate. For we do not understand the meaning of the parables by understanding either the author's intentions, or the community's, or Jesus' life-situation. What historical criticism does achieve is the reconstruction of texts whose meaning (its sense *and* its referent) the interpreter must now determine through other methods of analysis. Recent New Testament studies of parables have incorporated explicitly semantical and literary-critical methods. Inasmuch as the parables are narrative expansions of a basic metaphor, it becomes imperative for any interpreter of parabolic texts to explain the structure and nature of such a narrative genre and the nature and structure of metaphor itself as a linguistic expression. In short, as the recent work of Amos Wilder, Robert Funk, Norman Perrin, Dan O. Via, and Dominic Crossan shows,[43] the interpreter of the parables of Jesus must enter into the task here called "explanation" in order to determine first the "sense" of the parable itself.

The question remains, however, whether semantical, or structuralist, or literary-critical explanations of the sense of a text can really determine the entire theological meaning of the text. In the present theory of interpretation, a further task is required: the task of understanding the extra-linguistic referent of the text.[44] To what aspects of reality, ordinary or perhaps extraordinary, do these texts refer the reader? These referents of the text do not refer to the meaning "behind" the text (such as the author's real intention or the social-cultural situation of the text). Rather, as noted briefly in the previous chapter, the referent of the text expresses the meaning "in front of the text." More exactly, we can determine both an object-referent of some existential import (viz., that way of perceiving reality, that mode of being-in-the-world which the text opens up for the intelligent reader) and a subject-referent (viz., the personal vision of the author implied by the text). In the latter case, one can establish the meanings present in the basic vision of the world of that "implied author" (for example, the vision of the "world" of Jesus as referred to by the parabolic texts).

Although this latter understanding of "referent" is not divorced from either prior historical or semantical investigations, still "referent" here is clearly distinct from those prior factors. Further, the referents of the text are *the* factor demanding a properly hermeneutical as distinct from either a historical or a literary-critical exercise. In this sense, the final moment of interpretation of a text (namely, the hermeneutical determination of the referents of the text) is not involved in one subject trying to understand another subject. Rather this final moment of interpretation is properly defined by what Hans-Georg Gadamer labels the fusion of horizons (*Horizontverschmelzung*): the reader overcomes the strangeness of another horizon not by empathizing with the psychic state or cultural situation of the author but rather by understanding the basic vision of the author implied by the text and the mode-of-being-in-the-world referred to by the text.[45]

On this understanding of the task of interpretation, the following consequences for the theologian's interpretation of the meanings of Christian texts seem to follow. First, the psychologizing tendency of much theological interpretation is challenged in favor of an approach which, although informed by psychological and historical consciousness, is nevertheless committed to an understanding of the objectivity or ideality of meaning fixed in written texts and even in oral texts by various modes of discourse. This approach, it must be candidly admitted, favors a reversal of priority from the "historicity" of religious texts to their "logicity." The full implications of this shift may perhaps best be examined by studying how this theory of interpretation can be employed to determine the limit-language (the sense) and limit-experience (the referents) of explicitly Christian texts in Part II of this work.[46]

Secondly, the tendency in contemporary theology to imply that hermeneutics can encompass the entire field of theology is eliminated by this understanding of the limited but highly important task of hermeneutics (namely, to determine the sense and the referents of texts).[47]

Thirdly, the tendency in much contemporary theological hermeneutics to include a "decision element" in the hermeneutical task itself and to give relatively little attention to the question of the aesthetic meanings uncovered by theological hermeneutics is challenged.[48] Indeed, this theory of interpretation appeals primarily to the imagination (by disclosing a possible way of being-in-the-world as a project for our imagination to envision) rather than to the will (an ethical enterprise).[49] By means of that aesthetic differentiation, the theologian is free to develop his further tasks of the ethical and metaphysical appropriation of the meanings referred to by the text as genuinely distinct inquiries.[50]

There seem solid reasons for accepting this theory of interpretation both on general theoretical grounds and as a possible corrective to some of the major difficulties of the present theological moment. This theory of interpretation can eliminate the psychologizing tendencies of the dominant "divination" theory of interpretation without challenging either the need for prior historical work in the reconstruction of the texts to be interpreted and without a wholesale negation of any interest in the author of texts—as the "implied author." [51] This theory of interpretation can also allow the properly hermeneutic task to be clearly differentiated from the further ethical and metaphysical examinations of the meanings disclosed by the interpreter. This factor could well lead to a reexamination of the important role of the imagination for any study of religious texts. Such otherwise different theologians as Hans Urs von Balthasar, Nathan Scott, Justus George Lawler, and Ray Hart[52] have argued thusly for some years with a conviction and eloquence that seems matched only by the stunningly silent response of many of their fellow theologians. Such a properly theological role for the imagination, in its turn, could lead to a renewed recognition of the distinct roles of appropriation: ethical inquiry into the value of the "meanings disclosed" (Is this way of being-in-the-world a valuable one for the ethical human being?); metaphysical inquiry into the cognitive claims of the meanings disclosed (Are these meanings internally coherent and adequate to the rest of our experience?).

A revisionist theologian, moreover, may well find this recent hermeneutical theory particularly helpful for his/her own enterprise. This theory allows the theologian to employ a method capable of explicating the principal existential meanings of Christian texts without involving one in the difficulties of either psychologizing those meanings or of expecting "hermeneutics" to carry the impossible burden of ethical and metaphysical analysis.

THE TASK OF CRITICAL CORRELATION

The application of criteria of adequacy to the first "source" of theology and criteria of appropriateness to the second "source" need not imply that criteria of adequacy are only applicable to the first and criteria of appropriateness to the second. Indeed, the final revisionist task of critical correlation is an attempt to allow for the application of the other set of criteria to each analysis. On the one hand, the meanings discovered as adequate to our common human experience must be compared to the meanings disclosed as appropriate to the Christian tradition in order to discover how similar, different, or identical the former meanings are in relationship to the latter.[53] In the present work, the most obvious example of this application is the argument in chapters five and six that the limit-character of the "religious dimension" present to our common human experience is similar in meaning to the limit-character of the religious meaning of the New Testament language. Insofar as this claim can be maintained, the first set of meanings may also be declared appropriate to the Christian tradition and the second set of meanings may also be declared adequate to our common experience.[54]

Such a correlation may be present not only for the questions of the logical character of both implicit and explicit *religious* language and experience (chapters five and six) but also for the question of the metaphysical character of the theistic referent of both our common experience and Christian experience (chapters seven and eight). However, as the concerns of fundamental theology move out of their orbit of primarily logical and metaphysical concerns to the orbit of dogmatics (i.e., to a greater concern with the explicit particularity of the Christian symbol-system), the concerns of fundamental theology itself may shift from criteria of metaphysical adequacy to criteria of relative experiential adequacy. As the christological chapter of this work (chapter nine) may serve to show in an initial manner, the major concern of the fundamental theologian at this later level of study is to show how the earlier determination of the legitimacy of religious theism leads naturally to a search for and an investigation of the relative experiential adequacy of various symbol-systems representative of those religious and theistic meanings. As such pioneering works as Reinhold Neibuhr's *The Nature and Destiny of Man*, Paul Ricoeur's *The Symbolism of Evil*, Langdon Gilkey's *Naming the Whirlwind: The Renewal of God-Language*, or John Cobb's *Structures of Christian Existence* may serve to suggest, the dominant criteriological concerns of an investigation of various symbol-systems is to show the relative experiential adequacy of one symbol-system (e.g., the Christian) both to the *meaning* and *truth* of religious theism and to the *meaningfulness* of this particular symbol-system for the human situation.[55] In the latter case, ethical and aesthetic criteria are clearly relevant to this matter-of-fact experiential discussion. Furthermore, as chapters nine and ten shall suggest, criteria of "meaningfulness" to our matter-of-fact situation can be further specified as "criteria of the relative adequacy" of a given symbol-system both to maintain a fundamental fidelity to religious theism ("meaning" and "truth") and to advance more encompassing modes of personal and societal transformation ("meaningfulness").[56]

It is true that once fundamental theology takes this more matter-of-fact, this clearly more "historical" turn, then fundamental theological reflection begins to approach the task of a properly Christian dogmatics. Yet a factor of no little importance still remains: the basic criteria and the basic modes of argumentation for dogmatics itself will remain those developed in fundamental theology. A central dogmatic concern, after all, is to determine the meaning, meaningfulness, and truth of a given Christian symbol for contemporary experience.

In fundamental theology itself, the shift in importance in its later stages to "criteria of relative adequacy" is indeed, as the chapters on christology and *praxis* will try to show, a shift of both criteriological and material importance. But these latter criteria, as much as the former, are in principle open to public discussion, to more than "Christian" scrutiny.[57] Finally, I do not believe that all the criteria outlined above under the general rubric of "philosophical reflection upon the meanings present in our common human experience and language and the meanings present in Christian texts" are purely methodological or formal. But probably only the risk of testing this model on the questions of certain religious, theistic, and christological meanings can hope to provide reasons for my belief.

Notes

(1) Since most of the issues treated in this chapter will be treated in the analyses of later chapters, the references here will be limited to presently essential sources of information. For the Anglo-American tradition on experience here, cf. John E. Smith, *Experience and God* (New York: Oxford University Press, 1968), esp. pp. 21–46; for a succinct formulation of the Whiteheadean position on experience (involving the crucial categories "perception," "subjectivist principle," "causal efficacy," and "presentational immediacy"), cf. the summary by Schubert M. Ogden, "Lonergan and the Subjectivist Principle," *Journal of Religion* 51 (1971), 159–63; cf. also notes in chapter eight for more extensive examples.

(2) This seems true not only of the classical British empiricist tradition of David Hume but also of the linguistic refinement of that "sensationalist" model into a "verificationist" model in the modern "verification" and "falsification" discussions; cf. chapters six and seven for references to these discussions.

(3) For a classical example of a phenomenological account of feelings, cf. Max Scheler, *The Nature of Sympathy* (New York: Anchor, 1970).

(4) The phrasing here follows the analysis of the structure of human consciousness developed by Bernard Lonergan as applied to the question of values. On the former, cf. *Method in Theology* (New York: Herder and Herder, 1972); pp. 3–27; on the latter, ibid., pp. 30–41.

(5) For examples of the phenomenological tradition on the "life-world," cf. *Patterns of the Life-World*, ed. James M. Edie and others (Evanston: Northwestern University Press, 1970); cf. also Maurice Natanson, *Edmund Husserl: Philosopher of the Infinite Tasks* (Evanston: Northwestern University Press, 1973), pp. 126–47, for a summary on Husserl's notion of "life-world." For an analysis of the relationship between the phenomenological tradition and the Anglo-American tradition of "radical empiricism," cf. John Wild, *The Radical Empiricism of William James* (New York: Doubleday, 1969), esp. pp. 359–417.

(6) For a clear exposition of the notion of "mediating immediacy," cf. Emerich Coreth, *Metaphysics* (New York: Herder and Herder, 1968), pp. 40–42.

(7) On "feelings" as our original apprehension of values, cf. Bernard Lonergan, *Method in Theology*, pp. 30–34.

(8) The manner in which Josiah Royce developed the important concept of the "community of interpretation" in relationship to both German Idealism and to the radical empiricism of William James is analyzed in John E. Smith, *Royce's Social Infinite: The Community of Interpretation* (New York: Anchor, 1969), pp. 3–109.

(9) The now familiar American expression "consciousness-raising" seems an apt expression not only for the self-appropriation of one's feelings (as in psychoanalysis) but also for what Bernard Lonergan in *Insight: A Study of Human Understanding* (London: Longman's, 1957), invites the reader to perform when he pleas for the "self-appropriation of one's intelligent and rational consciousness" (esp. pp. 319–39). The cultural import of the related Latin American notion of *"conscientização"* is articulated in Paulo Freire's *The Pedagogy of the Oppressed* (New York: Herder and Herder, 1970).

(10) For a major example of this "broad" use of phenomenology, cf. the analysis of the relationship between "symbol" and "experience" in Langdon Gilkey, *Naming the Whirlwind* (New York: Bobbs-Merrill, 1969), pp. 266–76.

(11) Cf. Emerich Coreth, *Metaphysics*, pp. 17–45.

(12) The phrase is not, of course, accurate for most representatives of the analytical tradition in philosophy (cf. later discussions in chapters six and seven). It remains accurate for three contemporary philosophical traditions: the phenomenological, the Anglo-American empirical, and the reformulated "transcendental method" of Coreth, Lonergan, and Rahner.

(13) Cf. Emerich Coreth, *Metaphysics*, pp. 22–41.

(14) Ibid., p. 37.

(15) Cf. Schubert M. Ogden, "Lonergan and the Subjectivist Principle," pp. 163–66; cf. also chapter five, n. 54, and chapter eight, n. 5, for some remarks on the openness of the later positions of Lonergan and Rahner to the more comprehensive notion of experience. For a classical exposition, cf. Alfred North Whitehead, *Process and Reality* (New York: Free Press, 1969), pp. 167–81.

(16) For a clear and summary account of the Husserlian notions of "phenomenon," "intentionality," and "constitution," cf. Robert Sokolowski, "Edmund Husserl and the Principles of Phenomenology," in *Twentieth Century Thinkers*, ed. John K. Ryan (New York: Alba, 1965), esp. pp. 138–41.

(17) For signally clear and systematic presentations of Husserl's complex thought, cf. Robert Sokolowski, *The Formation of Husserl's Concept of Constitution* (The Hague: Mouton, 1964); idem., *Husserlian Meditations* (Evanston: Northwestern University Press, 1974).

(18) For the history of the development of that tradition, cf. Herbert Spiegelberg, *The Phenomenological Movement*, 2 vols. (The Hague: Nijhoff, 1965); for more recent developments, cf. Paul Ricoeur, "New Developments in Phenomenology in France: The Phenomenology of Language," *Social Research* 34 (1967), 1–30. For Bernard Lonergan's analogous notion of "intentionality-analysis," cf. chapter two, n. 1.

(19) Although it may be technically inappropriate to describe Heidegger's ontology (or even his "retrieval" of Kant) as "transcendental," the clearly ontological (and not existentialist) character of Heidegger's thought seems to allow for this interpretation. For Heidegger's formulation of his ontological question, cf. the penetrating essay by Thomas Prufer, "Martin Heidegger: *Dasein* and the Ontological Status of the Speaker of Philosophical Discourse" in *Twentieth Century Thinkers*, pp. 159–75; see also, William Richardson, *Heidegger: Through Phenomenology to Thought* (The Hague: Nijhoff, 1967).

(20) The linguistic categories "metaphor" and "concepts" will be discussed in chapters six and seven. For a masterful analysis of religious "images" in several cultures, cf. the works of Mircea Eliade, esp.; *Images and Symbols: Studies in Religious Symbolism* (New York: Sheed and Ward, 1969).

(21) We shall employ various analysts in this tradition in chapters five and six. For a summary-analysis of the tradition, cf. Frederick Ferré, *Language, Logic and God* (New York; harper & Row, 1961).

(22) Cf. chapter five for examples.

(23) Inter alia, cf. Robert Bellah, "Civil Religion in America" in *The Religious Situation*, ed. Donald R. Cutler (Boston: Beacon, 1968), pp. 331–56; Martin E. Marty, *Righteous Empire: The Protestant Experience in America* (New York: Dial, 1970), esp. pp. 244–66; Sidney Mead, "The Nation with the Soul of a Church," *Church History* 36 (1967), 262–83; Michael Novak, *Choosing Our King: Powerful Symbols in Presidential Politics* (New York: Macmillan, 1974), esp. pp. 105–63.

(24) This criterion, which refers to *logical* coherence or incoherence within a system of concepts, although less radical than the criterion of "coherence with experience" itself, is of considerable importance in investigating alternative concepts for theism: cf. discussion in chapter eight.

(25) Cf. chapter eight on the process theologians.

(26) As I trust is clear from the text itself, there are no claims here that the specific formulation of "philosophical reflection" as comprised of phenomenological and transcendental moments is an "exclusive" formulation of the possibilities of "philosophical reflection."

(27) The logical order of these questions is also of some importance: from religion to theism, not vice versa. This order is followed in Part II of the book.

(28) As noted in the discussion of the "revisionist model" in chapters three and four, a plea for criteria of appropriateness is not identical with a plea against a *Sach-Kritik* of traditional statements in scripture or tradition.

(29) Cf. the excellent summary statement from Altizer's *The Gospel of Christian Atheism*, "The Self-Annihilation of God," anthologized in *The New Christianity: An Anthology of the Rise of Modern Religious Thought*, ed. William Robert Miller (New York: Delacorte, 1967), pp. 367–76.

(30) This insistence on "tradition" and not merely "the text" continues to seem to me one of the most important insights maintained by the Catholic theological tradition. Although that latter tradition sometimes uses this insight to disallow a criticism of the *tradita*, it remains the case that a recognition of the reality of *traditio* should encourage (and does encourage as the contemporary, remarkably diverse theological life of Catholicism shows) an enriching recognition of the fuller reality of the "Christian fact."

(31) The "interpretation theory" employed here may be found in the work of Paul Ricoeur and Hans-Georg Gadamer. As the citations will clarify, I am following Ricoeur's own summary statement in "Interpretation Theory" (presented to a colloquium of the faculty at the University of Chicago Divinity School, May 1971). Since this important essay has not, to my knowledge, been published, the reader may find most of the elements employed here in the following recent publications of Ricoeur: the essays "Creativity in Language," "The Task of Hermeneutics," and "The Hermeneutical Function of Distanciation," in *Philosophy Today* 17 (1973), 97–142; "Philosophy and Religious Language," in *Journal of Religion* 54 (1974), 71–86; cf. also the published and unpublished works cited in chapter six as well as several of the essays in *Le conflit des interprétations* (Paris: du Seuil, 1969), esp. pp. 31–101 and pp. 233–65. For Gadamer, the *locus classicus* remains *Wahrheit und Methode* (Tübingen: J. C. B. Mohr, 1965). For interpretations of the interpreters here: on Ricoeur, cf. the works of Gerhart, Idhe, and Rasmussen cited in chapter nine, n. 47; for Gadamer, cf. Richard Palmer, *Hermeneutics: Interpretation Theory in Schleiermacher, Dilthey, Heidegger and Gadamer* (Evanston: Northwestern University Press, 1969); David E. Linge, "Dilthey and Gadamer: Two Theories of Historical Understanding," in *Journal of the American Academy of Religion* XLI (1973), 536–54; idem, "Editor's Introduction" to a collection of Gadamer's essays to be published by Northwestern University Press in 1975. For two comparative studies of Gadamer's achievements, cf. Frederick Lawrence, "Self-knowledge in History in Gadamer and Lonergan," in *Language, Truth and Meaning*, ed. Philip McShane (Notre Dame: University of Notre Dame Press, 1972), pp. 167–218; and Theodore F. Peters, "Method and Truth: An Inquiry into the Philosophical Hermeneutics of Hans-Georg Gadamer and the Theology of History of Wolfhart Pannenberg" (unpub. dissertation, University of Chicago Divinity School, 1973); cf. also the Gadamer *Festschrift* published under the title *Hermeneutik und Dialektik*, 2 vols. (Tübingen: J. C. B. Mohr, 1970)—note especially Ricoeur's contribution "Qu'est-ce qu'un Texte?" pp. 181–201. For a critical interpretation of Gadamer (and, by implication, Ricoeur) on Dilthey, cf. Matthew Lamb, "Wilhelm Dilthey's Critique of Historical Reason and Bernard Lonergan's Meta-methodology," in *Language, Truth and Meaning*, pp. 115–67. Finally, the critical exchange between Hans-Georg Gadamer and Jürgen Habermas will be significant for the concerns of chapter ten: inter alia, cf. *Continuum* 8 (1970), pp. 77–96 and 123–28; and Jürgen Habermas, *Zur Logik du Sozialwissenschaften* (Frankfurt: Suhrkamp, 1970), pp. 251–85. The other major tradition of interpretation theory is best represented in the contemporary period by Emilio Betti, *Teoria generale della interpretazione* (Milano: Giuffrè, 1955); and E. D. Hirsch, Jr., *Validity in Interpretation* (New Haven: Yale University Press, 1967). Hirsch is particularly important for continuing the insistence of "Romantic Hermeneutics" (Gadamer's phrase) upon the "mind of the author."

(32) For an analysis of Troeltsch here, cf. Thomas W. Ogletree, *Christian Faith and History: A Critical Comparison of Ernst Troeltsch and Karl Barth* (Nashville: Abingdon, 1965), pp. 17–81; and B. A. Gerrish, "Jesus, Myth, and History: Troeltsch's Stand in the 'Christ Myth' Debate," *Journal of Religion* 55 (1975), 13–36; on Bultmann, cf. Van A. Harvey, *The Historian and the Believer*, pp. 139–46; for Lonergan, inter alia, cf. *Method in Theology*, pp. 153–75 (on "interpretation"); pp. 175–235 (on "history"); on Lonergan here, cf. Bernard McGinn, "Bernard Lonergan and the Crisis in Historical Knowledge," to be published in *Essays in Methodology*, ed. Philip McShane (Dublin: Gill and Macmillan, 1975).

(33) For the hermeneutical significance of Barth's *Romans*, cf. James M. Robinson, "Hermeneutic Since Barth" in *The New Hermeneutic*, ed. James M. Robinson and John B. Cobb, Jr. (New York: Harper and Row, 1964), esp. pp. 25–33; on the difficulties of Barth here, cf. Van A. Harvey, *The Historian and the Believer*, pp. 153–59; for an example in Karl Rahner, note his almost a-historical use of the categories "apocalyptic" and "eschatology" in "The Hermeneutics of Eschatological Assertions," in *Theological Investigations*, IV (Baltimore: Helicon, 1966), 337. This is not to deny the extraordinary import of either Barth's or Rahner's hermeneutical methods; on Barth, cf. the Robinson essay cited above; on Rahner, note how his use of a Heideggerian method of "retrieval" has allowed him, in the volumes of the *Investigations*, to retrieve the contemporary "meaningfulness" (in my terms) of several major moments in the Roman Catholic tradition.

(34) Cf. Hans-Georg Gadamer, *Wahrheit und Methode*, esp. pp. 185–205; Paul Ricoeur, "The Task of Hermeneutics," esp. pp. 120–28.

(35) The following sections represent, to a large extent, a summary of Paul Ricoeur's analysis in "Interpretation Theory." Unless otherwise indicated the points made may be found in a more extended and technical form in that important essay and in the essays cited in n. 31 above.

(36) Ibid., pp. 1–8, for this whole section.

(37) One may note here Ricoeur's own shift from the emphasis upon written texts in "Interpretation Theory" to the wider category of "modes of discourse." On the latter, cf. "Philosophy and Religious Discourse," pp. 73–75, 78–79; and "The Hermeneutical Function of Distanciation," pp. 130–39.

(38) "Interpretation Theory," p. 8, for Ricoeur's development of the four different manners in which "event" surpasses itself in the "meaning."

(39) Ibid., pp. 8–12.

(40) Although this concept is not employed by Ricoeur, I believe it is faithful to his meaning. For the category, cf. Wayne Booth, *The Rhetoric of Fiction* (Chicago: University of Chicago Press, 1961), esp. pp. 71–76 and 211–21.

(41) For examples here in New Testament studies, cf. the special issue on "Structuralism" in *Interpretation: A Journal of Bible and Theology* (1974); for Ricoeur's own position, cf. his essays on the interpretation of parables cited in chapter five. His position there is summarized as follows: "The analysis of the parables will give us an opportunity to try the more difficult way, according to which a *structural analysis—*

disconnected from structuralist ideology—may enrich an existential hermeneutics," in "Structuralism and Structuralist Ideology" (privately printed lecture for a course at the University of Chicago Divinity School, Spring 1973), p. 1. On structuralism, cf. *Structuralism, Yale French Studies*, 36 and 37 (1966); Richard Macksey and Eugenio Donato, *The Structuralist Controversy: The Languages of Criticism and the Sciences of Man* (Baltimore: Johns Hopkins Press, 1970).

(42) Cf. discussion on parables as limit-language in chapter six for references to the works mentioned in this summary section.

(43) This is not to suggest that these authors employ Ricoeur's interpretation theory outlined here. Such, indeed, is not the case; but all of these critics do employ modern methods of literary criticism for their work: cf. chapter six for citations.

(44) "Interpretation Theory," pp. 12–19; also, "Philosophy and Religious Language," pp. 79–84.

(45) Cf. *Wahrheit und Methode*, pp. 289–90.

(46) Cf. especially chapter six on religious language and chapter nine on christological language.

(47) Although a different "interpretation theory" is employed there, this point is made methodologically by Bernard Lonergan with his concept of "hermeneutics" as one of the "functional specialties" in theology: cf. *Method in Theology*, p. 153.

(48) The hermeneutical tradition of Fuchs and Ebeling seems relevant here: cf. the summary-analysis of that stance provided by Robert W. Funk, *Language, Hermeneutic and Word of God*, esp. pp. 60–71.

(49) This formulation seems more faithful to the German Kantian tradition (so influential on German Protestant theology) than it does to the Anglo-American tradition of Peirce, James, Whitehead, and Hartshorne, wherein ethical (value) categories are largely interpreted in aesthetic (e.g., "appreciation") terms. This aspect of the Anglo-American tradition may prove especially significant for the development of ethical criteria here. For a major attempt to link the hermeneutical tradition itself to the imagination in a theologically revisionist way, cf. Ray L. Hart, *Unfinished Man and the Imagination* (New York: Herder and Herder, 1969), esp. pp. 267–315.

(50) As noted in chapter six, n. 67, Ricoeur himself is wary about any use of metaphysics here. Ricoeur's own appeal to Schleiermacher's classical distinction between the task of hermeneutics and the task of ethics, however, seems to suggest that he does favor the possibility of introducing ethical criteria here.

(51) Cf. n. 40 above for the concept. For an argument that Pannenberg's concept of "universal history" provides a more comprehensive context than "hermeneutics," cf. Wolfhart Pannenberg, "Hermeneutics and Universal History," in *History and Hermeneutic*, ed. Robert W. Funk (New York: Harper & Row, 1967), pp. 122–53; for Gadamer's own reflections, cf. "On the Scope and Function of Hermeneutical Reflection," in *Continuum* 8 (1970), esp. pp. 91–92. For an extensive study of this debate, cf. Theodore F. Peters, "Method and Truth."

(52) Cf. Hans Urs von Balthasar, *Herrlichkeit* (Einsiedeln: Johannes Verlag, 1961); Justus George Lawler, *The Christian Image: Studies in Religious Art and Poetry* (Pittsburgh: Duquesne University Press, 1966); Nathan A. Scott, Jr., "Prolegomenon to a Christian Poetic," *Journal of Religion* 35 (1955), 200 ff.; Ray L. Hart, *Unfinished Man and the Imagination.* This is not to imply that these diverse thinkers hold the same judgments on either "imagination" or theology. Quite clearly, they do not.

(53) For a clear formulation of the methodological need for a discipline engaged in this dialectical study, cf. Bernard Lonergan, *Method in Theology*, pp. 235–67. Lonergan's own resulting "foundations" (in Lonergan's expression) are quite different than those formulated in this work. Still the task of "dialectics" is, I believe, so concisely formulated by Lonergan as to be available even for those who may not accept Lonergan's own "foundations."

(54) This may also be formulated, as it is in later chapters, as involving a hermeneutical correlation between the two sets of meanings. For example, the meaning of the limit-situation of reflection on death as one's own destiny provides a "hearing" context for the symbolic language employed in a Christian funeral service. Alternatively, that latter language can only be heard (or, to use Merleau-Ponty's suggestive phrase, "over-heard") in the context of an appreciation of the limit-situation disclosed: cf. the discussions in chapters six and seven.

(55) All four of these works are cited throughout this text. They serve, I believe, as excellent examples of the search for existential "meaningfulness" in terms of "criteria of the relative adequacy" of a particular symbol system for our concrete experience: cf. especially the methodological discussion of "experiential meaning" as disclosed by an analysis of the relationship between "symbol and experience" in Langdon Gilkey, *Naming the Whirlwind*, pp. 266–76; cf. also Paul Ricoeur's observations on how we may avoid becoming merely "Don Juans of the myth" by developing what I call criteria of relative adequacy and Ricoeur labels "existential verification" in *The Symbolism of Evil* (Boston: Beacon, 1967), pp. 306–46; cf. also John Cobb's methodological remarks on the possibilities of comparative analyses of differing "structures of existence" in his *The Structure of Christian Existence* (Philadelphia: Westminster, 1967), esp. pp. 13–24 and 137–50; for a succinct formulation of Niebuhr's methodological position here, cf. his essay, "Coherence, Incoherence and Christian Faith," *Christian Realism and Political Problems* (New York: Scribner's, 1953).

(56) Cf. the discussions in chapters nine and ten as initial applications of criteria of relative adequacy for personal (chapter nine) and societal (chapter ten) transformation.

(57) As manifested, I believe, in the work of Cobb, Gilkey, Niebuhr, and Ricoeur mentioned in n. 55 above. The need for determining how we may have a "confessional" position that is still open to "public" discourse remains, I believe, the chief question for an adequate revisionist model for dogmatic theology. Insofar as this work tries to spell out "public" criteria and apply them to the questions of "fundamental theology," it may be said to initiate that discussion. Until several further questions are addressed, however, (e.g., "values," *"praxis,"* authority, church, doctrine, etc.), the discussion in this entire work of a model for dogmatics remains at best initiated.

Part II

Chapter 5

The Religious Dimension of Common Human Experience and Language

FOREGROUND: **Purpose and Structure of Part II**

The present work is principally concerned to outline a new model and method for fundamental theology—a model which can be faithful to some of the more important pluralist possibilities of the present day. It remains then to determine whether that formal claim—the revisionist model—may receive some initial and tentative material articulation.[1] Consequently, the following chapters will recall and reinterpret certain familiar positions in the contemporary theological context in accordance with that model. The consistent use of the general revisionist formal model to reinterpret specific material positions from a broad spectrum of traditions may also serve to show how different thinkers can share both certain conclusions and a basic vision of theology's present task.

A factor of some importance, the basic structure of Part II, is provided by the revisionist model itself. Throughout, there will be summary-interpretations of the two principal sources of theological reflection, common human experience and language, and Christian texts. In each case a comparison and a correlation of the two distinct interpretations will also be initiated.[2]

Another structural characteristic can be described in more substantial or material terms: when one has a concern for the questions articulated in Part I and wishes to sort out the more basic substantive questions for the application of the model, the following logical order of questions seems correct. How and in what senses is the religious interpretation of our common human experience and language meaningful and true? How and in what senses is the theistic interpretation of religion meaningful and true? How and in what senses is the christological interpretation of theistic religion meaningful and true? These concerns seem not only reasonable but even logically necessary for any thinker wishing to test any model of the revisionist kind upon the existential and cognitive claims of the Christian religion.[3] In fact, these questions emerge with notable frequency in contemporary religious thought. When the questions are differentiated in the manner and order suggested above, each question may be tested individually and in its logical interrelationships with the other questions.

The first question is the question of this chapter: how and in what senses is the religious interpretation of common human experience and language meaningful and true?

THE CONCEPT OF LIMIT

There is no universally agreed upon single definition for the human phenomenon called "religion." [4] To be sure, certain attempts at definition continue to claim serious attention. In theological circles, the tradition initiated by Schleiermacher's pioneering attempt to differentiate religious experience as a "feeling of absolute dependence" has been developed both by Rudolph Otto's phenomenological description of the "holy" as *mysterium fascinans et tremendum*" and by Paul Tillich's ontological analysis of this Schleiermacher-Otto tradition in his justly famous analysis of "ultimate concern" as constitutive of the religious dimension of our experience.[5]

The social sciences have also developed certain classical approaches to the "functions" and sometimes the "essence" of religions, classically formulated in the works of Max Weber and Emile Durkheim.[6] Recently, for example, the social functions of religion have been articulated by Peter Berger under the general category of how religions function to provide basic "social constructs" for reality.[7] In the tradition of cultural anthropology, a very helpful understanding of "religion" has been proposed by Clifford Geertz in a definition which nicely unites certain dominant philosophical and theological interests in the character of religious symbols with social scientific interest in the important individual and social functions which "religions" can express.[8] For Geertz a religion is:

1) a system of symbols which acts to
2) establish powerful, pervasive, and long-lasting moods and motivations in men by
3) formulating conceptions of a general order of existence, and
4) clothing these conceptions with such an aura of factuality that
5) the moods and motivations seem uniquely realistic.

Examples of the various approaches to the meanings and functions of "religion" could be multiplied almost indefinitely. However, a need to agree upon a single universal definition[9] for the term "religion" is neither necessary nor particularly desirable in the present pluralist situation. There is no longer, nor need there be, any one universally agreed upon "religious perspective." To be sure, there are what Wittgenstein labelled "family resemblances" among the religious perspectives which are sufficiently distinct from various moral systems or aesthetic expressions to continue to justify our ordinary use of such familiar and acceptable expressions as "religion," "morality," and "art." [10]

What seems essential in the present context, therefore, is not to attempt a single all-encompassing definition of "religion." Instead, as either the Schleiermacher-Otto-Tillich tradition attempts in one way, or the Weber-Berger-Geertz tradition in quite another, contemporary analysts are content to describe certain basic factors which characterize a religious as distinct from a moral, an aesthetic, a scientific, or a political perspective. As the reader shall discover in this and the following chapter, I have come to believe that the concept "limit" can be used as a key (but not exhaustive) category for describing certain signal characteristics peculiar to any language or experience with a properly religious dimension.[11] Whether that dimension be explicit or implicit is not, in fact, the central issue. My contention will be that all significant explicitly religious language and experience (the "religions") and all significant implicitly religious characteristics of our common experience (the "religious dimension") will bear at least the "family resemblance" of articulating or implying a limit-experience, a limit-language, or a limit-dimension.

Now it seems sufficient merely to note a more ordinary usage of the category "religion." Employed in our common discourse, "religion" usually means a perspective which expresses a dominating interest in certain universal and elemental features of human existence as those features bear on the human desire for liberation and authentic existence.[12] Such features can be analyzed as both expressive of certain "limits-to" our ordinary experience (e.g., finitude, contingency, or radical transience) and disclosive of certain fundamental structures of our existence beyond (or, alternatively, grounding to) that ordinary experience (e.g., our fundamental trust in the worthwhileness of existence, our basic belief in order and value).

We can often both experience and articulate the "limits-to" aspect of the religious perspective. On such occasions, we may also find the ability occasionally to speak, more often to "show" or "disclose" the horizon, ground, or "limit-of" such language and experience.[13] In either case, we need to reflect upon both the explicit limits-to our ordinary experience (the everyday and the scientific, the moral, aesthetic, and political) and the implicitly disclosed dimension which functions as limit-of or ground to[14] (e.g., *fundamental* faith or trust) our more ordinary ways of being-in-the-world.

Clearly all explicitly religious language and experience (the religions) remain the most important expressions of the meaning of religion.[15] Still the claim can be made that a certain basic horizon or dimension of our common experience can justly be described *as* religious. To understand how this claim might be maintained, the rest of this chapter will analyze the phenomena of certain "limit-questions" and "limit-situations" which several contemporary critics believe provide the surest clues to a disclosure of the properly religious horizon to our everyday, our scientific, aesthetic, and moral experience. By providing examples of such analyses, I hope to be able to determine with greater exactness both the meaning and the possible meaningfulness[16] of the expression "the religious dimension" of our common human experience and language.

LIMIT-QUESTIONS IN SCIENCE

The religious dimension can perhaps best be viewed by reflection upon certain limit-questions to the scientific and moral enterprises and by reflection upon certain limit-situations in our everyday lives. That dimension, moreover, does not depend upon a single philosophical tradition for its mediation. Rather, in the present pluralist situation it may prove more helpful to examine interpretations of such phenomena from representatives of four major philosophical traditions: process thinking, transcendental method, linguistic analysis, and existential phenomenology. Each of these traditions could in principle be employed to mediate the significance of both the phenomena of limit-questions to the scientific and moral enterprises and limit-situations in everyday life. In what follows, however, each analysis will employ diverse traditions for the mediation of a given phenomenon. Such a pluralist choice may serve to provide more convincing evidence for the claim to a religious dimension that bears the logical meaning of limit and the existential weight of disclosive meaningfulness.

By initiating that analysis with a study of the phenomenon called limit-questions,[17] I hope to show how, at the limit of both the scientific and the moral enterprises, there inevitably emerge questions to which a response properly described as religious is appropriate. In searching out such responses, another service may be rendered to the inquiry: a clarification of how the very concept of limit provides a logical key for understanding the distinction between scientific and religious meaning on the one hand and the distinction between moral and religious meaning on the other.

Science and Religion: Their Relationship[18]

It is now clear that the centuries-old dispute between "religion" and "science" is largely past history. Except for fundamentalists in both fields, the emerging consensus is so clear as almost to have become a cliché: both fields have their own specific data, methods, and languages. The disputes from Galileo through Darwin are tragedies unlikely to be repeated. The somewhat desperate moves of some religious thinkers to find "gaps" in scientific theories for the now discredited "God of Gaps" to enter are in widespread disrepute.[19] Correlatively, since the emergence of the literally non-imaginable theories of modern physics, the mechanical models of classical scientific theory no longer need refutation by troubled religious humanists.[20]

The present relationship between science and religion, however, is far more complex. A whole range of issues has emerged in the natural and human sciences which are of considerable import for the study of religion. And yet—with a few notable exceptions—the attitudes of a Laplace or even a Freud or T. H. Huxley seem curiously dated. The present situation is more correctly described as a search for the significant similarities and differences between the scientific and the religious dimensions of our common humanity.

Many, perhaps most, contemporary scientific and religious thinkers hold some variation of what might be labelled the "two-language" approach to this question.[21] On the one hand, many linguistic philosophers argue that religious language is "participant" or "self-involving" language (Austin, Evans) in a manner which scientific language as "spectatorial" cannot be.[22] On the other hand, most religious thinkers influenced by neo-orthodox theology hold to their own variation of the two-language approach. Karl Barth, as the clearest exponent of this variously articulated position, held that theology is concerned only and solely with "revelation" and is therefore neither encouraged nor distressed by the "neutral" discoveries of science.[23]

Despite the demise of both neo-orthodoxy and the earlier versions of linguistic philosophy, the two-language approach to the question of religion and science probably still remains the majority opinion among thinkers in both disciplines. Still, for a growing number the two-language approach to the question of the relationships between science and theology, however comforting to both groups, is not really an accurate description of the relationship. Several recent thinkers argue that there are significant similarities between the two disciplines. So much is this the case that some are willing to argue not only for the scientific study of religion (a commonplace) but also for a "religious dimension" to science itself.

That most thinkers who hold to some version of this latter "mediating" position are philosophers and theologians with a good grasp of contemporary scientific methods and conclusions seems a fair generalization. Indeed whatever their philosophical positions—process philosophy (Ian Barbour, Bernard Meland, Schubert Ogden) or transcendental method (Bernard Lonergan) or general reflection on the nature of scientific method (Michael Polanyi, Langdon Gilkey) or phenomenology (Louis Dupré, Paul Ricoeur) or even some versions of linguistic philosophy (Stephen Toulmin)—all may conclude to what may be interpreted as a "religious dimension" to the scientific enterprise itself.[24]

Assuredly many cultural factors are operative here. The gradual and steady reemergence of the positive need for symbol and even myth has rendered earlier discussions of demythologizing in accordance with the prevailing scientific world-view not so much incorrect as incomplete. The recurrent pattern of technological and ecological crises has rendered the curiously optimistic and manipulative "end of ideology" discussions of the

1950's as dated as other cold-war rhetoric of that period. Indeed, most parties to the present discussion—theologians, scientists, philosophers of religion and of science—are by now somewhat chastened in their former self-assurance. They have learned too well both the lessons of the tragic relationships of the past and the legitimate demands of the more recent two-language approach. They have learned to be careful to articulate the significant differences in methods and data in science and theology before approaching a question like the "religious" dimension of science itself.[25] Finally, there is a growing consensus among several of these thinkers on the need for the discipline of metaphysics to mediate the cognitive claims of any horizon-factor labelled the "religious dimension" of science.

These are some of the principal factors which render the present pluralist situation notably different from either the "science *vs.* religion" disputes of the past or even the two-language approach of the very recent anti-metaphysical, neo-orthodox, and linguistic hegemony on this question. Rather than providing another survey of the shared conclusions of these different "mediating" thinkers, we might best understand those conclusions by interpreting the argument of one major participant in the discussion, the Canadian philosopher and theologian, Bernard Lonergan.[26] Lonergan's argument is probably best understood by clarifying certain concepts and their relationships step by step. Thus reinterpreted, I will claim that Lonergan's own enterprise may be used as a contribution towards the analysis of limit-questions in science.

The Religious Dimension of Science: Self-Transcendence as Scientific Authenticity

The central category involved in Bernard Lonergan's analysis is the concept of "self-transcendence." [27] The major reason for the choice of "self-transcendence" as the central model (as distinct, for example, from "self-fulfillment") is clear and, I believe, sound. One lives authentically insofar as one continues to allow oneself an expanding horizon. That expansion has as its chief aim the going-beyond one's present state in accordance with the transcendental imperatives: "Be attentive, be intelligent, be reasonable, be responsible, develop and, if necessary, change." On the simplest level, one transcends oneself first by sensitivity. As a sensitive being, like the other higher animals, a human being is related not merely to himself or herself but to all surrounding realities. Yet humankind does not possess only the habitat of the animals. We also live in a world of meaning, a "universe."

We understand this self-transcending possibility best when we reflect upon our ability to ask questions, especially scientific questions.[28] Scientific questioning impels one past an experienced world of sensitive immediacy to an intelligently mediated and deliberately constituted world of meaning. Insofar as we ask and answer questions for intelligence—Is it clear? What is it?—we learn to understand and unify, to relate and construct, to generalize some view of the whole. Insofar as we go on to ask and answer questions for reflection—Is it so? Why? For what reasons? By what criteria? With what force of evidence?—we learn to affirm some reality beyond ourselves, our desires, needs, fears, and even acts of understanding. We learn, in our judgments, to affirm an unconditioned "yes" or "no": a fact, a reality, a truth not constructed by our own needs but demanded by our critical intelligence.[29] We learn that the real world is constituted not only by our experiences of sound and taste and sight and hearing and touch of what is "out-there," nor only by our desires and fears and needs and feelings for what is "in-here." Especially for the scientist, the "real world" is also constituted by what we understand and affirm with evidence. For example, we literally cannot imagine the theories of quantum mechanics;[30] but we can understand and affirm them. All scientifically probable judgments, it is true, only allow for a cognitive self-transcendence. Yet the fact demanding clarity is precisely that scientific judgments really are examples of cognitive self-transcendence. In a word, they are objective.[31] Our judgments are the inevitable and critical products of our own self-transcending subjectivity.

Ordinarily, however, we do not remain satisfied with a merely cognitive self-transcendence. We are not, for example, prepared to allow technology to develop unhampered by consideration of ethical factors. Except for "Dr. Strangelove" or Adolf Eichmann types, most scientists and technologists are determined to find ways to act and live in accordance with critically determined values. We cannot but raise questions of value for our deliberation, evaluation, decision, and action. Insofar as we answer these questions of value in a critical manner, we know that we are again involved in self-transcendence. We have decided for some ideal of what is truly good and not merely for what gives us pleasure and helps us to avoid pain. We really do know when and how we have moved past a level of merely cognitive self-transcendence to one of real, moral, existential, and communal self-transcendence.[32]

The Religious Dimension of Science: Self-Transcendence and Limit-Questions

The increasing complexity of the scientific drive for self-transcendence—from sensitivity through intelligent and critical reflection to deliberate action—also manifests certain transcultural factors in the scientific enterprise itself. Indeed the questions for intelligence, for reflection, for deliberation so clearly involved in science are genuinely transcendental notions insofar as they can be recognized as the existential conditions of the possibility of being an authentic human being. To mediate these conditions as transcendental, to be sure, requires an extended exercise in transcendental reflection (as Lonergan himself attempts at length in *Insight* and more summarily in the opening chapters of his recent *Method in Theology*).[33]

For present purposes, it will be sufficient to reflect upon certain widely shared demands for continuing self-transcendence in the scientific community itself in order to understand the presence and character of certain limit-questions in that context. The facts of everyday good and evil, of scientific, technological, and ecological progress and decline do eventually give rise to questions about the basic character of this universe for the authentic scientific inquirer.[34] Unless he wishes to abandon the search for authentic self-transcendence the scientist cannot silence the question of the final horizon of scientific inquiry. On the contrary, he may reflect upon each level of self-transcending inquiry to understand what horizon or dimension it presupposes.[35]

On the level of questions for intelligence the authentic scientific inquirer can inquire into the very possibility of fruitful inquiry. In his scientific research a scientist can and does reach intellectually satisfying answers. Yet he can also ask such limit-questions as the following throughout his inquiry: Can these answers work if the world is not intelligible? Can the world be intelligible if it does not have an intelligent ground? In more technical terms, once the scientist has reflected upon the conditions of possibility for his inquiry, he may find himself face to face with a question properly described as a limit-question. Here that question is initially formulated as the question of both a limit-to his inquiry and possibly disclosive of a limit-of that drive (viz., an intelligent ground for intelligibility). In that logical sense, the question can be described as a religious-as-limit question.[36]

On a second level, the scientist can reflect on his scientific judgments as distinct from his intelligible hypotheses. In Lonergan's technical vocabulary, the scientist may reflect upon his ability to reach a virtually unconditioned affirmation, i.e., a conditioned whose conditions happen to be fulfilled by scientific evidence.[37] Yet he may also note that each virtually unconditioned judgment reached is not the ultimate ground of itself or other such judgments but merely one case of such. Scientific judgment, to repeat, is a conditioned whose conditions happen to be fulfilled to a high degree of probability. Hence the scientist might also ask whether there can be any virtually unconditioned judgments unless there exists also a formally unconditioned (i.e., an unconditioned in the strict sense of no conditions whatsoever). Once again the scientist may be driven by his own critical intelligence to ask a limit-question implying both a limit-to his scientific inquiry and a limit-of it—a final or grounding horizon for all his judgments.[38]

On a third level, the scientist can deliberate about his own need to evaluate his findings in accordance with ethical values. At this point, the scientist (especially the social scientist) may well ask limit-questions like the following: Is it worthwhile to ask whether our goals, purposes, and ideals are themselves worthwhile (a limit-to question)? Can we understand and affirm such a demand for worthwhileness without affirming an intelligent, rational, responsible source and ground for them (a limit-of question)? [39]

Since these limit-questions legitimately follow from scientific inquiry itself, they are not imposed extrinsically upon scientists by "religious" types but rather are well within the scientific inquirer's own horizon.[40] In fact, the scientist can seem to deny the need for such limit-questions into the intelligent, rational, and responsible grounds of the scientific enterprise only at the unwelcome price of self-contradiction.[41] No inquirer can commit himself to the task of authentic self-transcendence (i.e., intelligent, rational, and responsible thought and action) and then deny his own need to seek the ultimate intelligent, rational, and responsible grounds for such inquiry and action. When recognizing that fact, the scientist may, as Stephen Toulmin reminds us, elevate some scientific theory (e.g., evolution or entropy) to the level of a "scientific myth." Then the theory functions as a final, a limit (i.e., religious) interpretation of all existence.[42] Short of self-contradiction the scientist cannot fail to recognize reflectively the need for some such dimension, however he may wish to label it. It also seems to follow that the scientific inquirer can no longer rest satisfied with a two-language approach. Rather he may attempt to mediate that final or ultimate limit-dimension in some manner: through symbol, or myth, or philosophy.[43] By all such mediations, he may well find that such a final horizon or dimension as disclosive of a limit-to his inquiry and a possibly ultimate limit-of that inquiry may legitimately be described as suggesting a religious dimension to scientific inquiry.

It is true, of course, that Lonergan's own analysis depends upon his transcendental method for its final mediation. Although I am convinced that Lonergan's method is fundamentally sound on this point,[44] I am (as I indicated above) by no means reluctant to have the same argument mediated by other and quite different philosophical approaches. Although space does not permit an extensive analysis of them, the fact remains that other philosophical positions also mediate a recognition of a religious dimension or horizon of science. Either Louis Dupré's Hegelian phenomenology or Alfred North Whitehead's process philosophy or Stephen Toulmin's linguistic analysis of the "limiting questions" in science all mediate a similar understanding. Toulmin's analysis, for example, is particularly helpful in mediating that logically distinct and prior domain of existential fundamental reassurance and confidence in the worthwhileness and intelligibility of our existence.[45]

Just as the "existentialist" rediscovery of the category limit-situation helped to mediate a recognition of the peculiar limit-character and necessity of religious meaning for humanists, so a careful application of the category limit-questions to scientific inquiry can mediate a recognition of an authentically religious dimension of that most human of enterprises, contemporary science. Neither theology nor science really has anything to fear from a future collaboration which recognizes the autonomy and the mutual interrelatedness of these two sorely needed conversation partners for our critical present and future. All they have to lose by such dialogue is the memory of their past tragic history and the unpromising spectre of a future non-conversation between a dehumanized science and a "ghettoized" theology.

More immediate to our present purposes, the phenomenon called limit-questions to scientific inquiry can allow one to see what can be called a religious dimension in that scientific component so important to our modern cultural experience. A similar religious dimension can be discovered by reflection upon the limit-questions ineluctably present to our common moral experience.

LIMIT-QUESTIONS IN MORALITY

Religion and Morality: Identical or Distinct?[46]

A familiar complaint against classical liberal and modernist theologies was that they tended to explain religion in general and Christianity in particular as, without remainder, an ethical system.[47] Clearly this charge does not seem universally applicable to the major figures in the liberal theological tradition. Certainly the charge is nonsense if applied to Schleiermacher, Otto, and Tillich. For other "liberal" thinkers, however, the charge does have some real substance. One might recall the familiar results of the early liberal quest for the historical Jesus. That quest collapsed not only because of Schweitzer's exposé of its failure to take the apocalyptic context of Jesus' teaching and person seriously. Rather, the classical liberal participants in the "old quest" were led almost inexorably to a model that may well have fit the nineteenth-century liberal bourgeois ideal of the good moral life. But it is difficult to find any adequate articulation there of any dimension peculiarly religious—certainly not in the sense of those limit-experiences and limit-languages described by Otto and Tillich.[48] Part of the reason for this cul de sac may be that the classical liberals—of whom Albrecht Ritschl may still be considered the paradigmatic figure—were hampered by certain narrowly neo-Kantian approaches to the questions of science, morality, and religion and trapped by their ethical fear of anything smacking of "mysticism" or "apocalypticism." [49] Perhaps it is too harsh a judgment upon the heroic efforts at theological reconstruction of the classical Protestant liberals and Catholic modernists to claim that their failure to specify the religious factor as clearly distinct from the moral was as complete as these brief remarks may suggest.[50]

The fact remains, however, that (again with such notable exceptions as Schleiermacher, Otto, von Hugel, and Tyrrell) it is difficult to discover in either the classical Protestant liberals or the classical Catholic modernists an analysis that clearly and systematically differentiates the religious realm from the moral in other than narrowly neo-Kantian, i.e., basically ethical, terms.[51] This same liberal difficulty reemerges in more contemporary terms when one recalls the position of such linguistic analysts of religious language as R. B. Braithwaite and R. M. Hare.[52] In either case, the reader is hard pressed to find a qualitative difference between religious and moral language. In Hare's case, both such languages express our "bliks" or basic attitudes towards the world. In Braithwaite's case, religious language is really moral "attitudinal" language expressing the speaker's intention to act in a certain manner and articulating and internalizing that attitude through parable and story. Yet the contemporary analyst of the religious use of language cannot but ask whether the use of parable and story provides the sole characteristic of religious language distinguishing it from moral "attitudinal" language.

This familiar criticism of the liberal failure to interpret the specifically religious aspect of religious experience and language seems to remain a basically sound historical judgment. Even that partial failure was not without its real triumphs: thanks in large measure to liberal efforts, there remain few if any defenders of a position claiming that religion does not involve an ethical dimension. Fewer still would wish to rob ethical concerns of their autonomy from religion.[53] Yet the question recurs whether there is some clear and qualitative distinction between moral and religious language and hence between the "forms of life" which each discloses.[54] For the conventional wisdom in the secularist culture at large, it seems fair to observe, religion is widely considered a reasonably useful if somewhat primitive way of being moral.[55] One *can* be moral without it; yet, by providing paradigms, parables, stories, and rituals, religion serves the helpful function of stimulating us—or, at least, our children—to perform the right, the ethical action.

In fact, given the societal role of such religious leaders as Gandhi, King, and Chavez in recent years, one scarcely needs to insist that a religious vision can invest ethical commitments with real staying power. In principle, both individual and social ethics are a constitutive dimension of any authentically religious world-view. What may need further consideration, however, is the question of exactly how one may best distinguish religious from moral discourse and experience. With that task in mind, we may return to the category limit-questions, now in relationship to our moral discourse. Moreover, we shall now depart from a use of Lonergan's transcendental method in order to engage in an interpretation of two distinct philosophical methods: the analytic philosophy of Stephen Toulmin and the process philosophy of Schubert Ogden.[56]

The Logic of Limit-Questions in Moral Discourse

Our interpretation of the analyses of Ogden and Toulmin may indicate a factor of no little importance for the discussion of pluralist possibilities: a philosopher of the process tradition (Ogden) can articulate his Anglo-

American empirical position in strictly linguistic terms. That reformulation, to be sure, demands that the linguistic philosopher be representative of what has been called the "third stage" of analytic philosophy: the examination of the meaning of a particular kind of discourse through an analysis of its actual uses in ordinary speech. Toulmin is particularly helpful here since he has examined the basic kinds of argument involved in several modes of discourse in his larger work *The Uses of Argument*. He has also examined the use of explicitly ethical and religious discourse in his shorter work *An Examination of the Place of Reason in Ethics*.[57] In fact, these two books are Ogden's principal resources for his own linguistic reformulation of the process tradition's insight into the radically experiential character of religious discourse. Summarily stated, the argument may be interpreted as follows.[58]

Limit-Questions in Morality

In keeping with the "third stage" of the analytic tradition, Toulmin argues against a confinement of the concepts "truth" and "reality" to the narrowly defined principle of verification.[59] Rather the analyst must try to "unpack" the differing uses of argument (and hence of "truth") present in the distinct uses of everyday language (aesthetic, moral, religious, scientific, etc.). In keeping with Toulmin's own dependence on the later Wittgenstein's approach to the use of language, he also insists upon the linguistic need to uncover those "forms of life" or distinct situations of human existence which the various uses of language function to manifest. Moral language, for example, serves to use arguments (and utter true—or good—moral judgments) in order to allow us "to correlate our feelings and behavior in such a way as to make the fulfillment of everyone's aims and desires as far as possible compatible." [60]

In the final analysis, and in a manner analogous to Lonergan's, neither scientific nor moral uses of argument are entirely self-contained. When we ask a question like "Why ought I keep my promise anyway?" we ask a question which still has the form of a moral question ("ought") but which does not actually function ethically. In fact there is no moral argument for answering that question. Such questions, therefore, may be described as limit-questions: questions emerging at the limit of the usual kinds of moral questions and arguments. More summarily, we cannot really produce a moral argument for being moral. The limit-character of the logic of such questions (and hence the type of arguments to which they will appeal) suggests to Toulmin that they be described as "religious" or "theological" questions. Our own natural "desire for reassurance, for a general confidence about the future" impels us to *use* religious language and to develop theological arguments. Once we do so, we may also recognize that the logical peculiarity of all such "limiting questions" is logically correct. Given that insight, an analyst of religious and theological language may recognize that this language, when used properly, is neither a simple misuse of scientific language (as implied by Flew in the "Theology and Falsification Debate"),[61] nor simply reducible without remainder to moral language as implied by the classical "liberal" analyses or by E. B. Braithwaite's linguistic analysis. Religious and theological language, on the contrary, is a language of limit-questions and, to extend Toulmin's point, limit-answers.

The next crucial step in the argument is supplied by Ogden's ability to develop Toulmin's conclusions in the direction of greater empirical specificity.[62] In my judgment, Ogden's use of the resources of the Anglo-American empirical tradition frees him to explicate the "reassurance" aspect of Toulmin's analysis in a more specified and more experiential manner. In initially linguistic terms, Ogden develops Toulmin's own insistence that we use religious language to "reassure" ourselves that the "whole" and the "future" are trustworthy in order to argue that all religious *language* thereby bears the linguistic form of *re-presentation*.[63] We misunderstand the function of religious language if we claim that it *causes* (presents) our general confidence or trust in the meaningfulness of existence. We understand such language correctly only when we recognize that the use of religious language is *an effect* (a *re*-presentation) of an already present basic confidence or trust. The kind of experience which religious language discloses is thereby clarified: an already present basic confidence has been threatened (e.g., in some "boundary situation" or by reflection upon the limit-questions of morality) and needs the reassurance which religious re-presentative language may bring.[64] Empirically, the "form of life" disclosed by religious and theological language can be further specified as the experience of a basic or "limit" confidence or trust, a common human faith—which, when threatened, can find the reassurance it seeks from neither science nor morality but only from those attitudes we name religious. In Ogden's words, religions "provide us with particular symbolic forms through which that faith (i.e., our basic confidence and trust in the meaningfulness of existence) may be more or less adequately re-affirmed at the level of self-conscious belief." [65] In my own vocabulary, whatever else may be true of either the re-assuring character of religious experience or the re-presentative character of religious language, both that experience and language manifest a distinctively limit-character. This seems true in reference to both the limit-to character of limit-questions (Why ought I keep my promise anyway?) and the limit-of character of religious limit-answers. The latter may be either that basic (or limit-of) confidence or trust which specifies a major experiential aspect of the religious dimension of human existence or it may be those "re-assuring," self-conscious religious beliefs and symbol-systems which, to various degrees of relative adequacy, provide explicitly religious experience and explicitly theological answers.

An obvious argument against this position is to suggest that the notion of a basic (limit) trust, a "common human faith," is imported from another and, perhaps, an alien philosophical tradition.[66] Yet such an argument does not really command agreement. One may, in fact, be informed by another philosophical tradition in such manner that one may legitimately employ its concepts to render explicit the implicit assumptions of another tradition (as, I believe occurs throughout Ogden's use and development of Toulmin's linguistic analysis or in my own reinterpretation of both their positions into the limit-language vocabulary of this present work).

A positive case can also be made that precisely Ogden's use of the analytic tradition allows for an explication *otherwise not clearly present* in the Anglo-American empirical tradition itself.[67] Analytical philosophy's characteristic mode of reflection upon the differing uses of argument, the logical peculiarity of limiting-questions, and the relationship between "uses" of language and "forms of life" allows one way to render precise the Anglo-American tradition at exactly the point where that tradition probably most needed aid.[68] Analytic philosophy may clarify the fact that when we use the word "religion" we mean the use of language to re-present certain limit-answers to certain limit-questions; when we use the phrase basic—or limit —confidence we mean that "form of life" (that mode-of-being-in-the-world) manifested by religious as re-presentative language.[69] In either case, we are dealing with a language and an experience whose logically limit-character distinguishes its use from other uses of language and from other dimensions of experience or forms of life.

It might be helpful to repeat that this particular discussion has been chosen merely as one example of a kind of philosophical analysis which suggests, to me at least, the legitimacy of pointing to "limit" as a defining characteristic of a religious dimension of our experience and language. A completion of a revisionist fundamental theology would, of course, need to do more than analyze the limit-questions of moral and scientific discourse. The "more" needed would include at least the following: analyses of the limit-situations in everyday life; an analysis of the claims involved in the classical "hermeneutics of suspicion" upon all religious language (Feuerbach, Marx, Freud, Nietzsche et al.); finally, strictly philosophical discussions of positions which reduce religious and theological language to either misused scientific language (Flew and Ayer), disguised moral language (Braithwaite), or action-oriented aesthetic language (Santayana).[70] That full revisionist task is an imposing, even overwhelming one; however, short of strict fideism, there is really no other option. Indeed, the recognition of fideism's unacceptability as a theological option is the clearest reason to attempt to develop a revisionist model for fundamental theological reflection. In later chapters we will attempt to deal more explicitly but still only partially with the problems raised by the first two "needs" listed above. At the present we must remain content to complement the analyses of the presence of limit-questions in science and morality with a study of certain limit-situations in our everyday experience.

LIMIT-SITUATIONS IN THE WORLD OF THE
EVERYDAY

Rather than engaging in extended analysis of the many thinkers who attempt in various ways to disclose a religious dimension or horizon to our
common experience, this chapter signalizes two categories to make that
claim. Those categories are those limit-situations in everyday life analyzed
by existentialist thought and those limit-questions to scientific and moral inquiry analyzed by various philosophies of science and ethics. Since I have
already investigated examples of the latter category, I shall now turn to a
brief investigation of the former category.

The concept limit-situation is a familiar one in the existentialist philosophy and theology of the very recent past.[71] Fundamentally, the concept refers to those human situations wherein a human being ineluctably finds
manifest a certain ultimate limit or horizon to his or her existence. The concept itself is mediated by "showing" the implications of certain crucial positive and negative experiential limit-situations. More exactly, limit-situations
refer to two basic kinds of existential situation: either those "boundary" situations of guilt, anxiety, sickness, and the recognition of death as one's own
destiny,[72] or those situations called "ecstatic experiences"—intense joy,
love, reassurance, creation.[73] All genuine limit-situations refer to those experiences, both positive and negative, wherein we both experience our own
human limits (limit-to) as our own as well as recognize, however haltingly,
some disclosure of a limit-of our experience.[74] The negative mode of limit-
situations can best be described with Karl Jaspers as "boundary-situations." Such experiences (sickness, guilt, anxiety, recognition of death as
one's own destiny) allow and, when intense, seem to demand reflection
upon the existential boundaries of our present everyday existence. When an
announcement of a serious illness—whether our own or of someone we
love—is made, we begin to experience the everyday, the "real" world, as
suddenly unreal: petty, strange, foreign to the now real world. That "limit"
world of final closure to our lives now faces us with a starkness we cannot
shirk and manages to disclose to us our basic existential faith or unfaith in
life's very meaningfulness.

The positive mode of limit-situations can be described, as they are by
Abraham Maslow, as "peak experiences" or, as I prefer, as "ecstatic experiences." Undeniably, such experiences (love, joy, the creative act, profound
reassurance) are authentically "self-transcending" moments in our lives.[75]
When in the grasp of such experiences, we all find, however momentarily,
that we can and do transcend our usual lackluster selves and our usual everyday worlds to touch upon a dimension of experience which cannot be
stated adequately in the language of ordinary, everyday experience. Authentic love, both erotic and agapic, puts us in touch with a reality whose

power we cannot deny. We do not work ourselves into a state of love, as we might into a habit of justice. We "fall," we "are" in love. While its power lasts, we experience the rest of our lives as somehow shadowy. The "real world" no longer seems real. We find ourselves affirming the reality of ecstatic experience, but not as something merely decided upon by us. In all such authentic moments of ecstasy, we experience a reality simply given, gifted, happened.[76] Such a reality, as religious mystics remind us, may be a taste of that self-transcending experience of a "being-in-love-without-qualification" familiar to the authentically religious person.[77]

At the very least, such ecstatic experiences can sensitize one to the possibilities of an existential grounding for those everyday experiences of self-transcendence which disclose the most deeply held meanings of our lives. To reassure a child crying in the night that all is well;[78] to experience the self-and-other transcendence of loving sexual expression; to experience an "unattended moment" with friends, music, or nature. All such *ec-static* experiences may, by their "limit-disclosing" character, serve as "signals of transcendence," as "rumors of angels," or, less metaphorically, as a "showing" if not a "stating" of a limit-dimension to our lives. That limit-to the everyday also seems to disclose—in the same *ec-stasis*—a limit-of whose graciousness bears a religious character.[79] For the moment, however, let us recall such experiences of ecstasy merely to remind ourselves of certain human experiences which most of us have had with greater and less frequency and which many of us can recognize as expressive of a "world of meaning" beyond the everyday. Such a "world," by its strange ability to put us in touch with what we believe to be a final, a "trustworthy," meaning to our lives may also disclose to us, however hesitantly, the character of that ultimate horizon of meaning which religious persons call "gracious," "eventful," "faith-ful," "revelatory."[80] To be sure, such experiences need not be understood in explicitly religious terms as the mystic's experience of an unrestricted religious love would be.[81] Rather, as we have insisted throughout this chapter, such experiences are more properly described not *as* explicitly *religious* but as disclosive of a "limit," a "religious" dimension or horizon to our lives.

However intense an expression of our common experience both boundary-situations and ecstatic experiences may be, such experiences are clearly common *human* experiences. The temptation to exclude such considerations from an analysis of common human experience as neurotic symptoms (the way to avoid, for example, the truth of Kierkegaard's analysis of *Angst*) is to miss their real significance. An appeal to these phenomena is not an appeal to a neurotic guilt, an obsessive anxiety, an alienated sickness, a morbid preoccupation with death, a romantic infatuation with love, creativity, and ecstasy.[82] On the contrary, an appeal to such phenomena as disclosive of our actual situation is fundamentally an appeal to experiences such as responsible guilt, authentic anxiety, responsible recognition of death as one's ownmost destiny, and authentic self-transcending human love. Clearly, such experiences, however ambiguous, are not in principle merely "strange" experiences. Uncommon they are. Yet they are uncommon mainly because we try to keep them from surfacing in our everyday lives by our strategies of inauthenticity: *"divertissement,"* distraction, *Gerede*.[83] Beginning with Kierkegaard,[84] the classical existentialist analyses of such experiences have provided a powerful way to clarify the human situation as intrinsically a limit-situation: a situation wherein we find ourselves not the masters of our fate but radically contingent or limited (boundary-situations). At the same time, we may also find ourselves radically out-of-our-everyday-selves as ecstatic, as gifted, even as "graced."[85]

Perhaps the clearest way to understand the "religious" implications of such existentialist analysis is to recall a familiar instance of its exercise: the phenomenological analysis of basic anxiety as distinct from the phenomenon of fear.[86] The point of that analysis is subtle but important for understanding the basic character of a religious dimension to our common existence. Fear as a phenomenon[87] (that is, as that which appears to human consciousness) manifests itself as a *fear of a specific object.* Fears are manifested when we pay heed to the various kinds of phobias to which each of us may be prone: a fear of the dark, of heights, of electricity, etc. Anxiety (or *Angst*), on the other hand, is a *qualitatively different* phenomenon in its very manifestation. Anxiety is *not* a fear of some specific object (or even of the sum total of specific objects). Anxiety is a fear of *no-object*-in-the-world-alongside-other-objects. Anxiety is literally, as Heidegger reminds us, a fear of No-thing.[88] More positively stated, anxiety is a fear disclosive of our often forgotten but never totally absent consciousness of our own radical contingency. In anxiety, we do not merely consider, we know that we neither create ourselves nor can we assume the continuance of existence. Instead we find ourselves—as the metaphors of the existentialists and the mystics alike remind us—poised over an abyss, a chasm, whose exact nature we do not know but whose experiential reality we cannot deny.[89]

What, really, does this analysis of anxiety and similar existentialist analyses manifest? At the very least, the analysis discloses that the final dimension or horizon of our own situation is neither one of our own making nor one under our control. In analyzing anxiety, we may also see that our very situation is, in fact, correctly described as a limit-situation. We are grounded or horizoned by no other thing in the universe, but rather by No-thing. In terms of the language we employ for such experiences, the analysis may also manifest that at a certain point the language of conceptual analysis begins to falter. Instead, the human spirit begins to search for metaphors expressive of the experience (abyss, chasm, limit) and for narratives capable of expanding and structuring these metaphors (parables, myths, poems). Such metaphors, images, symbols, and myths seem linguistically necessary to express that literally unspoken, and perhaps unspeakable, final dimension to the end of our lives. In a word, the language initially most appropriate for expressing that experience is symbolic as distinct from strictly conceptual. Such language, as symbolic, involves a double intentionality which expresses both a literal meaning (for example, an actual physical abyss) and a non-literal meaning which otherwise remains unsaid and unspoken (in this case, the disclosure of an other, a final dimension, which serves as limit-to our experience of the everyday and limit-of the rest of our existence).

As suggested previously, symbolic language may find further though partial expression in the conceptual language of metaphysics—especially the analogical language of metaphysics.[90] However helpful a later metaphysical language may be, all authentic limit-language seems to be initially and irretrievably a symbolic and a metaphorical one. Insofar as the hidden dimension of an ultimate limit is not merely hidden but not even expressible in the language of the everyday (as no-*thing*, no object in the world alongside other objects), that language retains the linguistic structure of metaphor and symbol. At the very least, metaphorical and symbolic language is proper to the originating expression of this disclosed but not adequately conceptualizable dimension of our common existence. In fact, as I shall argue in the next chapter, even *explicitly* religious language (e.g., the language of the scriptures or of the Christian mystics) is intrinsically symbolic and metaphorical limit-language.

It does not seem improper to suggest, therefore, that all authentic religious language and experience—precisely as that limit-language re-presentative of a final dimension or horizon of meaning to our existence—is also autonomous. The religious dimension of existence is not, I believe, adequately described as simply another human activity coordinate to such activities as science, morality, or culture. By its limit-character, a religious dimension is more accurately described by some such phrase as ultimate ground to or horizon of all other activities—as Paul Tillich, perhaps more than any other contemporary thinker, has tried to show by his several analyses of the peculiar character and force of the "ultimate concern" implicit in every human concern and uniquely disclosive of a religious dimension to all human existence.[91] I am content to leave the powerful and still evocative expression "ultimate concern" to Tillich and simply suggest that reflection upon limit-questions and limit-situations does disclose the reality of a dimension to our lives other than the more usual dimensions: a dimension whose first key is its reality as limit-to our other everyday, moral, scientific, cultural, and political activities; a dimension which, in my own brief and hazy glimpses, discloses a reality, however named and in whatever manner experienced, which functions as a final, now gracious, now frightening, now trustworthy, now absurd, always uncontrollable limit-of the very meaning of existence itself. I find that, although religiously rather "unmusical" myself, I cannot deny this reality. I also find that reflection upon limit-questions and limit-situations helps me to locate, if not adequately to name, that reality. A neologism does not really seem needed here: that reality is religious. One of its characteristics seems to be its authentically limit-character in all its manifestations.

As my earlier analyses of limit-questions suggest, there remain other and quite distinct routes to the question of a religious dimension to our existence. Throughout I have attempted to clarify the meaning of the phrase "philosophical reflection upon common human experience"[92] by analyzing selected examples of such reflection in our present pluralist situation. This reflective task is a phenomenological one in the broad sense of an analysis of the "meaningfulness" for our common experience of religious language as re-presentative of a final horizon to our common experience. Two categories, limit-situation and limit-question, are helpful indices to what may be called the "religious dimension" of our everyday, our scientific, and our moral experience.[93] Finally, such analysis may serve to suggest how "religion" continues to operate in our common secular lives as an authentic disclosure which both bespeaks certain inevitable limits-to our lives and manifests some final reality which functions as a trustworthy limit-of life itself.

Whether the cognitive claims involved in religious language are true is a further question. That question can be raised only after one addresses two additional questions: what does explicitly Christian religious language mean and how does that meaning relate to the limit-character of the "religious dimension" of our common experience; how may one specify the cognitive claims of either implicit or explicit religious language in order properly to investigate their claims to truth. The principal cognitive claim involved in religious language, I shall argue, is the explicitly theistic claim: that the objective referent of all such language and experience is that reality which religious human beings mean when they say "God." If this is the case, the proper set of questions for fundamental theology become: first, the question of the "limit" meaning and existential meaningfulness of a religious dimension to our common lives; second, the question of the meaning and meaningfulness of explicitly Christian language as limit-language; third, the question of the referential-as-theistic meaning and truth of religious language. This chapter has tried to speak only to the first of these questions.

Notes

(1) The revisionist model itself is not, of course, purely formal: yet a legitimate distinction remains between an articulation of the model and its application. Part II of this work represents only one possible application of the model. In principle, one may accept the model without accepting these particular applications.

(2) The phrase "initiated" is important insofar as each question gives rise to further questions not answered simply on the basis given. For example, discussion of the di-

polar character of God does not, of and by itself, answer the legitimate further questions of analogical and literal God-language or of a fully adequate concept of God as creator. On the first, cf. David Burrell, *Analogy and Philosophical Language* (New Haven: Yale University Press, 1973); on the second, cf. Langdon Gilkey, "The Eternal God: Eternal Ground of New Possibilities."

(3) The "necessity" is a logical one insofar as at least these three questions (and in that order) must be addressed by anyone accepting the revisionist model.

(4) For surveys of various aspects of this question, cf. Ninian Smart, *The Phenomenon of Religion* (New York: Herder and Herder, 1973), esp. pp. 1–79; idem, *The Science of Religion and the Sociology of Knowledge* (Princeton: Princeton University Press, 1973), esp. pp. 3–24, 49–92; Mircea Eliade and Joseph M. Kitagawa (eds.), *The History of Religions: Essays in Methodology* (Chicago: University of Chicago Press, 1959), esp. the essays by Joseph M. Kitagawa (pp. 1–31), Wilfred Cantwell Smith (pp. 31–59), Jean Daniélou (pp. 67–86), and Mircea Eliade (pp. 86–108). For the important contributions of Eliade himself, cf. esp. Mircea Eliade, *Patterns in Comparative Religion* (New York: Sheed and Ward, 1958); idem, *Myth and Reality* (New York: Harper & Row, 1963); idem, *The Quest: History and Meaning in Religion* (Chicago: University of Chicago Press, 1969), esp. pp. 1–72. For interpretations of Eliade, cf. Jonathan Z. Smith, "The Wobbling Pivot," and Douglas Allen, "Mircea Eliade's Phenomenological Analysis of Religious Experience," *Journal of Religion* 52 (1972), 134–50 and 170–86. In the same issue, cf. the important survey-discussion on "definitions" of religion by Hans H. Penner and Edward A. Yonan, "Is A Science of Religion Possible?" (pp. 107–34). Cf. also Louis Dupré, *The Other Dimension: A Search for the Meaning of Religious Attitudes* (New York: Doubleday, 1972), esp. pp. 1–148.

(5) Inter alia, cf. Tillich, *Systematic Theology*, I (Chicago: University of Chicago, 1951), 11–15. In a more popular vein, cf. D. Mackenzie Brown, *Ultimate Concern: Tillich in Dialogue* (New York: Harper & Row, 1965), esp. pp. 1–19. The *loci classici* in Schleiermacher and Otto are: Friedrich Schleiermacher, *On Religion* (New York: Harper & Brothers, 1958); and Rudolph Otto, *The Idea of the Holy* (New York: Oxford University Press, 1958).

(6) *Loci classici* here: Emile Durkheim, *The Elementary Forms of Religious Life* (New York: Macmillan, 1915); Max Weber, *The Sociology of Religion* (London: Methuen, 1965). For a helpful survey-analysis of the Durkheim and especially the Weber traditions, cf. Michael Hill, *A Sociology of Religion* (New York: Basic Books, 1973).

(7) Cf. Peter Berger, *The Sacred Canopy: Elements of a Sociological Theory of Religion* (New York: Doubleday, 1967), esp. pp. 3–53 and 175–89.

(8) Cf. Clifford Geertz, "Religion as a Cultural System," in Donald Cutler (ed.), *The Religious Situation: 1968* (Boston: Beacon Press, 1968), pp. 639–88. The direct quotation may be found on p. 643. Note also the use and development of Geertz's position advanced by Andrew M. Greeley, *Unsecular Man: The Persistence of Religion* (New York: Schocken, 1972), esp. pp. 55–84.

(9) The desire for a "universal definition" may, in fact, be a remnant of what Bernard Lonergan nicely labels a "classical consciousness": cf. Bernard Lonergan, *Method in Theology* (New York: Herder and Herder, 1972), pp. xi and 70.

(10) For some examples of the use and development of Wittgenstein's own cryptic sayings on "religion," cf. D. Z. Phillips (ed.), *Religion and Understanding* (Oxford: Blackwell, 1967); idem, *The Concept of Prayer* (London: Routledge & Kegan Paul, 1965); Paul Holmer, "Nygren and Linguistic Analysis: Language and Meaning," in *The Philosophy and Theology of Anders Nygren*, ed. by Charles W. Kegley (Carbondale, Ill.: Southern Illinois University Press, 1970), pp. 70–93. For a criticism of "Wittgensteinian fideism," cf. Kai Nielsen, "Wittgensteinian Fideism," in *Philosophy* XLII (1967).

(11) Some important qualifications should be mentioned here. First, "limit" is argued to be *a* characteristic, not a universal definition of religion. Indeed such further characteristics as the "dialectical" character of religious experience and language involve further questions implied but not treated here. On the latter, cf. esp. Louis Dupré, *The Other Dimension*, esp. pp. 1–61; and Thomas J. J. Altizer, *Mircea Eliade and the Dialectic of the Sacred* (Philadelphia: Westminster, 1963). Second, the argument is not that *all* limit-language is *eo ipso* religious, but rather that all religious (dimension or explicit) experience and language has a limit-character. In general terms, there can be "limit-to" language which is not disclosive of a final "limit-of" dimension. Third, a historical observation may prove clarifying here: the emphasis on the limit-character of religious language and experience is closer to the classical Kantian analysis of religion in the *Critique of Practical Reason and Other Writings in Moral Philosophy* (Chicago: University of Chicago Press, 1949), and *Religion Within the Limits of Reason Alone* (New York: Harper & Row, 1960), than it is to what I understand to be the legitimate further questions from the Hegelian-dialectical analysis emphasized by such thinkers as Dupré and Altizer. For an analysis of the historical context, cf. James Collins, *The Emergence of Philosophy of Religion* (New Haven: Yale University Press, 1967), pp. 89–212 (on Kant) and pp. 212–350 (on Hegel); and Emil Fackenheim, *The Religious Dimension in Hegel's Thought* (Bloomington, Ind.: Indiana University Press, 1967), esp. pp. 160–223. Fourth, such a more modest enterprise may, I hope, reopen rather than close off such further philosophical and theological questions as "analogical" and "dialectical" languages. Fifth, the Kantian motif does not call for a retreat from the insistence upon the post-Kantian notion of experience outlined in the prior chapter's description of philosophical reflection including both a phenomenological and a transcendental moment. Sixth, the major but not sole influences upon my own interpretation of the limit-character of religious language are Ian Ramsey and Paul Ricoeur (yet without the latter's emphasis upon a return "to Kant through Hegel"). On this last, cf. Paul Ricoeur, "The Specificity of Religious Language" (unpublished lecture delivered at University of Chicago Divinity School, Spring 1974), p. 30: "As I say in the 'outline,' this suggestion leads in the direction of Kant rather than that of Hegel. Or—if I dare say so!—it calls for a post-Hegelian return to Kant." Further analysis of both Ricoeur's and Ramsey's positions will be conducted in the following chapter.

(12) Cf. Van A. Harvey, *The Historian and the Believer* (New York: Macmillan, 1966), p. 261. Note how Harvey employs the cautionary tack of not attempting a universal definition of *the* religious perspective but employs the Wittgensteinian formulation of "family resemblances."

(13) This distinction between "stating" and "showing" a reality is familiar to Wittgenstein and, in a different way, to the later Heidegger. I am indebted here to David Burrell's own frequent and careful use of this distinction in analyzing religious language. For examples of Burrell's own mode of analysis, cf. his *Analogy and Philo-*

sophical Language, p. 258. The distinction is employed extensively by Burrell in *Exercises in Religious Understanding* (Notre Dame: Notre Dame University Press, 1975).

(14) "Ground" seems to remain a suggestive metaphor despite its frequent reference (in German uses of *Grund*) to mystical and perhaps irrational use (as in Jacob Böhme). Our more empirical or perhaps more domesticated English language tradition may be better able to avoid this temptation. For Paul Tillich's sometimes German, sometimes English use of the "ground" metaphor, cf. his *Systematic Theology*, I, 112–117, 155–58.

(15) The discipline of history of religions is especially relevant to the theologian here. For an example of this use, cf. Bernard Lonergan's use of Friedrich Heiler in *Method in Theology*, pp. 108–10. Heiler's own essay may be found in M. Eliade and J. Kitagawa (eds.), *The History of Religions*, pp. 142–53.

(16) Recall the specific meanings accorded these criteriological concepts in chapter four.

(17) Cf. Stephen Toulmin, *An Examination of the Place of Reason in Ethics* (Cambridge: Cambridge University Press, 1950), pp. 204 ff. Toulmin's own phrase is "limiting question."

(18) This section represents a revised version of my essay "The Religious Dimension of Science," in *The Persistence of Religion*, Concilium 81, ed. by Andrew Greeley and Gregory Baum (New York: Herder and Herder, 1973), pp. 128–35; cf. p. 129, n. 1, for references to the extensive literature on this subject. Especially noteworthy are Ian Barbour, *Issues in Science and Religion* (Englewood Cliffs, N.J. Prentice-Hall, 1966); idem, *Science and Religion: New Perspectives in the Dialogue* (New York: Harper & Row, 1968); and Langdon Gilkey, *Religion and the Scientific Future* (New York: Harper & Row, 1970).

(19) Bonhoeffer's critique here has been especially influential in recent theology: cf. Dietrich Bonhoeffer, *Letters and Papers From Prison* (London: Fontana, 1956), esp. pp. 145–7.

(20) Cf. Bernard E. Meland, *The Realities of Faith: The Revolution in Cultural Forms* (New York: Oxford University Press, 1962), esp. pp. 109–70.

(21) Cf. Ian Barbour, *Issues in Science and Religion*, pp. 115–25.

(22) Donald Evans, *The Logic of Self-Involvement* (London: SCM Press, 1963).

(23) Barth's references are ordinarily to historical methods but are applicable to the natural sciences as well: cf. Barbour, *Issues in Science and Religion*, pp. 116–21.

(24) This is, of course, an interpretation of their position. For references, cf. n. 18 above.

(25) The expression "religious dimension" is my own. Each of these thinkers have alternative formulations.

(26) As students of Lonergan's thought will note, the present analysis serves as a reinterpretation rather than paraphrase of Lonergan's own position. For example, Lonergan's more traditional formulation of the question as "the question of God" is here reinterpreted into a question of "the religious dimension of science." Further, the conjunction of Lonergan's concept of "self-transcendence" and Toulmin's concept of "limit-questions" is interpretative. I trust, however, that this very brief analysis remains a legitimate reformulation and interpretation of Lonergan's position. For Lonergan's own formulation, cf. *Method in Theology*, pp. 101–5.

(27) Ibid., pp. 104–5.

(28) For a succinct formulation of Lonergan's position here, cf. Bernard Lonergan, "Metaphysics as Horizon," in *Collection* (New York: Herder and Herder, 1967), pp. 202–21.

(29) *Method in Theology*, p. 101–3; cf. also the more extensive analysis in *Insight: A Study of Human Understanding* (London: Longmans, Green, 1957), pp. 271–319.

(30) Cf. the important extension of Lonergan's position on this issue by Patrick Heelan, *Quantum Mechanics and Objectivity* (The Hague: Nijhoff, 1965).

(31) Cf. *Insight*, pp. 375–85.

(32) For Lonergan's own notion of value, cf. *Method in Theology*, pp. 34–41.

(33) Ibid., pp. 3–27. The central sections of *Insight* here may be found in pp. 319–431.

(34) Cf. *Method in Theology*, pp. 102–5.

(35) For Lonergan, fidelity to the spirit of inquiry does not allow one *authentically* to rest content on any one level: hence his development of the model "self-transcendence"; and his crucial insistence that method (which reflects upon both logical and non-logical operations), not logic, is the primary factor needing full explication by the "authentic inquirer."

(36) It should be noted that I have changed Lonergan's own argument here from his formulation of the question as the "question of God" to my own present, more limited claim that the logic of this kind of question involves both an authentically "limit-to" and "limit-of" character. For Lonergan's own formulation, cf. *Method in Theology*, pp. 101–3.

(37) This notion of judgment as a "virtually unconditioned" is one of Lonergan's most important technical innovations: cf. *Insight*, esp. pp. 279–81.

(38) For Lonergan's earlier formulation of his position here, cf. *Insight*, pp. 634–87. It might be noted that the formulation of *Method*, however brief, does articulate the question in the context of a discussion of values, including religious values: a context whose absence impedes the argument for "general transcendent knowledge" in *Insight*. The use of the formulation in terms of "limit-questions," although not Lonergan's own, seems faithful to his argument.

(39) For the development of Lonergan's notion of value from his *Insight* period to his *Method in Theology* period: cf. Frederick Crowe, "An Exploration into Lonergan's New Notion of Value" (to be published as *Proceedings of Lonergan Workshop, June, 1974*, by Darton, Longman & Todd). Briefly stated, Lonergan's work continues the tradition of Aristotelian *phronesis* into an explicitly contemporary formulation: cf. *Method in Theology*, p. 41, n. 14, for the Aristotelian background.

(40) For Lonergan's concept of horizon-analysis, cf. David Tracy, *The Achievement of Bernard Lonergan* (New York: Herder and Herder, 1970), pp. 1–21.

(41) In Lonergan's transcendental formulation, the basic contradictions are not to be found between conflicting concepts but between the performance of the intelligent, rational, and responsible inquirer and the concepts he employs to thematize that performance. This "dialectic of concept and performance" provides the central clue to Lonergan's insistence that the question of a transcendental method is a more radical question than that of logic. For a summary statement of Lonergan's notion of the "dialectic between performance and concept," cf. his essay-review of Emerich Coreth's similar position in "Metaphysics As Horizon," in *Collection*, esp. pp. 214–20, and Lonergan's own application of this transcendental dialectic to the position of Hume in *Method in Theology*, pp. 20–21.

(42) Cf. Stephen Toulmin, "Contemporary Scientific Mythology," in Alasdair MacIntyre (ed.), *Metaphysical Beliefs* (London: SCM Press, 1957), pp. 13–81; and Langdon Gilkey, *Religion and the Scientific Future*, pp. 65–137.

(43) For a discussion of these possibilities, cf. Gilkey, *Religion and the Scientific Future*, pp. 101–37.

(44) Its basic formulation remains the argument of *Insight* as a whole; a summary version may be found in *Method in Theology*, pp. 3–27. It might also be noted that, although Lonergan's notion of experience does not explicitly articulate the Anglo-American tradition's revised notion of experience, still his notion seems clearly open to that development. Note, for example, how Lonergan's original list of the operations for experience as the five senses (*Method*, p. 6) is later expanded (p. 17) to include "imagining," "perceiving," "feeling," and "moving." This is not to suggest that Lonergan's position already develops this more comprehensive notion of experience but that his position is not dependent upon a sensationalist view of experience as are several more strictly Kantian formulations of "transcendental method." For a rigorous critique of Lonergan from this viewpoint, see Schubert M. Ogden, "Lonergan and the Subjectivist Principle," *Journal of Religion* 51 (1971), 155–73. Although I share Ogden's Whiteheadian view on the relationship of "experience" and "consciousness," I do not share what seems to be his interpretation (p. 162) that Lonergan's notion of consciousness is constituted by an almost Cartesian clarity and distincness. Indeed, Lonergan's own formulation of the distinction between "consciousness" and "knowledge" (cf. *Insight*, esp. pp. 319–39) is crucial for understanding his position, and his notion of "experience," although undeveloped, seems clearly open to the Whiteheadian understanding.

(45) Cf. n. 17 above; Dupré suggests a symbolic mediation of the religious dimension as the "other dimension." He is negative towards "arguments" for the existence of God; for example, cf. *The Other Dimension*, p. 128.

(46) Amidst the extensive literature on this subject, cf. the valuable collection of survey articles and original contributions in Gene Outka and John P. Reeder, Jr. (eds.), *Religion and Morality* (New York: Anchor, 1973).

(47) For example, cf. H. Richard Niebuhr's use of his own principle of "radical monotheism" to reformulate the liberal notion of responsibility as responsibility to God, in H. Richard Niebuhr, *The Responsible Self* (New York: Harper, 1963), pp. 108–26.

(48) On the history of this development, cf. Norman Perrin, *The Kingdom of God in the Teaching of Jesus* (London: SCM Press, 1963).

(49) Rudolph Otto can also be described as neo-Kantian, of course, but the influence of Schleiermacher on his position seems to have broken the more usual "moral" bounds imposed by *The Critique of Practical Reason* to allow for Otto's own development of the notion of the "numinous" in his classical treatment, *The Idea of the Holy*. On Ritschl, recall his use of ethical rather than metaphysical (or mystical) categories in his theology as perhaps typified by his justly famous comment: "I, too, recognize mysteries in the religious life, but when anything is and remains a mystery, I say nothing about it," in *Justification and Reconciliation* (Edinburgh: T. & T. Clark, 1902), p. 607, n. 1.

(50) The achievement of Ritschl, for example, is surely not to be explained in these terms without remainder. His great work *Justification and Reconciliation* remains a classical locus of invaluable insights into the history of religious doctrine.

(51) This remains the case for those liberal theologians principally influenced by Kant's *Critique of Practical Reason* and his *Religion Within the Limits of Reason Alone*: not, however, for the more recent interest in and employment of Kant's third critique; nor for the Heidegerrian reinterpretation of the achievement of Kant in Martin Heidegger, *Kant and the Problem of Metaphysics* (Bloomington, Ind.: Indiana University Press, 1962); nor, finally, for the revisionist return to Kant via a reinterpretation of the category "limit."

(52) Cf. R. B. Braithwaite, *An Empiricist's View of the Nature of Religious Belief* (Cambridge: Cambridge University Press, 1955); R. M. Hare in *New Essays in Philosophical Theology*, A. Flew and A. MacIntyre (eds.) (London: SCM Press, 1955), pp. 99–105.

(53) Cf. *Religion and Morality*, pp. 295–428.

(54) The Wittgensteinian expression "forms of life" will be used as roughly equivalent to the phenomenological category "mode-of-being-in-the-world" employed throughout this work.

(55) This seems a fair observation on the "popular" image of the secularist culture at large as expressed in popular form in publications like *Playboy* and as expressed in philosophical form in American naturalism. On the latter, cf. Yervant Krikorian (ed), *Naturalism and the Human Spirit* (New York: Columbia University Press, 1944).

(56) In principle, of course, other analyses could be cited. Reasons of brevity impel one to choose a single example of each analysis for each sub-section.

(57) Cf. Stephen Toulmin, *The Uses of Argument* (New York: Cambridge University Press, 1958); idem, *An Examination of the Place of Reason in Ethics.*

(58) Cf. Schubert M. Ogden, *The Reality of God* (New York: Harper & Row, 1966), pp. 27–44, for the analysis interpreted throughout this section.

(59) Ibid., pp. 27–8.

(60) Ibid., p. 29.

(61) Cf. n. 52 above.

(62) Ogden, *The Reality of God*, pp. 32–4.

(63) Ibid., p. 33.

(64) Ibid., pp. 32–4. Note Ogden's development of Toulmin's own position on reassurance.

(65) Ibid., p. 34.

(66) The avoidance of this temptation is especially important when one attempts to do theology in the present pluralist setting. The alternative of a common-sense eclecticism is not so much pluralistic as chaotic.

(67) The suggestion, once again, is that the Anglo-American empirical tradition can make "the linguistic turn" without surrendering its own profound insights into the nature of experience. For a recent example, cf. John E. Smith, *The Analogy of Experience* (New York, Harper & Row, 1973).

(68) Ogden's own commitment to the Anglo-American empirical tradition may prove illustrative of that tradition's ability to employ the modes of analysis rendered available by the "third stage" of analytical philosophy. For a more extensive interpretation of the latter, cf. chapter six.

(69) The importance of this notion of the "re-presentative" function of religious language is analyzed in relationship to christological language in chapter nine.

(70) Inter alia, cf. George Santayana, *Skepticism and Animal Faith* (New York, Dover, 1955), esp. pp. 214–33, 287–311. The other alternative positions are referred to throughout this text.

(71) Inter alia, cf. Karl Jaspers, *The Perennial Scope of Philosophy* (New York, Philosophical Library, 1949), pp. 85–87, 168–80.

(72) Cf. Karl Jaspers' position on "ciphers" in *Philosophical Faith and Revelation* (New York: Harper & Row, 1967), esp. pp. 104–48, 234–47, 302–15; idem, on "boundary-situations" in *Philosophy*, vol. 2 (Chicago: University of Chicago Press, 1970), pp. 177–218.

(73) In psychology, cf. Abraham H. Maslow, *Religions, Values and Peak Experiences* (New York: Viking, 1970); cf. also Peter Berger, *A Rumor of Angels* (Garden

City, N.Y.: Doubleday, 1969), esp. pp. 95–125; and Sam Keen, *Apology for Wonder* (New York: Harper & Row, 1969); idem, *To A Dancing God* (New York: Harper & Row, 1970). Among the existentialists the pioneering works of Gabriel Marcel should also be cited here: inter alia, cf. Gabriel Marcel, *Being and Having* (London: Dacre, 1949). Throughout the text I prefer the use of the word *ec-stasy* as disclosive of the ability to be outside the "everyday" limits on such occasions.

(74) In the language employed earlier, this could be formulated as "stating" the "limits-to" in order to "show" the "limits-of."

(75) Note that the model remains "self-transcendence," not "self-fulfillment" nor "self-abnegation."

(76) For an example of this as part of mystical experience, cf. William Johnston, *The Mysticism of the Cloud of Unknowing* (New York: Desclée, 1967); for the parallel in more ordinary experiences, cf. Abraham H. Maslow, *Toward A Psychology of Being* (Princeton: Van Nostrand, 1962); idem, *Religions, Values and Peak Experiences*.

(77) Cf. Bernard Lonergan, *Method in Theology*, pp. 101–10.

(78) Cf. Peter Berger, *A Rumor of Angels*, pp. 67–70; cf. also Charles A. Carr, "Peter Berger's Angels and Philosophy of Religion," *Journal of Religion* 52 (1972), 426–37.

(79) The final appeal here is an appeal to "experience" in the sense described in chapter four: a disclosure of a final dimension to the self's experience of the self—a "showing" to oneself; rarely an adequate "stating."

(80) At such moments, we also recognize how our language and our experience are liberated together or, often enough, not at all. Often what Heidegger names a "destruction" is necessary in order for a "retrieval" to take place. The hermeneutical circle described here suggests a twofold relationship: on the one hand, a limit-situation finds an explicitly religious language important (as when one faces the reality of one's own or a friend's death); on the other hand, an explicitly religious language (e.g., the language of the Christian funeral service) cannot really be "heard" unless the limit-situation is comprehended. The banalization and flight from the reality of death in modern technological societies is one of the surest signs of the impoverishment afforded by a dual failure to comprehend either limit-situations or religious limit-language.

(81) On the phenomenology of mystical experience, cf. Georges Morel, *Le Sens de l'existence d'après St. Jean de la Croix*, 3 vols. (Paris: Aubier, 1960).

(82) This is not to deny the presence of neurotic symptoms in a figure like Søren Kierkegaard; it is to deny that their presence adequately explains the extraordinary person of Kierkegaard as well as his analyses.

(83) Cf. Martin Heidegger, *Being and Time* (London: SCM, 1962), pp. 203–25, on certain modern strategies of inauthenticity, including *Gerede* (idle talk), curiosity, and ambiguity.

(84) For incisive analyses of Kierkegaard, especially on his use of pseudonyms for developing the "stages of existence," cf. Stephen Crites, *In The Twilight of Christen-*

dom: Hegel vs. Kierkegaard on Faith and History (Chambersburg, Pa.: American Academy of Religion, Studies In Religion, 1971); idem, "Pseudonymous Authorship as Art and as Act," in *Kierkegaard: A Collection of Critical Essays*, ed. by Josiah Thompson (Garden City, N.Y.: Doubleday Anchor, 1972), pp. 183–230; and Her-mann Diem, *Kierkegaard's Dialectic of Existence* (London: Oliver and Boyd, 1959).

(85) A familiar example of the hermeneutical difficulty mentioned in n. 80 above may prove helpful here. The hymn "Amazing Grace" seems to have remarkable res-onance for secular audiences; indeed in a manner which liberal Baptists, who have different memories of its origins, often seem to find puzzling. Yet precisely the secu-lar willingness to use a phrase like "amazing grace" is indicative, I believe, of the basic correctness of the central theological insight into the giftedness of life itself as the latter is formulated in the doctrine of grace with the latter's twofold components of a doctrine of creation and redemption.

(86) This is, of course, an interpretation of merely one aspect of Heidegger's pro-found analysis of the Being-Question as present to *Da-sein*. For Heidegger's analy-sis, cf. *Being and Time*, esp. section 40, pp. 228–41.

(87) Ibid., pp. 179–82.

(88) Ibid., p. 231: "Nothing which is ready-to-hand or present-at-hand within the world functions as that in the face of which anxiety is anxious. . . . Accordingly, when something threatening brings itself close, anxiety does not 'see' any definite 'here' or 'yonder' from which it comes. That in the face of which one has anxiety is characterized by the fact that what threatens is nowhere. . . . In that in the face of which one has anxiety, the 'It is nothing and nowhere' becomes manifest. . . ."

(89) Note throughout how such unusual "limit-insight" demands a distortion (de-struction-retrieval) of the language, as in Heidegger's own tearing-apart of the Greek and German languages.

(90) On the latter, cf. especially, David Burrell, *Analogy and Philosophical Language*, esp. pp. 7–35, 119–71, 213–69.

(91) On Tillich, cf. n. 5 above.

(92) In terms of the criteria developed in chapter four, the "meaning" of the "reli-gious dimension" disclosed by limit-questions and limit-situations may be described as a meaning with a logically "limit" character (as limit-to and limit-of); its "mean-ingfulness" may be found in the existential disclosure (e.g., reassurance) which such situations and language allow. The "truth" claims of such language will need the ex-plicit raising of the question of God as the objective referent in reality for such expe-riences (cf. chapters seven and eight). The "meaning" and "meaningfulness" of such "religious dimension" experience and language, however, may find some alignment with Heidegger's insistence upon truth-as-*aletheia*—at least in the more modest terms of the present insistence upon a "disclosure model" meaningfulness. On *aleth-eia* in Heidegger, cf. William J. Richardson, *Heidegger: Through Phenomenology to Thought* (The Hague: Nijhoff, 1967), pp. 484–90.

(93) In the modified sense as disclosive of the "limit" character of such a dimension. This neither affirms nor negates the further question of the dialectical character of such experience articulated by Louis Dupré in *The Other Dimension*.

Chapter 6
Religious Language in the New Testament

The central category of the last chapter was the concept of "limit." In either the limit-situations of the everyday or in the limit-questions of moral and scientific inquiry, a dimension limiting (as limit-to) and grounding (as limit-of) the ordinary is disclosed. For that basic dimension to our lives a language re-presentative of the basic faith disclosed in moments of crisis and of ecstasy seems appropriate. That basic faith in the worthwhileness of existence, in the final graciousness of our lives even in the midst of absurdity, may be named the religious dimension of our existence. The meaningfulness of both religious language and of the form of life it re-presents is grounded in the experience of a basic faith and is mediated cognitively by reflection upon limit-situations and limit-questions. The present discussion will continue that suggestion by arguing that a signal peculiarity of authentic explicitly religious language also lies in its character as a limit-language disclosive of certain limit-experiences.[1]

To test this hypothesis, I shall interpret certain recent developments in linguistic theory and in New Testament analysis primarily by means of the hermeneutical theory set forth in chapter four.[2] The following steps seem essential to establish the character of Christian religious language as limit-language re-presenting our most basic faith: First, one may recall those developments in recent linguistic analysis of religious language which can show the concept of the logically odd (or limit) character of religious language. Second, one may turn to some recent interpretations of how certain New Testament language forms share the limit-character proper to the religious use of language. Third, one may return to the hermeneutical theory developed earlier in order to suggest one way of describing that possible mode-of-being-in-the-world referred to by New Testament language. Finally, one may suggest how an existential verification of such a mode-of-being-in-the-world might proceed. Once these steps have been taken, we may be prepared for the central question of the next chapter: the truth of the central cognitive claim of New Testament religious language that the objective referent of such language is properly named God.

119

BACKGROUND: Analytic Philosophy and Religious Language

To keep the discussion within reasonable limits, this section shall concentrate upon two representative contemporary analysts of religious language, Ian Ramsey and Frederick Ferré.[3] At the same time, Ramsey and Ferré must be understood in the context of the wider discussion of religious language by linguistic analysts. Both Ramsey and Ferré represent the "third stage" of the analysis of religious language. The obvious question, then, is just what were the first two stages and what are the distinguishing characteristics of this "third stage."

The issue posed by the analytic tradition is a clear one: before anyone can begin to examine the truth-claims of religious language one must first see whether such language even has meaning.[4] Surely there is little point in investigating claims to truth of intrinsically meaningless or nonsensical language. For the first two stages of the analytic movement, religious language was cognitively meaningless; for the third stage, religious language is not meaningless since it has specific meaningful uses, including a properly cognitive one.

The first two stages of the linguistic tradition were applications of the "verification principle" and the "falsification principle" respectively to religious language. In the first stage, represented by A. J. Ayer's *Language, Truth and Logic*,[5] the principle for meaningful statements was clear: all meaningful statements must either be verified in sense experience or be the logically necessary and non-existential statements of mathematics and logic. On either count, Ayer concluded, religious statements (along with metaphysical and most ethical ones) fail and are strictly meaningless. Since even Ayer has modified this rigorous (and non-verifiable!) principle of verification,[6] it seems fair to say that very few analysts any longer feel content simply to apply this principle to religious language.

Though the second stage of the linguistic analysis of religious language developed a more sophisticated criterion of meaning, it also concluded that religious language was meaningless. The best representative of this second view remains Antony Flew and his application of the principle of falsifiability to religious language.[7] In logical terms, Flew maintains that if the statement "God loves us" asserts that such is the case, then it must also logically deny that its contradictory is not the case (i.e., it must be falsifiable). In empirical terms, if the speaker of this statement cannot tell us what event or series of events would have to occur for us to conclude that the statement "God loves us" is false, we must conclude that such a statement is in fact non-falsifiable and hence meaningless.

Flew's challenge and its subsequent discomfiture for defenders of the meaningfulness of religious statements probably helped to impel the third stage of the discussion. The fundamental character of this stage is perhaps best represented by the statement of one of Flew's respondents in the original "Theology and Falsification" debate, Basil Mitchell: "In place of the dogmatic assertion that those statements alone have meaning which are empirically verifiable, the latter movement asks the question 'what is the logic of statements of this kind? . . . What is their use and function, what jobs do they do?' " [8]

Several analysts in this third stage of the discussion often maintain that the principal *use* of religious language is a moral or attitudinal one.[9] One may recall Hare's famous reply to Flew that religious statements are not assertions about the world. Rather such statements express our "bliks," i.e., our different attitudes toward the world.[10] One may also recall R. B. Braithwaite's more developed analysis on the intrinsic connection between religious and moral statements. For Braithwaite, religious statements are like moral statements in that they are non-descriptive but still have a use and hence a meaning.[11] The logic of religious statements is none other than to express the intention of the asserter to act in a particular way. Religious statements do not describe the world but express our attitudes and behavior in that world. In fact, for Braithwaite, the major difference between moral and religious statements is that the latter statements are more internalized inasmuch as religious statements are tied together into a whole system of statements via metaphors, stories, and parables. Though Braithwaite's claim that religious statements do not have a properly cognitive use may be challenged, his analysis illustrates an important conclusion of the third stage: the very logic of religious statements does involve various "uses," one of which is the expression of the intention of the asserter *to act* in a particular way.[12]

The development of this "third stage" of the linguistic analysis of religious statements is principally concerned to determine the *use* of such statements. For what I have earlier called questions on the "meaning" and "meaningfulness" of religious language, the linguistic tradition is invaluable.[13] The value of that tradition for expressing both the attitudinal and descriptive uses of religious language may be seen in the more developed positions of Ian Ramsey and Frederick Ferré.

Ian Ramsey sets forth his central understanding of the "uses" of religious statements in his book *Religious Language: An Empirical Placing of Theological Phrases.*[14] As the title indicates, Ramsey is principally concerned to answer two questions about religious language: to what kind of empirical situation does religion appeal; for such situations, what kind of language is appropriate. Ramsey's answers to these questions seem uniquely helpful ones for determining a *logical* answer to the question of both the descriptive and attitudinal uses of religious language. To his first question, Ramsey responds that the kind of situation which religious language discloses is a situation which involves both an "odd discernment" and a "total commitment." [15] More exactly, religious language points to the kind of highly personal situation which cannot be described in straightforward indicative language. Like poetic metaphors, [16] religious language discloses an odd personal discernment which cannot be described literally but whose reality cannot be denied. In those situations where we find ourselves discerning the meanings of our lives, Ramsey suggests (through his own metaphors: "the penny drops," the "ice breaks," the "light dawns"), we find religious language useful and thereby meaningful. Moreover, we notice that the kind of situation to which religious language points has two further distinguishing characteristics. Unlike poetic or ethical language, religious language expresses a *total* commitment (*the* meaning of my life) as well as a meaning which has univeral significance (this meaning—e.g., fundamental trust—is applicable to all human life). Such a combination of an odd personal discernment, a total commitment, and a universal significance is the *empirical* "place" for religious and theological statements. [17]

Ramsey's analysis, then, is helpful in analyzing how religious statements do logically point to situations which involve at least the actions of odd personal discernment and total commitment. His analysis can provide still another clarification of the present question. That clarification can best be seen in Ramsey's second question and his reply. What kind of language is appropriate to such a situation? Ramsey's fuller response is intriguing. He observes that an "odd" language will be needed for the odd personal discernment situation. This fact, in turn, demands that we find a language that is an "object-language," yet more than object language. In his early work, Ramsey appealed principally to the odd logic of nicknames as an example of such odd (i.e., non-literal) language. We employ nicknames to allow for disclosures of an odd personal sort. In his later and more developed work, Ramsey appeals to the logic of metaphorical language. [18] He recalls the contemporary understanding of metaphor not as a substitute for literal meanings but as an emergent meaning occasioned by the tension or interaction between various "literal" words. To articulate odd personal disclosures, either poetic or ethical or religious language may prove appropriate.

Why then is religious language uniquely appropriate to certain situations? Recall that, for Ramsey, the empirical place of religious language involves not only an odd discernment or disclosure but also a total commitment and a claim to universal significance. What kind of language would be appropriate for such situations? Ramsey's ingenious response is that a language with a peculiar kind of "qualifier" is needed. We find the need to *qualify* our normal object language to the point of infinity in order to express a *total* commitment and a *universal* significance. When religious persons say, for example, that God is infinitely good, they point to an empirical situation where they have loved and been loved in return. Then they remind us that a total commitment to the one religiously loved (God) demands that we qualify this love as distinct from all our other loves (friends, country, church, etc.) by expressing ourselves in such odd language as "God is infinitely loving."[19]

Ramsey's analysis, I believe, allows one to clarify both the unique attitudinal uses involved in religious language and the genuinely if oddly descriptive character of its odd logical language. Insofar as we experience odd discernments expressing both the attitude of a total commitment and a description of a universal applicability, we find ourselves impelled to use religious language. Correlatively, insofar as we use religious language with logical propriety we find ourselves impelled to note both that attitude of total commitment and those descriptions of odd discernment and universal applicability which serve as the empirical placing for religious language.

A word of caution is necessary here. Though Ramsey's analysis seems genuinely helpful for the present question, I do not think that he really resolves the full problem of the cognitive status of religious language. That question is more properly treated in the next two chapters where we shall also see why Ramsey's analysis of theological language may prove far too sanguine about the disclosure power of any and all traditional theological language—as Ramsey's analysis of God's "impassibility" and "immutability" most clearly reveal.[20] For challenging traditional theological language, I find Frederick Ferré's position both more revisionist and more helpful.[21]

Ferré conducts his criticism in accord with what a revisionist theologian considers fully legitimate criteria. If such language is not merely logically odd but also internally incoherent, it should be revised.[22] How, for example, does one coherently speak both the language of the biblical God's immutability and the language of his relationship to history? Is such language appropriate to our experience? Does not the language of God's impassibility qualify to the point of meaninglessness the disclosure situation it intends to allow? Although Ramsey and Ferré share a similar analytical method and several similar conclusions, Ferré's approach to the question of traditional religious language serves as a worthwhile check upon Ramsey's more traditional theological stance.

At the moment I am concerned to show only that linguistic analysis of the logic of religious language does manifest characteristics that may legitimately be described by the favored category "limit": the employment of such "odd" qualifiers as "infinitely"; a qualitatively *odd* discernment; a *total* commitment; a *universal* applicability.[23] Insofar as my development of Ramsey's logical analysis in the direction of limit-language is sound, a singular instance of present pluralist possibilities suggests itself. The major modern philosophical tradition (linguistic analysis) which began its study of religious language in a negative, indeed hostile, manner has, through the work of Ramsey and Ferré, now provided good logical reasons for affirming the propriety of my own use of the expressions "limit-language" and "limit-experience" for explicitly religious expressions. Limit-language seems a correct way to indicate the logically odd character of religious language and the qualitatively different empirical placing for that language in our common experience. It remains to be seen whether the originating religious language of the Christian religion can legitimately be described as a limit-language manifesting certain qualitatively different limit-experiences.[24] With that question in mind, I shall now turn to several recent interpretations of the linguistic "oddness" of the New Testament usage of certain traditional literary forms. Just what are these forms and what linguistic peculiarities do they involve? Is it fair to label such forms "limit-language" manifesting, both logically and empirically, explicitly Christian limit-experiences?

NEW TESTAMENT LANGUAGE: The Breaking of Forms

The following analysis does not pretend to describe the enormous variety of languages and forms of life which the New Testament texts disclose. My interest is to focus attention upon certain language forms ("senses") and certain modes-of-being-in-the-world ("referents") made available by recent New Testament scholarship.[25] Employing the method of interpretation outlined in chapter four, this section will be concerned to understand whether the "sense" of the New Testament use of certain important language forms may legitimately yield an authentically Christian limit-language. The next section will be concerned to see whether the basic existential "referents" of such forms yield limit-experiences disclosive of an authentically human mode-of-being-in-the-world.[26] The final section shall also attempt to spell out some forms of validation for those New Testament modes-of-being-in-the-world.

The first question concerns both the sense and the limit-language character of the New Testament usage of certain language forms. The basic hypothesis is this: several recent interpretations of the New Testament uses of proverbs, eschatological sayings, and parables show how the *sense* of such languages can properly be described as fitting the earlier description of religious language as a limit-language.[27] As that process is described in literary critical terms by New Testament scholars like Amos Wilder, William Beardslee, Dan O. Via, Robert Funk, Norman Perrin, and Dominic Crossan,[28] and as that process is philosophically analyzed by Paul Ricoeur, the basic structure of this hypothesis can be stated with clarity: the New Testament consistently modifies the traditional use of the language of proverbs, eschatological sayings, and parables through such procedures as intensification, transgression, and "going to the limits" of language;[29] these modifications allow the interpreter to propose that the sense of this language should be described as a limit-language of a genuinely religious character. Some instances of such procedures in operation may illustrate this claim.

Proverbs

As William A. Beardslee interprets this process at work in the New Testament usage of the traditional Jewish language form, the proverb,[30] one may note the peculiar "intensification" of that traditional language form which occurs. Recall, for example, such a classical New Testament proverb as "Whoever seeks to gain his life will lose it, but whoever loses his life will preserve it" (Lk 17:33; cf. Mk 8:35). The reader is jarred by paradox. We are not told that we should simply give up the project of finding some continuity of meaning for our lives. Otherwise, we might find a skeptical, an ironical, or even cynical negation of traditional folk wisdom's attempts to formulate proverbs helpful to the search for a meaningful life. Instead we are advised that the way of wisdom is not found by seeking to "gain" life's meaning on our own. Even at its best, our everyday way of being in the world—our moral projects, our intellectual strivings, our traditional proverbial wisdom, our hopes, and struggles—will not suffice. The everyday with all its ambiguity including all its wisdom and goodness must be "intensified" to the point where we reach the limit of all present efforts, where we are jarred into "letting go" of even our best struggles:[31] to "lose our life" in order to gain it. That intensification of ordinary proverbial language by the linguistic strategies of paradox and hyperbole alerts one to the limit of the ordinary use of such language and thereby discloses the properly limit-sense of New Testament proverbs. Its sense is the sense of all authentically religious language: the strange, jarring, paradoxical, and unnerving sense of a limit-language beyond the morality of traditional proverbial wisdom into the limit-domain of authentically religious speech. The referent of such language, as we shall see in the next section, may have a similar limit-character. At the moment, we are concerned only with noting linguistically just how we cannot but call such an intensified usage of proverbial wisdom a limit-language.

Proclamatory Sayings

As Norman Perrin interprets this same process of intensification, transgression, and "going to the limit" of language in the proclamatory sayings of Jesus, the same analogous procedure seems operative.[32] The proclamatory saying of Lk 17:20–21 will serve as an example: "The kingdom of God is not coming with signs to be observed; nor will they say, 'Lo, here it is!' or 'there!' for behold, the kingdom of God is in the midst of you." Most contemporary interpreters of these sayings have been concerned principally with understanding the exact nature of the temporal order proclaimed by Jesus. Is the kingdom "wholly future" (Schweitzer and "consequent eschatology"); already here (Dodd and "realized eschatology"); both present and future in the process of realization (Jeremias, Perrin)? Surely, these are legitimate questions. With equal surety, these questions, as Perrin's own earlier work demonstrates, have now received something like a definitive answer.[33] However, as Perrin further suggests, only when our linguistic sensitivities are sharpened do we realize that such questions are *not* the central questions which the language of the proclamatory sayings contain.[34]

In fact, the proclamatory sayings of Jesus break the traditional apocalyptic usage by transgressing altogether its literal temporal character. In terms of the present analysis, I interpret the significance of Perrin's discovery as follows: only when the interpreter recognizes linguistically that he is dealing here with an authentically religious use of language, will he be willing to abandon both an interpretation which ties that language to traditional apocalyptic usage and an interpretation which has as its chief concern the determination of the literal "when" of the eschatological occurrence. In proclaiming "the kingdom of God is among you," this language does not disclose an everyday "when," even one of great everyday significance (as Oscar Cullmann's "D-Day" analogy for such language suggests).[35] The very language of the proclamation breaks all concern with "literal" time. That language intensifies the recognition that the everyday, even at its most significant, is utterly unable to disclose the final meaning of the everyday. It brings the listener/reader to a point which can only be described as beyond the limits of the everyday.

In this use of language we find again a limit-language which upsets our finest temporal predictions and our most significant temporal events: a limit-language which forces us to hear the evocation not of a super-everyday, a beyond and out-of-this-world, a "super-natural" world. Rather in these proclamatory sayings we find a religious use of language which challenges, provokes, jars alike our wisdom, our morality, and our sense of everyday time. Literalize that language and that super-everyday world of supernaturalism called fundamentalism emerges. Observe that language transgress the ordinary apocalyptic language it employs and a disclosure occurs. "Another" world opens up: not an apocalyptic, super-everyday world; but a "limit" dimension to *this* world, *this* experience, *this* language.[36] A more exact description of that limit-experience waits upon an examination of the classical New Testament limit-language, the parable.

Parabolic Language

Since the emergence of historical consciousness in the last century, perhaps no greater advance has been made in the remarkable history of New Testament reinterpretation than the recovery of the meaning of the parables of the New Testament.[37] Indeed, the historical reconstruction of the parabolic texts as the parables *of Jesus* (as exemplified in the work of Joachim Jeremias[38]) has become one of the most important components in the historical quest for Jesus of Nazareth. The principal interest of the present analysis, however, is not to study the parables as clues for that historical quest. Rather, our interest in the parable remains the crucial one of determining whether this key New Testament language form also fits the category of limit-language.[39]

Before suggesting how recent New Testament scholarship would seem to validate this claim, it may prove helpful to contextualize the discussion on the parabolic form by summarizing its basic moments. As students of Christianity know well, the earliest and longest-lasting interpretation of the New Testament parables by the Christian community was an allegorical one. In the New Testament itself, in the exegeses of Alexandria, Antioch, and Augustine, in the medieval tradition of the "four senses" of scripture, parables, until fairly recently, have been widely interpreted as allegories.[40] This traditional allegorical attempt to find a point-by-point "spiritual" interpretation of each element in each parable received a death-blow in the last century from the pioneering work of Adolph Jülicher.[41] Jülicher demonstrated that parables are not in fact allegories, but a unique literary genre recounting a story of ordinary life. Moreover, each story, for Jülicher, manifests a moral dictum. If Jülicher's attempt to find a central moral teaching for each parable has not survived the moral *Weltanschauung* of the religious liberalism of his age,[42] his argument for the uniqueness of the literary genre, the parable, as distinct from the allegory did survive.[43]

The next major stage of modern parabolic interpretation, best represented by the work of C. H. Dodd and Joachim Jeremias, encompassed two major foci.[44] The first focus was the employment of sophisticated historical linguistic analysis to determine the actual life-situation (*Sitz im Leben*) of either Jesus, or of the early Christian community, or of the redactor of the various parables.[45] The major accomplishment of this stage was the historian's ability to achieve a historical reconstruction of the parables *as* the parables of Jesus. Indeed, so much is this the case that Norman Perrin does not exaggerate when he states: "When we study the parables of Jesus, we are really studying the historical reconstruction of those parables by Joachim Jeremias." [46] The second major focus as well as the other major accomplishment of this "historical" study of the parables was its articulation of the eschatological (not the "liberal-moral") vision of the parables.[47] That conclusion eliminated classical liberalism's strictly moral interpretation of the New Testament parables and thereby allowed a reinterpretation of the religious-as-eschatological vision of Christianity. That same conclusion also tied the basic eschatological vision of the parables to the eschatological vision disclosed in the proclamatory sayings and deeds of the "implied author" of the parables, Jesus of Nazareth.[48] In that sense, this stage of parable-interpretation already discloses the unique "limit-vision" of Christian eschatology as a religious not merely ethical vision for the contemporary reader. That disclosure does not take place by any appeal to a tropological "sense" of the parables, but by a careful historical investigation into the cultural and religious life-situation of the text and a careful historical reconstruction of the parables as the parables of Jesus himself. However, this second stage of parable-interpretation lacks precisely what our present investigation seeks: the ability to show how the actual language form of the New Testament parables linguistically discloses the limit-vision of Christian eschatology; the ability to show how that limit-vision in turn can be adequately articulated only in a limit-language.[49]

This third and still developing stage of parable-interpretation is characterized by the use of contemporary literary criticism and linguistics to understand the linguistic form of the parables. This stage—with all its present excitement, complexity, and internal differences[50]—has reached certain central conclusions: foremost, the fundamental linguistic form operative in the narrative genre of parable is the metaphor. In one sense, this insight was already present in Jülicher's de-allegorizing of the parables. But a crucial difference has now emerged. Jülicher, along with his contemporaries, assumed that a metaphor is fundamentally a simile expressing a likeness which, in principle, can be rearticulated in literal (for Jülicher, ethical) terms. The present generation of New Testament scholars, following their colleagues in general literary criticism, now reject this "substitution-theory" understanding of metaphor.[51] In fact, a metaphorical meaning—at least one still alive[52]—is not simply a strange or a merely ornamental substitute-meaning for a literal (e.g., ethical) meaning based upon some resemblance between the "literal" and the "metaphorical" meanings. Rather, following the lead of such literary critics and linguistic analysts as I. A. Richards, Monroe Beardsley, and Max Black,[53] these New Testament scholars employ some version of the "tension or interaction theory" for understanding metaphorical meaning. Briefly stated, this "interaction or tension" theory to understanding metaphorical meaning holds that the key to any good metaphor lies in the "tension" between the key terms in a metaphorical statement. Aside from now dead metaphors ("the arm of the chair," "man is a wolf"),[54] the careful analyst of metaphorical statements (not words!) notes that a new non-dictionary meaning emerges from the "twist" which occurs when certain unlikely terms are allowed to interact, usually with no little semantic impertinence.[55]

If one wishes to understand certain events of recent American history, for example (events like the Democratic and Republican conventions of 1968 and 1972, or the peace-march on the Pentagon of 1967), one may turn not only to the scientific (and, in that sense, literal) analyses of professional sociologists, political scientists, and psychologists, but also to such literary interpretation as Norman Mailer's.[56] Why? The reason seems obvious: Mailer is able to capture a new meaning in such events—and, often, it seems the *real* human meaning—by his remarkable ability to produce dazzling metaphors which excite imagination, challenge the literal understanding, and jar the perceptions. Mailer's basic metaphor for the events of the Pentagon march in *Armies of the Night*, his series of provocative metaphors for such public personalities as Senator Hubert Humphrey, Mayor Richard Daley, or Senator Eugene McCarthy, cannot really yield to literal substitutes.[57] Yet these metaphors do so forcefully disclose new meanings to familiar events and personalities that the reader continues to read on. Alas, all good metaphors, if repeated often enough, too soon become dead metaphors and are buried in our dictionaries. But each of us recognizes a living metaphor and its emergent meaning whenever we read or hear one.[58] Indeed, when a good metaphor "hits" us we feel that we have discovered something really new about reality; something which we cannot without loss of meaning translate into strictly literal terms. With a similar understanding of the "tension theory" of metaphor, a present generation of New Testament scholars insists that the basic linguistic form for the parable is the metaphor. Not only is allegorical interpretation improper; even Jülicher's residual "substitution-theory" understanding of parabolic metaphors as illustrating moral maxims is thereby rendered inadequate for analyzing these familiar parabolic metaphors.

However, parables are not only metaphors. They are also narrative extensions of a basic metaphor.[59] As such, their linguistic form bears a further complexity. Can we find in these seemingly ordinary and realistic narratives of the New Testament, these "metaphors of normalcy" as Dominic Crossan aptly labels them,[60] certain characteristics which transgress the poetic form of the narrative metaphor up to that "limit" proper to a religious use of language? To repeat our now familiar question: even granted the metaphorical character of these seemingly ordinary stories, can we legitimately claim that the New Testament use of parables involves a limit-language? With the intensification-process which Beardslee found in the New Testament use of proverbs, with the overturning of chronological time which Norman Perrin discovered in the eschatological proclamation sayings, there seemed solid linguistic reason to suggest that these New Testament uses of language were legitimately described in limit-language terms. Can the parable also be properly described as involving a limit use of language?

For at least one philosophical interpreter of New Testament parables, Paul Ricoeur, that claim can legitimately be made. In an interpretation of this complex question as intriguing as it may prove tentative,[61] Ricoeur claims to find a parallel form of "going to the limits of language" occurring in those widely heralded "metaphors of normalcy," the New Testament parables. With that characteristic of the parables which New Testament scholars describe as their "realism" (Perrin), their "ordinariness," their normalcy (Crossan), there seems every good linguistic and historical reason to agree.[62] Surely these stories—the Wicked Husbandmen, the Great Feast, the Prodigal Son—could have happened and in several cases probably did. Even now in a non-agrarian and non-first century setting, a contemporary reader can recognize the parable's fidelity to the experience of ordinary life.

Yet, Ricoeur argues, the very "realism" and "everydayness" of the narratives heighten the eccentricity of those modes of behavior to which the "kingdom" is compared.[63] The very ordinariness of the narrative form seems to force the tension of the underlying metaphor to a limit beyond morality and everydayness: indeed to a limit-vision of human possibilities. If one recalls the basic hypothesis of this entire study that the religious dimension of our lives is not another super-everyday, super-natural life but rather a final, a limit-dimension to the whole of everyday life itself, this suggestion by Ricoeur may be said to make existential as well as linguistic sense.

Existentially, the extraordinary does emerge from and illuminate the ordinary. Linguistically, the underlying metaphor of the parable explodes by means of the extraordinary elements in this "ordinary" narrative form. If such is indeed the case, one finds the peculiar religious "limit" use of language operative even in the New Testament parables. In short, the parables too are a limit-language. In linguistic terms, one need not appeal merely to an additional "theological" interpretation of the parables after a "literary" interpretation has been completed, as does Dan O. Via after completing a brilliant literary interpretation by employing the classical forms of comedy and tragedy to illuminate the narrative structure of the various parables.[64] One need not appeal only to the general eschatological religious vision enunciated by Jeremias, Dodd, or Bultmann as the parabolic horizon of meaning in order to understand that eschatological, limit horizon.[65] Rather one may note that, even linguistically, these narratives, for all their ordinariness, force the underlying metaphor to a limit which can be described as a "religious" use of language. The parables, as stories, take the reader to the point where the course of ordinary life is broken; an intensification of the everyday emerges; the unexpected happens; a strange world of meaning is projected which challenges, jars, disorients our everyday vision precisely by both showing us the limits to the everyday and projecting the limit-character of the whole.

To see this possibility in linguistic terms, Ricoeur argues that there are seldom-noted clues in the narrative itself to justify the description "limit-language." [66] These clues are found in the "extravagant" behavior of several of the characters which clash with the ordinary narrative. In the parable of the Wicked Husbandmen, for example, is it not in everyday terms absurd for a man to send his son after already losing his servants? Are we not still affronted by the extravagant action of the "employer" in the Laborers in the Vineyard parable? In that perhaps most arresting of all, the parable of the Prodigal Son, the father's actions towards both sons is strange and disconcerting. By "everyday" standards surely more sympathy is owed the responsible elder son in the sub-plot of this tale. By "everyday" standards surely something less than the "great feast" seems fitting for the irresponsible prodigal's return in the main plot of the tale. One suspects that even as extravagant a modern cult-figure as Zorba the Greek would not be quite that extravagant in dealing with a faithful (by all ordinary standards) elder son and a faithless (by all ordinary standards) younger one.

Ricoeur's linguistic case seems sound. Even in the parables, those perhaps too often heard narratives, those metaphors of normalcy, a limit-language may be found. Whatever the "kingdom" means,[67] its meaning emerges as an extraordinary, indeed an extravagant, possibility which the tension of the metaphors express in a narrative whose characteristic quiet normalcy is broken by the extravagant action of the characters. This linguistic clue may lead the reader to a major linguistic and existential discovery. Simply to say, for example, that the meaning of the Prodigal Son is that it represents a metaphor for the "Father's love without limit" (Jeremias) is to say much but not enough.[68] To read the story, to watch the intertwining of the sub-plot of the elder son and the plot of the prodigal son is to await and receive the surprise of an ordinary story become extraordinary; to witness a common, possibly now dead metaphor explode with a linguistic power that discloses possibilities for human existence which seem and are beyond the limit of what our ordinary language and experience might imagine. What that experience might be we shall now attempt to describe.

NEW TESTAMENT LIMIT-EXPERIENCE: A Possible Mode-of-Being-in-the-World

Before attempting an initial description of the character of the limit-experience which seems manifested by these limit-languages of the New Testament, it may prove helpful to relate this discussion to two prior analyses: the analysis of religious language articulated by Ian Ramsey and the analysis in the preceding chapter of the "religious dimension of our common human experience." By the first, we achieve a further clarification of the logical character of religious language as limit-language; by the second, we may specify how even the limit-experience described in New Testament language remains within the realm of authentically *human* experience.[69]

Ramsey's argument concluded that religious language was logically "odd." Its "oddness" consists largely in its use of extreme qualifiers (*"first* cause," *"creatio ex nihilo," "infinitely"* wise) which serve the analyst as indicators of the possible presence of a "disclosure" involving odd discernments, total commitments, and universal significance. Though the designation "odd" seems a legitimate way to express the logical peculiarity of all genuinely religious language, as I suggested above, I hesitate to accept it without some modification. If it be correct to say that the "empirical placing" of religious language involves an odd personal discernment, a total commitment, and a universal significance, then a simpler, less ambiguous expression than "oddness" is to designate religious language a limit-

language disclosive of certain limit-experiences.[70] "Limit" seems a less ambiguous expression than "odd" when one recalls, as Ramsey's own earlier
work suggested, that there are other "odd" languages—for example, the
language of nicknames. Only the religious use of language has what one
might call that final "oddness" of bringing ordinary language forms (proverbs, sayings, parables) to the limit of language by such strategies as intensification and transgression. In a parallel fashion, other human experiences
are also "odd." True joy, for example, is correctly described as an event, a
happening, an odd, unexpected occurrence. But only an explicitly religious
experience seems logically to involve either an explicitly *total* commitment
for the participant and a self-conscious belief in the *universal* significance of
the experience itself. To be sure, both those limit-situation and limit-question experiences described in the preceding chapter involve not only explicit
recognitions of the limits-to our everyday world but also implicit acknowl-
edgments of some final limit-of dimension that seems to ground all our experience. And yet it seems that only an explicitly religious experience adequately perceives and only an explicitly religious experience appropriately
articulates the fullness of the limit-vision disclosed in the earlier experiences
of a religious dimension of experience.[71]

There is indeed an "oddness" about explicitly religious experience and
religious language. That oddness, I suggest, is first found in the ineluctably
limit-character of all authentically religious experience and language. The
point is not simply that "oddness" is too ambiguous—and perhaps too British—an expression to describe either the language or the experience appropriate to the phenomenon called religion. If one does not employ a category
like "limit," one cannot help wondering just how does religious language
and experience qualitatively differ from other language and experience.[72]
Only a limit-language can and does appropriately disclose that final realm
of meaningfulness to our lives, that "other" trusting faithful dimension to
our existence, which may adequately allow the explicit acknowledgment
that the whole of our existence is other than a "getting and spending," other
than absurd, other even than the real, the "everyday" world. That other dimension may be perceived fleetingly but with some immediacy in limit-situations. Its presence may be mediated by reflection upon the meaning of the
limit-questions of scientific and moral activity. At those moments, we may
find ourselves turning to the limit-languages of religion in order to see how
they try to re-present that "other," that limit-dimension of our lives.[73]

To turn to the second point, how can one conceptually express just how
explicitly religious experience is both authentic human experience (not
trans-worldly, super-natural flights of fancy), and yet not strictly correlative
with, but basic horizon to, our ordinary activities in the everyday, in science, culture, morality, and art? The recurring suggestion of these analyses
is that here we must use some concept like the category "limit." For "limit"
implies not only that our ordinary language, our ordinary knowledge, and

our ordinary experience are limited (limit-to); the category also acknowledges that there is a language, an experience, and even a knowledge which correctly be-speaks, dis-closes, and e-vents that limit as a final limit-of dimension of all our existence. The concept "limit" warns us as well against all attempts to domesticate religious language and experience.[74] With the category "limit" one may reject both supernaturalist trading in the extraordinary-ordinary "world of religion" and all too easy, too lazily liberal claims that the "real" meaning of religion is an ethical, or an aesthetic, or a pseudo-scientific one.

This understanding of religious language and experience as limit-language and limit-experience is admittedly a revisionist formulation.[75] Yet the major religions, save where they lapse into fundamentalism, have always recognized this central limit characteristic of religion. One need not appeal only to a religion like Buddhism,[76] nor need one appeal only to what William James recognized as the "limit-cases" of religion—that mystical strain which, even when under suspicion, emerges in all the major religions.[77] Rather one can appeal to language less strange, indeed perhaps now all too common, to Western Christian ears: the language of "mystery" and "scandal." When Catholic Christians speak of mystery they either mean an uninteresting and basically irreligious datum, muddle, or puzzle.[78] Or they mean—as Karl Rahner so clearly means—that radically mysterious dimension to our lives which limits and grounds the rest of our activities.[79] When Protestant Christians speak of the "scandal of Christianity" they either mean some uninteresting and basically irreligious tenet of fundamentalism.[80] Or they mean—as Bultmann means—the dialectical, the limit scandal that this God of Jesus the Christ is also and always *my* God.[81]

The categories limit-language and limit-experience, therefore, seem useful, tentative, and admittedly revisionist formulations of the genuinely religious dimension of both our common faith and our explicitly Christian faith.[82] As such, the category may help free us from the reduction of religion to that revelational positivism called fundamentalism which proclaims intellectually untenable tenets as the meaning of a particular religion. That category may also free us from the too ready and too ideological denial by modern technological man of that "other" dimension to our lives. In fact, there seem good reasons to suspect that no minor cause for the sometimes desperate thinness of much of our contemporary technological existence[83] lies in our seeming inability to allow that other dimension in our lives. The liberation of our language and the liberation of our experience go hand in hand.[84] If we could hear—or "over-hear"—the limit-language of the Christian gospel anew, we might experience again a dimension to life which renders it whole. If we could at least listen to the "hints and guesses" disclosed to us in limit-situations, we might have some intimation of the odd, mysterious, indeed scandalous limit-experience which that gospel proclaims as an authentic human possibility.[85]

In that gospel, proverbs do not function to orient us to our everyday lives. "A stitch in time saves nine" is a helpful proverb yet hardly "discloses" a wholeness of meaning to us. But "Let the dead bury the dead" does not give us common-sense advice for orienting us toward grief and loss. Such a proverb deliberately disorients us, disconnects us from the ordinary, the acceptable, the "respectable." [86] If we allow New Testament proverbial language to disclose its genuinely religious meaning, such proverbs can reorient us to that dimension of life which restores a wholeness of meaning to all our basic activities. In that same gospel, the proclamatory sayings of Jesus do not provide us time-plans for the kingdom as future, as past, or as present. Rather, in the evocative phrase of Ernst Fuchs, these sayings actually bestow on us the e-vent of an authentic time: time as the e-vent, the happening, for the disclosure of God's gracious and trustworthy action to happen now.[87]

The parables do not merely tell a pleasant (or unpleasant) story to evoke a moral maxim. They are fictions. As with all good fiction, they redescribe ordinary reality in order to disclose a new, an extraordinary possibility for our lives.[88] In the peculiar limit-use of narrative and metaphor in the parables these fictions redescribe the extraordinary in the ordinary in such manner that the ordinary is transgressed and a new and extraordinary, but possible mode-of-being-in-the-world is disclosed. Religious language in general re-presents that basic confidence and trust in existence which *is* our fundamental faith, our basic authentic mode of being in the world.[89] Further this religious parabolic language, as fiction, does not merely re-present such faith. Those fictions redescribe ordinary existence to show how authentic existence itself may occur: a life lived totally in and by the event, the gift of faith and faith alone.

In reading the parables, we may suddenly find our imaginations conceiving the possibility that, after all, it may yet be possible to live as if in the presence of a God whose love knows no limits.[90] We find our sensitivities alert to the possibility that the mystics may indeed have found that this God can be loved in return without restriction.[91] We find the occasional hints, signals, rumors received in the too fleeting moments of limit-situations now re-presented and redescribed in a story, a fiction, which tells us that one possible mode-of-being-in-the-world is to live with explicit faith, with complete trust, with unrestricted love.[92] We find stories, proverbs, sayings, letters, poems which transgress even their ordinary literary genres to disclose an authentically religious mode-of-being-in-the-world (one whereby we self-consciously acknowledge and attempt to live by that basic faith we otherwise too fleetingly and too nervously find). We may also find that such a "way" does not ask us to leave this world for some "greater" supernatural realm.[93] Rather the "religions" themselves, I believe, fundamentally ask us to allow the limit-experiences of trust and confidence in the final graciousness of reality itself to provide the basic orientation to our lives.

Is such a mode of existing, this explicit faith, this risk to go to the limits, simply inhuman, non-experiential, meaningless? Although the entire argument of this book is to the effect that this question can and should be answered negatively, I do not hesitate to second the reluctance with which many in our culture will respond to it. It is well to remind ourselves, however, that this question is not identical with the more usual question on "religion" in our culture. As that latter query is ordinarily formulated, the participants in the discussion—secularists and religionists alike—assume that one must speak of "religion" either with a vacuousness that masks some other agenda or with a supernaturalist precision that exposes an unacceptable demand for a *sacrificium intellectus*. To state the matter with the bluntness needed, for many of us fundamentalism and supernaturalism of whatever religious tradition are dead and cannot return. At their best, Western Christians have learned too well—as Nietzsche reminds us—the truth that Christianity taught. That truth was and remains that one's fundamental Christian and human commitment is to the value of truth wherever it may lead and to that limit-transformation of all values signalized by the Christian demand for agapic love.[94] Fundamentalism of whatever tradition and by whatever criteria of truth one employs seems to me irretrievably false and illusory. Christian fundamentalism cannot and will not withstand the force for truth and the transformative power of self-sacrificing love which its own originating limit-language and its own past and present religious dynamism has set loose in our history.[95]

Whatever its ambiguities and shortcomings, the history of modern theology is largely the often painful and always partial articulation of that insight. As modern and post-modern religious thought in general and as these two chapters, however summarily and tentatively, may serve to suggest, the collapse of religious fundamentalism is not the end of religion. Religious language and religious experience promise, restore, and liberate a dimension to our lives which we can destroy only at the unwelcome price of self-deception and human impoverishment.[96] Religious language does not present a new, a supernatural world wherein we may escape the only world we know or wish to know. Rather that language re-presents our always threatened basic confidence and trust in the very meaningfulness of even our most cherished and most noble enterprises, science, morality, and culture.[97] That language discloses the reassurance needed that the final reality of our lives is in fact trustworthy. Such reassurance seems sorely needed when in various personal, communal, and historical situations we find our faith in the very meaningfulness of existence threatened. Such language allows us to re-present with something approaching adequacy those major irruptions of unmerited and eventful reorientations to our lives experienced in authentic love, joy, and even despair.

Religious language, whenever it is authentically related to a religious insight of extraordinary force as in the New Testament,[98] employs and explodes all our ordinary language forms in order to jar us into a recognition of what, on our own, can seem only a desirable but impossible possible mode-of-being-in-the-world. As proverbial, that religious language disorients us and forces us to see another, a seemingly impossible way of living with authenticity. As parabolic, that language redescribes our experience in such manner that the sense of its meaning (its now limit-metaphor) discloses a limit-referent which projects and promises that one can in fact live a life of wholeness, of total commitment, or radical honesty and agapic love in the presence of the gracious God of Jesus the Christ.[99]

Are such limit-experiences and limit-languages true? We are still not able to answer that question fully. And yet, in terms of criteria of existential meaningfulness there seem good reasons to affirm the reality of both a religious dimension of our common experience and the existential significance of the originating language of the Christian religious heritage. In terms of the criteria of coherent logical meaning, there also seem solid reasons to affirm that the category "limit" is a useful if merely initial index to religious meaning. There remain, to be sure, several central questions which must be raised before any fuller claims to truth may be advanced. As the argument of the entire first part of this book suggested, Christian religious language and experience make claims other than claims to existential meaningfulness. That language also makes claims that are legitimately labelled cognitive. Central among such historical claims is the insistence that the objective ground or referent of all limit-experience and limit-language is that reality Christians name God.

Notes

(1) Note the qualifications introduced in the last chapter, especially that "limit" is a single defining characteristic of religion, not a definition. Since these two chapters form a unit, full bibliographic data for many titles here may be found in the notes of chapter 5.

(2) Especially influential, therefore, is Paul Ricoeur's essay "Interpretation Theory" (presented to a colloquium of the faculty at the University of Chicago Divinity School, May 1971) on written texts; cf. also Hans-Georg Gadamer, *Wahrheit und Methode: Grundzuge einer philosophischen Hermeneutik*, p. 367. For published texts of Ricoeur that contain most of the material of his interpretation theory, cf. his essays "Creativity in Language," "The Task of Hermeneutics," and "The Hermeneutical Function of Distanciation" in *Philosophy Today* 17 (1973), 97–142.

(3) Cf. especially, Ian Ramsey, *Religious Language: An Empirical Placing of Theological Phrases* (New York: Macmillan, 1963); idem, *Models and Mystery* (London: Oxford, 1964); idem, *Christian Discourse* (New York: Oxford, 1965); idem (ed.), *Words About God* (New York: Harper & Row, 1971); Frederick Ferré, "Mapping the Logic of Models in Science and Theology," in *New Essays on Religious Language*, ed. by Dallas M. High (New York: Oxford University Press, 1969), pp. 54–

97; idem, "Metaphors, Models and Religion," *Soundings* LI (1968), 327–45; Robert P. Scharlemann, "Theological Models and Their Construction," in *Journal of Religion*, 53 (1973), 65–82; cf. also the recently published collection by Ian Ramsey, edited by Jerry H. Gill, *Christian Empiricism* (Grand Rapids: Eerdmans, 1974), pp. 59–143.

(4) For the history of these developments, inter alia, cf. J. A. Martin, Jr., *The New Dialogue Between Philosophy and Theology* (New York: Seabury, 1969); Raeburne S. Heimbeck, *Theology and Meaning: A Critique of Metatheological Skepticism* (Stanford: Stanford University Press, 1969); John Macquarrie, *God-Talk: An Examination of the Language and Logic of Theology* (New York: Harper & Row, 1967), esp. pp. 9–147. For an important original contribution to the discussion, cf. William A. Christian, *Meaning and Truth in Religion* (Princeton: Princeton University Press, 1964); Edward MacKinnon, "Linguistic Analysis and the Transcendence of God," *Proceedings for the Catholic Theological Society of America* 23 (1968), 28–45; idem, *Truth and Expression* (New York: Newman, 1971).

(5) A. J. Ayer, *Language, Truth and Logic* (New York: Dover, 1946), esp. pp. 114–20.

(6) Cf. Frederick Copleston, *Contemporary Philosophy: Studies in Logical Positivism and Existentialism* (London: Burns and Oates, 1956), pp. 41–60 passim.

(7) Antony Flew and Alasdair MacIntyre (ed.), *New Essays in Philosophical Theology* (New York: Macmillan, 1955): cf. especially his charge that the expression "God loves us" dies "the death of a thousand qualifications," p. 97. Note how Flew's position actually includes two principles, one logical and one empirical; cf. Schubert M. Ogden, "Reply to Flew's 'Theology and Falsification' in Retrospect," to be published in *Theology and Verification*, ed. Malcolm L. Diamond and Thomas Litzenburg, Jr. (Indianapolis: Bobbs-Merrill, 1975). For a more recent expression of the tradition, cf. Alastair McKinnon, *Falsification and Belief* (The Hague: Mouton, 1970).

(8) Cf. Basil Mitchell (ed.), in *Faith and Logic: Oxford Essays in Philosophical Theology* (London: Allen and Unwin, 1957), p. 5.

(9) On Wittgenstein's meaning as "use," cf. Garth Hallett, *Wittgenstein's Definition of Meaning as Use* (New York: Fordham University Press, 1967).

(10) R. M. Hare in "Theology and Falsification," in *New Essays in Philosophical Theology*, pp. 99–103.

(11) Cf. R. B. Braithwaite, *An Empiricist's View of the Nature of Religious Belief* (Cambridge: Cambridge University Press, 1955); for van Buren's use of Braithwaite, cf. Paul van Buren, *The Secular Meaning of the Gospel* (London: Macmillan, 1963), pp. 92–99.

(12) This "use" of religious (dimension and explicit) language has special relevance for this work to the criterion of "meaningfulness" described in chapter four.

(13) As the following section attempts to show, Ian Ramsey's work, for example, may be said to show both the "meaning" (odd logic) and "meaningfulness" (empirical placing) described in the section on criteria in chapter four.

(14) Cf. n. 3 above.

(15) Ian Ramsey, *Religious Language*, pp. 11–54.

(16) This is more representative of Ramsey's later work; cf., for example, his essay in *Words About God*, pp. 202–23.

(17) For an alternative formulation, note how Ramsey could claim to "show" these realities even when they cannot be "stated" except by an "odd language."

(18) Especially important here is the influence of Max Black in *Models and Metaphors* (Ithaca, N.Y.: Cornell University Press, 1962), esp. pp. 25–47.

(19) *Religious Language*, pp. 75–101. Note the parallel to the hermeneutical circle of limit-situations and explicitly religious limit-language suggested at the end of chapter five as *the* hermeneutical circle needing intrinsic "correlation" for the revisionist model of theology.

(20) Ibid., pp. 57–60.

(21) Cf. especially his clearly revisionist comments in "Metaphors, Models and Religion," and to the position articulated in his important texts *Language, Logic and God* (New York: Harper & Row, 1961), and *Basic Modern Philosophy of Religion* (New York: Scribner's, 1967).

(22) Cf., for example, his observations in "Mapping The Logic of Models," esp. pp. 74–85. The insistence of Robert Scharlemann in "Theological Models and Their Construction" that Ramsey's and Ferré's differing positions should employ a distinction between models and religious symbols as a difference in kind (p. 68) strikes me as a helpful suggestion for removing some unnecessary ambiguities in Ramsey and Ferré.

(23) Note how, for example, Paul Ricoeur shifts Ramsey's British expression of "oddness" to his own more Continental and Kantian expression "limit" in "The Specificity of Religious Language" (unpublished lecture, University of Chicago Divinity School, Spring 1974), esp. pp. 16–18.

(24) *Mutatis mutandis,* the language of Buddhism and Hinduism could be studied to disclose their limit-character. The present study is not restricted in principle but only in fact to the limit-character of Christian religious language. To repeat our consistent insistence, even the limit-character of Christian religious language is, I believe, an important but not exclusive characteristic of that language. The present analysis does not investigate, for example, the further claim that religious language is intrinsically "dialectical," although it seems to set a context for a new investigation of that claim.

(25) I am deeply indebted for what follows to the philosophical analysis of Paul Ricoeur and the exegesis of Norman Perrin. Wherever possible I shall refer to their published work on this section. This will often not be possible, however, since many of the major insights were formulated in privately circulated notes of Professors Ricoeur and Perrin for a course in which the three of us investigated the question of "Religious Language" from the viewpoints of our distinct disciplines (University of

Chicago Divinity School, Spring 1974). Since the published versions are not available at this time, I shall refer to the unpublished. However, Ricoeur's three lectures will be published in revised form in *Semeia* (Missoula: Scholars' Press, Summer 1975), and Perrin's work will appear in a book entitled *The Kingdom of God and the Parables of Jesus* (Philadelphia: Fortress, 1975).

(26) More exactly, of the particular limit-character of that Christian mode-of-being-in-the-world.

(27) Cf. chapter four, the section on "Interpretation Theory," for the meanings of "sense," "referent," etc., and for references to Ricoeur's essay on "Interpretation Theory."

(28) Inter alia, cf. Robert Funk, *Language, Hermeneutic and the Word of God* (New York: Harper & Row, 1966); Dominic Crossan, *In Parables* (Harper & Row, New York, 1973); Norman Perrin, "The Parables of Jesus as Parables, as Metaphors and as Aesthetic Objects," *Journal of Religion* 50 (1970), 340–46; idem, "The Modern Interpretation of the Parables of Jesus and the Problem of Hermeneutics," *Interpretation* 25 (1971), 131–48; idem, *The New Testament: An Introduction* (New York: Harcourt, Brace Jovanovich, 1974), esp. pp. 3–39; Dan O. Via, *The Parables: Their Literary and Existential Dimension* (Philadelphia: Fortress, 1967); Amos N. Wilder, *Early Christian Rhetoric: The Language of the Gospel* (New York: Harper & Row, 1964); William A. Beardslee, *Literary Criticism of the New Testament, New Testament Series*, ed. by Dan O. Via (Philadelphia: Fortress, 1970); *Semeia: An Experimental Journal for Biblical Criticism*, vol. I (Missoula: Scholars' Press, 1974).

(29) Cf. Paul Ricoeur, "The Specificity of Religious Language," pp. 1–15.

(30) Cf. William A. Beardslee, "The Uses of the Proverb in the Synoptic Tradition," *Interpretation*, 24 (1970); 61–76; idem, *Literary Criticism of the New Testament*, pp. 30–42; Ricoeur, "The Specificity of Religious Language," pp. 5–8.

(31) As in the sense of that phrase in Heidegger. For an extensive and independent use of Heideggerian categories, cf. Dominic Crossan, *In Parables*. On the use of Heidegger in the work of Fuchs and Ebeling, cf. Paul J. Achtemeier, *An Introduction to the New Hermeneutic* (Philadelphia: Westminster, 1969), esp. pp. 26–55; and James M. Robinson, "Hermeneutics since Barth," in *The New Hermeneutic*.

(32) Cf. Norman Perrin, *Rediscovering The Teaching of Jesus* (New York: Harper & Row, 1967) for his full survey; idem, *A Modern Pilgrimage in New Testament Christology* (Philadelphia: Fortress, 1974), esp. pp. 1–10, 41–57, 104–22; on Perrin's work, cf. Hans Dieter Betz (ed.), *Christology and A Modern Pilgrimage: A Discussion with Norman Perrin* (Claremont: New Testament Colloquium, 1971). For Ricoeur's interpretation of Perrin's work here, cf. "The Specificity of Religious Language," pp. 3–5.

(33) Cf. Norman Perrin, *The Kingdom of God in the Teaching of Jesus* (London: SCM, 1963), for the historical survey; idem, *Rediscovering The Teaching of Jesus*, for Perrin's own constructive exegetical resolution.

(34) Cf. Norman Perrin, "Presidential Address," *Society for Biblical Literature*, 1973.

(35) Inter alia, cf. *Christ and Time: The Primitive Christian Conception of Time and History* (Philadelphia: Westminster, 1950), for Cullmann's development of his christological *Heilsgeschichte*.

(36) Note how this insistence parallels the conclusion of chapter five on the reciprocal hermeneutical dependence of limit-situations and religious limit-languages.

(37) Besides the works of Perrin, Via, Crossan, and Funk listed in n. 28 above, the still towering achievement of Joachim Jeremias remains a classic; cf. Joachim Jeremias, *The Parables of Jesus*.

(38) Ibid., esp. Part II, pp. 23–115.

(39) As ordinarily preached in the Christian churches, clearly not; as present in the New Testament, yes.

(40) For an extensive history of the development of the "four senses" of scripture, cf. the monumental four-volume work of Henri de Lubac, *Exégèse mèdiévale* (Paris: Aubier, 1959–63). For a comparison of de Lubac, Ricoeur, and Lévi-Strauss on symbolism, cf. M. Von Esbroeck, *Herméneutique, structuralisme et exégèse* (Paris: Desclée, 1968), esp. pp. 101–97 on de Lubac.

(4)Adolf Jülicher, *Die Gleichnisreden Jesu* (Darmstadt: Wissenschaftliche Buchgesellschaft, 1963). Cf. the helpful discussion of the significance of Jülicher's work in Joachim Jeremias, *The Parables of Jesus*, pp. 16–20; and Werner Georg Kümmel, *The New Testament: The History of the Investigation of Its Problems* (Nashville: Abingdon, 1972), pp. 186–8.

(42) Cf. the discussion in chapter five on the liberal difficulty in equating religion and morality. Perhaps this liberal handicap can serve to remind the contemporary post-liberal theologian of the importance of developing a hermeneutical relationship between limit-situations and the limit-questions to morality and the explicitly religious language of the New Testament tradition. For the reverse side of the difficulty (viz., conservative Christians' temptation to "moralism"), cf. the suggestive analysis of Charles Davis, *Temptations of Religion* (New York: Harper & Row, 1973), pp. 72–89. I am impressed by the oral remarks of Bernard Meland that Christian theologians should demand "gold coinage" (i.e., radical experiential use—or, in my own categories, "meaningfulness") for their often too familiar words. For a good example of such "gold coinage," cf. Meland's own post-liberal formulation of the Christian doctrine of forgiveness in Bernard E. Meland, *The Realities of Faith: The Revolution in Cultural Forms*, pp. 242–7.

(43) This is not to suggest, as is sometimes done, that allegories cannot have a religious use: for examples, cf. de Lubac's work on the four senses cited above. It is to suggest that parables are ordinarily not allegories.

(44) On Jeremias, cf. n. 37 above; for Dodd, cf. C. H. Dodd, *The Parables of the Kingdom* (London: James Nisbet, 1935).

(45) For an analysis of scriptural methods of interpretation here, cf. Edgar V. McKnight, *What Is Form Criticism? New Testament Series* (Philadelphia: Fortress, 1969); and Norman Perrin, *What Is Redaction Criticism? New Testament Series*

(Philadelphia: Fortress, 1971). For an excellent summary of the results of historical study of the New Testament, cf. Robert M. Grant, *A Historical Introduction to the New Testament* (London: Collins, 1963).

(46) Oral comment of Perrin in course on "Religious Language" cited above.

(47) For the history of the rediscovery of the eschatological-religious, not ethical, cast of New Testament thought from Wrede and Schweitzer to the present, cf. Norman Perrin, *The Kingdom of God in the Teaching of Jesus*. The classical expression of this eschatological insistence remains the exegetically dated but still powerful picture portrayed by Albert Schweitzer in *The Quest of the Historical Jesus* (New York: Macmillan, 1964). The more recent debate is summarized in James M. Robinson, *A New Quest of the Historical Jesus* (Naperville, Ill.: Allenson, 1959).

(48) The category "implied author" I import from the literary criticism of Wayne Booth, in *The Rhetoric of Fiction*, esp. pp. 71–76 and 211–21, in order to avoid the unnecessary difficulties associated with reconstructions of Jesus of Nazareth's consciousness. This issue will be discussed in chapter nine: cf. Van A. Harvey, *The Historian and the Believer*, pp. 164–204, 246–93.

(49) The problem, once again, is the need to correlate the limit-experiences of our common human experience and the limit-vision of the New Testament, as in the correlating efforts of these two reciprocal chapters.

(50) For references, cf. n. 28 above: the more recent influence of structuralist analysis, especially upon the work of Dan O. Via may prove especially important here.

(51) Cf. Paul Ricoeur, "The Metaphorical Process" (unpublished lecture, University of Chicago Divinity School, Spring 1974), pp. 1–4 (on Jülicher), 4–10 (on theories of metaphor). Ricoeur's own extensive work on metaphor will be published by the University of Toronto Press in 1975.

(52) A "dead metaphor"—itself perhaps a dead metaphor!—is one which no longer allows any real disclosure. Cf. Paul Ricoeur, "Creativity In Language: Word, Polysemy, Metaphor," in *Philosophy Today* XVII (1973), esp. 105–112. Recall, for example, G. K. Chesterton's remark on the then (1930's) popular metaphor "off-color" that it sounds like "it was invented by Henry James in an agony of verbal precision."

(53) Inter alia, cf. Monroe Beardsley, "The Metaphorical Twist," in Warren Shibles (ed.), *Essays on Metaphor* (Whitewater, Wisc.: The Language Press, 1972), pp. 73–93; I. A. Richards, *Philosophy of Rhetoric* (New York: Oxford, 1936), esp. pp. 90–94 on the "transaction theory" of metaphor; Max Black, *Models and Metaphors*, pp. 25–48; Philip Wheelwright, *Metaphor and Reality* (Bloomington: Indiana University Press, 1962).

(54) Max Black, *Models and Metaphors*, pp. 32–3, 40–2. Ricoeur's criticism of Black's use of these tamed metaphors seems appropriate here.

(55) Monroe Beardsley, "The Metaphorical Twist," p. 74: "According to its rival, the Verbal-Opposition Theory, no such importation or composition occurs at all, but instead a special feat of language, or verbal play, involving two levels of mean-

ing in the modifier itself. When a predicate is metaphorically adjoined to a subject, the predicate loses its ordinary extension, because it acquires a new intension—perhaps one that it has in no other context. And this twist of meaning is forced by inherent tensions, or oppositions, within the metaphor itself." Cf. also Paul Ricoeur "The Metaphorical Process," for the application of the "metaphorical process" to parables.

(56) Cf. Nathan A. Scott, Jr., *Three American Moralists: Mailer, Bellow, Trilling* (South Bend: University of Notre Dame Press, 1974), pp. 81–97.

(57) Some examples from Norman Mailer: *Miami and the Siege of Chicago: An Informal History of the Republican and Democratic Conventions, 1968* (New York: Signet, 1968), pp. 123 (on Humphrey), 130–1 (on McCarthy).

(58) Which is, perhaps, why we recognize the truth of Aristotle's famous dictum: "The greatest thing by far is to be a master of metaphor."

(59) Cf. Paul Ricoeur, "The Metaphorical Process," pp. 4–24.

(60) Cf. Dominic Crossan, *In Parables.*

(61) Cf. the lectures "The Metaphorical Process" and "The Specificity of Religious Language."

(62) Cf. Norman Perrin's analysis of the history of parable interpretation, "The Modern Interpretation of the Parables of Jesus and the Problem of Hermeneutics," for a summary-analysis of the work of Jülicher and Jeremias leading up to the work of Wilder, Funk, Via, and Perrin himself; idem, *The New Testament: An Introduction,* on Crossan's contribution, p. 291.

(63) Cf. Paul Ricoeur, "The Specificity of Religious Language," p. 8: "It is what I call the extravagance within the parables. This trait has not been emphasized, even where the 'realism' of the parables has been insisted upon. The parables tell stories that could have happened or without a doubt have happened, but it is this realism of situations, characters and plots that precisely heightens the eccentricity of the modes of behavior to which the kingdom of heaven is compared."

(64) Dan O. Via, *The Parables.* For examples, cf. esp. pp. 110–76.

(65) This is not to suggest that "limit" and "eschatological" are synonymous terms. Further discussion of this matter may be found in chapter ten's analysis of various eschatological theologies.

(66) Paul Ricoeur, "The Specificity of Religious Language," pp. 8–15.

(67) Note how "Kingdom of God" can function as either an "image" (i.e., a non-linguistic reality), a metaphor, a symbol (i.e., an image or myth with the characteristic of permanency), or a myth (i.e., a narrative extension of an image, metaphor, or symbol). The expression, however used, also includes cognitive claims (e.g., there is a God and he has some relationship with humanity). Those latter claims, as chapters seven and eight argue, can be specified and should be examined on metaphysical grounds. Ricoeur himself has expressed some serious cautionary remarks to this po-

sition of mine (ibid, pp. 22–4). At least two of those cautions should be quoted as directly relevant to the entire argument of this revisionist model: "I am more reluctant to characterize by this phrase 'method of correlation' the content itself of a theology ruled by this polarity of 'sources.' The history of Western culture shows abundantly that this polarization very often became a dramatic confrontation between opposite claims, exacerbated by the demonic passions of clericalism and 'free thinking.' . . . The 'conflict of interpretations' seems to be the unavoidable existential trait which a 'method of correlation' assumes today. . . . This implies that the conceptuality which would express the concrete stage of confrontation characteristic of our situation should take into account the tensions and paradoxes which rule this dramatic confrontation. We must concede that this kind of conceptuality is still lacking, because we have received from the tradition mainly the conceptual expressions of the *hautes époques*, i.e., from the high moments when our culture dreamt of its complete integration and projected these dreams in systems where harmony overcame war, at least in discourse. . . . In fact, we 'think' with the débris and the offspring resulting from the wreckage of these systems and—perhaps—of the dreams which these systems brought to language." A few brief observations on these important criticisms: First, the criteria for the present revisionist model are not only metaphysical but include criteria of relative adequacy for meaningfulness (especially chapters four, nine and ten). Second, the metaphysical criteria seem demanded by the cognitive uses of religious language (like "Kingdom *of God*"); they do not *exhaust* such language but they are implied by it (chapters seven and eight). Third, my hope is that the present revisionary metaphysical position is not one from the *hautes époques* but a legitimate revision of those earlier "dreams" (chapters seven and eight). Indeed, these modern forms of metaphysics may perhaps even meet the excellent demands for "limit-concepts" developed by Paul Ricoeur, ibid., pp. 30–36.

(68) Joachim Jeremias, *The Parables of Jesus*, pp. 128–32.

(69) Hence a hermeneutical correlation between the meanings found in these two "sources" may be possible.

(70) Namely, those limit-situations disclosive of the religious dimension of our common human experience.

(71) Different religious traditions, to be sure, will articulate these explications differently. For a suggestive analysis of Christianity and Buddhism here, cf. John B. Cobb, *The Structure of Christian Existence* (Philadelphia: Westminster, 1967), esp. pp. 60–73, 107–37.

(72) The qualitative difference is determined by the limit-character of either an autonomous religious dimension to the rest of our experience or an explicitly religious language as transformative of the rest of our experience.

(73) For an explicitly dialectical formulation of that "other," "limit" dimension, cf. Louis Dupré, *The Other Dimension.* For an analysis of the hermeneutical aspects of the question, cf. Edward Schillebeeckx, "The Crisis in the Language of Faith as a Hermeneutical Problem," and for another formulation for the use of narrative as primary religious language, cf. Johann Baptist Metz, "A Short Apology of Narrative," in *The Crisis of Religious Language*, eds. Johann Baptist Metz and Jean Pierre Jossua, Concilium 85 (New York: Herder and Herder, 1973), pp. 31–46 and 84–99 respectively.

(74) As in many "official" uses of religious language and many "Hollywood" versions of contemporary *Angst* in contemporary religion.

(75 In the sense spelled out criteriologically in chapter four.

(76) Buddhism, like Christianity, is not exhaustively defined by the characteristic "limit" character to its language and practices but seems clearly involved with that character.

(77) William James, *The Varieties of Religious Experience* (New York: Collier, 1961), pp. 52–3, for James' defense of his appeal to mystical states as "the most one-sided, exaggerated and intense" forms of religious experience.

(78) One may recall the dictum cited by Frank Sheed on the Trinity: "I wish there were four of them, so I could believe more of them." On the more serious side, one may recall Gabriel Marcel's important distinction between a "mystery" and a "problem": inter alia, cf. Gabriel Marcel, *The Philosophy of Existence: A Metaphysical Journal* (Chicago: Regnery, 1962), pp. 1–25.

(79) Inter alia, cf. Karl Rahner, "The Concept of Mystery in Catholic Theology," *Theological Investigations*, IV (Baltimore: Helicon, 1966), pp. 36–77. On Rahner's position, cf. Ann Carr, "Theology and Experience in the Thought of Karl Rahner," *Journal of Religion* 53 (1973), 359–77; and Peter Mann, "The Transcendental or the Political Kingdom?" *New Blackfriars* 50, 51 (1969–1970), 805–12, 4–16; idem, "Masters in Israel IV: The Later Theology of Karl Rahner," *Clergy Review* 54 (1969), 936–8.

(80) The "Scopes trial" in Tennessee in the thirties was perhaps the clearest if not the most shocking recent example of this possibility.

(81) Inter alia, cf. Rudolf Bultmann, "Preaching: Genuine and Secularized," in *Religion and Culture: Essays in Honor of Paul Tillich*, ed. by Walter Leibrecht (London: SCM, 1959), esp. pp. 241–2.

(82) The significant differences should also be determined. A beginning in that direction (the direction of a dogmatic as distinct from a fundamental theology) is made in chapter nine's employment of criteria of relative adequacy on the question of christology. The German philosophical tradition's use of the paradigm of "identity and difference" (as employed by Karl Rahner and Johann Baptist Metz) may prove especially fruitful for that dogmatic exercise in dialectics. For an example of its employment, cf. Johann Baptist Metz, "Erlösung und Emanzipation," in *Erlösung und Emanzipation*, ed. by L. Scheffczyk, *Quaestiones Disputatae* (Freiburg: Herder, 1974), pp. 120–40.

(83) For example, cf. Robert Heilbroner, *An Inquiry into The Human Prospect.*

(84) Perhaps it is not too much to hope that at least an initial indication of this has been provided by these two chapters; the further social-transformative issues emerge in chapter ten.

(85) Cf. Herbert Braun, "Der Sinn der neutestamentlichen Christologie," *Gesammelte Studien zum Neuen Testament und seiner Umwelt* (Tübingen: J. C. B. Mohr, 1962), pp. 243–62.

(86) Paul Ricoeur, "The Specificity of Religious Language," pp. 5–8.

(87) Inter alia, cf. Ernst Fuchs, *Glaube und Erfahrung* (Tübingen: J. C. B. Mohr, 1965), esp. pp. 247–51.

(88) Chapter nine will treat the question of the redescriptive power of fiction more extensively.

(89) That christological language adds a decisive "more" to that representation (of religious theism or theological anthropology) is also discussed in chapter nine.

(90) One may recall how the interpretation theory articulated in chapter four and employed here appeals primarily to the imagination rather than the will as in the more ethically oriented hermeneutical methods of Bultmann and the post-Bultmannians.

(91) Cf. William James, *The Varieties of Religious Experience*, esp. pp. 21–39, 299–337; for James' own "over-belief," cf. pp. 396–402.

(92) Cf. chapter nine for an initial spelling out of the "Christian story."

(93) "Supernatural" is employed here, as throughout this work, as a rough equivalent of "fundamentalist."

(94) Note how a commitment to the value, truth, may allow for the emergence of other values, including the sublation of agapic love: cf. Bernard Lonergan, *Method in Theology*, pp. 27–57, 235–45.

(95) The dilemma of the fundamentalist seems to be that he must domesticate his own religious language and experience (for example, through obscurantism) in order to disallow the demands for truth in that language and experience from erupting into his own secure and tamed world.

(96) The basic dialectic remains that of performance and concept, not merely concept and concept. A welcome result of the "third stage" of the analytical discussion may be its ability to free one from the latter dialectic and for the first.

(97) Inter alia, cf. the essays in Andrew Greeley and Gregory Baum, *The Persistence of Religion*, Concilium 81 (New York: Herder and Herder, 1973); Paul Ricoeur, "The Critique of Religion," and "The Language of Faith," *Union Seminary Quarterly Review* XXVIII (1973), 203–25; Langdon Gilkey, "Religious Dimensions of Scientific Inquiry," *Journal of Religion* (1970), 245–67.

(98) For a summary description, cf. Norman Perrin, "Ways of Being Religious in the New Testament," in *The New Testament: An Introduction*, pp. 305–9.

(99) It might be noted that the Christian tradition has consistently recognized the distinctively Christian character of "faith, hope, and love," as in Thomas Aquinas' definition of the latter as the "theological" virtues distinct from such "moral" virtues (a necessary pleonasm) as prudence, temperance, and justice. The discussions surrounding Anders Nygren's *Agape and Eros*, for example, could be retrieved in the attempt to determine the Christian mode-of-being-in-the-world for a Christian dogmatics.

Chapter 7

The Question of God: Metaphysics Revisited

INTRODUCTION: Limit-Language and Limit-Concepts

The two preceding chapters addressed one principal issue: the meaning and meaningfulness of religious language and experience. Two conclusions were advanced from the standpoint of a basically phenomenological analysis of our common human experience and of a hermeneutical analysis of the New Testament language of the Christian religion: first, the meanings of both religious language and experience are helpfully characterized by the concepts limit-language and limit-experience;[1] second, the existential meaningfulness of such language may be described as its ability to allow for the disclosure of certain possible modes-of-being-in-the-world which, *qua* religious, are not trans-worldly but recognizably and authentically human.

Such initial responses do not, of course, entirely fulfill the aim of the enterprise called revisionist theology. As the earlier methodological sections insisted, however important the attitudinal and character-forming aspects of religion may prove to be, still the cognitive claims of that experience and language must also be analyzed. Indeed, in the Christian religion such cognitive claims have played a central constitutive role for the practice of the religion itself.[2] For modern and contemporary critics of Christianity, moreover, the challenge to traditional cognitive claims has been forthright and often devastating. From a yet more basic viewpoint, there seems no good reason to abandon the position of common sense and philosophy alike that experience and understanding mutually imply one another. We do not, in fact, experience without some understanding of that experience and we do not understand *in vacuo*: we always understand some experience. The implications of this commonplace dictum are considerable. The centuries-long effort to articulate in explicitly cognitive terms the correct understanding of Christian religious experience and language has resulted in the development of certain "doctrines" or explicit articles of belief. Such doctrines are not in fact peculiar to an understanding of religious experience and language. Rather, any understanding of any experience—moral or aesthetic, for example—inevitably gives rise to the development of explicit cognitive doctrines for a given ethical, scientific, aesthetic, or religious tradition.[3]

To many contemporary analysts of Christian experience and language, moreover, the central, indeed the constitutive cognitive claim of that religion is its articulation of the Christian God as the sole and single objective ground of all reality.[4] With that judgment I am in full agreement. Indeed, as suggested earlier, not the least merit of the recent "death of God" critics was their ability to pinpoint the central cognitive claim of Christianity as its understanding of God.[5] In a still wider context, not the least merit of the various "hermeneutics of suspicion" on religion that have emerged in the last two centuries—of which Feuerbach, Freud, Nietzsche, Marx, and Dewey are among the clearest expressions—is the consistent insistence of contemporary thinkers that the traditional Christian understanding of God must be explicitly defended or rejected by Christian thinkers. That defense, for the fundamental theologian at least, must be conducted on grounds other than his own or his community's vision of faith, or even his own or his community's defense of the continuing existential meaningfulness of religious experience and language.[6] It is well to remember that not only can other authentically religious traditions—such as Buddhism—deny the need to maintain the theistic claim;[7] even some Christian theologians—and, one suspects, many Christians in practice if not in theory—effectively deny that claim.[8]

This and the next chapter on theism, therefore, will attempt a summary-interpretation of certain selected contemporary positions on the question of the Christian God. At the very outset, I must state that the position defended in these chapters is not identical to that of classical Christian theism.[9] For reasons advanced in the next chapter, the classical position seems untenable from either an analysis of our common experience or an analysis of Christian self-understanding as expressed in its scriptures. Within the pluralism of positions on the question of alternatives to classical theism, I will suggest that the position called neo-classical theism[10] is a position worthy of more serious attention than it has ordinarily received from either the critics or the proponents of classical Christian theism. More importantly, that position may also be capable of validating its cognitive claims from the point of view of both "sources" of religious reflection. Indeed, for the several neo-classical thinkers whose important work that chapter will attempt to summarize and interpret, the meaning and truth of the theistic claim of the Christian religion can be validated both by an analysis of our common experience and by a hermeneutical analysis of the Christian scriptures.

An important methodological note must be entered at this point. In the analysis of the religious dimension of our common experience, we claimed only that a phenomenological analysis can show a meaning ("limit") and a meaningfulness for that experience. In the present analysis of the theistic claim, however, an explicitly metaphysical (or transcendental) analysis is also demanded.[11] If the argument for the need for that second form of analysis articulated in Part I was sound, no further extensive argument for the use of metaphysics should be required. Here I shall simply rearticulate those points which seem more exigent at this further material stage of the inquiry than they did in the more formal and methodological analysis of Part I.

If religious language and religious experience are correctly described as limit-language and limit-experience, then any attempt to judge the explicit cognitive claims involved in that language would seem to demand two factors: first, those cognitive claims should be explicated with as much *conceptual* clarity as possible. The analysis must depart from the properly metaphorical, proverbial, common-sense, and symbolic language of the originating religious language and must develop an explicitly conceptual language. This latter language does not claim to capture the full existential meaningfulness of the originating language.[12] Conceptual language does claim to articulate certain cognitive beliefs (or doctrines) that are either clearly implied by or even explicitly referred to by such language. The second factor is more historical in character: an explicit cognitive belief in the objective reality of God has historically been central to traditional Christian religious language. Given the prior analysis of religious language and experience, it seems fair to conclude that, for the Christian religion at least, the word "God" has a primary use or function to refer to the objective ground in reality itself for those limit-experiences of a final confidence and trust disclosed in Christian God-language.[13]

As this analysis proceeds, I shall give more detailed conceptual clarity to the Christian theistic concept. For the moment, I am concerned only to indicate the need for such conceptual clarity and the need for metaphysical analysis to investigate the theistic claim. Initially, consider the following possibility: if it be proper to speak of God as the objective ground in reality itself for the limit-experience and limit-language of the Christian religion, then it also seems logically necessary to describe this concept "God" as a limit-concept.[14] One may then ask whether there is in fact a mode of analysis which can investigate the cognitive claims of that kind of limit-concept. Neither the disciplines of empirical science, nor ethics, nor aesthetics, nor general cultural analysis make any such claim.[15] One mode of analysis, metaphysical or transcendental analysis, does. Does that claim hold?

As the earlier discussions of the "verification" and "falsification" debates indicated, the claim for metaphysics is often under as great a suspicion of intellectual irresponsibility as is the claim for the objective reality of God. That earlier and more formal analysis indicated some general reasons why the suspicion of all metaphysical inquiry as a legitimate, indeed necessary, enterprise seems ill-founded. At the present state of inquiry, let us return to this widely disputed claim for a metaphysical analysis of theistic language by presenting an argument in more immediate relationship to the prior analyses of religious language and experience.[16]

This "detour" from the explicit question of God to the prior question of metaphysics seems necessary if the metaphysical analysis of the next "theistic" chapter is to merit any consideration at all. If this detour through certain representative cases for and against the use of metaphysical analysis for investigating the theistic claims of religious language is successful, then the succeeding chapter's revisionist understanding of Christian theism may seem more probable than either the proponents or the critics of classical Christian theism ordinarily allow.

Moreover, if it be the case that the revisionist model for fundamental theology must validate the cognitive claims for the religious language under investigation, it becomes imperative that the theologian develop criteria for meaning and truth which can validate or invalidate those claims. For that means of validation, in my judgment, the theologian must turn to metaphysics. Such a turn, to be sure, cannot be made too rapidly. The historical fact remains that most contemporary theologians seem either to distrust or completely reject this use of metaphysical thought in theology.[17]

The ambition of this chapter is not to attempt a reply to the several philosophical and anti-philosophical (e.g., historicist and fideist) charges against the use of metaphysics in theology.[18] Rather, I wish to continue the discussion of the prior chapters on the limit-language of religion in order to see whether metaphysics is useful from that standpoint. In line with this aim, the remainder of the present chapter has three principal sections, each of which will attempt to articulate certain major questions on the use of metaphysical discourse. The first will investigate the "tentative claims" for metaphysics advanced by Ian Ramsey and Frederick Ferré as well as the "strong claims" for metaphysics advanced by Schubert Ogden. Ramsey and Ferré have been chosen for investigation to give the present analysis a clearer continuity with the earlier analyses of religious language. The choice of Ogden may facilitate the analysis of neo-classical theism in the chapter to follow.

The next section will investigate the recent and important charge of Anders Nygren that metaphysics is not only meaningless as scientific language but that its theological use is self-destructive. Since Nygren's recent work *Meaning and Method: Prolegomena to a Scientific Philosophy of Religion and a Scientific Theology* both summarizes and advances the linguistic discussion on the theological use of metaphysics, his work provides a unique opportunity to see the issues clearly.

Finally, I will attempt to articulate some crucial relationships between the properly conceptual language of metaphysics and the ordinarily metaphorical, symbolic, parabolic, and mythical languages of the originating religious discourse upon which metaphysics reflects. At that point, we may achieve some further clarification for a central question of this entire work: the relationship between the conceptual language of theology and the originating and usually metaphorical, symbolic, parabolic, and mythical languages of the religious tradition which theology is designed to reflect upon.

RELIGIOUS LANGUAGE AND COGNITIVE CLAIMS: The
Possibility and Necessity of Metaphysics

Many analytic philosophers of the third stage seem to make what can be labelled "tentative claims" for the need for metaphysics. That need is more clearly defined as the use of metaphysical thought to investigate the cognitive claims of religious languages (e.g., Baelz, Richmond, Martin).[19] As was the case with their influential analyses of religious language, Ian Ramsey and Frederick Ferré provide representative and important formulations of this general question.

Ian Ramsey: The Prospect for a "Theological Metaphysics" [20]

Since we have already examined Ramsey's basic analysis of the "empirical placing" of religious language and the "disclosure" functions which religious and theological language allow, we shall assume that prior discussion in order to see what "prospects" for metaphysics Ramsey believes his position allows. Ramsey's basic concern here may be found in his attempt to show how the word "God" functions both religiously and metaphysically. His fundamental argument for metaphysics is entirely consistent with his general position: the word God functions as the supreme "integrator" word for the "cosmic mapping" of *all* experience.[21] The word God has a properly *metaphysical* use for Ramsey, since metaphysics itself is that function of language which provides a "word map" with reference to which we may both *plot* our "cosmic position" and *integrate* both our scientifically observable and non-observable (e.g., "I") languages. Just as an awareness of the "I" as the non-observable integrator of all my experience is ordinarily evoked and disclosed through circumstances (e.g., limit-situations) that cause "the ice to break" or the "light to dawn," so too an awareness of the non-observable God as the *supreme integrator of all experience* may be evoked and disclosed through a modified use of the traditional "proofs" for God's existence.[22]

Perhaps this brief analysis has already indicated why I label Ramsey's position a "tentative case" for metaphysics. Ramsey does *not* hold that the "proofs" are really logical or classically metaphysical "demonstrations." [23] Rather, the "proofs" are best approached as occasions for "disclosure." They evoke our sense of the ultimate mystery of the world (for example, by disclosing our real contingency). They perform this disclosive function by leading through their odd logic to the point where "the light dawns," and we may now "see" the presence and role of the non-observable God as the supreme integrator of all experience. For Ramsey, the disclosure of God is directly parallel to the disclosure of the non-observable "I" as the "integrator word" of all my personal experience. This position does not really provide an argument for the use of metaphysics to examine the cognitive claims of religious language. For Ramsey, however, his analysis does show that the word God can function in a disclosive manner which may be described linguistically as a "theological metaphysics." [24] Whether Ramsey's position can really meet Nygren's charge of "category-mixing" is a challenge which can only be clarified after Nygren's own position is analyzed.[25] For the moment, it may prove sufficient to note the highly tentative character of the case for metaphysics which Ramsey advances as his proposed solution to the "cognitive claim" question of religious language.

Frederick Ferré: The Logic of Theistic Language and the Place of "Metaphysical Facts" [26]

On the question of the use of metaphysics for examining religious cognitive claims, Ferré's analysis differs significantly from Ramsey's. Although there is still a "tentative" character to Ferré's own argument, he does in fact argue that the very logic of theism implies, indeed demands, a strictly metaphysical resolution. Moreover, Ferré raises this question in the context of his own highly sophisticated linguistic analysis of the various "functions" of religious language. More exactly, Ferré develops the notion of three basic modes of analysis for any adequate investigation of religious language:[27] first, "syntactics" determines the "internal language games" of "first order" religious utterances. The analysis can and should be made of the various uses (e.g., devotional) of religious language by those who engage in that particular "language-game." Second, "interpretics" can analyze the non-cognitive uses of religious language insofar as such uses disclose certain feelings or attitudes, certain affirmations of policy, or certain performances. Third, "semantics" completes the analysis of religious language by explicitly raising the question of what is the meaning of and what is the ontological status for the *referent* of religious language.

This third mode of analysis is demanded by the other two. "Syntactics" demands "semantics" since religious and theological language precisely as a "language-game" with its own internal "syntactic rules" is not itself simply "about" the religious language game. In fact, engagement in syntactics should eventually impel the interpreter to raise the question of the "referent" of the language. This position, it may be noted, would seem to be in basic harmony with Paul Ricoeur's more hermeneutically oriented analysis of how the interpretation of the "sense" of a text (e.g., via structuralist analysis) should lead to an explicitly hermeneutical analysis of the "referent" of the text.[28]

"Interpretics" also demands "semantics." For we need some understanding about "what is known and what is real" for religious language in order to use successfully such language in moral, aesthetic, and psychological ways. A general understanding of "what is known and what is real" can be arrived at through some form of critical reasoning. In principle, critical reflection can formulate what is known as "fact" in the natural and social sciences and what is *referred to* as "fact" by religious and theological language. At this point in his analysis, Ferré makes the intriguing suggestion that the "facts" referred to by religious and theological language are correctly described as "metaphysical facts." [29] Hence the role of semantics will involve two principal functions: a specification of the "metaphysical facts" referred to by religious and theological language; a specification of the criteria for that reflective discipline (metaphysics) which critically investigates the cognitive claims involved in any genuine "metaphysical facts."

There remains, of course, the need to clarify the concepts, "metaphysical facts" and "metaphysical criteria," employed by Ferré. Yet here is where what I would call the suggestive but still tentative character of Ferré's case for metaphysics appears. On the one hand, it is clear that he does hold that religious and theological language semantically refers to "metaphysical facts." On the other hand, the exact nature of the cognitive claims involved in such "facts" (and thereby for the "referents" of religious and theological language) is not entirely clear.[30]

Certain factors, to be sure, do seem clear. Like scientific facts, metaphysical facts are both "given" in and by experience ("facts"), and *yet not simply* given but dependent upon our conceptual (here "metaphysical") interpretations. Furthermore, the nature of this kind of interpretation is best described as "conceptual synthesis": "A metaphysical system is a construct of concepts designed to provide coherence for all 'the facts' on the basis of a theoretical model drawn from among the facts." [31] Finally, the criteria for determining the truth of "theism," like the truth of any "metaphysical fact" are coherence and the adequacy of the "metaphysical" model (here theism) for all our experience. However, when one asks just how he might determine the "adequacy" of any metaphysical "fact" for all experience he seems to be left with the thought that ultimately this is a matter of "belief." Such "metaphysical" belief, to be sure, can be supported by the ability of the "fact" to survive the "tests of experience." [32]

In the next section, we may be able to find a way to specify further both those criteria and the character of that belief in a manner fundamentally faithful to Ferré's suggestive comments. For the moment, however, we might simply note that, however tentative Ferré's final case for metaphysical facts may be, his analysis, in my judgment, does advance Ramsey's position at three crucial points. Ferré continues to insist that however useful religious and theological language may be "syntactically" and "interpretively," those uses are *dependent* upon establishing the semantic referent of such language as a cognitive one.[33] That referent can be designated logically as a metaphysical referent.[34] All such referents should be adjudicated in accordance with the same general criteria for all metaphysical concepts (coherence and adequacy to experience) and should be articulated in strictly conceptual terms (surely a step beyond Ramsey's "maps" of "cosmic positions.")

Schubert Ogden: Faith, Religious and Theistic Representative Language, and Metaphysics

Thus far we have examined what I have called two tentative claims advancing the case for the use of metaphysical language for examining the cognitive claims of religious language. The analysis now will focus on what I label Schubert Ogden's non-tentative, indeed "strong" argument for the use of metaphysics in theology. Although Ogden has advanced this argument in several contexts (as has his principal mentor, Charles Hartshorne),[35] the present interpretation will confine its attention to his argument in a representative essay entitled "The Task of Philosophical Theology." [36] Ogden's position, I believe, can clarify the earlier discussion at the three points where that discussion most needed clarification: first, the more exact meaning of the "beliefs" [37] which metaphysics reflectively represents; second, the meaning and nature of metaphysics; third, the meaning and nature of the use of metaphysics for examining the cognitive claims of religious and explicit theistic language. My examination will proceed by an interpretation of Ogden's analysis *in relationship to* the three issues specified for clarification.[38] The first issue is the more exact meaning of "belief" and "faith."

On the first issue, Ogden maintains that "faith" or "belief" is a fundamental factor in the life of every human being, not simply every explicit religious believer.[39] On a first level, which human beings share with the other animals, there exists what Santayana named "animal faith," i.e., that instinctive confidence of an animal in the environment as permissive of its struggle to live and reproduce its kind.[40] On a second, distinctively human level, one finds the phenomenon of "self-consciousness," i.e., the ability to understand and reflect upon that instinctive confidence. We never experience without some understanding and we never understand without some experience. The primary experience in question, moreover, is that "belief" or "faith" (synonymous terms here), that "basic trust" or "confidence," which, precisely as directly related to all understanding, can be recognized as fundamental. This remains the case even if all such basic beliefs cannot be "justified" (i.e., proved) in strictly deductive terms since all understanding *presumes* just that faith.

On the basis of these primary distinctions, two further specifications may be introduced: an "existential faith" constitutive of all human existence as such and a "reflective understanding" wherein existential faith can be represented in an express, thematic, and conceptually precise way. In place of Ferré's relatively broad appeal to "beliefs," or of Ramsey's reference to "cosmic disclosures," we now find a clear and, I believe, sound formulation of the nature of the "existential faith" which can and should be mediated through some mode of reflection and discourse.[41]

The next logical question concerns the mode of reflection and discourse which can fulfill that task. On strictly logical terms alone, that mode of reflective understanding is correctly described as metaphysical.[42] All such reflection involves raising to "express, thematic and conceptually precise" expression ("full self-consciousness")[43] those basic beliefs that are (to formulate the question in explicitly transcendental terms) the condition of the possibility of our existing or understanding at all.[44] For example, scientific language presupposes the basic belief that events are so ordered that our experience of such events in past and present *warrants* our maintaining certain expectations of the future.[45]

In historical terms, of course, metaphysical analysis in the West has been principally concerned with the three "basic realities" of self, world, and God. For present systematic purposes, it is necessary to affirm only that some mode of reflection and some correlative mode of representative discourse is needed to explicate in as conceptually precise a manner as possible all the basic beliefs which ground our existing or understanding at all.

The principal interest of this chapter remains the task of understanding what basic belief is explicated in the cognitive claims implied by the religious use of the word God. That general question can now be stated with greater exactness: granted the existence of "basic beliefs," granted too the need of a mode of reflection and discourse which can investigate all claims to provide adequate re-presentation of such beliefs, is explicitly theistic language an adequate re-presentation of those basic beliefs?[46] To answer that question the analysis must turn to the question of the cognitive meaning of all religious, especially theistic, language and to the allied question of the role of metaphysical language and reflection in judging those cognitive claims. Does theistic language adequately re-present the most basic faith presupposed by all our existing and understanding? Properly understood, that *is* the philosophical question of God.

That question may be reformulated in the following manner: why are the issues of religious theistic cognitive claims in the final analysis metaphysical questions?[47] Ogden, following Whitehead, maintains (in harmony with the position advanced in chapters five and six of this work)[48] that religion is not simply coordinate with other cultural fields (science, art, morality, politics), but is correctly understood as fundamental to all cultural fields. This position can be formulated still more sharply by recalling Ogden's own previous arguments: religion is a word best reserved for those *re-presentative expressions* of human beings which do not intend to explicate some single "belief" presupposed by a particular language (for example, scientific language's presupposition of a belief in the order and thereby predictability of events). Rather, religious language, indeed all religious expression, is used to represent the most basic belief (more exactly, that basic common human confidence and trust in existence) which underlies all our other basic beliefs (for example, the belief that it is ultimately meaningful to pursue a moral life).[49] Religion, in short, is basically a representative phenomenon whose cognitive claims can be investigated only by a mode of reflection (metaphysics) whose task is precisely the investigation of all claims to re-present our basic beliefs as the conditions of the possibility of all our existing and understanding.[50]

This position may be further clarified by recalling how an explicitly theistic self-understanding is both demanded by religious experience and language and open to critical investigation only by an explicitly metaphysical inquiry. Ogden advances this position by recalling Whitehead's well-known dictum: "the doctrines of rational religion aim at being that metaphysics which can be derived from the supernormal experience of mankind in its moments of finest insight."[51] Alternatively, one might also recall another Whiteheadian dictum in *Religion in the Making*: "Christianity . . . has always been a religion seeking a metaphysics."[52]

Whitehead, Hartshorne, and Ogden seem to be on solid historical grounds when they point to the Judaeo-Christian concept of God as the signal example of this general principle.[53] However, it may prove helpful to note that the argument need not be confined to the "radically monotheistic" concept of Western religion. If religion be in fact the kind of re-presentative expression explicated by Ogden,[54] or the kind of limit-experience and limit-language explicated in my own prior analysis, then we are logically impelled to ask whether the explicitly theistic representation of that faith is both possible and necessary. That latter issue is more systematic than historical. Historically it is not, of course, the case that all religious language is God-language. In systematic terms, however, one cannot but ask whether the cognitive character of all religious language does not imply the reality of God as the objective referent of that language.[55]

The concept God is the central and the clearest expression of the general metaphysical character of religious language itself. Where God is conceived radically (as in such monotheistic religions as Judaism, Christianity, and Islam), God is conceived metaphysically. In Ogden's own language, which I see every reason to endorse, God is conceived as "the ultimate creative ground of anything that is so much as even possible, and hence to be in the strictest sense necessary, not merely a being among others, but in some way "being-itself." In fact, the God of theism in its most fully developed forms is the one metaphysical individual, the sole reality whose individuality is constitutive of reality as such; the sole being who is, therefore, the inclusive object of all our faith and understanding."[56]

A formulation of this point from the opposite side might also be noted: not only are the cognitive claims of religious and explicitly theistic language adequately investigated only by metaphysical reflection and adequately expressed (i.e., in a conceptually precise way) only in metaphysical language, but metaphysical inquiry itself is completed only when the concept of God is explicitly accepted or rejected. If one recognizes the strictly metaphysical claims which the radically theistic concept of God involves, one may recognize as well that precisely that concept also provides a basic category for metaphysics itself: *the* single metaphysical referent to our most basic faith or trust. In exactly that sense, Charles Hartshorne's otherwise puzzling comment makes sense: "Neutrality as to God means no metaphysics; . . . if metaphysics knows anything, it must either know God, or know that the idea of God is meaningless." [57]

A summary of the limited purpose of this brief analysis of Ogden's position may be helpful here: I have not pretended to present a metaphysical argument for accepting the cognitive claims of religion and theism.[58] Rather I have been solely concerned to clarify the central question which the analytic tradition has explicated for any use of religious language: what that language means *cognitively* and what mode of reflection can investigate its claims.[59] I have suggested that either Ramsey's "prospects for a theological metaphysics" or Ferré's suggestion of the presence of "metaphysical facts" by means of a "semantic" analysis of religious language are suggestive but tentative explications of the claim that metaphysical language is the proper language for explicating the cognitive claims of religious language. I have then suggested that Schubert Ogden's representative analysis of the metaphysical character of the language of radical theism, supplemented by my own earlier argument for the limit-character of religious language in general,[60] provides the clarifications which Ramsey's and Ferré's earlier analyses lacked: the meanings of "basic beliefs" and "basic faith"; the meaning of metaphysical reflection and thereby of metaphysical language; the logical reasons why the cognitive claims of radically theistic language (and, by implication, the limit-language of any religious tradition) can only be adequately investigated by transcendental (metaphysical) analysis;[61] the same logical reasons why religious language can only be adequately re-presented conceptually by explicitly metaphysical language.

Although this general position on metaphysics and religious language is shared by such proponents of a reformulated "transcendental method" as Maréchal, Coreth, Rahner, and Lonergan and by such neo-classical philosophers as Whitehead, Hartshorne, and Ogden, this position has been widely rejected by linguistic philosophers.[62] It should then prove helpful to examine one of the most clearly developed articulations of this dominant antimetaphysical tradition in contemporary theological literature, the recent *magnum opus* of Anders Nygren, *Meaning and Method.*[63]

RELIGIOUS LANGUAGE AND THE IMPOSSIBILITY OF
METAPHYSICAL LANGUAGE: Anders Nygren

The intention of this section is not to investigate the impressive and complex systematic position which Anders Nygren develops for what he calls a "scientific" (basically an "objectively argued") philosophy of religion and a "scientific" ("motif-research") theology.[64] My present concern is to focus solely upon Nygren's rejection of metaphysics as a cognitively meaningful mode of inquiry for either philosophy or theology. As his several critics and admirers have noted, this anti-metaphysical stance is a major factor in Nygren's own linguistic alternative for philosophical and theological reflection.[65] Since the principal question of this entire chapter remains the use of metaphysics for investigating the cognitive claims of religion, I think this narrow focus is justified.[66]

The basic charge leveled by Nygren in his several critical discussions of the meaning (ultimately, for him, the "scientific meaninglessness") of metaphysics can be stated as follows: all metaphysical language is involved in one form or another of what Gilbert Ryle has labelled a category-mistake.[67] These mistakes present facts belonging to one category or subject in an idiom that is appropriate to some other category. The central category-mistake of metaphysical language consists in the mistaken assumption that metaphysics, as it is usually presented, is in some meaningful sense "scientific." His most extended analysis of this charge may be found in his insistence that metaphysics *as scientific* must be either "deductive" or "inductive." Nygren's own proposed alternative is to suggest that the proper use of metaphysical language is as "conceptual poetry."

Deductive Metaphysics[68]

Metaphysics, for Nygren, has traditionally worked with a deductive method which, it claimed, allowed for a basic and comprehensive science. In advancing its claims, metaphysics employed the axiomatic method of mathematics in order to deduce its metaphysical conclusions from its self-evident axioms. Yet precisely here is where the difficulty lies: the axiomatic mode of argumentation, a *proper* scientific (i.e., objective) method for mathematics, is improper for any metaphysics claiming to possess self-evident axioms as the basic presuppositions of all thinking. As the different choices of historical "self-evident" axioms show, no axioms are in fact self-evident even to other metaphysicians. For example, is being or becoming the primary and self-evident axiom? Is substance or relation the primary category? Nygren's argument is clear and, as far as it goes, sound. Insofar as we use the term metaphysics to mean those classical rationalist systems epitomized in the work of Christian Wolff (Nygren's own favorite example is Leibniz)[69] and probably forever laid to rest *as scientifically meaningful* by the critique of Kant,[70] Nygren's conclusion seems both historically and methodologically correct. Moreover, insofar as any contemporary theological position (for example, the few remaining strictly "neo-Scholastic" positions) [71] argue for the metaphysical investigation of religious cognitive claims by using a deductive-rationalist model, such positions are open to the charge of cognitive meaninglessness. Yet, that this description of metaphysics does not fit the transcendental formulation of the task of metaphysics at least seems clear.[72] Still, for Nygren there are at least two other "uses" of metaphysics on the contemporary scene which are also cognitively meaningless.

Inductive Metaphysics[73]

Inductive metaphysics makes the same *kind* of category-mistake as deductive metaphysics but with different "scientific" categories and modes of argumentation. More exactly, an inductive metaphysics lays claim to a scientific status by appealing, not to the axiomatic mode of mathematical argumentation, but to the empirical mode of scientific verification. For Nygren, several modern "metaphysical" positions lay claim to scientific status in the following manner: there is always something incomplete about the results of the special sciences. These results can serve as the basis of induction for a metaphysical world-view.[74] Inductive metaphysics proceeds by inductively developing a unified world-view or general hypothesis about reality (e.g., "process" as the fundamental characteristic of all reality).[75] This induction occurs by constructing a world-view from the implications of the more particular results of one or several of the empirical sciences (e.g., evolutionary theory in the life sciences).[76] This use of inductive method, however, is not scientific in the empirical sense. Strictly speaking, such general world-views or world-hypotheses cannot be verified or tested through any recognized empirical method of science. Such metaphysical world-views, whatever their other legitimate uses (e.g., moral or aesthetic),[77] are not actually scientific.

I think that Nygren has provided an excellent analysis of a frequent misuse of the word metaphysics. Indeed, it is quite possible that when that word is used in much theological literature (e.g., in the criticisms of metaphysics by Karl Barth), the meaning of metaphysics is exactly what Nygren analyzes it to be: a substitute for the vague phrase "Philosophy of life." [78] More tellingly, such a mode of discourse cannot really claim a properly scientific status (as distinct from its use as expressing a "blik" or attitude, an aesthetic use, a moral use, etc.). *A fortiori*, anyone attempting to investigate critically the cognitive claims of religious language should hardly appeal to a mode of investigation and a language which itself has no real scientific or even objectively cognitive status!

Metaphysics as Conceptual Poetry[79]

For Nygren, the proper use (i.e., meaning) for the word metaphysics is its function as a kind of conceptual poetry. Although metaphysics may employ concepts, such concepts are meant to express aesthetic (poetic) meanings and not scientific meanings. In keeping with his own revisionary interpretation of Wittgenstein, Nygren maintains that meaning has various "uses" determined by various "contexts." [80] Consequently, only a narrow and mistaken (for him, a "metaphysical" in the pejorative sense) criterion of meaning (e.g., Ayer's "verification" principle) would confine the use of "meaning" to strictly scientific meaning.[81] Therefore metaphysical language is not meaningless if it is used as conceptual poetry. Metaphysics is, however, utterly meaningless as scientific language for it does not correctly employ either an axiomatic mode of mathematical argumentation nor an empirical mode of scientific verification.

Perhaps it is already clear why Nygren's critique of metaphysics may be a valuable if reluctant ally of the view advanced in this book. From the latter perspective, we can summarize the value of Nygren's analysis. He exposes the fact that when the word metaphysics is employed in contemporary discourse it may have any one of three distinct uses: inductive metaphysics, deductive metaphysics, or conceptual poetry. In any one of those three uses, metaphysical language does not function as a legitimate form of objective meaning.[82] This suggestion seems particularly helpful since any wide reading in contemporary theological literature will reveal that many cases "for" and "against" metaphysics in theology assume that one or the other of Nygren's three "meanings" or "uses" for metaphysics is indeed the meaning assigned to that slippery word.

However, none of the meanings analyzed by Nygren as exhaustive of the "uses" of metaphysics can be used to characterize the position advanced in this work. Metaphysics is neither axiomatic nor inductive argumentation.[83] Rather its mode of argument can be more properly described as transcendental in the exact sense that metaphysical argument shows that certain basic beliefs must necessarily be maintained as basic conditions of the possibility of our understanding or existing at all. Such basic beliefs (not "self-evident axioms" or "world-views") can be shown to be basic by demonstrating the self-contradictory character which their denial involves for any intelligent and rational ("reflective") inquirer.[84] Insofar as this mode of reflection and discourse can investigate all basic beliefs, it can (indeed, it alone can) investigate the cognitive claims made in religious language (as itself re-presentative of our basic existential confidence or trust). In terms more directly related to the analyses of our prior chapters, metaphysics provides that mode of analysis which can explicate and judge those limit-concepts needed to explain the cognitive claims of the originating religious limit-language and limit-experience.

Yet this latter formulation of the metaphysical task (represented, in differing ways, in either contemporary transcendental method, or process thought, or even, however tentatively, in such linguistic philosophers as Strawson and Passmore) [85] is nowhere so much as mentioned, much less analyzed, in Nygren's otherwise extensive study. Perhaps, then, it may not seem too peremptory to suggest that Nygren's own alternative for theology (an analysis of the logical but not ontological conditions of the possibility of the uses of various basic concepts in different contexts) can be shown to be self-contradictory unless some reality claims ("basic beliefs" not merely "logical conditions") are in fact assumed.[86] Perhaps also it may not be too arbitrary a judgment to suggest that Nygren's claim to a "scientific theology" through "motif-research" may prove to be a hermeneutically sophisticated "fideism" [87] and his "scientific philosophy of religion" may be a major logical refinement of, but not major advance upon, Wittgenstein's earlier analysis of meaning as use-in-a-context.[88] And yet, insofar as Nygren's analysis of metaphysics really does serve the purpose which we claim for it (viz., to clarify and eliminate *improper* uses of metaphysical language),[89] his elaborate and important study can legitimately be said to provide a major clarification to the contemporary discussion.

THE USES AND ABUSES OF RELIGIOUS LANGUAGE

A primary task of metaphysical reflection should be the investigation of the cognitive claims of religious language.[90] That metaphysical interest need not become the occasion for failing to note the non-cognitive uses of religious language. The latter, for example, may be studied under the aegis of criteria for existential meaningfulness and are ordinarily better represented in uses of religious language other than the conceptual.[91] In a parallel manner, an acceptance of the contemporary meaningfulness of the non-cognitive uses of religious language and experience need not become the occasion to disregard the possibility of a strictly conceptual-metaphysical analysis of religious and theistic cognitive claims. The more exact relationship of these two factors can be appreciated more fully after an analysis, in a later chapter, of explicitly christological language. At present, my concern is simply to insist upon the need for *both* forms of analysis (phenomenological-linguistic and transcendental) in order to determine both non-cognitive and cognitive uses for implicit and explicit religious language.

Metaphysics and Metaphor

A secondary task of metaphysical reflection will be to explicate in strictly conceptual terms the thematic meanings of the primary religious metaphors, images, and symbols of any particular religious tradition. For example, if a primary metaphor employed in Christian religious texts is "God is love," one may analyze which metaphysical concepts can articulate the cognitive meaning of that metaphor in a manner which affirms rather than effectively negates the originating metaphor itself.[92] In fact, that concern informs the argument of such neo-classical thinkers as Charles Hartshorne and John Cobb that the categories of process thought can articulate the Christian understanding of the God-humanity relationship ("God *is* love") without negating the original symbol.[93] In contrast, the metaphysics of classical theology seems to be left with the unacceptable option of declaring the original scriptural metaphor a "mere metaphor" (e.g., for Aquinas, an analogy of improper attribution), a "mere symbol," or a "useful anthropomorphism" which should be eliminated when formulating a strictly conceptual understanding of the God-humanity relationship.[94] Most traditional Christian and Jewish theologians employing classical Greek metaphysics did (and, by the logic of that metaphysical position, must) deny that God is really affected by human actions *("ratio entis")*; even if it be anthropomorphically, metaphorically, symbolically, or logically helpful to express those meanings, in that earlier, scriptural fashion *("ratio rationis").* [95] On the contrary, process thinkers need make no such judgment. Indeed, the use of process metaphysical categories for God, humanity, and the relationship of love (e.g., dipolarity, internal relations, becoming) renders conceptually explicit the tensive meanings of the metaphor itself.

Parenthetically, I do not understand the common fear that such an employment of metaphysics will eliminate the "mystery" which the religious use of metaphors are intended to disclose. The correct employment of metaphysics *can* eliminate incoherence and self-contradiction in the concepts used to explicate the "disclosure" which the "interaction" of the metaphorical statement is meant to evoke. Since a classical task of Christian theology has been the attempt to show either "where the mystery lies" (Aquinas), or how the "scandal of faith" is properly articulated (Kierkegaard), there seems good reason to believe that the proper use of strictly metaphysical concepts genuinely aids reflection upon the cognitive claims of any given religious language.[96]

It may prove helpful to add that the position defended here is not identical to the Hegelian position on *"Vorstellung"* (re-presentation) and *"Begriff"* (concept) insofar as the latter position, as I understand it, claims that the *"Aufhebung"* which the concept provides renders the earlier representations unnecessary, whereas the former makes no such claim.[97] Indeed, the process concepts may allow the metaphors and symbols of the originating re-presentative religious language to be rendered conceptually intelligible (e.g., coherent in themselves and adequate to our basic "beliefs"). In sum, the present argument for the use of the properly limit-concepts of metaphysics is intended to provide a third alternative to a discussion which still seems largely dominated by the classical models "rationalism" (e.g., Hegel and the "right-wing" Hegelians) and "fideism" (e.g., Kierkegaard, Barth, and the Wittgensteinian fideists).[98]

Metaphysics and Myth

The word "myth," even more than the word "metaphysics," has many uses. However, if one first clarifies what he means by such categories as metaphor, concept, and metaphysics as applied to religious and theological language, then one may be in a better position to clarify the principal positive and negative meanings of myth. Some scholars of religious language, notably Bultmann, Eliade, and Ricoeur, have attempted distinct definitions of myth. Still others hold that the very word "myth" now has so many different meanings that it is arguable whether one can speak of a proper meaning for the word at all. My own position is that a legitimate meaning for the language of myth can be found *if* some prior classification of religious language as re-presentative language and as limit-language is maintained; and if the prior uses of the terms "metaphorical language" (through "interaction-theory") and "metaphysical language" (as "transcendental" reflection employing limit-concepts) are maintained.[99] In the context of those clarifications, the key issue for any analysis of mythical language becomes the prior questions of how our basic beliefs are either adequately or inadequately re-presented in the religious use of metaphors and the theological use of metaphysical concepts.

Myths (which linguistically may include metaphors, symbols, and concepts in a *narrative form*) can also be analyzed as intending adequate representations of basic beliefs (the positive meaning of myth) even if that intention is sometimes misapplied (the negative meaning of myths). More exactly, myths, insofar as they function as the first narrative re-presentations of our experiences as selves holding certain basic beliefs,[100] have a fully positive meaning. Indeed, precisely in that function myths should be taken "seriously but not literally." The problem (the "literalization" of myth) can, therefore, be seen as the same kind of fundamental linguistic mistake as an improper understanding of the religious use of metaphors as "substitutes" for literal and non-limit meanings; as the improper understanding of the theological use of models as "picture" models; and of the improper understanding of the theological use of metaphysical language as "deductive" proofs of axiomatic beliefs. Since all these mistaken options are well described as "category-mistakes," it does not seem difficult to understand the correctness of Rudolf Bultmann's demand for demythologizing as an integral moment in the task of contemporary theology. It may be true that Bultmann explicitly holds to a relatively narrow understanding of myth (basically a re-presentation of the "transcendent" in terms of the "immanent").[101] It is precisely this narrow understanding that frees Bultmann, at the very least, to develop his notion of a genuinely *improper* use of myth, viz., as mythological. In present categories, that use can be described as a literalization (i.e., through re-presentations determined by "immanent," external sense-perception categories) of "serious" but not "literal" meanings (those basic beliefs of the self and the basic referent of those beliefs—God —which cannot be adequately re-presented in the linguistic categories of the immanent).[102] In a similar fashion, the more positive and wider interpretations of the meaning of myth advanced by scholars like Mircea Eliade and Paul Ricoeur can also be affirmed, I believe, as further specifications of the authentically limit-character of both the language and the disclosure present in those religious narratives we call myths.

These brief comments on myth do not pretend to provide anything like a final word on this complex historical, philosophical, and theological subject. Rather the present proposal for understanding both the positive and negative uses of myth is designed to parallel the prior discussions of metaphor, model, and metaphysics. Just as the latter have proper and improper uses for religious and theological language, so too has myth. Indeed, all such uses can be summarized again (but perhaps with more linguistic exactitude) under the familiar consensus-quotation of Reinhold Niebuhr: "Myths, too, are to be taken seriously but not literally."

I have tried in this chapter to articulate the limited but important need for metaphysical analysis of Christian religious language. Such analysis, by its ability to engage in authentically transcendental reflection and to develop genuine limit-concepts for the theistic referent of religious limit-language and limit-experience, should aid the analyst to adjudicate any cognitive claims present in that language. When correlated to the earlier analysis of the meaningfulness of religious language and experience itself, metaphysical reflection may also come to be recognized not as an academic, but an existential question for the reflective contemporary person. Without religious meaningfulness, theism tends to become merely a dead and uninteresting issue. Without the truth of theism, religion tends to become an existentially useful but not cognitively serious question. The existential meaningfulness of the theistic question, to be sure, emerges only from an authentically religious base. But the final truth of religion, I believe, is in fact its objective ground in theism. How that claim might be validated, the next chapter will attempt to show.

Notes

(1) This applies, in their differing ways, to both the discussion of a religious dimension of our common experience (chapter five) and explicitly religious language (chapter six). The two are meant to comprise a hermeneutical correlation.

(2) A classical illustration of this principle remains the pioneering work of John

Henry Cardinal Newman, especially as articulated in his *Apologia Pro Vita Sua* (New York: Random House, 1950), esp. pp. 237–76.

(3) As in the generic meaning of the doctrine of utilitarianism. For the religious use of the categories "doctrine" and "dogma," cf. Avery Dulles, *The Survival of Dogma* (New York: Image, 1973), esp. pp. 155–92.

(4) In fact, this seems a fair historical statement for traditional Christianity; in principle it seems a necessary element of the Christian religion.

(5) This is especially true of Paul van Buren in *The Secular Meaning of the Gospel* (London: Macmillan, 1963), esp. pp. 1–23, 63–74.

(6) For such a defense in relationship to the analyses of the "death of God" theologians, cf. Langdon Gilkey, *Naming the Whirlwind: The Renewal of God-Language* (New York: Bobbs-Merrill, 1969), pp. 107–79.

(7) More exactly, certain forms of Buddhism.

(8) "Effectively" insofar as even an "orthodox" believer may lack theistic *faith* and thus be involved in "atheism of the heart." Correlatively, one may have such "faith" and still lack reflective self-understanding of that faith as a belief in God. On the latter, cf. the suggestive analysis of Henri de Lubac in *The Drama of Atheistic Humanism* (New York: Sheed and Ward, 1951); Johann Baptist Metz (ed.), *Is God Dead?* Concilium 16 (New York: Paulist, 1966); Schubert M. Ogden, "The Strange Witness of Unbelief," in *The Reality of God* (New York: Harper & Row, 1964), pp. 120–44.

(9) As examples, the classical theism articulated by either Thomas Aquinas for the Catholic tradition or by John Calvin for the Reformed tradition.

(10) For the fullest expression of this in relationship to classical alternatives, cf. Charles Hartshorne and William L. Reese (eds.), *Philosophers Speak of God* (Chicago: University of Chicago Press, 1953), esp. pp. 1–29, and 499–517 (the latter for a discussion of the neo-classical theism alternatively named panentheism).

(11) For an articulation of transcendental-metaphysical analysis, cf. Emerich Coreth, *Metaphysics* (New York: Herder and Herder, 1968).

(12) As distinct from Hegel's seemingly larger claims for the *Aufhebung* provided by his philosophical concepts: on Hegel, cf. Emil Fackenheim *The Religious Dimension in Hegel's Thought* (Bloomington, Ind.: University of Indiana Press, 1967), esp. pp. 160–223; and Albert Chapelle, *Hegel et la réligion*, 3 vols. (Paris: Aubier, 1963). It is this aspect of Hegel's claim for *Begriff* (concept) over religious representation *(Vorstellung)* which is, in Karl Rahner's apt phrase, "the mad and secret dream of Hegel." Although this aspect of Hegel's thought is correctly considered unavailable for contemporary retrieval, other aspects of his thought (especially its dialectical analyses) are widely considered permanent achievements needing contemporary retrieval. For an example of a post-Hegelian return to Kant and Hegel, cf. Paul Ricoeur's formulation of limit-concepts in "The Specificity of Religious Language," pp. 21–36; idem, *Freud and Philosophy: An Essay in Interpretation* (New Haven: Yale University Press, 1970), pp. 459–553.

(13) Cf. Schubert M. Ogden, *The Reality of God* (New York: Harper & Row, 1966), p. 37.

(14) Cf. Paul Ricoeur, "The Specificity of Religious Language," pp. 21–36. The further characteristics of this conceptual language as "negative," "analogical," and "dialectical" would require the formulation of those further questions not treated here. On these possibilities, cf., inter alia, Battista Mondin, *The Principle of Analogy in Protestant and Catholic Theology* (The Hague: Mouton, 1963).

(15) This is an *in principle* statement. In fact, anthropologists, for example, in spite of their methodological strictures, often speak of the results of their study for our "humanity."

(16) The earlier analyses may be found in chapters three and four.

(17) Inter alia, cf. the excellent summary in Langdon Gilkey, *Naming the Whirlwind*, pp. 435–44; Gordon D. Kaufman, *Relativism, Knowledge and Faith* (Chicago: University of Chicago Press, 1960), pp. 95–117.

(18) For an example of a brief but cogent reply to the historicist critique, cf. Emil L. Fackenheim, *Metaphysics and Historicity* (Milwaukee: Marquette University Press, 1961).

(19) Inter alia, cf. Peter R. Baelz, *Christian Theology and Metaphysics* (Philadelphia: Fortress, 1968); esp. pp. 1–16, 79–135; James A. Martin, *The New Dialogue Between Philosophy and Theology* (New York: Seabury, 1966), esp. pp. 130–207; James Richmond, *Theology and Metaphysics* (New York: Schocken, 1971), esp. pp. 1–49, 93–155; cf. also the important arguments for metaphysics advanced by such Whiteheadian thinkers as Frank B. Dilley, *Metaphysics and Religious Language* (New York: Columbia University Press, 1964); and Dorothy Emmet, *The Nature of Metaphysical Thinking* (London: Macmillan, 1949).

(20) Cf. Ian Ramsey (ed.), *Prospects for Metaphysics* (London: Allen and Unwin, 1961), pp. 164–76.

(21) Ibid., p. 174.

(22) On the integrating function of the "I" in personal discourse, ibid., p. 166.

(23) Ibid., pp. 173 ff.

(24) In terms of the criteria outlined in chapter four, Ramsey may show a "meaning" and a "meaningfulness" to religious language, but not the "truth" of its cognitive claims.

(25) The category "category-mixing" is Gilbert Ryle's in *The Concept of Mind* (London: Hutchinson, 1949), wherein he examines the mind-body problem in terms of the traditional category-mistake of assuming a "ghost in the machine."

(26) Frederick Ferré, *Language, Logic and God* (New York: Harper & Row, 1961); idem, *Basic Modern Philosophy of Religion* (New York: Scribner's, 1967), esp. pp. 301–441.

(27) Ferré, *Language, Logic and God*, pp. 146–50.

(28) Ibid., pp. 159 ff.; the references to Ricoeur's position may be found in chapter four.

(29) Ibid., p. 161. Although suggestive, the very expression "metaphysical facts" serves to becloud the fact that metaphysics deals not with facts but with the nature of any fact (i.e., factuality).

(30) What, for example, is the exact meaning to be assigned the "metaphysical fact" of theism?

(31) Ibid., p. 161.

(32) Ibid., p. 165.

(33) In the terms employed in this work: besides the employment of criteria of "meaning" and "meaningfulness" (like Ramsey, see n. 24 above), Ferré's position may be said to move beyond Ramsey's to the demand for criteria of truth for cognitive claims.

(34) The argument is, at the moment, one of the logic of the nature of the referent. Alternatively, one may state the need for a limit-concept (cf. Ricoeur citation in n. 12 above).

(35) For Hartshorne, inter alia, cf. esp. Charles Hartshorne, *Man's Vision of God and The Logic of Theism* (Chicago: Willett, Clark, 1941); *A Natural Theology for Our Time* (La Salle, Ill.: Open Court, 1967); *Reality as Social Process: Studies in Metaphysics and Religion* (Glencoe: Free Press, 1953); *Creative Synthesis and Philosophic Method* (La Salle, Ill.: Open Court, 1970). For significant similarities and differences between Hartshorne and his chief mentor, Alfred North Whitehead, on these issues, cf. Lewis S. Ford (ed.), *Two Process Philosophers: Hartshorne's Encounter with Whitehead* (Missoula, Montana: AAR Studies in Religion, 1974).

(36) Schubert Ogden, "The Task of Philosophical Theology," in Robert A. Evans (ed.), *The Future of Philosophical Theology* (Philadelphia: Westminster, 1971), pp. 55–85.

(37) The expression "beliefs" is Ogden's. In terms of the distinction between "faith" and "beliefs" employed throughout this work, the actual referent is to "faiths." In this section, however, to avoid unnecessary terminological confusion, we shall follow Ogden's own terminology.

(38) Ogden's concerns are broader than the three issues under discussion; for example, he is also concerned with the question of revelation, cf. ibid., pp. 72–79.

(39) Ibid., p. 56.

(40) Ibid. Note the shift of terminology from "belief" to "faith."

(41) Note, that in terms of my present use of criteria of "meaning," "meaningfulness," and "truth," Ogden's analysis may be said to advance not only Ramsey's set-

ting forth of the "meaning" and "meaningfulness" of religious language, but also refines Ferré's move forward into criteria for truth as criteria of meaning (as internal coherence) and criteria of adequacy to experience (as basic faith). On the notion of experience assumed here, cf. the discussion in chapter four.

(42) Ibid., p. 59. Note the fundamental harmony between this position and the one outlined in chapter four on philosophical reflection as phenomenological-transcendental.

(43) For a linguistic formulation of this point, note Ogden's reference (ibid., p. 61) to John Passmore, *Philosophical Reasoning* (London: Duckworth, 1961), p. 78 (as cited by Ogden, p. 83, n. 10).

(44) Recall the discussion in chapter four on how transcendental reflection need not be limited to its Kantian origins for its formulation.

(45) Ogden, "The Task of Philosophical Theology," pp. 62–63; cf. also Ogden's earlier use of Stephen Toulmin's analysis of the uses of argument in Schubert M. Ogden, *The Reality of God*, pp. 28–37.

(46) In the terms employed earlier in this work, the question can also be formulated as: Is God the objective referent in reality for those basic beliefs (or faith)?

(47) Ogden, "The Task of Philosophical Theology," p. 65.

(48) Cf. the discussion in those chapters of the autonomously limit-character of the religious dimension of our experience.

(49) Cf. the discussion of limit-questions in chapter five.

(50) Cf. the discussion of metaphysics in chapter four.

(51) Ibid., p. 66. The reference is to Alfred North Whitehead, *Religion in the Making* (New York: Macmillan, 1926), p. 33 (as cited by Ogden, p. 83, n. 13).

(52) Alfred North Whitehead, *Religion in the Making*, p. 50. The contrast is completed by Whitehead's complementary if historically dubious remark: ". . . in contrast to Buddhism which is a metaphysic generating a religion."

(53) For a classical formulation of this insistence in more historical terms, cf. H. Richard Niebuhr, *Radical Monotheism and Western Culture, With Supplementary Essays* (New York: Harper, 1960). For an analysis of the significant similarities and differences between H. Richard Niebuhr's theology and that of the process thinkers, cf. Donald E. Fadner, "The Responsible God: An Analysis of The Theology of H. Richard Niebuhr" (unpublished dissertation, University of Chicago Divinity School, 1974).

(54) Cf. also Schubert M. Ogden, *The Reality of God*, pp. 31–33.

(55) As in the discussion of the image, metaphor, symbol, and myth "Kingdom of God," in chapter six, n. 67.

(56) Ogden, "The Task of Philosophical Theology," p. 67.

(57) Ogden's reference is to Charles Hartshorne, *Reality As Social Process: Studies in Metaphysics and Religion*, p. 176; *A Natural Theology for Our Time*, p. 32; cited by Ogden, "The Task of Philosophical Theology," p. 84, n. 15.

(58) For the latter, cf. Charles Hartshorne, "The Formal Validity and Real Significance of the Ontological Argument," *The Philosophical Review* 53 (3), 230 ff.; idem, "Can There Be Proofs for the Existence of God?" in *Religious Language and Knowledge*, ed. Robert H. Ayers and William T. Blackstone (Athens, Ga.: University of Georgia Press, 1972), pp. 60 ff.; idem, "Six Theistic Proofs" in *Creative Synthesis*, pp. 275–97; idem, "The Theistic Proofs," in *Natural Theology*, pp. 26–65.

(59) "Solely concerned" in this section on metaphysics; the interests of the work as a whole include an interest in the non-cognitive uses of religious language, cf. the discussion in chapter four.

(60) The principal need for that supplement is the showing of the "meaningfulness" of that language and its logically unique "meaning" as a limit-language.

(61) For a comparison of two "transcendental" accounts, cf. John C. Robertson, "Rahner and Ogden: Man's Knowledge of God," *Harvard Theological Review* 63 (1970), 377–407.

(62) The major difference between the "transcendental method" tradition and the process tradition on this question is the claim by the latter and denial by the former that God is experienced, not inferred, by such reflection. This issue revolves around the notion of "experience" in question, cf. the discussion in chapter four. It should also be noted, however, that the commitment of the "transcendental" Thomists since Maréchal to the centrality of the dynamism of the subject does not make their position on "inference" and "experience" identical to the more strictly inferential procedures of, say, R. Garrigou-Lagrange.

(63) Anders Nygren, *Meaning and Method: Prolegomena to a Scientific Philosophy of Religion and a Scientific Theology* (Philadelphia: Fortress, 1972); for discussion of Nygren's wide-ranging contributions to philosophy of religion and theology, cf. *The Philosophy and Theology of Anders Nygren*, ed. Charles W. Kegley (Carbondale, Ill.: Southern Illinois University Press, 1970); for a critical appraisal of Nygren's earlier works in philosophy of religion, cf. William Johnson, *On Religion: A Study of Theological Method in Schleiermacher and Nygren* (Leiden: Brill, 1964), pp. 75–163.

(64) On the former, cf. Nygren, *Meaning and Method*, pp. 65–127; on the latter, cf. ibid., pp. 351–79, and the articles by Walter Lindstrom (pp. 95–101), Bernhard Erling (pp. 101–20), Erik M. Christensen (pp. 120–28), Jacob Heikkinen (pp. 128–41), and Philip S. Watson (pp. 223–38) in *The Philosophy and Theology of Anders Nygren.*

(65) Cf. Ragnar Bring, "Anders Nygren's Philosophy of Religion," *The Philosophy and Theology of Anders Nygren*, pp. 33–70; Robert T. Saudin, "Theology Without Metaphysic," *Journal of Religion* 52 (1972), 450–57.

(66) The importance of Nygren's development of motif-research, for example, does not depend upon his philosophy of religion.

(67) Nygren, *Meaning and Method*, pp. 165, 282, and 315.

(68) Ibid., pp. 47–48.

(69) Ibid., pp. 41, 85–87, 92–97.

(70) Ibid., esp. pp. 201–5.

(71) For a survey of neo-Scholastic opinions on this, Cf. Thomas C. O'Brien, *Metaphysics and the Existence of God* (Washington, D.C.: Thomist Press, 1960), esp. pp. 19–99, 240–65.

(72) It is perhaps significant that Nygren's extensive analysis of the contemporary range of opinion includes no mention of this neo-Thomist reformulation of transcendental method. On the latter, cf. Otto Muck, *The Transcendental Method* (New York: Herder and Herder, 1968).

(73) Nygren, *Meaning and Method*, pp. 48–50.

(74) Ibid., p. 45, n. 18. In the American context, for a similar position, cf. Stephen Pepper, *World Hypotheses* (Berkeley: University of California Press, 1942).

(75) Yet this is surely not the nature of metaphysical argumentation for the leading contemporary process philosopher, Charles Hartshorne. On the latter, cf. Charles Hartshorne, "What Metaphysics Is" and "Non-Restrictive Existential Statements" in *Creative Synthesis and Philosophic Method*, pp. 19–42 and 159–72, respectively. Hartshorne's position is also unexamined in Nygren's wide-ranging survey.

(76) As suggested above in n. 75, this is not a relevant observation on Hartshorne. It may prove to be a fair observation upon such thinkers as Samuel Alexander, C. Lloyd Morgan, or, more recently, Teilhard de Chardin.

(77) This would probably be Nygren's judgment upon a position like Teilhard de Chardin's in *The Phenomenon of Man* (New York: Harper & Row, 1965).

(78) Nygren, *Meaning and Method*, under the idea of a "metaphysical system," p. 50.

(79) Ibid., pp. 51–57. For Nygren, Heidegger's philosophy would be an example of this tendency.

(80) Note Nygren's use and reformulation of Wittgenstein here, ibid., pp. 243–65.

(81) Ibid., pp. 142–46.

(82) On scientific meaning, cf. ibid., pp. 65–78 and 123–27 on science; pp. 219–27 on "objective argumentation in philosophy" as a logical analysis of presuppositions.

(83) Nor, even for Heidegger, aptly described as "conceptual poetry"; cf. Martin Heidegger, *Introduction to Metaphysics* (New Haven: Yale University Press, 1959). On axiomatic, empirical, and philosophical argumentation in Nygren, cf. *Meaning and Method*, pp. 102–23.

(84) Again the basic dialectic is between performance and concept, not concept and

concept. For a succinct formulation here, cf. Bernard Lonergan, "Metaphysics As Horizon," in Emerich Coreth, *Metaphysics*, pp. 197–221. For Coreth's method, cf. *Metaphysics*, pp. 31–45).

(85) On Passmore, cf. n. 43 above; for Strawson's concept of a "descriptive metaphysics," cf. his *Individuals* (London, 1961), p. 9.

(86) What, for example, happens to Frege's concept of reference when Nygren reformulates the *Sinn-Bedeutung* distinction in terms of "contexts" of meaning? Is his own position merely the reverse side of the flaw he analyzes in Bertrand Russell's restriction of Frege ("atomism")? Cf. *Meaning and Method*, pp. 254–61.

(87) For disallowing critical questions in this "scientific theology." For the classical instance of Nygren's neo-orthodox position here, cf. his important study *Agape and Eros* (New York: Harper & Row, 1969). For Nygren's theology in the context of Swedish theology, cf. Nels F. S. Ferré, *Swedish Contributions to Modern Theology* (New York: Harper, 1967). These comments are not intended to deny the importance of motif-research itself as a possible component for a systematic theology.

(88) The major influence here seems to be the Uppsala school of logical analysis, cf. *Meaning and Method*, pp. 141–3; pp. 146–8 for Nygren's critical relationship to the thought of Hägerström.

(89) Namely, what Nygren aptly labels "inductive" and "deductive" metaphysics and "metaphysics as conceptual poetry" outlined above.

(90) Cf. discussion in chapter five.

(91) Cf. also discussion of "meaningfulness" in chapter four and applications in chapters nine and ten.

(92) As in any use of the "theory of substitution" for metaphor; cf. discussion of metaphor in chapter six.

(93) Inter alia, cf. John B. Cobb, Jr., *A Christian Natural Theology* (Philadelphia: Westminster, 1965), pp. 247–48; idem, *The Structure of Christian Existence*, pp. 125–37; Schubert M. Ogden, *The Reality of God*, pp. 47–70, esp. 67–68.

(94) On the question of Thomas Aquinas, cf. the critically positive treatment of David Burrell, *Analogy and Philosophical Language* (New Haven: Yale University Press, 1973), pp. 119–71; for Burrell's own constructive position cf. "Analogy, Metaphor and Models," ibid., pp. 252–64. For a contrasting account, cf. Charles Hartshorne and William L. Reese (ed.), *Philosophers Speak of God*, pp. 119–33.

(95) Cf. Schubert M. Ogden, *The Reality of God*, pp. 47–51. The reference to Thomas Aquinas is to *Summa Theologica*, Ia, 13, 7.

(96) In the terms employed earlier, metaphysical concepts may serve as the proper limit-concepts needed to explicate the meanings of the originating limit-languages proper to the religious dimension of our common experience and explicitly religious language.

(97) Cf. n. 12 above.

(98) For an example of an argument for the revisionist model in the wider theological context, cf. John B. Cobb, Jr., *Living Options in Protestant Theology: A Survey of Methods* (Philadelphia: Westminster, 1957), esp. his account of "Theological Positivism," pp. 121–99 and his own conclusions, pp. 312–24.

(99) This sentence is not understood to introduce new factors, but simply to summarize certain central conclusions of this study thus far.

(100) Cf. Schubert M. Ogden, "Myth and Truth," in *The Reality of God*, pp. 99–120; on the narrative function of myths, cf. Paul Ricoeur, *The Symbolism of Evil* (Boston: Beacon, 1967), pp. 3–10, 161–75. For a survey of the interpretations of myth from the viewpoint of history of religions, cf. Mircea Eliade, "Myth" in *Encyclopaedia Britannica*, Vol. 15 (1968), pp. 1132–42; for a brief formulation of Eliade's own influential and important position here, cf. Mircea Eliade, *Myth and Reality* (New York: Harper & Row, 1963).

(101) On Bultmann, cf. Schubert M. Ogden, *Christ Without Myth* (New York, Harper & Row, 1961), pp. 24–44; cf. also Ogden's reply to Bultmann's critics (Macquarrie, Owen, and Hepburn) that Bultmann's notion of myth is too narrow, ibid., pp. 166–70.

(102) Cf. Schubert Ogden, "Myth and Truth," esp. pp. 116–19.

Chapter 8

The Meaning, Meaningfulness, and Truth of God-Language

THE PHILOSOPHICAL SITUATION: The New Metaphysics

The former chapter indicated both what metaphysics is *not* and the general character of a contemporary metaphysical analysis. I shall now summarize and expand upon the meaning of metaphysics by articulating a specific metaphysical position. In the most basic sense, any metaphysical analysis must meet two general criteria for metaphysical statements: coherence and fidelity to experience broadly and fairly understood.[1] In most modern forms of strictly metaphysical analysis, this second experiential criterion is best fulfilled by taking the now famous "turn to the subject."[2] As indicated in the earlier methodological analysis of chapter four, this turn is representative of all those metaphysical traditions whose self-understanding has been deeply influenced by the Kantian critique of classical rationalist metaphysics. In one of its clearest and soundest reformulations, this turn to the subject has been employed by Karl Rahner and Bernard Lonergan to develop various formulations of a "transcendental method" leading to a reinterpretation and, to a large extent, a reestablishment of traditional Aristotelian and Thomist categories.[3] Although I have the highest respect for the aim and the solid accomplishments of this modern transcendental tradition,[4] I shall not in fact employ it here. The reason for that reluctance may be more clearly grasped at the end of this chapter. For the moment, it may be sufficient to state that this transcendental tradition—thus far at least—is unwilling to break with the classical theistic concepts of Aquinas.[5] Hence, whatever its other merits as an authentic method of metaphysical inquiry, the transcendental methods of Rahner and Lonergan will not prove helpful to any theologian sharing the present revisionist conviction that classical Christian theism is neither internally coherent nor adequate as a full account of our common experience and of the scriptural understanding of the Christian God.

One modern reformulation of the tasks of both metaphysics and the question of theism, ordinarily described as process thought,[6] remains in sev-

172

eral of its major formulations a mode of metaphysical analysis appropriate to the modern task of theistic restatement. To be sure, this mode of metaphysical analysis is as committed to the modern "turn to the subject" as is the transcendental tradition. Classically formulated in Whitehead's "reformed subjectivist principle," [7] the constitutive principle of the process tradition insists that philosophers note their experience as experiencing selves rather than their sense-perception of objects as the fundamental experiential and, thereby, metaphysical ground of all their basic concepts. In an achievement too little noted by other philosophers, the classical Anglo-American tradition of James, Peirce, Dewey, and Whitehead has challenged the classical understandings of experience.[8] In either the modern empiricist tradition of Hume or the transcendental criticism of empiricism initiated by Kant, the common understanding of experience as sense-experience of other objects or of the self as object has remained a largely unchallenged doctrine.[9] For the Anglo-American tradition, on the contrary, the concept of experience is far richer and more wide ranging.[10] Here experience refers to our primary experience of our selves as moving, feeling, sensing, thinking, acting, and deciding. As this process tradition, in the work of Whitehead and Hartshorne,[11] metaphysically refined the categories appropriate to this understanding of the self and of the self's multi-dimensional experience, a new set of metaphysical categories was developed to replace those of classical rationalisms, empiricisms, and transcendental methods.

A firm grasp of those central categories is crucial for any understanding of the new theism. If one shifts one's focus away from the sense-perception of objects ("experience") as the paradigm case for reality to the self's full range of unconscious, conscious, and knowing experiences of the self as the paradigm case for reality, a change in basic metaphysical categories also occurs. In place of the essentially non-temporal and non-relational categories of "substance" and "being" of the classical metaphysical tradition, the categories "process," "sociality," and "time" emerge. The very meaning and hence reality of the self's full experience is intrinsically and systematically relational, social, and temporal.[12] The self as we actually experience that self is an illusion if it is not a process of change and continuity: a process which precisely as process involves both internal relations with all reality and the distinct temporal modes of present, past, and future. This shift of basic paradigms, away from the secondary phenomenon of the world constituted by the experience of our senses to the primal phenomenon of a social and temporal self, involves a radical shift in the kind of metaphysical categories developed.[13]

Here, one might say, that "turn to the subject" characteristic of modern metaphysics has been taken to its logical and liberating conclusion.[14] For the central criterion of properly metaphysical analysis—that it be truly adequate to all experience—now finds itself fulfilled by a direct relationship to the "conditions of the possibility" of the experiencing self in its full multi-dimensional radicality.[15] Correlatively, the central categories of this meta-physics—process, becoming, relation, sociality, and temporality—are artic-ulated in direct dependence upon the metaphysical analysis of the experi-encing self as the paradigm case of all reality. As we shall see below, even God is to be understood not as an exception to these categories but rather as the chief, indeed, the constitutive exemplification of the categories them-selves.[16] For the moment, however, I am concerned only to clarify why and how this metaphysical tradition might be said to continue and perhaps complete[17] that "Copernican revolution" in metaphysical thought initiated by Kant's "turn to the subject." Of secondary but real importance to the theologian, this metaphysical tradition has developed categories which seem both more faithful to the kind of limit-concepts needed to explicate the religious limit-dimension of our common experience and more faithful to the actual related and temporal God referred to by the limit-language of the Christian scriptures themselves.

Indeed there seems every good reason to assume that the specific work on the metaphysical question of God formalized in the work of Charles Hart-shorne will merit far more critical attention from both the critics and propo-nents of Christian theism in the future than it has to date.[18] This is not the place to review the complex and pioneering work of Hartshorne himself, however much his work demands the critical attention of Christian theolo-gians and metaphysicians. To my knowledge, no other single thinker in mo-dernity has proposed as carefully formulated and evidential a series of alter-natives to the classical dilemmas of theists and non-theists alike.[19] Hartshorne's position argues, for example, as clearly as does that of classi-cal or modern Thomism, that metaphysics demands theism for its own vali-dation. For Hartshorne, as was previously noted, "neutrality as to God means no metaphysics."

At the same time, the process tradition poses a coherent, clear, and new meaning to the concept "God" (the variously labelled neo-classical, panen-theistic, or dipolar theism discussed below); a concept, moreover, not in-cluded in the more usual alternatives (basically classical theism, pantheism, agnosticism, and atheism).[20] Finally, Hartshorne's position reopens the question of the "proofs" of God's existence with the analytical tools of a modern process metaphysics. On the one hand, Hartshorne does not at-tempt to introduce the kind of deductivist and purely inductive methods of "proof" which our earlier discussion of Nygren has disallowed. On the other hand, as Hartshorne's reinterpretation of Anselm's ontological argu-ment shows,[21] he is concerned to show how the proper concept for the real-ity of God is demanded by our most basic beliefs. More exactly, only the re-ality of God, itself reinterpreted in process metaphysical categories, can account for that original and ineluctable confidence in the worthwhileness of existence which the earlier analyses of the religious dimension of our common experience portrayed.[22] Just how such a claim for the truth of the reality of God might be defended we will reconsider after the exact meaning which this new metaphysics posits for the Christian God has been clarified. For the present, I have only suggested why metaphysical analysis is needed by theologians and what kind of metaphysics seems best fitted to present philosophical and theological concerns.[23]

THE THEOLOGICAL SITUATION: The Search for an Appropriate Formulation of the Meaning and Truth of God

On no single question does the choice of a basic theological model so determine one's response as on the question of God. From the classical theism present in either fundamentalist or sophisticated philosophical theologies following the orthodox model, through the various liberal and neo-orthodox models for the proper conceptualities for the Christian God, through the negation of that theistic reality altogether by the major proponents of the radical "death of God" theologies, to the quiet and ambivalent silence upon the entire subject present in several theologies of culture, the question of the Christian God is fashioned by the aims and methods of one's general theological model.[24] For the revisionist model for fundamental theology the question of God is equally central. If the revisionist theologian is to be faithful to the demands of his own model, he must develop a conceptuality for the Christian God that may show its necessity for a proper understanding of our common experience and its fundamental continuity with the God proclaimed in the Christian scriptures.

In this context, then, the process conceptuality for the Christian God deserves the most serious consideration by all reflective contemporary persons.[25] A major importance of the process thinkers is that they force this issue of God on two fronts: on the first, they analyze our common human experience in order to make both an affirmation and a negation of the more usual contemporary self-understanding. Affirmatively, the process thinkers unhesitatingly assert the need for all contemporary men and women to assent to the major positive characteristics of the modern experiment since the Enlightenment. The genuine values of modernity—openness, autonomy, change, critical investigation of all our traditions, personal responsibility for one's judgments and beliefs, constant struggle for authentic liberation—are precisely those characteristics of the modern experiment which cannot be set aside.[26]

Some of the process thinkers, it is true, have a sometimes disturbing tendency to ignore the ambiguities and serious limitations of modernity.[27] Modernity, at least since its own self-critique in figures like Marx, Freud, and Nietzsche, is not nearly as sanguine about the possible outcome of the human experiment as was the Enlightenment. In a word, process is not to be identified with progress. Any effort to slide over that distinction cannot but involve a disservice to the modern attempt at full-scale liberation.[28] Yet, upon careful reading, most of the process thinkers cannot be convicted of a naive modernity. Whitehead, Hartshorne, Cobb, Meland, Ogden, Loomer, et al., are neither merely Enlightenment figures nor nineteenth-century liberals. They are, in fact, quite aware of the ambiguities of modernity.[29] Most of them, for example, affirm the liberating insights into the fundamental ambiguity of our actual situation expressed by the existentialists. In general, so unintimidated are most process thinkers by the easy, perhaps even lazy liberalism on religion of so many of our contemporaries that most of them do not hesitate to challenge modernity on the question of God.[30] They argue that precisely the modern affirmations of openness, change, and liberation[31] demand a belief in God as the ground of these and all our other most particularly modern aspirations.

In short, the process thinkers' position on modernity is neither an easy one nor one widely shared: they affirm the authentic values of secularity and deny the ideology of secularism.[32] They do not run for cover when, say, Antony Flew or Jean-Paul Sartre or Gore Vidal disbelievingly inquire how a truly modern person can affirm the existence of God. Rather they affirm it and they argue with considerable persuasion that the very commitment to the authentic values of modernity forces that affirmation upon all reflective persons.[33]

On this first front of the understanding of our common human experience as modern men and women, the process thinkers are clear and, I believe, sound. Still more ambitious, on a second front, they challenge and reinterpret the understanding of God of the classical Christian tradition. They affirm with the tradition that the existence of God is the only possible final understanding of our human situation, but deny that the nature of God as understood and expressed by that tradition is sound.[34] They affirm that God is the supremely perfect one, but they deny that the concept of perfection excludes change and process in God himself.[35] They affirm with the scriptural tradition that fundamentally God is love, but insist that Christians can only really *mean* this statement when they reject the concept of a changeless, non-relative being articulated by classical Christian theism.[36] On this second front, they affirm the theism of the classical Christian tradition while they deny that the most usual concept employed to communicate that tradition—namely, the understanding of God as self-subsistent being unaffected by our actions[37]—is either coherent or scriptural. The process theologians are committed to no less an enterprise than clarifying the justification and meaning of the most fundamental aspirations and affirmations of contemporary human beings, *and* clarifying the justification and meaning of the most basic Christian affirmation, the reality of God.[38]

It may also be worth noting that the work of the process thinkers may be coming to the fuller attention of the American theological community at precisely the right moment in its history. Process thought is a consistent and systematic theological option which has been developed almost exclusively in our own highly empirical Anglo-American culture. Here is a position which gives no mere lip service to modernity's demand for radical critique, fundamental change, and personal responsibility. Process thought argues that only a full-fledged commitment to the authentic values of the modern experiment can be a serious option for all those—most of us, I suspect— who now see no authentic way to deny this commitment. The demand for Christian "relevance" is, at heart, the demand that Christians manage somehow to affirm their Christian self-understanding without negating their commitment to their positive experience as modern and post-modern men and women. My own suspicion is that those theologians who tell us that the problem is to render Christianity relevant to our contemporaries have profoundly missed the full dimensions of the present dilemma.[39] For we are now our contemporaries, and our task is really to make our Christian self-understanding meaningful in our own life styles and our own reflection.

All reflective persons should, then, investigate the process thinkers' charge that the major affirmation of the classical Christian theological tradition, namely its understanding of God, may be missing the point of the scriptural understanding of God's relationship to man. This is, to be sure, no minor point in any program. There are few more highly developed and philosophically impressive traditions than the traditional Christian theological understandings of God as one, as triune, as creator.[40] And yet—the troubling questions of the process thinkers cannot be silenced even on an existential level: Is not the God of the Jewish and Christian scriptures a God profoundly involved in humanity's struggle to the point where God not merely affects but is affected by the struggle? Is Bonhoeffer's famous cry that only a suffering God can help merely a rhetorical flourish of a troubled man?[41] Can the God of Jesus Christ really be *simply* changeless, omnipotent, omniscient, unaffected by our anguish and our achievements? Was the magnificent move of classical patristic and medieval Catholic Christianity from the *quoad nos* of the scriptural interest in God's relationship to humanity to the *quoad se* of the patristic and medieval interest in God-in-himself a fully positive move?[42] Or did its impressive intellectual achievements conceal certain inherent religious and conceptual difficulties? My own suspicion is that all authentic Christians live and pray and speak as if God were really affected by their action.[43] They live as if, to use the expression of one process theologian, God really were Pure Unbounded Love struggling, suffering, achieving with humanity.[44] Yet the question recurs: Christians may live and say this, but can they *mean* it. Can they render it conceptually coherent if they continue to employ the concepts of classical theology? Can Christians mean the most fundamental religious affirmation of Christian self-understanding if they simultaneously affirm the usual understanding of classical Christianity that God is the self-subsistent, changeless, omniscient, all-powerful one who is not really *(relatio entis)* but only notionally *(relatio rationis)* affected by human actions?

Such are some of the questions which process theology poses to classical Christian thought on God. The basic answer which the process theologians themselves affirm is that God must be considered a dipolar reality.[45] We might best understand this initially difficult concept by recalling two further questions.

Is not intelligent and responsible change a positive not a negative factor in all our experience? For example, does not Newman's famous dictum "To live is to change and to be perfect is to have changed often" [46] find resonance in our most fundamental outlook upon our lives? How then do we move from this modern self-understanding to the insistence that God precisely as *the perfect one* must be changeless? Of course, to a Greek or medieval Christian, the move is a relatively easy one. For to the Greek and medieval mind, change, history, temporality are all imperfections when compared to the stable, self-subsistent being affirmed in genuine philosophical thought.[47] Indeed, only a freedom from history and from change really frees the classical mind for an authentic contemplative approach to God, the perfect and changeless one. Such a classical route to an understanding of God does not seem to be so readily available to any modern who really does affirm change as a genuine perfection. For a consistent modern Christian, the process theologians argue, change like all perfections should be applied to God.

In addition, do we not all share the basic understanding of the self-as-relative which modernity in all its major expressions, its literature, psychology, philosophy, sociology, insists upon? [48] The answer of process thinkers to this question is clear: we are authentic selves only in direct proportion to our ability to be affected by and related to other selves. The substance-self of the classical tradition is at best an abstraction.[49] I am the person I am precisely because of my relationship to this history, this family, these friends, those mentors, these ideas appropriated and experiences shared. I am, in a word, a profoundly relative not substantial being. Whether I know it or not, I am the person I am because this idea has taken hold in me, this friend has literally entered my life, this set of historical experiences has affected me. Indeed, love, the most human and the most religious of all experiences, is by definition a *relative concept.*[50] Is not love as an experience a manifestation of our innate demand for relatedness to others? And is not love as a concept the clearest concept by which authentically Christian thinkers have tried to understand God's relationship to man as manifested in the event of Jesus the Christ? What is the meaning of that event other than the overwhelming scandal and mystery of a gracious, loving God fully related to all humanity? We take it for granted that a person who cannot be reached, cannot be affected by the ideas of others, the experience of the historical moment, the love of other persons, the wonder and anguish of existence, is one closed, frightened, dead. Are we then to affirm with the ordinary understanding of classical Christian theology that God alone is in no real way affected by others? [51] Or should we say that God is both absolute (as the one whose *existence* depends on no other being) and relative (as the one whose *actuality* is relative to all other beings)? [52]

This final suggestion is the one which, following the lead of Alfred North Whitehead and Charles Hartshorne, most process thinkers affirm.[53] As strange as it may sound to the classical mind, the concept of a dipolar God is not really a difficult one to grasp. Dipolarity, in fact, is less difficult a concept if we consider first not God's but our own analogously dipolar structure.[54] In one aspect of my person—that highly abstract aspect whereby I simply *exist*—I am not affected by others. I simply exist. Yet, in another aspect of my reality, my actual, concrete person, I am intrinsically and deeply related to others. As a feeling, thinking, willing, acting self, I am related to my own body (as my first environment), to other persons, to my historical moment, to such other historical moments as I can appropriate and so forth. In a word, I am myself dipolar. As merely existing with certain defining characteristics, I am relatively unrelated to others. As this concrete person (my "actuality") I am through and through a relative creature. This dipolar understanding of the self is the one employed analogously to try to make meaningful—that is, conceptually coherent—the scriptural understanding of God. The dipolar concept for God is real but analogous, for in *both* "poles" of his reality God alone is *supremely* perfect. In an abstract pole God alone is absolute. God alone among all realities is not dependent on others for existence. In a concrete pole, however, God, like us, is relative. Again a qualitative difference is introduced: God alone is relative to all other beings. God alone affects and is affected by all others.[55]

Even such crucial world figures (that is those thinkers or activists who affect lives on a major scale) as Aquinas or Marx were affected by and affect a still relatively small number of other persons. On the contrary, as "Pure Unbounded Love," in Schubert Ogden's expression, or as "the fellow sufferer who understands" and "lures us on to the good" in Whitehead's famous formulations,[56] God alone is relative to all. God alone affects all (by providing the relevant possibilities) and is affected by all (by changing as our actual decisions and actions occur and affect God).[57] This dipolar God alone is *both* absolute *and* supremely relative. This dipolar concept, a limit-concept when applied analogously to God, seems a genuinely coherent way to affirm the central scriptural insight that a loving and related God alone is God.

We can summarize this brief and thus far fairly untechnical statement on the meaning and existential meaningfulness of the "process God" by concentrating upon the questions of the more exact logical meaning and claims to truth proposed for this understanding of God. It may be recalled that the process claim—a claim in harmony with the general aims of the revisionist theological model—insists that the dipolar concept of God is at once internally coherent as a concept, true to our common experience, and true to the scriptural meaning of God.[58]

Dipolarity

The insistence that the dipolar understanding of the Christian God is meaningful includes several negative and positive arguments. The negative arguments concentrate upon the difficulties of classical theism. One such argument insists that the monopolar "prejudice" of traditional classical theism, operative in its understanding of God as the Wholly Absolute One, renders meaningless the central modern insight that all reality is constituted by both external and internal relations.[59] In the classical view, creatures are really related to the world and to God. God, as purely and wholly "absolute," is related to creatures only externally or nominally. Yet that concept, for any thinker who recognizes internal relationships as intrinsic to all reality, cannot but strike one as incoherent in itself and as not in harmony with the rest of experience.[60] In that sense, classical theism fails to meet legitimate criteria for logical meaning.

The classical theist's problem, moreover, seems compounded by the question of existential meaningfulness: Can a Wholly Absolute God, unrelated internally to creatures and thus literally unaffected by their actions, seem anything other than an existentially intolerable burden for humanity?[61] If the heart of our authentic secularity is its consistent insistence that our life here and now is that which is of ultimate significance,[62] can we really hold that our ultimate commitment is to a God literally unaffected by that life? Is the real Christian belief one in a "super-natural" world whose existential lure too often removes its believers from the struggle for truth and justice in this world?[63] In terms of existential meaningfulness, at least, the "wholly absolute" God of classical supernaturalism cannot but seem repugnant to the secular spirit. That existential difficulty—probably far more than the possible incoherence of the concept of the Wholly Absolute itself—has rendered atheism a seemingly unavoidable option for some of the paradigmatic witnesses of the modern struggle for liberation.[64]

A third problem for the classical concept of God presents itself as a more explicitly hermeneutical one. Can the classical theist render conceptually meaningful the scriptural attributes for God other than by effectively denying them? If all the "attributes" of the classical Absolute—immutability, aseity, omnipotence, impassivity, etc.—are interpreted as denying that God bears an internal relationship to anything beyond divine Absolute being, how can one render conceptually meaningful the scriptural assertions of a God really affected by the actions of humanity? Are these constant spiritual assertions merely anthropomorphisms, "only" symbols, "merely" metaphors whose real conceptual meaning is quite the opposite? To be sure, the classical theist has always insisted that the final understanding of the relationship between God's power and knowledge and human freedom is a "mystery."[65] With that final assertion there seems no philosophical or theological reason to disagree. Yet as the scholastics noted time and time again, the philosophical theologian's principal task was to try to clarify just "where the mystery lies."[66] It seems unlikely that the conceptual expression of the mystery of the reality of the Christian God need lie in the concept "Wholly Absolute": a concept which seems to make meaningless our understanding of reality as constituted by internal relationships; which seems to force some of those among our contemporaries most firmly committed to such traditional Christian orientations as the struggle for truth and justice and love[67] in this world to turn away in existential repugnance from a God literally unaffected by this struggle; which seems to find an interpretation of the scriptural insight into the profound, abiding, loving, and reciprocal relationship between that God and this world only through concepts which seem to substitute negative literal meanings for the positive disclosures of the Jewish and Christian religious limit-language.

Given this negative critique of the problems of both meaning and meaningfulness involved in classical theism, the concept of a dipolar God would seem to merit careful consideration as a positive alternative. Does that dipolar concept itself meet the criteria for meaning, meaningfulness, and truth set forth by the revisionist model? Assuming that the earlier discussion of dipolarity is basically clear, such concepts may now be applied more technically to the question of God. On a first level the meaning-as-coherent-concept of the dipolar God can be stated.[68] Given the fact that the basic metaphysical analogy for reality is the self and the self's own experience as intrinsically social and temporal, God too—precisely as real—is to be understood as social and temporal. More exactly, God as the eminently relative one is the perfect, and hence unique, instance in reality of creative becoming.[69] God alone is supremely or eminently social and temporal. As such, God alone is related to all reality through immediate participation in a manner analogous to the self's immediate relationship to its own body.[70] God, as social, both eminently affects and is affected by all reality. In a similar manner, the dipolar God as eminently temporal may be understood to be in a continual process of self-creation, again analogous to the self's own temporal creation. As eminently or supremely temporal, the divine process of self-creation is also genuine but only analogous to our process. Where, in each new moment of our experience, we synthesize much of our past actuality through memory and the unconscious with our several projects of future possibilities, God alone synthesizes in each new moment all the actuality already achieved with all the true possibilities as yet unrealized.[71] God as the eminently social and temporal one is unsurpassable in principle by all reality save self. Precisely as unsurpassably temporal and social—and, in that revised sense, as changeless—God alone is God.

The concept of God as the eminently social and temporal one seems both a coherent and a meaningful metaphysical concept based upon the analogy of the self's own temporal and social reality.[72] Precisely as such this conceptuality seems to be the kind of genuine limit-concept which our entire investigation thus far has sought. Yet surely, it seems fair to say, the history of Western thought on God cannot have been wholly wrong in insisting upon the need to declare God "absolute." As Paul Tillich suggested in his reaction to Charles Hartshorne's theism, the seeming loss of this absoluteness for understanding the radically monotheistic God of Judaism and Christianity would seem to render the insistence upon the social and temporal character of God religiously, if not philosophically, unacceptable.[73] This "religious" objection, at first glance, seems well-taken. But what may be overlooked here is that the eminently social and temporal God of process thought, precisely as a limit-concept, is also coherently conceived as absolute.[74] Let us recall that the understanding of the self provides the central clue to this analogous understanding of God's self. That understanding, as outlined above, insists not only that our selves are properly understood as social and temporal, but also that those selves are dipolar. We can legitimately abstract certain characteristics from our concrete "actuality" to an understanding of our existence and essence. Yet if we are consistent, we do not hold that such characteristics (e.g., our mutability, our passivity, our materiality) are exhaustive of the concrete persons whose actuality our friends know. The same distinction—again analogously—applies to the process understanding of God.

Indeed, by returning to the understanding of God as the eminently social and temporal one, we might see how in fact this analogy to the self functions to allow a genuine affirmation of "absoluteness" in God. Before that, however, we might note an important procedural difference in the very raising of the question of God's absoluteness. The present concern is to understand how the already personal (as social and temporal) God may also be understood as absolute—not the reverse.[75]

The point of this shift in the very formulation of the question is worth dwelling upon. In the case of self-understanding, we best understand certain attributes of our own person (our passivity and mutability, for example) only after we have first understood as best we can the concrete social and temporal constitution of our own experience. Similarly, we best understand certain attributes of God's person (immutability and impassivity, for example) only after we have analogously understood God's concrete, eminently social and temporal person.[76] If we follow this procedure, the attributes of God's absoluteness can be stated with clarity and coherence: the fact of God's eminent relativity—a relationship to *all* reality—is itself relative to nothing. Precisely as such, the eminently relative God is the absolute ground of all relationships, ours and the divine. In short, absoluteness—and the traditional metaphysical attributes which serve to articulate that absoluteness—can be truly affirmed about God.[77] Yet the key to understanding that affirmation remains that the absolute is the abstract pole of God. We cannot coherently conceive of God as the eminently relative and temporal one unless we also affirm the presence of absoluteness as the abstract principle and, in that sense, central attribute of God. The concrete, actual God, to be sure, is not to be identified with the absolute—or with any of those attributes (immutability, impassivity, aseity, etc.) which serve to clarify the fuller meaning of the concept absolute as "related to no other." [78] The concrete God is the eminently social and relative one affecting and affected by all reality; the abstract principle which renders coherent this concept of a divine self really analogous to our selves is the affirmation of God's absoluteness as the abstract principle of the divine concrete identity.

When we affirm that God is dipolar, therefore, we affirm that God has both a concrete pole which is eminently social and temporal, an ever-changing, ever-affecting, ever-being-affected actuality, and an abstract pole which is well-defined—if "concretely misplaced"—by traditional Western reflection upon the metaphysical attributes of the Wholly Absolute One. [79] By means of the metaphysical employment of the analogy of the social and temporal self's own dipolar structure, this dipolar understanding of God presents one with what seems to be a coherent and thereby a meaningful concept for the reality of God. For the dipolar concept insists that God alone is both absolute and supremely relative, both ground of all reality and affected by all reality. In terms of the first criterion for "meaning," internal coherence, the dipolar concept of God seems clearly meaningful. [80]

The second criterion for meaning, we may recall, was the need not merely for internal coherence but for existential meaningfulness. That criterion too seems to be fulfilled by this process understanding of God. Precisely as the eminently social and relative one, God is affected by or internally related to all creatures. No contemporary secular thinker with a real commitment to the ultimate significance of our actions for good or evil here and now need fear that this God—the only God, I believe, whom Christians know—is indifferent to or unaffected by that commitment or that struggle. [81] The Christian God is involved in that struggle to persuade us to the good; to aid us by that immediate participation we call love to choose the true and right possibility; to be affected by the actual choice made. [82] Yet that actual personal choice—the actualization of the possibility for good or evil—is ours. [83] There is no monarchical God who first decides for us and then is indifferent to our choice and its consequences. [84] There is a God—the God of Abraham, Isaac, Jacob, and Jesus Christ—which a process metaphysics can aid us to understand in strictly conceptual terms. [85] If, as we insisted above, the primary existential use of the word "God" is to refer to the objective ground in reality itself for those limit-languages and limit-experiences of an ultimate worth of our existence, our commitment to the good, and our struggle to achieve it; if the primary logical need for explicating this reality is a coherent limit-concept, then, on secular grounds alone, one need not hesitate to articulate that existential faith in explicitly theistic terms. [86] In terms of criteria for existential meaningfulness, the dipolar understanding of God's reality is as meaningful as its ability reflectively to articulate the objective basis of those limit-experiences and limit-languages found in both our common existence and the Christian faith. [87] Both our common existence and our Christian faith seem to find adequate reflective articulation only when they are explicated in self-consciously theistic terms. Such theistic understanding in turn can serve to maintain the existential meaningfulness of Christian theism only when it is formulated by means of some kind of coherent limit-conceptuality.

3.   The third question of meaning remains the explicitly hermeneutical one implied by criteria of appropriateness. Here merely a few summary comments seem in order since it is difficult to envisage how the dipolar understanding of God can be judged out of harmony with the biblical picture of God's "actions." On the contrary, by means of this metaphysics, one may render conceptually coherent the clear insistence of the Christian scriptures that God is qualitatively distinct from creatures both as, in some meaningful way, absolute (i.e., not dependent on creatures at all) and as supremely related to, affecting, and affected by all reality.[88] In the final section of this chapter, I shall try to reflect further upon the possible uses of this dipolar concept for understanding the symbolic limit-language of the scriptures and for formulating new symbolic language. For the present I shall risk a simple, indeed a blunt statement of what seems, to me at least, fairly obvious: from a hermeneutical viewpoint, the interpreter of Hebrew and Christian texts seems on far more solid ground in appealing to the dipolar concept of God as more in harmony with scriptural meanings than any concept informed by the monopolar outlook.[89] Perhaps it need not always be the case that the God of the scriptures and the God of the philosophers are irreconcilable. In that revolution in theological reflection upon the meaning of God called process thought, perhaps that chasm has at last been bridged.

In fact, the most original metaphysical thinker in the process tradition, Charles Hartshorne, takes the discussion of the meaning of the dipolar concept of God a step further. That step is the strictly metaphysical insistence that a correct logical understanding of the "meaning" of the concept God is also an affirmation of its "truth." [90] Although it is not my purpose to argue for Hartshorne's complex position here, the main outlines of that position surely merit consideration. Nor are those main outlines unfamiliar ones to the contemporary student of philosophical theology. Indeed, as the title of Hartshorne's work, *Anselm's Discovery,* makes clear, the position is a reformulation of what Hartshorne believes to be the properly metaphysical-logical discovery in Anselm's ontological argument. Hartshorne's own reformulation involves several issues of considerable complexity. With two of those issues we shall not deal here: his subtle exegetical argument for his own interpretation of the proper meaning of Anselm's "second" argument along with his counter-argument against such classical and modern interpreters of Anselm as Aquinas, Descartes, Kant, and Gilson; his elaboration of the need for and the character of a modal logic and a theory of possibility to defend his position.[91] The other two major issues involved in Hartshorne's central argument, however, do demand some consideration in the present context: the logical relationship of the questions of meaning and truth when applied to the concept of God; the properly dipolar meaning of that theistic concept.[92]

It seems fair to state that the latter of these issues has been clarified above. For the dipolar (or pantheistic) understanding of God as both the supremely relative and the absolute one has been the major focus of this entire discussion. That conceptuality for the reality of God, moreover, seemed internally coherent and, in that sense at least, meaningful. The obvious further question is that of the truth of the reality of God. Here is where Hartshorne argues that Anselm did make a genuine discovery in formulating the ontological argument. Hartshorne challenges the prevalent notion that the ontological argument fails because it attempts to make a fallacious inference from an idea (a "meaning") to a reality (a "truth"). The point of that argument, he insists, is quite the opposite. Not just any idea warrants an inference to a reality (e.g., the idea of "man" or of "unicorn"). Only the coherently conceived idea of the radically monotheistic Judaeo-Christian God—precisely as the idea of a necessary existent—warrants that reality.[93] If one can coherently conceive the concept "necessary existent," he must, short of self-contradiction, affirm its reality. A central purpose of the dipolar conceptuality for the reality of God has all along been the attempt to articulate a coherent conception (relative and absolute, temporal and eternal) of that necessary reality.

The main lines of Hartshorne's argument can probably best be clarified by recalling the prior discussion of the internal incoherence involved in the classical monopolar concept for God and the coherence of the modern dipolar concept. Both conceptualities insist that the strictly metaphysical character of that theistic reality—at least as described in radical monotheism—can only be analyzed accurately if God is understood to be the one necessary existent. Yet the first set of concepts—laden, as Anselm's own concepts were by the monopolar prejudice[94]—could only describe that necessary existent as the Wholly Absolute One. That concept, ridden with the difficulty of how that reality can be real and yet lack internal relations to the world, can be described either positively as "mysterious" or negatively as incoherent. If the first route, the proclamation of mystery and paradox, is taken, one may find (as surely Anselm and the great mainline classical theistic tradition did find) religious meaningfulness but not coherent conceptual meaning. And yet, that incoherence can be removed by the insistence that the "Absolute One" is not in fact the concrete God of the Christian scriptures but rather is the abstract principle (or abstract pole) of the eminently social and temporal concrete God (the concrete pole). If that conceptual reformulation is legitimate, the central concept shared by classical and neo-classical metaphysics alike, the concept "necessary existent," may find a coherent explication.

What follows from that reformulation can be stated in more properly Anselmian ontological terms: to be able coherently to conceive *what* God is (the meaning) is also to know *that* God is (the truth or reality). As the coherently conceived sole necessary existent, God—and God alone—cannot but be experienced in anything that is so much as even possible.[95] In this single instance, the instance of coherently conceiving the necessary reality of God, meaning and truth are logically identical. The largely positivist contemporary criticism of theism (represented by the application of the verification and falsification principles to theistic meaning) seems unable to comprehend that even logically the meaning and truth of this concept "necessary existent" cannot be separated. Given the general positivist distrust for the meaningfulness of any metaphysical language, these same critics also fail to see that a recognition of the unique logical character of the concept "necessary existent"—once coherently explicated in dipolar terms—has the equally unique ontological or real character of either being necessarily true or necessarily false. If the latter be the case, then the internal incoherence of the concept must be articulated. If the former be the case, then there seems no good logical or ontological reason for denying the unique metaphysical reality of that unique logical-metaphysical concept.

Some necessary repetition may be helpful here. In the present pluralist situation of theology, there are admittedly very few theologians willing to defend the theological use of the classical "proofs" for God's existence. With the criticism of that tradition in either its deductivist or inductivist modes, I have already voiced my full agreement.[96] Yet the core of that tradition, as this all too brief delineation of Hartshorne's reformulation of the ontological argument may serve to indicate, lies elsewhere. The word "proof," bearing as it does the tones of a pre-critical age of deductivist, and, in that sense, rationalist metaphysics, is probably best consigned to the scrap-heap of spent concepts. And yet, what the properly ontological component in all the classical arguments for God's existence in fact explicated was the insight that only an affirmation of the reality of God as the one necessary existent can validate our very understanding of our selves as selves, our primordial and unconquerable basic faith in the ultimate worthwhileness of our existence.[97] That such basic faith does exist can be validated in the valiant struggles for the cause of humanity of such exponents of "absurdity" and "meaninglessness" as Sartre and Camus. That such basic faith can only find coherent reflective articulation by the development of limit-concepts which allow an affirmation of the objective reality of God has been the central insistence, variously formulated, in the tradition upholding the legitimacy of "arguments" for God's existence. That this same objective reality of God cannot be conceived coherently by means of the Wholly Absolute conceptualities of classical theism, but can be conceived coherently in the dipolar conceptualities of neo-classical theism we have already argued. That these latter limit-meanings also and necessarily involve an experiential affirmation of the truth of the objective reality itself is the fundamental logical and metaphysical insight needed to affirm, with something approaching reflective adequacy, that our most basic and common faith is not an illusion.[98] The question of God's reality, the divine necessity or impossibility, is not a question of interest only to those with a taste for arcane subjects. In fact, the question of properly conceiving God's reality—precisely as the objective ground of our most basic faith in the meaningfulness of our lives—is of crucial existential import for all concerned with the need to articulate an objective ground for that faith. Then the concern is the strictly reflective one of trying to render one's reflection upon life coherent with the actual "performance" of life.[99] From the perspective of the theist, only a clear and coherent affirmation of God's reality renders that common reflective task soluble.

For those unconcerned with the struggle to actualize this shared faith in the worthwhileness of existence, the problem is far more radical. In that case, whether God's reality is affirmed or denied makes little or no existential difference. Such persons—inside and outside the churches—seem involved not in disbelief but in un-faith. Their problem is one demanding nothing short of conversion to the commitment to actualize that common basic faith.[100] Here reflective beliefs—whether theist, agnostic, or atheist—are not the basic issue. The first and abiding issue for human beings is their faith or un-faith, commitment to value or failure to live a human life. A faith of this kind, as I have already suggested, is most immediately experienced in boundary-situations and peak experiences and most clearly mediated or represented in the limit-language of an explicitly religious self-understanding. If that common faith is shared, then what I dare to call the limit-question of God as the objective ground in reality for that very faith becomes a reflective issue of major existential import. At that point, the issues of metaphysics become of singular concern for the reflective human being. How that same reality may be self-consciously articulated with existential and symbolic adequacy has been the major concern of the religions. Whether and to what degree of adequacy symbolic language can re-present the conceptualities of the process tradition will be the concern of the remainder of this chapter and the heart of the "christological" reflections of the following chapter.

THE MEANINGFULNESS OF CHRISTIAN GOD-LANGUAGE: The Search for an Adequate Limit-Language

The proposals of this chapter thus far lead me to express a personal caveat. Although I have become convinced that process thought does provide the most adequate resource for contemporary theism, I remain unconvinced that process thought, of and by itself, provides as full a resolution of the contemporary theological situation as several process thinkers seem to suggest.[101] In the first place, there remain internal problems which the process tradition seems unable to resolve with anything like a lasting consensus. More important for my own purposes, there remain technical problems within process thought which need real clarification. Even if one grants the genuine importance of the articulation of the dipolar character of God's reality, still further technical clarification of that concept seems necessary. One needs, for example, further clarification of the hermeneutical and constructive issues at dispute between William Christian's articulation of God as "a single actual entity" and John Cobb's articulation of the same dipolar God as a "personally ordered society of actual entities." [102] Surely such issues must be clarified before the full conceptual articulation of what I believe to be this major modern discovery can receive the fully adequate technical articulation it demands. That such a need does not threaten the more primordial discovery of God's dipolar reality seems secure. But that such a need is a genuine one for the further elucidation of this tradition seems equally sure.

In a similar vein, it seems fair to state that the process thinkers' hermeneutical analyses of the complex meanings present in *the* "classical theist," Thomas Aquinas, need further reflection.[103] Hartshorne and others are too often satisfied with accepting some outdated neo-scholastic interpretation of Aquinas' meaning when more accurate and more contemporary formulations can be found in the work of such diverse thinkers and traditions as Rahner, Lonergan, Preller, and Burrell.[104] The basic dipolar criticisms of Aquinas' monopolar position may well still hold. Yet the fact remains that an adequate criticism of these more modern and more accurate interpretations of the subtle and complex position of Aquinas cannot, to my knowledge at least, be found in the process corpus. The present substantive dialogue on this central issue cannot but be advanced by the removal of the seeming misapprehensions, not to say non-conversation, between the newer forms of Thomism and the several forms of process metaphysics.

More externally, perhaps, at least two non-theistic issues deserve more careful attention from thinkers in the process tradition. A fuller process anthropology, more cognizant with and more articulate of the ambiguity, the tragedy, the sin involved in a truly contemporary as distinct from a modern model of humanity, is sorely needed.[105] It may well be the case that the seeming inability of process thought to have the wider existential impact which its revisionary concept of the Christian God's reality deserves may result from the presence of a kind of residual liberal optimism which the process image of man too often evokes. This anthropological difficulty, moreover, is increased when a second "external" issue is introduced: the relative lack of analysis of other than strictly conceptual language among process thinkers.[106] As the earlier chapters on religious language strove to indicate, the originating language of a religious tradition or of the religious dimension of our common experience is seldom strictly conceptual. As the remainder of this chapter will suggest, that insight may aid us to suggest how the conceptual language of process theology may find expression in a symbolic language more resonant with the sensibilities of contemporary humanity. If such symbolic language can be articulated then, perhaps, process theology may find the wider existential-religious impact which, in my judgment, its rich conceptual discoveries deserve. In the terms of the prior analysis of religious language as limit-language, one may state that the present need becomes that of finding symbolic language which can allow the disclosure of the Christian God to "happen" for the present actual situation.

For the purpose of disclosing the need for symbolic language, let us assume that the central paradigm of the Christian experience of God is that disclosed in the Johannine literature under the summary limit-metaphor "God is love." It seems a fair historical observation that classical metaphysics, given its stand against any notion of internal relations for the Wholly Absolute God, found it difficult to render this limit-metaphor of the Christian religion conceptually coherent. For example, neither the philosophical-theological "caritas synthesis" representative of Catholic Christianity nor the largely anti-philosophical agape insistence claimed by Anders Nygren as one of Luther's central discoveries seemed able to render this profoundly religious understanding of God's love both conceptually coherent and existentially meaningful.[107] In contrast, process metaphysics, given its insistence upon internal relations as constitutive of all, even the divine, reality, seems able to provide a coherent conceptual understanding of this crucial Christian insight.[108] This seems true whether one turns to that Protestant understanding of the God-humanity relationship as a dialectic of agapic love or to the Catholic emphasis upon the synthesis of eros and agape in Christian caritas. Either tradition here, I believe, could find articulate and coherent conceptual expression through a metaphysics whose crowning exemplification is precisely an eminently social, temporal, related—in a word, loving—God.

Such conceptual clarification of the disclosing Christian metaphor "God is love" by means of process categories would be no small theological achievement. What would still seem badly needed, however, would be symbolic forms of expression that might allow that insight to resonate more fully to the deepest sensitivities of our present multi-dimensional cultural situation. Yet for that task, the process thinkers seem, by and large, to be too ready to rest content with the suggestive symbolic expressions of Whitehead himself. In fact, the leitmotif of Whitehead's famous symbolic description of the process God as "the fellow sufferer who understands" and who "lures us on to the good" is a frequent symbolic refrain in the process thinkers' attempt to render symbolically meaningful their conceptual discoveries. There seems every good reason to continue to respect these symbolic formulations of Whitehead. Especially is this so in a culture where the majority of participants, theists, atheists, and agnostics alike, probably continue to picture God, when they think of God at all, through the symbol of an all-powerful, an all-knowing, often even a tyrannical monarch. The disclosure afforded by the symbol of the monarchical God seems neither *fascinans* nor particularly *tremendum*. Ordinarily that disclosure inclines human beings either simply to forget that reality as soon as possible, or to fight against it with the militancy of the symbolic *cri de coeur* that this God must die, or passively to submit to it with the equally desperate cry that "God's ways are not ours." In place of this monarchical image, surely the image of God's persuasive, non-coercive love is both more resonant to our own experience of human love and more faithful to the image of God disclosed in the Christian scriptures.

Yet my hesitancy about the power of these Whiteheadean symbols to evoke the full disclosure of the Christian God remains. If we recall the prior discussion of the limit-character of New Testament language, a further step may be taken in the search for adequate symbolic language. In symbolic terms, it seems hermeneutically sound to insist that God's love as described in the scriptures bears a persuasive, not a coercive character. It seems equally clear that the scriptual limit-language disclosure of that persuasiveness is not fully captured by the calm and vaguely Edwardian image evoked by Whitehead's "fellow-sufferer who understands." [109] The God of the Jewish and Christian scriptures is not simply described in images evocative of a compassionate, a somehow "liberal," fellow-sufferer. Although genuinely evocative, that image seems more disclosive of, say, the reasonable and compassionate mode-of-being-in-the-world represented by such a believable and admirable group of understanding fellow-sufferers as the Bloomsbury circle. The "fellow-sufferer" image scarcely seems to break the bonds of an admirably moral and aesthetic world into those dramatic and sometimes extreme limit-experiences explicitly re-presented in religion. The Whiteheadean images, moreover, may too easily lend themselves to the quiet and perhaps fatal optimism disclosed in liberal symbols of human development, rather than to the less readily optimistic, indeed explosive vision present in post-modern and post-liberal symbols of human liberation. Finally, a mere contentment with the "fellow sufferer" image can too often evoke the picture of a kind of "warm deism" which seems neither appropriate to our own experience of the religious dimension of existence, nor faithful to the scriptural portrait of a God who actually "acts" in history.[110] Those scriptural "acts of God," to be sure, are usually mythologically expressed. Yet, even in fidelity to the demands of demythologizing, can we not find symbols which eliminate the purely mythological elements while retaining the fully religious-as-limit existential disclosure that the Judaeo-Christian God really does act in history: God's promises of a radically new world; a raising of prophets to proclaim that newness; acts for and promise of a limit-liberation from social and individual forces whose power, indeed whose evil, bear at least as radical a character today as in biblical times? By all means, let us remain faithful to the symbol of God's persuasive, not coercive power of love. But can we not find more adequate symbolic expression for that very persuasiveness—for that Pure Unbounded Love—than the somehow distant image of a "fellow-sufferer who understands"? Can we not find more compelling and more liberating symbolic language for the plight of oppressed and oppressor alike? Can we not find some honest, i.e., some properly demythologized way, to express anew, as Ernst Bloch and his several Christian theological admirers suggest, the liberating, the radically new force of that divine love as represented in the limit-language of Jewish and Christian eschatology? [1] My own conviction is that such a way can be found if we look anew at the originating christological and eschatological limit-languages of the Christian religion in the dual context of an understanding of all authentically religious language as limit-language and in the context of what I believe to be the authentic limit-concept developed by the process thinkers: a conceptually coherent, a dipolar understanding of the Christian God of love.

Notes

(1) Inter alia, cf. Antony Flew, *God and Philosophy* (New York: Harcourt, Brace and World, 1966), pp. 27–29; Schubert M. Ogden, "The Task of Philosophical Theology," in *The Future of Philosophical Theology*, pp. 65–72, esp. 71–72; cf. also the discussion of "philosophical reflection" in chapter four. Since this chapter forms a unit with the preceding chapter, full bibliographic data for many titles here may be found in the notes of chapter seven.

(2) For the argument that this turn began with Thomas Aquinas, not Descartes, cf. Johann Baptist Metz, *Christliche Anthropozentrik: Über die Denkform des Thomas von Aquin* (München: Kösel-Verlag, 1962), esp. pp. 124–35; for the modern recovery of the "turn to the subject," cf. Bernard Lonergan, *The Subject* (Milwaukee: Marquette University Press, 1968).

(3) Inter alia, cf. Karl Rahner, *Spirit in the World* (New York: Herder and Herder, 1968); idem, "Theology and Anthropology," in *The Word In History*, ed. T. Patrick Burke (New York: Sheed and Ward, 1966), pp. 1–23; Bernard Lonergan, *Insight: A Study of Human Understanding* (London: Longmans, Green, 1957), esp. pp. 319–434; for surveys of this tradition, cf. Otto Muck, *The Transcendental Method*; and Helen James John, *The Thomist Spectrum* (New York: Fordham University Press, 1966), pp. 139–91.

(4) On Lonergan, cf. my *The Achievement of Bernard Lonergan* (New York: Herder and Herder, 1970); on Rahner, cf. the articles by Ann Carr ("Theology and Experience in the Thought of Karl Rahner," *Journal of Religion* 53 [1973], 359–77) and John C. Robertson ("Rahner and Ogden: Man's Knowledge of God," *Harvard Theological Review* 63 [1970], 377–407); for an excellent account of the philosophies of God in Rahner and Lonergan, cf. Gerald A. McCool, "The Philosophical Theology

of Rahner and Lonergan," in *God Knowable and Unknowable*, Robert J. Roth (ed.) (New York: Fordham University Press, 1973), pp. 123–57.

(5) Cf. Lonergan, *Insight*, pp. 634–87, for Lonergan's Thomist formulation of an argument for "general transcendent knowledge." For a critical defense of Lonergan's position here, cf. Bernard Tyrell, *The Philosophy of God According to Bernard Lonergan* (South Bend: University of Notre Dame Press, 1974); for Lonergan's own response to some of these criticisms, cf. *Foundations of Theology: Papers from the Lonergan Congress, 1970*, ed. Philip McShane (London: Gill and Macmillan, 1971), pp. 223–35. In Rahner, note how Thomist categories especially on the original unity of being and knowing still dominate in his *Hörer des Wortes: Zur Grundlegung einer Religionsphilosophie* (München: Kösel-Pustet, 1941), rev. ed. by Johann Baptist Metz (München: Kösel, 1963). The English translation is so seriously marred as to render it not dependable here. In the cases of both Rahner and Lonergan, however, there seems to be, in their later work, an operative but not fully thematized wider notion of "experience" than that present in their earlier, more neo-Thomist and transcendental formulations. For an example in Rahner, cf. his discussion of "mystagogical experience" in "Atheism and Implicit Christianity," *Theological Investigations*, IX, esp. pp. 154–64; on Lonergan, cf. chapter five, n. 44.

(6) For a good historical survey of this tradition, cf. Gene Reeves and Delwin Brown, "The Development of Process Theology," in *Process Philosophy and Christian Thought*, ed. Delwin Brown, Ralph E. James, Jr., and Gene Reeves (New York: Bobbs-Merrill, 1971), pp. 21–67; for a systematic presentation of the issues, cf. Bernard M. Loomer, "Christian Faith and Process Philosophy," ibid., pp. 70–99; for selections from these philosophers, cf. Douglas Browning, *Philosophers of Process* (New York: Random House, 1965): note especially the summary statement of Charles Hartshorne, "The Development of Process Philosophy," ibid., pp. v–xxii.

(7) Cf. Alfred N. Whitehead, *Process and Reality: An Essay in Cosmology*, p. 252: "The subjectivist principle is that the whole universe consists of elements disclosed in the analysis of the experiences of subjects."

(8) A parallel position may be found in the work of the existential phenomenologists: for an extended comparative analysis of these two traditions, cf. Calvin O. Schrag, *Experience and Being: Prolegomena to a Future Ontology* (Evanston: Northwestern University Press, 1969), esp. pp. 15–125.

(9) Cf. John E. Smith, *Experience and God* (New York: Oxford University Press, 1968), pp. 21–46; for an argument on the presence of an implicitly wider notion of experience in Hume and Kant, cf. James Collins, *The Emergence of Philosophy of Religion* (New Haven: Yale University Press, 1967), esp. pp. 29–49, 74–89 (on Hume), 129–212 (on Kant).

(10) John E. Smith, *Experience and God*, pp. 21–68; idem, *Themes in American Philosophy: Purpose, Experience and Community* (New York: Harper & Row, 1970).

(11) Cf. Bernard E. Meland, "The Empirical Tradition in Theology at Chicago," in *The Future of Empirical Theology*, ed. Bernard E. Meland (Chicago: University of Chicago Press, 1969), pp. 1–65, esp. 40–54. Note Meland's own cautionary remarks on this "third phase" of empirical theology at Chicago, pp. 41–42, 53–54. For Meland's own more Jamesian employment of the tradition of "radical empiricism"

inter alia, cf. Bernard E. Meland, *The Realities of Faith: The Revolution in Cultural Forms* (New York: Oxford University Press, 1962), pp. 118–22, 174–84, 198–99. This "radical empiricism" will be expressed in an important new work by Bernard E. Meland, tentatively entitled *Fallible Forms.*

(12) For a clear and systematic presentation of the Whitehead-Hartshorne tradition here, cf. John B. Cobb, Jr., *A Christian Natural Theology,* esp. pp. 1–176. The soundest guide to Whitehead's major work remains Donald W. Sherburne, *A Key to Whitehead's Process and Reality* (New York: Macmillan, 1966). An excellent bibliographical list of works in the Whitehead-Hartshorne tradition may be found in *Process Philosophy and Christian Thought,* ed. by Delwin Brown et al., pp. 475–89. More recent issues and bibliography in the process tradition are discussed in the important new journal *Process Studies.*

(13) This insight is what lies behind Whitehead's famous remark: ". . . the difficulties of all schools of modern philosophies lie in the fact that, having accepted the subjectivist principle, they continue to use philosophical categories derived from another point of view" (*Process and Reality,* p. 253).

(14) This represents my own value-judgment; that same insight can, I believe, be incorporated into the tradition of "transcendental methods" of Rahner and Lonergan; cf. the discussions of "experience" and "transcendental analysis" in chapter four and the discussions of Rahner and Lonergan in n. 5 above.

(15) Cf. chapter four for a defense of this transcendental formulation.

(16) Cf. the excellent summary of debates surrounding this issue, Gene Reeves and Delwin Brown, "The Development of Process Theology," pp. 36–49; for Whitehead himself, cf. "God is not to be treated as an exception to all metaphysical principles, invoked to save their collapse. He is their chief exemplification" (*Process and Reality,* p. 521).

(17) More precisely, on the question of experience. On questions of language one must, I believe, turn elsewhere. On the latter, cf. Richard Rorty (ed.), *The Linguistic Turn: Recent Essays In Philosophical Method* (Chicago: University of Chicago Press, 1967). The linguistic analyses of the Whitehead scholar, William A. Christian, should prove particularly important for further discussions between these two traditions: cf. William A. Christian, *An Interpretation of Whitehead's Metaphysics* (New Haven: Yale University Press, 1959); idem, *Meaning and Truth in Religion* (Princeton: Princeton University Press, 1964); idem, *Oppositions of Religious Doctrines* (New York: Herder and Herder, 1971). Also important here is the dialogue of Schubert M. Ogden with linguistic philosophers on these issues. Besides the references to Ogden's dialogues with Antony Flew and Stephen Toulmin already cited, cf. his recent discussion of the work of Alastair McKinnon's work "Falsification and Belief," *Religious Studies* 10 (1974), 21–43.

(18) For the principal works of Hartshorne, cf. chapter seven, n. 35. On Hartshorne, cf. William L. Reese and Eugene Freeman, *Process and Divinity: The Hartshorne Festschrift* (La Salle, Ill.: Open Court, 1964), esp. pp. 19–37 (John E. Smith), 493–515 (Schubert M. Ogden), 515–29 (J. M. Findlay), 533–61 (Howard L. Parsons). On various aspects of Hartshorne's work, besides those works already cited, cf. Malcolm Diamond, "Contemporary Analysis: The Metaphysical Target and the Theo-

logical Victim," in *Process Philosophy and Christian Thought*, pp. 143–70; Eugene H. Peters, *Hartshorne and Neo-Classical Metaphysics: An Interpretation* (Lincoln: University of Nebraska Press, 1970); Ralph E. James, Jr., *The Concrete God: A New Beginning for Theology—The Thought of Charles Hartshorne* (Indianapolis: Bobbs-Merrill, 1967); Thomas Richard Rice, "Natural Theology in the Thought of Charles Hartshorne" (unpublished dissertation, University of Chicago Divinity School, Spring, 1974). The last-cited work is, I believe, especially valuable for setting Hartshorne's work in the context of several important traditional and contemporary formulations of the task of natural theology.

(19) Cf. Charles Hartshorne and William L. Reese, *Philosophers Speak of God*. This important work, although ground-breaking and invaluable as a resource for Hartshorne's interpretations of the tradition of reflections on theism, is not, in my judgment, without some serious flaws: certain omissions (especially the omission of Hegel) are notably puzzling; certain failures to provide adequate historical context or to come to terms with more recent historical interpretations of the thinkers under study are equally puzzling—the almost a-historical interpretations of Aquinas (pp. 119–33) and Kant (pp. 142–50) are especially troubling. Yet when all is said and done, the work remains a gold-mine of texts and clear and systematic interpretation.

(20) Ibid., pp. 15–29 for the typologies.

(21) Charles Hartshorne, *Anselm's Discovery* (La Salle, Ill.: Open Court, 1965).

(22) Cf. Schubert M. Ogden, *The Reality of God*, pp. 21–70; cf. also our own earlier discussion in chapter five.

(23) This could also be formulated, as it was earlier, that limit-languages and limit-experience need limit-concepts for their explication. The latter, in turn, as metaphysical, need to maintain fidelity to that experience as well as to their own logical demands for internal coherence. For a negative formulation of this insight, cf. Charles Hartshorne, "Why There Cannot Be Empirical Proofs," in *A Natural Theology for Our Time*, pp. 66–89.

(24) Cf. the discussion of these models in chapter two.

(25) This initial and largely non-technical formulation of the issues is adapted from my earlier review of two anthologies on Process Theology in *The National Catholic Reporter* (July 23, 1972), reprinted in the *Anglican Theological Review* LV, no. 2 (April 1973), 218–24. The anthologies in question are *Process Theology*, ed. Ewert H. Cousins (New York: Newman, 1971) and *Process Philosophy and Christian Thought*. Both anthologies, it should be mentioned, contain valuable bibliographies in process thought and excellent selections of central "process" documents.

(26) Cf. the discussion of that context in chapter one.

(27) This seems especially true for the earlier empirical theologians of the "Chicago School" up to Henry Nelson Wieman. From the generation of Loomer and Meland forward, however, this familiar charge does not ring true. Even Wieman should be interpreted (especially in his still seminal work *The Source of Human Good* [Carbondale, Ill.: Southern Illinois University Press, 1946]), as a major reaction against and alternative to the dominant liberal tradition of his period. For an excellent sum-

mary of Wieman's own context and achievement, cf. Bernard E. Meland, "The Root and Form of Wieman's Thought" and Bernard Loomer, "Wieman's Stature as a Contemporary Theologian," in *The Empirical Theology of Henry Nelson Wieman*, ed. Robert W. Bretall (Carbondale, Ill.: Southern Illinois University Press, 1963), pp. 41–69 and 392–99 respectively. For an example of an analysis of the ambiguities of human existence from this tradition, cf. Bernard E. Meland, "The Source of Human Evil," in *Faith and Culture* (London: George Allen and Unwin, 1955), pp. 139–58. It is also important to note how Schubert M. Ogden appeals to the tradition of Heidegger and Bultmann for an anthropological counterpart to the process interpretation of God's reality, cf. his essay "Bultmann's Demythologizing and Hartshorne's Dipolar Theism," in *Process and Divinity: The Hartshorne Festschrift*, pp. 493–515.

(28) The need for the development of a social ethic by the process thinkers should be noted here: one in conversation with the dialectical analyses of the Frankfurt School (cf. chapters one and ten) seems especially needed. The primarily aesthetical background of process views on ethics needs explication here. Jürgen Habermas' own recent partial retrieval of the work of Charles Sanders Peirce may prove important as an initial step in this conversation. Cf. Habermas, *Knowledge and Human Interests* (Boston: Beacon, 1971), esp. pp. 121–39.

(29) Cf. n. 27 above.

(30) Besides those works already cited, cf. John B. Cobb, Jr., "The Possibility of Theism Today," in *The Idea of God: Philosophical Perspectives*, ed. Edward H. Madden, Rollo Handy, and Marvin Farber (Springfield, Ill.: Thomas, 1968), pp. 98–123; W. Norman Pittenger, "Christian Theology After The 'Death of God,' " *The Church Quarterly* (1969), 306–14; Bernard M. Loomer, "Empirical Theology Within Process Thought," in *The Future of Empirical Theology*, pp. 149–75, esp. 165–69; Schubert M. Ogden, "The Christian Proclamation of God to Men of the So-Called 'Atheistic Age,' " in *Is God Dead?* Concilium 16, pp. 89–99.

(31) On the relative lack of an adequate process articulation of symbols of liberation, cf. the later discussion in this chapter and in chapter ten.

(32) Cf. Schubert M. Ogden, *The Reality of God*, esp. pp. 6–12.

(33) Recall, for example, Schubert Ogden's analysis of the positions of Camus and Sartre in "The Strange Witness of Unbelief," in *The Reality of God*, pp. 120–44.

(34) For the classical texts in Hartshorne here, cf. *Philosophers Speak of God*, pp. 1–25 and 499–514; cf. also idem, "Relative, Absolute, and Superrelative: The Concept of Deity," in *Reality As Social Process*, pp. 110–25; ibid., "Three Ideas of God," pp. 155–62; idem, "Ideas of God: An Exhaustive Division," in *Creative Synthesis and Philosophic Method*, pp. 261–74.

(35) Cf. Charles Hartshorne, *The Logic of Perfection and Other Essays in Neo-Classical Metaphysics* (La Salle, Ill.: Open Court, 1962).

(36) The category "meaning" used here refers to conceptual meaning as involving both internal coherence and adequacy to experience as outlined in chapter four.

(37) Cf. the discussion of "classical theism" in *Philosophers Speak of God*, pp. 58–76.

(38) In the terms employed earlier, a clarification of the limit-language of religion (either as religious dimension or explicitly religious) leads to a clarification of the objective referent for such language, the limit-category, God.

(39) This is not to deny the need for "relevance"; it is to deny that a merely traditional Christian self-understanding will suffice.

(40) For examples, cf. Bernard Lonergan, *De Deo Trino*, I-II, *ad usum auditorum* (Rome: Pontifical Gregorian Press, 1964); or the masterful articles under these titles in the German Catholic encyclopedia, *Sacramentum Mundi: An Encyclopedia of Theology*, ed. Karl Rahner with Cornelius Ernst and Kevin Smyth (New York: Herder and Herder, 1969).

(41) Dietrich Bonhoeffer, *Letters and Papers from Prison*, ed. Eberhard Bethge (London: SCM, 1953), p. 164.

(42) For an analysis of this development, cf. Bernard Lonergan, *Method in Theology*, pp. 302–12, 335–51; *De Deo Trino* I, pp. 87–112.

(43) Note, for example, Hartshorne's appeal to the phenomenon of worship in *A Natural Theology for Our Time*, pp. 3–184, 102–4, as the religious phenomenon which supports his own philosophical view of theism.

(44) The expression is from a hymn by Charles Wesley as employed by Schubert M. Ogden, in *The Reality of God*, p. 177.

(45) For the basic concepts here, cf. Charles Hartshorne, "The Law of Polarity," in *Philosophers Speak of God*, pp. 1–15. For the importance of the law of polarity for Hartshorne's thought, cf. Eugene H. Peters, *Hartshorne and Neo-Classical Metaphysics*, pp. 53–7, 79–92.

(46) Cf. John Henry Newman, *An Essay in the Development of Doctrine* (London: Toovey, 1905), p. 39: "In a higher world it is otherwise but here below to live is to change and to be perfect is to have changed often." The introductory phrase makes it clear that Newman is not to be affirmed as a "pre-process" process theist! Yet the sentence also affirms a long-standing conviction of mine: that the enduring fascination with Newman's life and thought is occasioned by the singular fashion in which he incarnates the passions and clashes of both traditional dogmatic Christianity and the modern sensibility in his marvelously subtle thought and altogether attractive person. For fresh reinterpretations of Newman, cf. *The Rediscovery of Newman: An Oxford Symposium*, ed. John Coulson and A. M. Allchin (London: SPCK, 1967).

(47) This is, to be sure, a rather expansive generalization. And yet, as a generalization, it seems true to the realities of the struggle, for example in Augustine, between Judaeo-Christian historical elements and Neo-Platonic elements.

(48) For a summary-analysis of the sociological model, cf. David M. Rasmussen, "Between Autonomy and Sociality," in *Cultural Hermeneutics* 1 (1973), pp. 3–47.

(49) On the substance-accident set of categories of traditional Western metaphysics, cf. Alfred N. Whitehead, *Process and Reality*, esp. pp. 240–55.

(50) Cf. Daniel Day Williams, *The Spirit and the Forms of Love* (New York: Harper & Row, 1968), esp. pp. 111–30.

(51) This is the "ordinary understanding" insofar as the *concepts* employed in classical theism imply this understanding in contrast to the originating metaphors and symbols of the Christian scriptures and of the prayer and worship of ordinary Christians.

(52) Cf. Charles Hartshorne citations in n. 34 above, and "Philosophical and Religious Uses of 'God,' " in *Process Theology*, pp. 101–19. On "existence" and "actuality," cf. also Charles Hartshorne, *Reality As Social Process*, pp. 204–7.

(53) For Hartshorne's defense of Whitehead's position, cf. "Is Whitehead's God the God of Religion?" in *Ethics* LIII (1943), 219–27.

(54) For succinct formulations, cf. Charles Hartshorne, *Creative Synthesis and Philosophic Method*, pp. 254–60, 291; Schubert M. Ogden, *The Reality of God*, pp. 58–9.

(55) Cf. Charles Hartshorne, *Philosophers Speak of God*, pp. 1–25, 499–514.

(56) For the clearest expression of Whitehead's views here, cf. the brief, often technical, but religiously eloquent final section of *Process and Reality*. Part of that section demands quotation: "The action of the fourth phase is the love of God for the world. It is the particular providence for particular occasions. What is done in the world is transformed into a reality in heaven, and the reality in heaven passes back into the world. By reason of this reciprocal relation, the love in the world passes into the love in heaven, and floods back again into the world. In this sense, God is the great companion—the fellow-sufferer who understands" (p. 532). For the defense of the "religious availability" of Whitehead's concept of God, cf. Bernard M. Loomer, "Ely on Whitehead's God," in *Process Philosophy and Christian Thought*, pp. 264–86. For a concise summary of the relevant texts for Whitehead's doctrines on religion, cf. John B. Cobb, Jr., *A Christian Natural Theology*, pp. 215–52; for a similarly concise summary on Whitehead's doctrine on God, ibid., pp. 135–76. For differing views, cf. Donald W. Sherburne, "Whitehead without God," in *Process Philosophy and Christian Thought*, pp. 287–305; William A. Christian, "The Concept of God as a Derivative Notion," in *Process and Divinity: The Hartshorne Festschrift*, pp. 181–205.

(57) Note that the key concept is *not* change but creative synthesis, cf. Charles Hartshorne, "Whitehead's Novel Intuition," in *Alfred North Whitehead: Essays on His Philosophy*, ed. George L. Kline (Englewood Cliffs, N.J.: Prentice-Hall, 1963), pp. 161–70; idem, "A Philosophy of Shared Creative Experience" in *Creative Synthesis*, pp. 1–19.

(58) In the terms employed earlier (chapter five), this can be formulated as "true to the religious dimension of our common experience." It might also be noted that the literal and analogical use of the dipolar concept for God fits our earlier description of a proper theological use of limit-concepts.

(59) Cf. Charles Hartshorne, *Creative Synthesis*, pp. 52–3, 82–4, 167–70.

(60) The negative criterion "incoherence" here bears both the narrower meaning of

internal incoherence in concepts and the wider meaning of not coherent with the rest of our experience.

(61) A burden which may be summarized in the cultural fact of the "death of God" announced by the radical theologians, cf. discussion in chapter two.

(62) Cf. Schubert M. Ogden, *The Reality of God*, esp. pp. 38–40; note also the discussion of limit-questions in chapter five.

(63) Recall the constant plea of that other thinker in the process tradition, Pierre Teilhard de Chardin, against that temptation: cf. esp. his *Le Milieu Divin* (London: Collins, 1960). For a comparison of Teilhard and Whitehead, cf. Ian Barbour, "Teilhard's Process Metaphysics," in *Process Theology*, pp. 323–51.

(64) We shall suggest later in this chapter that this important insight of the process tradition needs symbolic articulation as well in order to disclose its existential power.

(65) For a brilliant modern reinterpretation of that tradition, cf. Karl Rahner, "The Concept of Mystery in Catholic Theology," in *Theological Investigations*, IV (Baltimore: Helicon, 1966), pp. 36–77.

(66) Note Bernard Lonergan's helpful notion of an "inverse insight" (*Insight*, pp. 19–25), and his application of that notion to the kind of insight the theologian seeks into "mystery," in *De Deo Trino* I, pp. 274–5. The crucial question remains not of "mystery" (or in the alternative Protestant formulations "paradox" and "scandal") but *where* and *when* and how the "inverse insight" occurs. Lonergan provides a convincing example of how an accumulation of theoretical insights could lead Aquinas to affirm the mystery of divine transcendence in his study *Grace and Freedom: Operative Grace in the Thought of St. Thomas Aquinas* (New York: Herder and Herder, 1971), esp. pp. 93–117. A process analysis of that interpretation of Aquinas' position and not merely of earlier interpretations of Aquinas on these matters is badly needed. I hope, in a future monograph, to compare critically the "process" and Thomist views on this and related questions (e.g., literal and analogical language for God-talk). For the present, I am concerned simply to communicate my own understanding of certain initial and signal process insights.

(67) Cf. John B. Cobb, Jr., "Man As Responsible Being," in *A Christian Natural Theology*, pp. 92–135; idem, "What is the Future? A Process Perspective," in *Hope and the Future of Man*, ed. Ewert H. Cousins (Philadelphia: Fortress, 1972), pp. 1–15; David Griffin, "Whitehead and Niebuhr on God, Man and World," *Journal of Religion* 53 (1973), 149–76; Franklin I. Gamwell, "Theism and Political Theory: Beyond Reinhold Niebuhr" (unpublished dissertation, University of Chicago Divinity School, 1973); Daniel Day Williams, "Love and Social Justice," in *The Spirit and The Forms of Love*, pp. 243–76.

(68) In terms of the criteria outlined in chapter four, one might also claim criteria of meaningfulness and truth here. Recall Hartshorne's own important criteriological dictum here: "There is no absolute disjunction between thought and experience. A thought *is* an experience of a certain kind, it means *through* experience. . . . A thought which does not mean by virtue of an experience is simply a thought which does not mean" (*Man's Vision of God*, p. 311).

(69) Cf. Charles Hartshorne, *Creative Synthesis*, pp. 261–74.

(70) Cf. Schubert M. Ogden, "What Sense Does It Make To Say, God Acts in History?" in *The Reality of God*, pp. 164–87, esp. 175–83.

(71) Cf. ibid., pp. 58–60.

(72) Hence, there seems to be a clear harmony here between the views set forth in chapters four and five and the present analysis.

(73) Cf. The Hartshorne-Tillich exchange in *The Theology of Paul Tillich*, ed. Charles W. Kegley and Robert W. Bretall (New York: Macmillan, 1952), pp. 164–95 and 330–32.

(74) Ogden, *The Reality of God*, pp. 60–66.

(75) Ibid., p. 66.

(76) Ibid., p. 61.

(77) Ibid., pp. 60–63.

(78) Ibid., p. 60: "Hence, just because God is the *eminently* relative One, there is also a sense in which he is strictly absolute. His being related to all others is itself relative to nothing, but is the absolute ground of any and all real relationships, whether his own or those of his creatures." This concept of God's "absoluteness" should provide a new context for the more familiar discussions between classical theists and secular philosophers on the possibility or impossibility of affirming the absoluteness of God. For eloquent examples of the more familiar discussion, cf. Maurice Merleau-Ponty, *Éloge de la philosophie* (Paris: Gallimard, 1953), esp. pp. 57–65; and Regis Jolivet, "Le probleme dè l'absolu dans la philosophie de M. Merleau-Ponty," in *Tijdschrift voor Philosophie*, 19 (1957), 53–100.

(79) For the law of polarity, cf. Charles Hartshorne, "A Logic of Ultimate Contrasts," in *Creative Synthesis*, pp. 99–130; for the "fallacy of misplaced concreteness," Alfred N. Whitehead, *Science and the Modern World* (New York: Free Press, 1967), p. 51.

(80) I am assuming here that the argument on the need for metaphysical concepts for the logic of theism (chapter seven) is acceptable; then the question of meaning as internal coherence becomes a paramount issue.

(81) The importance of this position for contemporary "theologics of *praxis*" is indicated in the discussion of chapter ten.

(82) Besides the text already cited, cf. the alternative formulation of Whitehead's position here of Lewis S. Ford, "Divine Persuasion and the Triumph of Good," in *Process Philosophy and Christian Thought*, pp. 287–305.

(83) I do not agree with the familiar charge that this Whiteheadian position can be simply labeled "Pelagian": in fact, the typologies "Pelagian," "semi-Pelagian" and "Augustinian" are all articulated in a context which assumes the classical theistic

doctrine of God. Once that doctrine is reformulated in neo-classical or panentheistic terms, it would seem to follow that the classical doctrines of grace and freedom would also need reformulation in a contemporary dogmatics. I do not pretend that these present remarks in fundamental theology resolve the question of the doctrine of grace but they do provide, it would seem, one element for an eventual reformulation of the doctrine in a contemporary Christian dogmatics. For further process suggestions along this line, cf. David R. Griffin, *A Process Christology* (Philadelphia: Westminster, 1973), pp. 241–66.

(84) Cf., inter alia, Alfred N. Whitehead, *Religion in the Making*, pp. 66–78; idem, *Process and Reality*, pp. 519–21.

(85) Cf. Charles Hartshorne, *Creative Synthesis*, p. 243: "The God of religion, as Pascal saw, is not the absolute of philosophy, any more than the richest concrete actuality can be identical with the most abstract of all individual characters. Yet both can form one transcendent being!" For a contrary view, cf. James Collins, *God in Modern Philosophy* (Chicago: Gateway, 1959), pp. 315–25.

(86) Cf. Schubert M. Ogden, *The Reality of God*, esp. pp. 37–44, and the discussions in chapter five of this book.

(87) Note, again, that the appeal here is to "faith" as prior to "beliefs."

(88) Cf. Daniel Day Williams, "How Does God Act?: An Essay in Whitehead's Metaphysics," in *Process and Divinity*, pp. 161–81; Schubert M. Ogden as cited in n. 70 above; for a major interpretation of the similarities between process categories and New Testament categories, cf. William A. Beardslee, *A House for Hope: A Study in Process and Biblical Thought* (Philadelphia: Westminster, 1972).

(89) A Kierkegaardian "thought-experiment" may be useful to mention here: what if process categories had been available to and employed by the original Greek and Latin Christians who formulated classical theism? Would present-day Christians be as baffled and sometimes scandalized by the seemingly unscriptural "strangeness" of some of the formulations of say, such great masters as Thomas Aquinas or John Calvin, as they now seem by the "untraditional" claims of the process theologians? For arguments that there are resources in the tradition for process categories, cf. Ewert Cousins, "Truth in Saint Bonaventure," in *Proceedings of the American Catholic Philosophical Association* 43 (1969), 204–10; Walter E. Stokes, "Freedom as Perfection: Whitehead, Thomas and Augustine," *Proceedings of the American Catholic Philosophical Association* 36 (1962), 134–42.

(90) Cf. esp. Charles Hartshorne, *Anselm's Discovery*. For an excellent survey of recent Anselm literature, cf. *The Many-Faced Argument: Recent Studies on the Ontological Argument for the Existence of God*, ed. John Hick and Arthur C. McGill (New York: Macmillan, 1967); cf. also the important logical study by Alvin Platinga, *God and Other Minds: A Study of the Rational Justification of Belief in God* (Ithaca: Cornell, 1967).

(91) On the complexity of Anselm's argument and its classical interpretations, cf. Arthur C. McGill, "Recent Discussions of Anselm's Argument," in *The Many-Faced Argument*, pp. 33–118; Charles Hartshorne, "The Second or Strong Form of the Proof," in *Anselm's Discovery*, pp. 33–6; for Hartshorne on the interpretations, ibid.,

pp. 154–64 (Aquinas), 164–73 (Descartes), 208–34 (Kant). Finally, for Hartshorne's argument on the need for a modal logic, cf. ibid., pp. 60–70.

(92) Ibid., pp. 22–33; pp. 41–53. The brief comments in the present chapter do not claim to provide Hartshorne's "proof" but merely to indicate its major components; the reference notes indicate the texts for the "proof" itself; for a recent Thomist critique of Hartshorne here, cf. E. L. Mascall, *The Openness of Being: Natural Theology Today* (Philadelphia: Westminster, 1971), pp. 48–58.

(93) Ibid., esp. pp. 25–33.

(94) Ibid., pp. 3–33.

(95) As early as in *Beyond Humanism: Essays in the New Philosophy of Nature* (Chicago: Willett, Clark, 1937), Hartshorne maintained that we have direct awareness of God (cf. pp. 284–6); since the theistic idea is identical to the idea of cosmic totality conceived as an integrated individual, Hartshorne has consistently held that God is always directly though vaguely present to experience (for example, cf. *Man's Vision of God*, pp. 126–7). Note, for example, the formulation in *Anselm's Discovery* (pp. 64–5): "Has the existence of God an experiential meaning? ('Experiential' is not the same as 'empirical': the latter connotes, 'compatible with some, but *not all* conceivable experiences'; the former, 'confirmed or manifested at least by some, perhaps by all, conceivable experiences'). . . . and, if all things require God's existence for their own, the occurrence of anything whatever—and so of any non-divine experience—implies the divine existence. Accordingly, whether or not in such experiences there is consciousness that God exists depends only upon the level of self-understanding of the experience. . . . And of course many mystics claim to experience God. Since their claim is compatible with the (proper) conception of God, and the claim of falsification is not thus compatible, Anselm's Principle seems to be vindicated. Greatness is conceivable only as existent, by the very criteria which allow us to conceive either the existence or the nonexistence of any island, dollar, devil, you please." This may be justly cited as a radicalization of what Paul Tillich called "the ontological approach" to philosophy of religion (cf. "The Two Types of Philosophy of Religion," in *Theology of Culture*, pp. 10–30, esp. 12–16 and 20–6). The "cosmological approach" (ibid., pp. 16–19) is ordinarily understood to deny direct experience of God but to argue for an inferred knowledge of God from created effects. For an argument that these typologies do not account adequately for the "transcendental Thomism" of Rahner and Lonergan, cf. John C. Robertson "Tillich's Two Types and the Transcendental Method" in *Philosophy and Religion: 1971,* ed. David Griffin (Chambersburg, Pa.: American Academy of Religion, 1971), pp. 48–57. For Hartshorne's own nuanced use of the "ontological proof" in relationship to the other classical "proofs," cf. his "Six Theistic Proofs," in *Creative Synthesis*, pp. 275–98.

(96) Cf. chapter seven, discussion of Anders Nygren's anti-metaphysical position.

(97) Cf. Schubert M. Ogden's reformulation of Hartshorne's insight in *The Reality of God*, pp. 21–43; cf. also Ogden's nuanced position on the place of the "proofs" of God's existence for the theologian, especially his quotation from Maurice Blondel: "This means that the proofs of God, as Maurice Blondel expressed it, 'are not so much an invention as an inventory, not a revelation so much as an elucidation, a purification and a justification of the fundamental beliefs of humanity' " (p. 43, n. 71).

(98) To continue the language of the earlier discussions, this point may be taken as a summary-observation on why what might be labelled the "limit-discipline" of metaphysics continues to be needed by fundamental theologians studying the cognitive claims involved in either the religious-as-limit-dimension of our common experience or the explicitly religious God-language of the Christian tradition.

(99) For a fine formulation of what might be called a modern dialectic of the concept and performance of "faith," cf. Paul Tillich, *The Dynamics of Faith* (New York: Harper, 1957). For an important theological criticism of Hartshorne's own occasionally "intellectualistic" understanding of "faith," cf. Schubert Ogden, *The Reality of God*, p. 24, n. 40.

(100) "Conversion" in the sense of the transformation model of self-transcendence outlined in chapter five.

(101) An example of this "over-claim" may be found in process systematic theology in the insightful work of Daniel Day Williams, *The Spirit and the Forms of Love*; more convincing is the appeal of the process thinker Schubert Ogden to alternative resources for a Christian anthropology in *Christ Without Myth*. My own belief is that process thought has made a major contribution on the doctrine of God and on a systematic understanding of other doctrines insofar as all Christian theological doctrines are influenced by the doctrine of God. On the other hand, there are other resources, both philosophical and theological, in the present pluralist situation which seem more genuinely promising for the development on such critical questions as language, dialectical *praxis,* and anthropology, than the process tradition. For a relevant suggestion from the viewpoint of the central process tradition, cf. Bernard E. Meland, "Can Empirical Theology Learn Something from Phenomenology?" in *The Future of Empirical Theology*, pp. 283–307. A major example of a revisionist theologian's willingness to employ process categories for certain major questions on the doctrine of God yet insistence upon the need for other resources may be found in the work of Langdon Gilkey. Besides the work of Gilkey already cited, cf. his "New Modes of Empirical Theology," *Vox Theologica* (January 1973), pp. 345–70; and "The Eternal God: Eternal Ground of New Possibilities." For one analysis of Whitehead's own views on the linguistic question, cf. Lyman T. Lundeen, *Risk and Rhetoric in Religion: Whitehead's Theory of Language and the Discourse of Faith* (Philadelphia: Fortress, 1972), esp. pp. 253–73.

(102) For these issues, cf. the interpretative essay and bibliographical citations in Gene Reeves and Delwin Brown, "The Development of Process Theology," esp. pp. 36–64, as well as the issues signalized from the viewpoint of a more Jamesian "radical empiricism" in Bernard E. Meland, "Introduction: The Empirical Tradition in Theology at Chicago," in *The Future of Empirical Theology*, pp. 1–65.

(103) Cf. comments in n. 19 and n. 66 above; cf. also the essays of David Burrell on the philosophical grammar of Thomas Aquinas in his *Exercises in Religious Understanding* (Notre Dame: University of Notre Dame Press, 1974), pp. 80–140; cf. also his important linguistic interpretation of Aquinas' position in *Analogy and Philosophical Language.* For Hartshorne's own position, cf. "The Idea of God—Literal or Analogical?" *The Christian Scholar* 39 (1956), 131–6. As mentioned above in n. 66, I hope to be able to comment on this issue of analogical language in a future monograph. Until that time, perhaps the reader will bear with an unevidenced statement of my belief on the present discussion, viz., that the position of Thomas Aquinas on

theism and analogical language is neither as unsubtle as Hartshorne and others seem to think it, nor as sound as Burrell and others seem to judge it.

(104) On Rahner, Lonergan, and Burrell, cf. the works already cited; for alternative formulations, cf., inter alia, Etienne Gilson, *The Christian Philosophy of St. Thomas Aquinas* (New York: Random House, 1956); Jacques Maritain, *Existence and the Existent* (New York: Pantheon, 1948); Edward Sillem, *Ways of Thinking about God* (London: Darton, 1961); Victor Preller, *Divine Science and the Science of God: A Reformulation of Thomas Aquinas* (Princeton: Princeton University Press) 1967.

(105) Alternatively (and, I suspect, more realistically) one may turn elsewhere for such resources—as suggested above by n. 101, this has already happened for some process thinkers, notably Schubert Ogden in *Christ Without Myth.*

(106) A clear exception here is the more "radically empirical" work of Bernard E. Meland. Besides the works of Meland already cited, for an example of his appeal to and notion of myth, cf. his essay, "Analogy and Myth in Postliberal Theology," in *Process Philosophy and Christian Thought*, pp. 116–28.

(107) That either Catholic "caritas" or Lutheran pure "agape" was operative in the lives of their proponents as existentially meaningful seems obvious; but that either the Thomist synthesizing notion of "caritas" or the Lutheran notion of "agapic love" is conceptually coherent with the classical theism of either position is a question which Anders Nygren in his monumental work of motif-research, *Agape and Eros*, does not consider.

(108) Cf. for example, Daniel Day Williams, *The Spirit and The Forms of Love*, esp. pp. 111–30.

(109) Perhaps a similar point is made by John Cobb's comment that in the matter of religion "Whitehead's own spirit was urbane rather than intense" (*A Christian Natural Theology*, p. 223).

(110) The expression "warm deism" is Prof. Don Browning's (oral comment). It should be recalled that the present comments (in keeping with the criteria of meaningfulness) are comments on the inadequacy of the symbols employed by the process thinkers to communicate their conceptual understanding, not on the concepts themselves.

(111) Cf. the discussion of the theologies of *praxis* in chapter ten. For an argument that process categories do provide an adequate understanding of the biblical symbols of hope, cf. William A. Beardslee, *A House for Hope: A Study in Process and Biblical Thought*. For an eloquent plea for "symbols" for hope, cf. Carl E. Braaten, "The Significance of the Future: An Eschatological Perspective," in *Hope and the Future of Man*, pp. 40–55.

Chapter 9

The Re-presentative Limit-Language of Christology

INTRODUCTION: The Question of Christology

The analysis of the metaphysical character of Christian theism concluded with an expression of the need to find symbolic religious language to re-present the truth of religious theism in a manner consonant with our actual situation.[1] For Christians such language does not need invention, but rediscovery and reappropriation. Since the New Testament period to the present, Westerners generally, and Christians specifically, turn to the story of Jesus as the illuminating symbol for their religious understanding of existence.[2] From the earliest language of the New Testament, the preaching, teaching, and deeds of Jesus of Nazareth himself, through the moment when the preacher becomes that which is preached,[3] a continuous series of interpretations of this singular story by theologians, painters, musicians, writers, teachers, ethicians, and even politicians, have dominated the religious consciousness of the West.[4]

Before deciding that this story has lost its power to disclose our present situation, to evoke those limit-experiences and that limit-image of a living and loving God which can transform and reorient our lives, one should see whether this historical symbol can be experienced anew.[5] My own conviction, which this chapter shall try to document, is that hearing that story—or perhaps better, "over-hearing" it anew—still allows for those singular moments of a redescription of life's possibilities and a transformative reorientation of life's actualities which Christians have suggested by such traditional phrases as redemption and salvation.[6]

By all means, let us hear with fresh minds those other stories—of the Buddha, of Mohammed, of Krishna—which we have too long and too ignorantly kept at a psychic distance.[7] But to hear again the story of Jesus the Christ we owe at least to the memories of our ancestors, and perhaps even to the memories of our earliest—our childhood—selves who once heard it freshly.[8] More importantly, we owe it to the authentic religious possibilities inherent in our own lives to see what mode-of-being-in-the-world this "supreme fiction," this re-presentative fact, might yet allow.

204

I shall employ the same criteria as those spelled out in Part I: just how, phenomenologically, can we understand the existential meaningfulness of this central Christian symbol for our common experience; just how, metaphysically, can we understand the nature of and the means of validation for the specific cognitive claims of christology.[9] The strategy of the present chapter can be described as a kind of "detour" through a discussion of the nature of "facts" and "fictions" to that question of existential meaningfulness. A detour seems demanded if the character of christology, at once factual and fictional, is to find contemporary clarification. In the Christian story of Jesus as the Christ we find ourselves presented with a story—a fiction—which needs reinterpretation,[10] and with a claim to fact which needs clarification and perhaps restatement. That christological fact, for example, is not really a metaphysical reality in traditional Christian self-understanding. A proper understanding of God is an understanding of a metaphysical reality. For the concept of God, when conceived coherently, is either necessary or impossible. The reality of God, for the Christian, is a reality which either necessarily touches all our experience or necessarily does not exist. Yet the christological reality—the reality of God's self-manifestation in Jesus as the Christ—is not a metaphysical reality but a fact. There was and is no strict necessity for that action.[11] Yet, for the Christian tradition, God did act in Jesus Christ. That action is represented in the limit-language of the New Testament by and about Jesus as the Christ. Before one can understand that action and that story, however, one must first ask whether any matters of fact—as distinct from metaphysical realities—can be described as appropriate disclosures of more than a particular cultural situation, as meaningful to our common human experience. On logical grounds alone, a matter-of-fact claim cannot be validated metaphysically in the manner of the theistic claim itself. Yet a factual claim can be validated as intrinsic to the life we all actually—as a matter of fact—lead.[12]

What facts, then, do we need to investigate? At least three suggest themselves: first, the fact of our common human need for story, fiction, and symbol; second, the fact of "evil" in the human situation; third, the fact that facts are not exhaustively defined in terms of actualizations of possibilities, but also include re-presentations of possibilities. If we can clarify the kinds of facts relevant to our factual situation and thereby meaningful to our common experience, then we shall be prepared to investigate some more specific meanings involved in the Christian proclamation of Jesus as the Christ.

Before our detour through the nature of facts and fictions begins, a presupposition of this entire discussion may well need some brief explanation. We presuppose as fact what history and common sense alike testify: that any specific religious tradition starts with some moment or occasion of special religious insight. This moment, if authentically religious, will be experienced as a limit-experience and will be expressed in a limit-language representative of that insight and that experience. If the language and the experience bear universal implications, if they are not purely at the mercy of psychological or sociological forces which adequately explain their meaning without remainder,[13] then we may describe this religious tradition as a universal, a major religion. Such a designation of universality implies two characteristics: the religion arises from a special historical occasion of religious insight, but the special religious experience and language are sufficiently evocative of our common experience to bear the claim of universal meaningfulness. As that claim is clarified—for example, through the *Logos* tradition of Christianity[14]—the full import of the special occasion is itself felt with more and more existential force. The special occasion of the preaching and person of Jesus of Nazareth seems clearly to meet these criteria; as the Christian religion develops in and beyond the New Testament itself, one finds that this process of universalization is radicalized to the point where he who preached the Kingdom becomes the focus of the preaching!

This strange history—an intensification process which includes at one and the same time a universalization of religious meaning and a radicalization of the special occasion itself—allows one to see something of the peculiar complexity of the Christian religion. As that complexity has been traditionally interpreted, one finds the insistence that all Christian self-understanding—of God, humanity, and cosmos—is irrevocably christocentric. As that complexity has been more coherently "unpacked" through the history of christological reflection, one finds the concept "christocentrism" accepted as constitutive of the Christian religion[15] in two radically different ways. In a first and still widely influential form, christocentrism means that only and solely God's "special revelation" in Jesus Christ is meaningful for a proper human self-understanding. This form of christocentrism, more accurately labelled "exclusivist" christology, may be found in most forms of Christian fundamentalism or in such sophisticated theological forms as the christology of Karl Barth.[16] Any exclusivist christocentrism, however, is unavailable to anyone who agrees with the basic purposes and criteria of a revisionist theology. The revisionist position holds that christocentrism is not the exclusive property of fundamentalists and Barthians. Rather, it insists that not only does our common experience deny such claims to exclusivity but so do the Christian scriptures! For there, as this chapter shall attempt to show, one finds a claim for Jesus Christ that does place an understanding of his role and person at the center of Christian self-understanding; that does believe that such understanding of Jesus Christ is universal in its applicability to the human situation; but does not find any exclusivist understanding of that reality to be meaningful.[17] For this second christocentric position, probably best described as an "inclusivist" christology, the disclosure manifested by the Christian proclamation of Jesus Christ is genuinely disclosive of all reality, is meaningful for our common existence, is central for a human understanding of the limit-possibilities of human existence.[18] What that special occasion ("special" or "categorical" revelation) manifests is the disclosure that the only God present to all humanity at every time and place ("original" or "transcendental" revelation) is present explicitly, actually, decisively, as my God in my response to this Jesus as the Christ.[19]

This tradition of an inclusivist christology, present implicitly in historical Catholic Christianity's fidelity to the theological motif of the "universal salvific will of God" and in liberal Protestant Christianity's reformulations of christocentrism, is the basic christological position which informs my interpretation.[20] Yet a contemporary interpretation, committed to a revisionist model for theological reflection, cannot remain content simply to announce its position in terms of God's universal salvific will. Rather one must try to show how and why this christological understanding, once reinterpreted in more explicitly contemporary terms, can be faithful to both the central meanings of our common experience and the central meanings of the New Testament texts. To the first step of that larger task we now turn by means of our detour through facts and fictions.

THE FACT OF THE NEED FOR FICTION

A variety of disciplines cite sufficient evidence to suggest that a near consensus has emerged on the human need for more than conceptual analysis for understanding human existence. More positively, human beings need story, symbol, image, myth, and fiction to disclose to their imaginations some genuinely new possibilities for existence; possibilities which conceptual analysis, committed as it is to understanding present actualities, cannot adequately provide.[21] This section shall briefly describe certain of such evidence on our need for fiction and suggest certain formulations which may allow us to describe the meaning and the intention of this crucial human fact.

A kind of evidence has already been investigated in the earlier discussion of the meaning of religious language. In summary terms, one of the major conclusions of the third stage of analytic philosophy's investigation of the uses (meaning) of religious language was its firm insistence upon the legitimately non-cognitive uses (evocative, aesthetic, attitudinal, performative, etc.) which religious language fills. Such language, as R. B. Braithwaite's distinguished analysis shows, ordinarily involves the use of some "story" or "parable" by means of which the attitude of the speaker can be more deeply internalized.[22] More specifically, the very notion of "fiction" may provide the first key to the present question.[23] Fictions do not operate to help us escape reality, but to redescribe our human reality in such disclosive terms that we return to the "everyday" reoriented to life's real—if forgotten or sometimes never even imagined—possibilities. The greatest works of fiction—even of that genre called "realism"—do not simply describe our lives as a merely journalistic or merely photographic account might.[24]

Rather by redescribing the authentic possibilities of human existence—through such structural strategies as plot, narrative, comic and tragic genres—fictions open our minds, our imaginations, and our hearts to newly authentic and clearly transformative possible modes-of-being-in-the-world.

Such fictions, precisely by means of this process of redescription, can and often do reorient our lives into possibilities which, left to ourselves, we would more than likely never imagine, much less attempt. The artist who can capture some moment in our common history and redescribe it through the traditional or novel structural genres of fiction does not merely capture that "moment." He often reorients it. In such ways do artists function, as Ezra Pound reminds us, as the "antennae of the race." Ernest Hemingway, for example, does not attempt a careful analytical account of ethical possibility in the manner of a Kant or an Aristotle. Yet Hemingway's creative ability to redescribe our experience through believable and transformative fictions allows us to understand and to feel what "grace under pressure" might mean as a real possibility. Probably more than we know, all of us are indebted to those artists who have captured moments in our common history and redescribed those moments in their full possibilities for authentic and inauthentic life. We often find ourselves more deeply transformed and more radically reoriented by such "supreme fictions" [25] than by the most careful analytical discussions of the distinction between "is" and "ought." [26] To capture how it feels to live a certain way, to provide by that distanciation process we call genre both a proper imaginative entry into and a psychic distance from the "world" of the novel, film, or poem frees us to experience that possibility in all its experiential reality. When those possibilities degenerate into a reader's mere literalization of them—desperate attempts to act out the life of a Hemingway character, a Bogart toughness, a Monroe vulnerability—then we may also recognize the pathetic consequences of taking symbols literally and not seriously. Yet when that possibility is allowed to function as a fiction—a redescription of what reality is and might be—we find that the consequence often includes a reorientation of our own most basic moods, feelings, reactions and actions, our very way of living in this world.

We have, in fact, learned too much about the primordial and all-pervasive impact of such orientating conscious and unconscious moods to dismiss either fiction or mood itself as mere escape in the manner of our Victorian forefathers.[27] Every generation in human history has needed fiction. Our own is one which ordinarily admits this explicitly. As Whitehead and Heidegger alike testify, our very fidelity to the need for careful conceptual analysis need not deter us from recognizing this fact of our need for fiction.[28] We need to analyze not merely descriptions of the everyday reality which is, but also those redescriptions of the everyday disclosed in the great symbols, images, stories, myths, and fictions of our culture. In this sense, we all recognize the existential correctness of Paul Ricoeur's oft-cited dictum:

"The symbol gives rise to [critical] thought; yet thought is informed by and returns to the symbol." [29] There is, to my knowledge at least, no strict metaphysical way to "prove" or demonstrate this need for fiction and story.[30] Yet there seems no need for such proof. The modern form of Pascal's wager may well have become the risk of entering imaginatively into those fictional worlds.[31] We do so best by trying to appropriate the possibilities of those worlds of the imagination critically through literary, social-scientific, psychological, philosophical, and even theological analysis. At the conclusion of such critical appropriation, restored perhaps by the liberating experience of a second "naiveté," we find ourselves returning once again to the symbols themselves, to reexperience their transformative possibility anew.[32]

This need for and this possibility of fictions remain, it seems, an uncommonly common matter of fact of our shared experience. If one demands a metaphysical necessity here, he will demand in vain. Yet few of us remain deeply troubled by this dilemma, for, even philosophically, the "risk," the "wager" of finding meaning in symbol, image, myth, story, fiction makes sense. Besides the metaphysical conditions of the possibilities of our common experience—besides, that is, such metaphysical realities as time and space and, yes, God—there remain those contingent facts of our actual lived time as we may experience them redescribed through the genius of a Proust; of space as we can experience it represented through the ever-changing vision of a Picasso; and even of God now experienced *as my God* as in the gospel proclamation that this Jesus is the Christ.

We find, as a matter of fact, that we need and want the disclosive power of symbols, images, myths, stories, and fictions to transform our common human experience into possibilities that remain deeply human because, somehow, those possibilities are more authentic than the everyday reality of our lives. To use a formulation reminiscent of Plato and Aristotle, we may then find that conceptual analysis alone will not suffice for character-forming action.[33] Rather, individually and societally, we need stories, fictions, and symbols to allow our own and our society's character to discover appropriate heuristic models.

We find as well that common honesty demands that we bring to bear upon the reality-claims of even our most cherished stories the most penetrating tools of critical analysis presently available. In that familiar theological word, we need to demythologize[34] in order to eliminate the literalizing temptations in our appropriation of myths which can at best becloud, at worst completely distort, the ways-of-being-in-the-world disclosed in the myths. We need to develop whatever scientific analyses are available—sociological, psychological, political, philosophical—to allow those stories to become critically purified of all that is not essential to their disclosure of an authentically human mode-of-being. Yet even at the end of our most rigorous critical endeavors, we all seem to find either that a second naiveté has been restored to us to allow the symbols, now purified of literalizing accretions, to speak again; or that our criticism has legitimately rendered these particular symbols, myths, fictions, no longer meaningful for the struggle to achieve authenticity. The latter case is evident in the powerful and new Christian theological myth developed in Thomas J. J. Altizer's post-death-of-God *Descent into Hell*,[35] or in the histories of some of our best contemporary critics of the Christian story such as Freud, Nietzsche, or Marx. As in these instances, we eventually discover that the myth-breaker must either create new and more adequate myths (as Nietzsche attempted) or suffer the fate of finding his own story become a myth for his successors (as happened to Marx and Freud alike).[36] Both the hermeneutics of suspicion and the hermeneutics of recollection[37] seem to end, however differently, in the same place: in a rediscovery of the need for some symbol, some myth, some fiction.

The criteria for judging the explicitly religious uses of symbolic, mythical, and fictional language remain the same as those employed throughout this work. Two exemplary formulations of this question may serve to suggest the general lines which a search for the meaningfulness of such language may presently take. One formulation we have already seen: for character-forming action we need metaphors, images, symbols, stories, parables, myths. This formulation, in fact, may lend itself to a ready adaption of the psychological and sociological analyses of the important role of symbol for individual and societal action. Admittedly, the formulation does not lend itself to the more easily formulated criteria for judgment of Aristotle's *Metaphysics*. But the tradition of Aristotelian ethical *phronesis*, a tradition continued in such diverse forms as Pascal's *esprit de finesse*, Newman's "illative sense," Bernard Lonergan's "judgments of value," reformulates the only criteria we have or need for judging the adequacy of character-forming symbols,[38] Only Aristotle's "just man" can adequately distinguish the stories of true justice from injustice. Only Lonergan's self-transcending human being can be trusted to weigh the relative real strengths and real weaknesses of competing character-forming myths.[39] Highly "subjective" criteria, to be sure. But criteria which somehow—as a matter of fact—suffice.

A second exemplary and perhaps more contemporary formulation will be tested at greater length in the following chapter. For the moment, perhaps the reader will be patient with its somewhat peremptory entry and its all too brief exemplification. The second formulation is as follows: for an adequate *praxis* we need both rigorous theory and appropriate symbolization.[40] This second formulation is obviously dependent upon the Hegelian-Marxist insistence that true *praxis* is only achieved by a union of correct theory and authentic practice. It develops that insistence on a single point, in the manner suggested by the revisionist Marxism of Ernst Bloch: besides theory and practice, true *praxis* also needs appropriate personal and societal symbols.[41] The symbols of eschatological "liberation" as distinct from the liberal symbols of "development" may be taken as an example. Those former symbols have been rearticulated by contemporary Christian theologians of *praxis* as symbols designed by the creative imagination in order to allow both a negation of present oppressive practice, and an articulation of the possibilities for transforming that practice in accordance with certain creatively imagined (either Utopian or eschatological) possibilities for human beings.

A central question for these other non-cognitive uses of religious language becomes, of course, just how can we validate them? The present answer, in keeping with the revisionist model, is clear: first, one can and should determine the cognitive claims in the religious language and judge those claims in accordance with the general criteria of metaphysics. Second, one should continue to develop those criteria for existential meaningfulness which can be labelled (as they are by Paul Ricoeur in *Symbolism of Evil*) criteria of "existential verification." [42] In sum, we should try to judge the relative adequacy of the various candidate systems of religious symbols in accordance with a contemporary understanding of the criteria of adequacy for "character" formation (principally ethical, aesthetic, and psychological criteria) and for *praxis* (principally ethical, political, and critical sociological criteria).[43] The attempts to formulate what I call "criteria of relative adequacy," is, I admit, notoriously difficult. Yet one may be encouraged by such studies as those of Paul Tillich (esp. on the "demonic" and the "kairos")[44] and of Paul Ricoeur (esp. his comparison of the adequacy of various mythic systems—e.g., the Orphic or Adamic—to deal with the problems of evil).[45] In such studies as these we find, however tentatively formulated, a way by means of which an "existential verification" of the relative existential adequacy of the non-cognitive uses of religious symbolic language may in fact occur. What surely can occur is the simple insight which this section has attempted to document: *as a matter of fact,* our common experience testifies to the need for such fictions, myths, images, stories, and symbols. As a matter of fact, we dismiss the seriousness of such fictions at the presumably unwelcome price of impoverishing our own humanity. A clear grasp of that fact is the first step needed to allow one to be willing to listen once again to the Christian story of Jesus Christ. Another fact also needs articulation if that story is to be heard properly. That fact, too,—the "fact" of evil—is not a metaphysical necessity. But that evil is a fact of our common situation seems to most of us, at the very least, highly probable.

THE FACT OF EVIL

The philosophical distinction between a metaphysical necessity and a matter of fact is also applicable to the discussion of evil. That humanity possesses both freedom and nature can be shown to be necessary characteristics of the human being: as, for example, Paul Ricoeur's *Freedom and Nature*, argues.[46] That human beings are also fallible, that we can commit error, is a direct consequence of the human reality as constituted by both freedom and nature.[47] But that we in fact commit not merely error but evil cannot be a necessary characteristic of our being. If, in fact, we are constituted by a metaphysical necessity to commit evil, then our freedom becomes a mere charade and our existential and reflective faith in either a good, loving God or in the very worthwhileness of existence becomes a lie.[48]

Yet the fact of evil seems too obvious a reality for any adult to allow its lack of metaphysical necessity to dim explicit awareness of its presence. That evil is a necessary constituent of our being, we may know we cannot state without contradicting the metaphysical necessity of our own freedom or the metaphysical and Christian theological belief in the loving actions of a good God.[49] But that physical and moral evil is our actual condition; that such evil is an omnipresent *fact,* whose inevitability we realize—in this century surely—on both individual and societal terms, is a reality which only the most unhappily and self-destructively innocent among us feels free to deny.[50]

The Christian theological tradition, I believe, has consistently attempted to be faithful to this insight into the inevitability but not metaphysical necessity of evil, or, in explicitly religious terms, of sin.[51] For example, underneath the subtleties of the medieval scholastic discussion of "original sin" lies the same basic insight:[52] we cannot logically say that each human being *must* sin with metaphysical necessity save at the unwelcome logical and theological price of destroying the reality of individual freedom. And yet, the tradition argued, each human being is responsible for the fact that eventually, indeed inevitably, he or she does personally sin. To resolve this dilemma, discussions of the constitution of human freedom emerged in the medieval period.[53] Does every free act demand explicit consent? Are not our habitual actions free and yet not necessarily explicitly consented to in each instance? To summarize a long and subtle discussion, the medievals claimed that there is something like a statistical necessity to personal sin (an inevitability, but not a metaphysical necessity). That inevitability allows one to understand how each human being, first trapped in a social situation where evil is clearly present,[54] then unable to continue the constant reflection needed to ward off the habitual inclination to evil ("original sin"), eventually cannot but sin *(non posse non peccare),* yet does so freely and responsibly.[55] The point of this medieval digression is not to defend either the traditional Christian understanding of "original sin" [56] or the traditional scholastic understanding of habits and freedom.[57] Rather the point is to indicate that the mainline Christian theological tradition has historically puzzled over the problem that evil—or, for the Christian, sin—is not a metaphysical necessity but is an inevitable matter of fact.[58]

A powerfully disclosive, an existential description of the reality of sin and evil remains, in my judgment, one of the permanent achievements of the recent philosophical and theological past.[59] On the occasion of the profound

crisis of Western liberal culture (the horrors of two World Wars, the exter-
mination of millions, the demonic outbursts of Fascist and Stalinist terror),
both existentialist philosophy and neo-orthodox theology retrieved the classical Christian image of man as alienated, estranged, fallen, sinful. That
classical Christian picture of humanity's radical possibilities for good and
evil was and is antithetical to both the classical Greek philosophical view of
humanity's inherent knowledge and goodness conquering error, and even to
the classical Greek dramatists' profound view of humanity's tragic situation.[60] The Christian image of humanity's actual state also proved to be, as
the neo-orthodox noted, antithetical to the soon fatuous optimism of the
modern liberal's belief in inevitable progress. As progress faded into apoca-
lypse, the liberal had finally to face the fact that not all human beings—perhaps not even he himself—were reasonable and well-intentioned. As
suggested symbolically by the still pathetic figure of Prime Minister
Chamberlain returning from Munich, umbrella and hope still in hand, liberalism—by its stark refusal to face the fact of evil—could no longer understand, much less control, such demonic outbursts of the human spirit as
Nazism.

In American culture, the pioneering work of Reinhold Niebuhr assured
the success of this post-liberal insistence on facing the fact of evil when attempting to transform the human situation. As Niebuhr's enduring work
The Nature and Destiny of Man argues,[61] this fact is present everywhere, to
all cultures, to all individuals. The contemporary task is not to deny our
true situation through a liberalism—Christian or otherwise—which cannot
admit one of the most glaring facts of our fate. Rather, if one admits the reality of evil, then he may investigate critically and comparatively those symbol-systems which promise a transformation of that fact on an individual,
societal, and a historical scale.[62] One need not continue to bless those Cold-
War, "realistic" politics which Niebuhr's work sometimes aided in order to
see the essential correctness of his vision and the realistic description he
portrayed of our actual destiny. In a similar fashion, one need not commit
oneself to the kind of seeming political naiveté which several of Jean-Paul
Sartre's political judgments suggest in order to see that his frozen vision of
man's limited, indeed nauseous, condition does disclose a truth unfamiliar
to his idealist philosophical predecessors.[63] In American culture, where the
terrors of the sixties, especially the twin evils of a now open racism and that
war upon the Vietnamese people and their culture which was not a "mistake" but was and is an evil, we hear almost daily that the surely too long
prolonged American "innocence" is finally dead.[64] And yet neither the
finally fatuous optimism of "consciousness III," nor the cries for "law and
order," for "normalcy," perhaps even for "innocence," from men whose
moral sensitivities can include Watergate as a merely "over-zealous" mistake and Cambodia as a needed exercise in military expertise, promise that
our own culture is yet willing to face the fact of evil, starting with its own.

One of the permanent achievements of the neo-orthodox theologians was their willingness both to face that fact and to attempt to find authentic Christian possibilities for its transformation. Their main accomplishment was the development of a powerfully disclosive, an existentially meaningful anthropology. If revisionist theology is to succeed materially, I believe, it should incorporate that neo-orthodox anthropological vision into its own twin vision of a common faith in the worthwhileness of existence which sustains us even beyond good and evil and a reflective belief in a credible, a suffering and loving Christian God.[65] A first step in that direction can be taken when, singly and as a society, we admit to the reality of that central fact of our own experience which we name evil or, in explicitly religious limit-language, sin. A second step can be taken when we follow that admission with a second one: that for character-forming action we need to study any symbols of transformation which both face and promise authentically to transform that situation. In the manner initiated by Paul Ricoeur's and Reinhold Niebuhr's comparative analyses of the existential adequacy of various symbol-systems for transforming personal and historical evil, the fundamental theologian needs to take the risk that a critical investigation of all such symbols, stories, images, myths, and fictions may yet disclose a means of authentic human transformation.[66] As a single step in that direction, the contemporary fundamental theologian might look anew at the story of Jesus the Christ and attempt to articulate some of its transformative existential possibilities. Before that task is attempted, one final discussion of "fact" remains: how facts themselves are constituted.

FACT AND POSSIBILITIES: Actualizations and Representations

The most obvious and legitimate logical alternative to a fact is a "mere" possibility. When we speak of facts, we mean that which actually is; the given; the "situation"; not a possible world but the actual one. Yet this familiar and necessary contrast between facts and possibilities includes an important ambiguity. Actually there are two ways by which possibilities may become facts.

The first and more familiar way is one which the Greek tradition of philosophy has so clarified that only that way ordinarily seems "factual" to us. The Greek insight can be succinctly formulated: a fact is an actualization of a possibility.[67] I project all sorts of possibilities for myself. Those few possibilities which I manage to actualize in my own life constitute the concrete facts (the actuality) about myself that, presently, I really am. With such facts, as actualizations-of-possibility, we are all familiar.

The second kind of fact, however, is less familiar to most of us, at least on a reflective level. Besides the actualization of a human possibility in human action, there remains the alternative of representing a certain possibility in disclosive symbolic language and action.[68] The category "re-presentation" was employed in the earlier discussion on religious language but now needs analytical clarification of its status as fact. On one level, one may recall that religious language is basically re-presentative as making present anew, through symbolic expression, a human reality (for example, our basic trust in the worthwhileness of existence) which somehow had become threatened or forgotten. On a second level, fiction, by redescribing our everyday experience, represents certain imaginative possible modes-of-being-in-the-world that can become actualized by us. Indeed, all the primordial symbols of our culture are not *mere possibilities.* They are facts: facts, to be sure, not as the actualization of a possibility but facts as ritual, as fictional, as symbolic representations of a real possibility. All genuine re-presentations are not to be assigned to the category "mere possibility" but to the category "fact."

The presence of this insight into the factual status of symbolic representations can also be found in several Christian traditions, in certain contemporary theories of interpretation, and in our everyday cultural lives. What does the Christian tradition mean by "sacrament" but a *fact,* not a mere possibility? [69] A Christian sacrament is traditionally believed to be a fact as the re-presentation of a real possibility which God has made present to humanity in Christ Jesus. At least since the time of Augustine's struggle against the Donatists, the major Christian traditions have not believed that the fact (or, for some traditions, the validity) of the sacramental rite depends upon the personal actualization by the minister of the possibility ritually re-presented. In principle, the minister, even while partaking in the ritual re-presentation, can live contrary to the religious possibility there re-presented without affecting the fact of an authentic sacramental re-presentation.[70] To be sure, the minister's own personal actualization of that possibility is eminently desirable. But the fact of the sacramental re-presentation itself does not depend upon it.

For the hermeneutical theory outlined in chapter four, moreover, the meaning of a text does not depend upon the author's own intention, much less his own actualization of the possibility which his text represents. The question of whether Ernest Hemingway was himself a "Hemingway character" (whether, for example, he actualized "grace under pressure" in his own life) is an interesting biographical question, but not a major one for understanding Hemingway's fiction.[71] That latter fictional fact represents a certain possibility for human existence by means of the process of redescription present in the various literary genres of fiction. In that representative sense, these possibilities are no longer mere possibilities but representative facts of our common experience. They remain so whether or not Hemingway himself—or any other person—personally actualized them. When we speak of fictional characters as "larger than life," more faithful to the meaning of our experience than everyday experience itself, we recognize that we do not find mere possibilities in the great symbolic representations of our culture. We find re-presentative facts, symbols, rituals which disclose to us possibilities that we might wish to actualize.

In our everyday cultural lives, we may also recognize this distinction between fact as actualization and fact as representation. For most of us certain historical personages begin to take on "symbolic dimensions." He or she begins to become representative of a certain human possibility for a particular cultural period. In recent history, for example, the slain Kennedy brothers and Martin Luther King, both before and especially after their deaths, began to take on this symbolic dimension for many in American culture. Dr. King was not simply a human being who actualized certain possibilities. He became a symbol, a cultural fact representative of a certain possible mode-of-being-in-this-world. That he himself actualized that possibility seems entirely likely. But that is not the fact of central cultural importance. Rather, as the culture experienced his preaching, his actions, his teaching, the culture's own memory-image of Martin Luther King became itself a cultural fact, a symbol, a representation of a particular authentic possibility. It appears evident that we ordinarily do not find the human reality we actually live exhausted by the more usual alternatives: either "facts-as-actualizations-of-possibility" or "mere possibilities." Rather we also find, most clearly in symbols as distinct from signs,[72] certain undeniable realities which are neither "mere possibilities" nor "personal actualizations of possibilities." These realities, these great representative images, symbols, rituals, stories, and myths of our cultural history, are not mere possibilities. They are the representative facts of a particular culture. Just this distinction between two kinds of "facts" can become of real theological significance when we ask ourselves the initial christological question: what kinds of factual claims are present in the Christian confession that Jesus is the Christ?

The following section will be one interpretative attempt to respond to that crucial Christian theological question.[73] For the present, it may be sufficient to remind ourselves that the title "the Christ" or "the Messiah" is the title of an office.[74] In other words, messiahship, like ministry in general, may be said to refer to that office which represents a certain possibility (here God's action for Israel and through Israel for humankind). It does not refer explicitly to the actualization of that possibility by the one who holds the office. In more familiar christological terms, the very question of the "Messianic self-consciousness" of Jesus is not really a primary question of fact for an adequate christology to answer.[75] What is primary is the meaning and truth of the claim that this Jesus is in fact the Christ; that the representational reality present in the office of Messiah may be found in the words, deeds, and destiny of Jesus of Nazareth.

The primary question of christology, therefore, does not take the form of attempting to establish the psychological state (the actualization of the possibility) of Jesus as the Christ.[76] Rather the primary question becomes the different but still factual one of understanding the inclusive claim to meaning and truth represented in the affirmation that this Jesus is the Christ; that in the proclamation through word and sacrament of the singular history of Jesus of Nazareth as the Christ the truth of human existence is re-presented with factual finality. Exactly what meanings that deeper re-presentation may include, the next section shall attempt to delineate. At present, however, it may now be possible to clarify why the two more usual modern articulations of the factual status of the Christian claim for Jesus the Christ are not, in fact, exhaustive options for contemporary christology.

The first of such routes, present in modern christology from Friedrich Schleiermacher and Albrecht Ritschl through Karl Rahner and Paul Tillich, effectively proposes a modern (sometimes metaphysical) psychologizing of the ontological high christology of Chalcedon and the Joannine *Logos* tradition.[77] However impressive these modern philosophical christological reconstructions may be (employing as they do with real originality that "turn to the subject" characteristic of modern metaphysics), they still seem to rest on a central assumption which the present alternative position challenges. That assumption holds that only an actualization of a possibility secures the status of fact for christological meaning. Hence the familiar modern theological route of analyzing Jesus the Christ's own actualization of the possibility he represented as the Christ and, more importantly, re-presented as God's self-manifestation, by means of a philosophical investigation of the "consciousness" of Jesus—whether as the primal religious, the Messianic, or the divine consciousness—becomes a primary form of modern christological reconstruction.[78]

Indeed that same assumption is operative in the other major modern route to the question of an adequate christology. In this second alternative, as expressed in the work of the New Hermeneutic and theologically articulated in the positions of Gerhard Ebeling and Ernst Fuchs,[79] the scriptural sources are studied with more sophisticated hermeneutical methods and with greater interest in the earliest christologies of the New Testament. The latter claim holds insofar as the practitioners of the New Hermeneutic argue their case not from the high christologies of the Joannine literature nor of Chalcedon but from the earliest christologies, implicit and explicit, in the synoptic accounts of Jesus' own preaching, teaching, and destiny.[80] Moreover, the hermeneutical sophistication of this position seems clear since the New Hermeneutic combines the high standards of traditional historical scholarship with a Heideggerian understanding of the primary relationship of language and existence.

Granted these solid gains, the new quest for the historical Jesus, so central for the proponents of the New Hermeneutic, still results in a psychologizing of the christological tradition. One ends the quest somehow assured that now one may understand the "faith" or "self-understanding" of Jesus himself. Thereby one is also assured a new, a more historically "factual" route to an adequate contemporary christology.[81] Yet even aside from the implicit and, it would seem, insuperable difficulties of claiming a historical reconstruction of the psychological state of any historical figure (especially one about whom we really know so little), a more basic question remains: does the factual status of the Christian affirmation of Jesus as the Christ really need this historical-psychological reconstruction? Admittedly something like the New Hermeneutic (or its alternative, a philosophical-psychological reconstruction of Jesus' consciousness) would be needed if the only kind of "fact" was an actualization of a possibility.

But if representations are also facts, we do not really need to understand Jesus' own consciousness of his actions and teaching in order to formulate a christology grounded in fact.[82] Rather we need to know what his words, his deeds, and his destiny, as expressions of his office of messiahship, authentically re-present as real human possibilities for genuine relationship to God. In a word, we need to know the existential meaning and truths re-presented for our present human experience by the christological affirmations. The need to study that christological affirmation seems especially pertinent to anyone who agrees with the earlier description of our present matter of fact condition. If we recognize both the fact of the presence of evil and the fact of the need for symbolic expressions in our lives, we may also recognize the desirability of studying the christological affirmation in terms of its symbolic, its re-presentative factual character in order to seek out its possibly transformative meanings. If that task can be successfully executed, then the positive existential meanings of christology (including those existential meanings delineated by both forms of modern christology described above) can be rearticulated.[83] That new articulation will be new, at least insofar as it will free the discussion from the insuperable difficulties present in any attempt to reconstruct Jesus' own actualization of those possibilities by either historical or modern philosophical methods.[84] An initial rearticulation in that line will be the primary aim of the final section of this chapter.

CHRISTOLOGICAL LANGUAGE AS RE-PRESENTATIVE LIMIT-LANGUAGE

The prior sections of this chapter attempted to set a context for a study of some of the existential meanings in the early christological affirmations: those meanings present in the representative language of the New Testament on the words, deeds and destiny of Jesus of Nazareth as the Christ. With that purpose in mind, this section will summarize some of the results of the historical reconstruction of the words and deeds of and about Jesus of Nazareth and delineate the primary existential meanings re-presented by those earliest christological affirmations. On that basis, this section will also summarize just how this interpretation of the re-presentative character of

christological language seems <u>both faithful</u> to our common experience and
<u>to the primary Christian scriptural meanings.</u>

In the earlier discussion of chapter six we advanced the claim that a principal fruit of the application of sophisticated methods of historical inquiry
to the scriptures was the reconstruction of the parabolic, proverbial, and
proclamatory words of Jesus.[85] When one recalls the work of Joachim Jeremias on the parables of Jesus, for example, he recalls a singular achievement of careful historical inquiry: the reconstruction of the present New
Testament parabolic texts into the parables *of Jesus*. That historical reconstruction, moreover, is not limited to the *words* of Jesus: in fact, the historical study of Jesus' words (especially the parables) remains the central clue
to his deeds and his destiny. As the work familiar to New Testament scholarship in such paradigmatic studies as Günther Bornkamm's *Jesus of Nazareth* and Norman Perrin's *Rediscovering the Teaching of Jesus* exemplify,[86]
that latter process seems secure in its main outlines: Jesus' teaching—as expressed in parable, proverb, and proclamatory saying alike—is dominated
by the powerful motif of the sovereignty or reign (the Kingdom) of God
which brings and demands a new righteousness.[87] By means of the various
gospel processes of intensification brought to bear upon the several literary
genres employed, this eschatological "Kingdom" language can be legitimately described as a limit-language disclosing certain limit-experiences of
fundamental faith, hope, and agapic love. That this limit-language of Jesus'
central teaching receives a parallel representation in the historically reconstructed deeds of Jesus also seems a fair conclusion to be drawn from the
dominant consensus of contemporary New Testament scholarship. There,
one finds, amidst a myriad of disagreement upon details, a clear main outline of the deeds and destiny of the historical Jesus:[88] his ministry in Gali-
lee, his baptism (probably a baptism of repentance) by John the Baptist; his
amazing conduct of open, unself-righteous, forgiving identification with the
despised of his society (publicans, prostitutes, the sick and weak, the "out-
casts" of his time), and his equally liberating conduct of righteous denunci-
ation of the established powers. The deeds of Jesus, in their turn, seem
clearly re-presentative of the central eschatological teaching proclaimed in
the parables. As the reign of God and his promise of a new righteousness
for humanity, a new, a faithful, an agapic mode-of-being-in-the-world is
proclaimed with existential urgency in the limit-language of Jesus' teaching,
so that reign and that new and liberating agapic righteousness—that limit-
experience—seems re-presented in the actual deeds of the historical Jesus.[89]

The existential re-presentative power of the words and the deeds of the
historical Jesus are summarized in that central representation of his life and
his destiny, his paradigmatic role as the crucified one. The passion narratives, when historically reconstructed as the original core of all four gospels,
allow scripture scholars to affirm that this man, whose words and deeds at-
test to a new possibility for human existence, met the dishonorable and ob-

scene fate of crucifixion. Not in vain have Christians signalized this fact of Jesus' disgraced destiny as the central symbol, the all-important representation of the central existential meaning of Jesus as the Christ.[90] Indeed, once that destiny is understood not *in vacuo* but in the context of the representative words and deeds of the historical Jesus, a mutual illumination of meaning is disclosed. The strangeness of the power of God as the power of love proclaimed in the teaching is decisively represented in the Christian symbol of the cross; God's very power seems weakness to the self-righteous, the secure, the established ones. In a directly parallel fashion, the strangeness of Jesus' liberating freedom in his conduct, his representation of a new and agapic possibility for existence, finds appropriate paradigmatic representation in a destiny where his self-sacrificing love seems destroyed by the stupidity and sin of the unloving, the self-righteous, the self-secure.[91]

The fact that the central representative symbol of the cross is always joined to the symbol of the resurrection is the final existential clue to the central meaning of Jesus' words, deeds, and destiny. For the resurrection as a representative symbol both recapitulates, reinforces, and intensifies the profound religious meaning of this representative figure, this Christ, this Jesus. Whatever the historical occasion of the resurrection-belief so central to the New Testament may be,[92] the basic existential meaning of that belief remains the same: the representative words, deeds, and teachings of this representative figure, this Jesus as the Christ, can in fact be trusted. He is *the* re-presentation, *the* Word, *the* Deed, *the* very Destiny of God himself. The God disclosed in the words, deeds, and destiny of Jesus the Christ is the only God there is—a loving, righteous Father who promises the power of this new righteousness, this new possibility of self-sacrificing love to those who will hear and abide by The Word spoken in the words, deeds, and destiny of Jesus the Christ.[93] In that limit-sense, the witness re-presented in those words, those deeds and that very destiny is true.[94] Its truth can still be heard by any human being (whether, in contemporary times, with the aid of historical reconstruction or, in prior ages, with the aid of mythological categories) [95] who "has ears to hear" that re-presentative Word which illuminates what an authentically human existence under the sovereignty of a living God may be. And yet this claim for the existential significance of those re-presentative words, deeds, and destiny does not depend upon a historical claim to have unraveled the consciousness or faith of Jesus himself. That latter study, in fact, is not needed; when attempted it seems to lead at best to historical claims with a low degree of probability. What *is* needed is precisely what the contemporary historical reconstruction of those words, deeds, and destiny of the historical Jesus provides: those historically reconstructed facts as providing the text for the proclamation of the signal re-presentative fact of God's true limit-representation of divine love in this representative, this Messiah, this Christ, this Jesus of Nazareth.

In keeping with the hermeneutical method employed throughout this work, one may formulate the principal meaning referred to by the histori-cally reconstructed re-presentative words, deeds, and destiny of Jesus the Christ as follows: the principal referent disclosed by this limit-language is the disclosure of a certain limit-mode-of-being-in-the-world; the disclosure of a new, an agapic, a self-sacrificing righteousness willing to risk living at that limit where one seems in the presence of the righteous, loving, gracious God re-presented in Jesus the Christ. The confession of either the signif-icance for my life of the representative words, deeds, and destiny of the his-torical Jesus, or the confession of this Jesus Christ as my Lord is not an in-vitation to live in the presence of the Christian god over against other "gods." [96] On the contrary, the summons proclaimed in that confession is an invitation to risk living a life-at-the-limits: a committed, a righteous and agapic life in the presence of the only God there is, here manifested as the "Father" of the Lord Jesus Christ.[97]

From the point of view of the present hermeneutical theory, one may ap-proach this Christian limit-mode-of-being-in-the-world as simply a *possible* one; one which one can at least imagine as a genuine human possibility. Yet once anyone judges that this possibility is one which appropriately and truly re-presents the fundamental actualities of his or her life—that com-mon faith in the worthwhileness of existence, that fundamental trust whose reflective clarification is a metaphysical affirmation of God's loving reality —one may find here not merely a project for the imagination, but a project which re-presents in and with truth *the* truth of our lives. In the confession of Jesus as the Christ, in the further confession of Jesus Christ as Lord, Christians find a true, a limit-re-presentation of their lives as lives whose basic faith is grounded in the action of a loving God.[98] They find that they can have faith and trust and love in the belief that even the power of sin can be transformed by the limit-forgiveness, the grace, of a loving God. What Christians find re-presented in the affirmation of Jesus Christ as Lord is no timeless truth of metaphysics.[99] Rather they find there the factual, symbolic re-presentation of the fundamental existential truth of existence: each Christian can—and in the affirmation of Jesus Christ commits himself to try to—live a life that dares to tread not merely beyond the bounds of the limits-to the everyday, but to sense something of the gracious character of the limit-of the whole of reality.[100] Nor does this manifestation cease with Jesus for the Christian tradition. Rather that very same re-presentation con-tinues to happen through the re-presentative words and sacraments of the community named the Christian church. The church has as its central par-ticular task the need to re-present in word and ritual that definitive limit-re-presentation of the life of God-with-humanity which Christians affirm when they proclaim that Jesus Christ is Lord.[101]

The heart of Christian self-understanding, therefore, remains radically christocentric. This is the case insofar as, for Christians, the symbolic fact of Jesus the Christ provides a re-presentative summary of their deepest understanding of themselves as religious, as before a gracious God, and as in a community which re-presents that possibility in word and sacrament. That christological language discloses those worlds of meaning with a decisiveness whose urgency was felt by the hearers of the historical Jesus, by the believers of the early church's proclamation of this Jesus as the Christ, by the Christian tradition's preaching of this Jesus Christ as Lord. To endorse christocentrism, however, is not really for Christians to speak of some new God radically different from the only God who lives.[102] To speak of the truth of the proclamation of Jesus the Christ renders more factual, more representative, more human one's basic faith in the God who always and everywhere is manifested.

That basic and universal faith in a loving God is not fundamentally arrived at as a conclusion from a phenomenological and transcendental analysis of common existence. Indeed, a fuller existential faith is clearly witnessed to in the Christian scriptures themselves: when Paul, for example, in Romans 1:18 ff proclaims that all are "without excuse" who refuse to witness to this God.[103] There Paul seems to be testifying to neither the presence of some personal "natural theology" nor some temporary lapse from his constant christocentric theme. Rather he can be interpreted as proclaiming that our limit-situation as human beings discloses our basic limit-faith in the gracious God who is manifested in Jesus the Christ. If that interpretation holds, then there is scriptural encouragement for the Catholic tradition's insistence upon the possibility of a reflective account of that universal experience (in that restricted sense, a "natural theology").[104] At the same time, the central Reformation insistence (crystallized in the image of humanity as *"simul iustus, simul peccator"*) seems equally faithful to the fuller complexity of Paul's vision. Precisely because of human failures—through error, through inattention, through self-righteousness and the false security of a mere adherence to some "natural" or "traditional" law, through destructive innocence, through forgetfulness and distraction, in a word, through that limit-reality Christians call sin—most Christians too rarely and too fleetingly allow the limit-reality of the presence of the God of Jesus Christ become the real orientation of their way of living in the world.

The fact of the matter of fact limit-situation and the fact of the need for symbolic expression may unite to allow Christians to hear again the stark re-presentative words and to see anew the strange disclosive power of the Christian limit-symbol, the cross-resurrection of Jesus the Christ. Then that symbolic and transformative re-presentation of the meaning of life may strike them anew with its full disclosive power.[105] Then one may recognize that this symbol's existential meaningfulness is not to be found by justifying miracles and prophecies, nor by historically validating some interpretation or other of the resurrection-belief, nor by developing a metaphysics which can spell out the "timeless truths" of this symbol's meanings, nor by formulating new laws and new beliefs to surround the symbol and becloud its existential meaning and power. Rather, when the full disclosive force of that symbol is existentially seen, one may realize that here any human being is asked to decide with an urgency for which that limit-language we call eschatological is an appropriate expression: to decide to risk living a life-at-the-limits, a faithful, hopeful, loving life, which the Christian gospel proclaims as both a true understanding of the actual human situation in its reality and its possibility and an ever-to-be-renewed decision.[106]

What is re-presented in the Christian proclamation of Jesus Christ as Lord is not, I believe, the exclusivist insistence that only and solely here may human beings find the meaning of their lives before a loving God. What is re-presented in this faith for Christians is the basic faith and the only God whom all humanity experiences. So appropriate does that christological limit-representation seem—both in the words, deeds, and destiny of Jesus of Nazareth, and in the proclamation and celebration of this Jesus Christ as Lord by the Christian community—that, for Christians, that Word has all the power of a complete and true manifestation of the fundamental meaning of authentic human existence.[107] As thus appropriate to the universal human situation, as thus disclosive of the struggle for an authentic humanity, christology does bear an inclusivist character. For Christians, christological language suffices because it fulfills certain factual understandings of human and divine reality: the fact that our lives are, in reality, meaningful; that we really do live in the presence of a loving God; that the final word about our lives is gracious and the final power is love.

Notes

(1) Cf. the discussion of the criteria of "meaningfulness" in chapter four: These criteria can be further specified here as an appeal to the transformative power (personal, societal, cultural) of a particular symbol-system; for an example of this use, cf. the analysis of the relations of symbols to lived experience in L. Gilkey, *Naming the Whirlwind* (New York: Bobbs-Merrill, 1970), pp. 268–76.

(2) Cf. discussion in section III of this chapter on "story" and "fiction." This is not intended to deny the important ecclesial context of all christologies, as emphasized in the many works of John Knox; cf. esp. his *Christ the Lord* (New York: Harper, 1945).

(3) A summary-analysis of what is at issue between Bultmann and the post-Bultmannians may be found in James M. Robinson, *A New Quest of the Historical Jesus* (Naperville, Ill.: Allenson, 1959).

(4) For examples, cf. the ground-breaking constructive analysis of how various christological understandings influence ethics in James M. Gustafson, *Christ and the Moral Life* (New York: Harper & Row, 1968); on general cultural issues, cf. the typologies developed by H. Richard Niebuhr in *Christ and Culture* (New York: Harper, 1951).

(5) The insistence remains that this should include a hermeneutical correlation, here between the limit-language of the New Testament and the limit-dimension of common human experience: cf. chapter four on "meaning," "meaningfulness," and "truth."

(6) Note that an employment of criteria of relative adequacy for meaningfulness does not imply an exhaustion of meaning, but does suggest a true location for existential meaning—for the former a full Christian dogmatics would be needed. For an example of a theological sensitivity to this issue, cf. Johann Baptist Metz, "Erlösung und Emanzipation," in *Erlösung und Emanzipation*, ed. L. Scheffczyk (Freiburg: Herder, 1974), pp. 120–40.

(7) This seems especially true of recent Christian theological attempts to interpret (and be interpreted by) the religious richness of various aspects of the Buddhist tradition. Inter alia, cf. John Cobb, *The Structure of Christian Existence* (Philadelphia: Westminster, 1967), pp. 60–73, 148–50; and Thomas J. J. Altizer, *Oriental Mysticism and Biblical Eschatology* (Philadelphia: Westminster, 1961).

(8) This could be reformulated in Paul Ricoeur's terms as our primary need to reappropriate our own "cultural memory" as in his own brilliant reappropriation of the "Pauline itinerary" of the "servile will" in *The Symbolism of Evil* (Boston: Beacon, 1967), esp. pp. 151–61.

(9) Less summarily, the concerns of the present chapter can be formulated as follows: first, to disclose the limit-character of christological language as religious language (hence its "meaning" as a logically limit-language); second, to disclose that the meanings of that language include the same cognitive claims of religious theism analyzed in the preceding chapters (hence, its meaning and truth as language about God and humanity); third, to disclose certain further claims to meaningfulness which the transformative character of that language may bear (hence, its existential "meaningfulness" as determined by criteria of relative adequacy). Once again, these questions and criteria do not exhaust the question of christological meanings but may serve to locate the questions proper to the fundamental theologian and thereby relevant to but not exhaustive for the dogmatic theologian.

(10) Recall the insistence of Hans-Georg Gadamer that interpretation demands a moment of "application" (over against the failure to realize this by what Gadamer calls the school of "Romantic Hermeneutics"), in *Wahrheit und Methode* (Tübingen: J. C. B. Mohr, 1960), esp. pp. 291–93. The work in historical theology of Gerhard Ebeling may be considered here as an example of the constant need for reinterpretation: inter alia, cf. his article "Hermeneutik," in *Die Religion in Geschichte und Gegenwart*, 3rd ed. (Tübingen: J. C. B. Mohr, 1959), vol. III, coll. 242–62. For an employment of the same insistence from the viewpoint of a theologian using a revisionist model, cf. Ray Hart, *Unfinished Man and the Imagination* (New York: Herder and Herder, 1968), esp. his reformulation of the "hermeneutical circle" as a "hermeneutical spiral," pp. 60–68.

(11) For the classical attempt to show necessity, cf. Anselm's *Cur Deus Homo?* in *Anselm: Basic Writings*, rev. ed. (La Salle, Ill.: Open Court, 1962); for a contemporary example of criticism of Anselmian arguments from necessity here, cf. Bernard Lonergan, *De Verbo Incarnato, ad usum auditorium* (Rome: Pontifical Gregorian University, 1964), pp. 497–98. The traditional scholastic distinction between a mat-

ter of metaphysical necessity ("Socrates, as a human being, is a rational animal") and a necessary matter of fact—or "contingent necessity"—("When Socrates sits, he necessarily sits") seems relevant here.

(12) Hence arguments here will be basically appeals to experience (chapter four) which argue for the relative adequacy of a particular symbol-system to disclose our existential situation.

(13) The key phrase here is "without remainder." All good historical interpretations of the Christian religion will, of course, attempt to take account of the sociological, economic, political, and cultural forces operative in the formation of the Christian religion. For an excellent example of this, cf. Robert M. Grant, *Augustine to Constantine: The Thrust of the Christian Movement into the Roman World* (New York: Harper & Row, 1970).

(14) Cf. Wolfhart Pannenberg, *Jesus—God and Man* (Philadelphia: Westminster, 1968), pp. 162–64, for an argument for the universalizing force of the *Logos* tradition; for the classical modern study of that tradition, cf. Aloys Grillmeier, *Christ in Christian Tradition* (New York: Sheed and Ward, 1965); note how even a revisionist theologian like Van Harvey will appeal to the *Logos* tradition here, cf. Van A. Harvey, *The Historian and the Believer* (New York: Macmillan, 1966), p. 288.

(15) This seems equally true of modern Catholic incarnational theologies where christological themes are employed to interpret the central meanings of such "Catholic" themes as "church" or "sacrament," as it is obviously true of the word-centered modern Protestant theologies. For an example of the former, cf. Edward Schillebeeckx, *Christ: The Sacrament of Encounter with God* (New York: Sheed and Ward, 1963).

(16) There remains, of course, great theological differences between the universalism explicated by Karl Barth's neo-orthodox exclusivist christology and the parochialism familiar to fundamentalist "exclusivist" positions. For a critical appreciation of Barth's position from a Catholic viewpoint on the issues, cf. Hans Urs von Balthasar, *The Theology of Karl Barth* (New York: Anchor, 1972), pp. 95–102 and 228–63.

(17) *Mutatis mutandis,* the same principle should hold true for such related Christian doctrines as justification and sanctification, church, sacrament, etc.

(18) For the criteria relevant here, cf. n. 9 above.

(19) For a recent Catholic interpretation of this tradition, cf. Karl Rahner, "Observations on the Concept of Revelation," in *Revelation and Tradition,* eds. Karl Rahner and Joseph Ratzinger (New York: Herder and Herder, 1966), pp. 9–25; for a contemporary reinterpretation of Schleiermacher's concept of original revelation, cf. Schubert M. Ogden, "On Revelation" (to be published in a *Festschrift* for Albert Outler); for modern Catholic interpretations of "revelation," cf. the papers by Avery Dulles, Myles Bourke, and Gabriel Moran to be published in *Proceedings of the Catholic Theological Society of America, 1974* (Yonkers: St. Joseph's Seminary, 1975).

(20) For an example of the use of this doctrine in the Catholic tradition, cf. Bernard

Lonergan, *Method in Theology* (New York: Herder and Herder, 1972), pp. 104–24; Karl Rahner, "History of the World and Salvation-History," in *Theological Investigations*, V (Baltimore: Helicon, 1966), pp. 97–114; idem, "Anonymous Christians," *Theological Investigations*, VI (Baltimore: Helicon, 1969), pp. 390–98; idem, "Atheism and Implicit Christianity," *Theological Investigations*, IX (New York: Herder and Herder, 1972), pp. 145–65. For a contemporary reformulation of the Schleiermacher-Troeltsch tradition here, cf. Paul Tillich's last public address, "The Significance of the History of Religions for the Systematic Theologian," in Paul Tillich, *The Future of Religions*, ed. Jerald C. Brauer (New York: Harper & Row, 1966), pp. 80–94. A classical contemporary expression of the Troeltsch tradition may be found in H. Richard Niebuhr, *The Meaning of Revelation* (New York: Macmillan, 1941). It seems puzzling that contemporary Catholic theologians, who employ the Catholic tradition's appeal to the "universal salvific will" of God to criticize classical Reformation exclusivist christologies, seem not to enter into dialogue with the classical liberal Protestant reinterpretations of the christological claims from Schleiermacher forward.

(21) The acceptance of this familiar cultural insight by theologians has come to play an increasingly important role in contemporary theology, especially in the work of John Dunne; cf. especially his *A Search for God in Time and Memory* (New York: Macmillan, 1969). Cf. also Michael Novak, *Ascent of the Mountain, Flight of the Dove* (New York: Harper & Row, 1971), esp. pp. 44–89. For an excellent analysis of modern studies in religion and literature, cf. Giles B. Gunn, "Introduction: Literature and Its Relation to Religion," in *Literature and Religion*, ed. Giles B. Gunn (New York: Harper & Row, 1971), pp. 1–37.

(22) Cf. R. B. Braithwaite, "An Empiricist's View of the Nature of Religious Belief," in John Hick (ed.), *Classical and Contemporary Readings in the Philosophy of Religion* (Englewood Cliffs: Prentice-Hall, 1964), esp. pp. 435–9.

(23) Inter alia, cf. the work of Wayne Booth, esp. his *The Rhetoric of Fiction* (Chicago: University of Chicago Press, 1961), esp. 3–67.

(24) The "new journalism" of Tom Wolfe, Truman Capote, Norman Mailer, et al. may serve as clear instances of the move to the higher roles of "fiction" by journalists themselves.

(25) This splendid expression is that of Wallace Stevens.

(26) One need not disparage the need for analytical study to recognize this common fact of our experience; for analyses of the ethical discussion, cf. *Religion and Morality*, ed. Gene Outka and John P. Reeder, Jr. (New York: Anchor, 1973).

(27) For a brilliant study of how theological motifs were secularized into the poetry and prose of the great Romantics, cf. M. H. Abrams, *Natural Supernaturalism: Tradition and Revolution in Romantic Literature* (New York: Norton, 1971). Among the Victorian theologians, Newman is clearly an exception to the wider rule of distrust of mood and fiction, although his own works of fiction, unlike his essays, are probably best forgotten.

(28) Recall Heidegger's use of the "myth of care" in the midst of his conceptual analysis of the structure of care in Martin Heidegger, *Being and Time* (London:

SCM, 1962), pp. 241–44; or Whitehead on the uses of symbolism, in Alfred N. Whitehead, *Symbolism: Its Meaning and Effect* (New York: Capricorn, 1955), pp. 60–88. Any reader of Plato will not be surprised at these modern formulations. For an analysis of the proper use of "rhetoric" by the philosopher, cf. Robert Sokolowski, *Husserlian Meditations: How Words Present Things* (Evanston: Northwestern University Press, 1974), pp. 269–70.

(29) Cf. Paul Ricoeur, "The Symbol Gives Rise to Thought," in *The Symbolism of Evil*, pp. 347–58.

(30) And yet, the ultimate appeal in both metaphysical and matter-of-fact questions is to experience (cf. discussion of the notions of "experience" in chapter four).

(31) Paul Ricoeur, *The Symbolism of Evil*, p. 355.

(32) Ibid., p. 351.

(33) I am indebted for this formulation to Prof. Robert Sokolowski in a lecture at a symposium held at The Catholic University of America, Summer 1972.

(34) The demand for "demythologizing" in Bultmann's sense should not be considered, as it often is, as an attack on the legitimate uses of myth. For a defense and reformulation of Bultmann's position here, cf. Schubert M. Ogden, "Myth and Truth," in *The Reality of God* (New York: Harper & Row, 1966), pp. 99–120.

(35) Cf. Thomas J. J. Altizer, *The Descent Into Hell: A Study of the Radical Reversal of the Christian Consciousness* (New York: Lippincott, 1970). A similar process may be found in feminist theologians' development of new Christian myths: for example, cf. Judith Plaskow Goldenberg, *The Coming of Lilith: Toward a Feminist Theology* (Loveland, Ohio: Grailville, 1972).

(36) For examples of this "fate," cf., inter alia, H. Gemkow, *Karl Marx: A Biography* (Berlin, 1970), for a semi-official hagiography; on Freud, cf. the brilliant if slightly hagiographical work of Philip Rieff, *Freud: The Mind of the Moralist* (New York: Anchor, 1961).

(37) These insightful phrases were coined by Paul Ricoeur; cf. *Freud and Philosophy: An Essay on Interpretation* (New Haven: Yale University Press, 1970), pp. 20–37.

(38) For the history (and appropriate citations) on Lonergan's relationship to Aristotle, Pascal and Newman here, cf. Frederick Crowe, "An Exploration of Lonergan's New Notion of Value" (to be published in Proceedings of Lonergan Workshop, Boston College, 1974, by Darton, Longman & Todd, 1975), pp. 1–43. For Lonergan himself, cf. *Method in Theology*, pp. 34–41 (esp. p. 41, n. 14, on Aristotle).

(39) Ibid., p. 240.

(40) Cf. the discussion of these issues in chapter ten.

(41) Inter alia, cf. Ernst Bloch, *Man on His Own: Essays in the Philosophy of Religion* (New York: Herder and Herder, 1970), esp. pp. 93–111.

(42) Paul Ricoeur, *The Symbolism of Evil*, pp. 164, 355–7.

(43) For examples of the development of what we have called "criteria of relative adequacy," cf., inter alia, Don S. Browning, *Generative Man: Psychoanalytic Perspectives* (Philadelphia: Westminster, 1973), esp. pp. 179–218, for an argument for the relative adequacy of Erik Erikson's account over those of Philip Rieff, Norman O. Brown, and Erich Fromm; in ethics, cf. James M. Gustafson, *Christ and The Moral Life*, esp. pp. 238–71, for Gustafson's own constructive statement taking account of the relative adequacies of the positions outlined elsewhere in the book; on *praxis,* cf. the works cited in chapter ten—for the moment, note the argument for the "relative adequacy" of his position on knowledge over against alternative formulations articulated by Jürgen Habermas in *Knowledge and Human Interests* (Boston: Beacon, 1971).

(44) On "kairos," cf. Paul Tillich, *The Protestant Era* (Chicago: University of Chicago Press), pp. 3–15; on the "demonic," idem, *Systematic Theology*, I (Chicago: University of Chicago Press, 1951), 139–40, 222–27. For a complete analysis of these concepts in Tillich's theology of culture, cf. James Luther Adams, *Paul Tillich's Philosophy of Culture, Science and Religion* (New York: Schocken, 1970). Further development of "criteria of relative adequacy" would, in my judgment, be a major concern in the development of a model for systematic theology.

(45) Paul Ricoeur, *The Symbolism of Evil*, pp. 306–79.

(46) Cf. Paul Ricoeur, *Freedom and Nature: The Voluntary and the Involuntary* (Evanston: Northwestern University Press, 1966), esp. pp. 355–486.

(47) Paul Ricoeur, *Fallible Man* (Chicago: Regency, 1965), esp. pp. 201–24. It should be noted that all three of the volumes cited form a part of a trilogy yet to be completed. The first phase of Ricoeur's philosophy of the will is the "eidetics of the will" in *Freedom and Nature*; the second phase is represented by the "empirics of the will" in *Fallible Man*, and the "symbolics and mythics of the will" in *The Symbolism of Evil*'s hermeneutical investigation of symbols and myths of evil. The third phase is to be completed by a "poetics of the will." These complex distinctions are relevant here only for locating the logic of the development of the phenomenology of will mentioned in the text. For Ricoeur's development, cf. Don Ihde, *Hermeneutic Phenomenology: The Philosophy of Paul Ricoeur* (Evanston: Northwestern University Press, 1971); David M. Rasmussen, *Mythic-Symbolic Language and Philosophical Anthropology: A Constructive Interpretation of the Thought of Paul Ricoeur* (The Hague: Nijhoff, 1971); M. J. Gerhart, "The Question of 'Belief' in Recent Criticism: A Re-examination from the Perspective of Paul Ricoeur's Hermeneutical Theory" (unpublished dissertation, University of Chicago Divinity School, 1973).

(48) Recall here the classical Christian theological and philosophical attempts to answer "the problem of evil" through such distinctions as God "permitting" but not "causing" evil. For a good summary-analysis of those discussions, cf. John Hick, *Evil and the God of Love* (New York: Harper & Row, 1966).

(49) As we indicated in the preceding chapter, this latter claim may also be held on strictly philosophical grounds, as in the work of Hartshorne.

(50) The alternative seems to be the kind of "dreaming innocence" analyzed by

Paul Tillich in *Systematic Theology*, II, 33–5, and dissected by such modern novelists as Graham Greene in *The Quiet American*. The recognition of this fact is communicated in highly personal and convincing terms in Langdon Gilkey's *Shantung Compound* (New York: Harper & Row, 1966); in more "world-historical" terms in Hannah Arendt's *Eichmann in Jerusalem: A Report on the Banality of Evil* (New York: Viking, 1963).

(51) Cf. for discussions of the distinctions between moral evil and sin James M. Gustafson, *Christ and the Moral Life*, pp. 66–70; H. Richard Niebuhr, *The Responsible Self: An Essay in Christian Moral Philosophy* (New York: Harper & Row, 1963), pp. 127–48; Charles E. Curran, "Christian Conversion in the Writings of Bernard Lonergan," in *Foundations of Theology*, pp. 41–59, esp. 51–3.

(52) Cf. Gustav Siewerth, "The Doctrine of Original Sin Developed and Presented in accordance with the Theology of St. Thomas Aquinas," in Marc Oraison et al. *Sin* (New York: Macmillan, 1962), esp. pp. 128–31, 137–48.

(53) Cf. Bernard Lonergan, *Grace and Freedom: Operative Grace in the Thought of St. Thomas Aquinas* (New York: Herder and Herder, 1970), pp. 17–19.

(54) This sentence conflates the medieval notion of sin as irrational with the implicitly medieval but explicitly modern notion of sin as social: on the first factor, cf. ibid. pp. 109–15; for the second, recall the familiar modern articulations from the "Social Gospel" through various theologies of liberation on the social character of sin.

(55) Ibid., pp. 139–45. I have tried to develop this interpretation of Thomas Aquinas in a paper entitled "The Religious Dimension of Experience: St. Thomas Aquinas on Sin" (to be published in *Proceedings, American Catholic Philosophical Society 1974* [Washington, D.C.]). Further discussion and textual documentation of this issue may be found there.

(56) In fact, the comments of Paul Ricoeur on this question seem to me entirely appropriate: "Hence, it is false that the 'Adamic' myth is the keystone of the Judaeo-Christian edifice; it is only a flying buttress, articulated upon the ogival crossing of the Jewish penitential spirit. With even more reason, original sin, being a rationalization of the second degree, is only a false column. The harm that has been done to souls, during the centuries of Christianity, first by the literal interpretation of the story of Adam, and then by the confusion of this myth, treated as history, with later speculations, principally Augustinian, about original sin, will never be adequately told. In asking the faithful to confess belief in this mythico-speculative mass and to accept it as a self-sufficient explanation, the theologians have unduly required a *sacrifium intellectus* where what was needed was to awaken believers to a symbolic superintelligence of their actual condition" (*The Symbolism of Evil*, p. 239).

(57) Cf. Bernard Lonergan, *Grace and Freedom*, pp. 41–46 (on habits), pp. 93–7 (on freedom); note also Lonergan's contemporary reformulation of this tradition from the viewpoint of his own categories of interiority in *Method in Theology*, pp. 288–91.

(58) Cf. Reinhold Niebuhr, *The Nature and the Destiny of Man*, I (New York: Scribner's, 1941), esp. pp. 251–55. Unfortunately, Niebuhr in this justly famous analysis continues the line of interpretation which suggests that the Roman Catholic tradi-

tion (in the work of Thomas Aquinas) is semi-Pelagian. For a refutation of that view, cf. Bernard Lonergan, *Grace and Freedom*, esp. pp. 51–2, on what Lonergan aptly calls Aquinas' development of a "statistical necessity" for sin. On the question of the contemporary use of the doctrine of "original sin" (n. 56 above), cf. Niebuhr's remarks in the "Preface for the Scribner Library Edition" (p. viii): "I used the traditional religious symbols of the 'Fall' and of 'original sin' to counter these conceptions. My only regret is that I did not realize that the legendary character of the one and the dubious connotations of the other would prove so offensive to the modern mind, that my use of them obscured my essential thesis and my 'realistic' rather than 'idealistic' interpretation of human nature."

(59) For an example of a later "revisionist" use of this neo-orthodox achievement, cf. Langdon Gilkey, *Naming the Whirlwind*, pp. 384–92.

(60) Cf. Charles N. Cochrane, *Christianity and Classical Culture* (New York: Oxford University Press, 1940).

(61) This work remains Niebuhr's most systematic theological statement. The insight itself runs through all his work as manifested in such a relatively early work as *Moral Man and Immoral Society* (New York: Scribner's, 1932).

(62) To restate this in terms of the criteria developed earlier: an appeal to experience can show the existential but not metaphysical meaning and truth of the fact of evil; an analysis of the disclosive power of the Christian understanding of "sin" can show the relative adequacy of that symbol-system's transformative power ("meaningfulness") over alternative possibilities. The major example of the latter kind of argument remains Reinhold Niebuhr's in *The Nature and Destiny of Man*, I, esp. pp. 93–150; for a critical analysis of Niebuhr's critique of Freudianism, cf. Peter Homans, *Theology After Freud: An Interpretive Inquiry* (New York: Bobbs-Merrill, 1970), pp. 23–66.

(63) For two Christian theological critical interpretations of Sartre's significance here, cf. Paul Ramsey, *Nine Modern Moralists* (Englewood Cliffs, N.J.: Prentice-Hall, 1962), pp. 111–49; David E. Roberts, *Existentialism and Religious Belief*, ed. Roger Hazelton (New York: Oxford-Galaxy, 1957), pp. 193–227.

(64) For a masterful historical perspective here, cf. Martin E. Marty, *Righteous Empire: The Protestant Experience in America* (New York: Dial, 1970); for a recent interpretation on the presence and ambiguity of symbols of innocence in present American culture, cf. Michael Novak, *Choosing Our King: Powerful Symbols in Presidential Politics* (New York: Macmillan, 1974), esp. pp. 105–23, 241–31.

(65) On that possibility, the following remarks by Paul Ricoeur, *The Symbolism of Evil*, p. 156, seem pertinent: "Then we shall understand that evil is not symmetrical with the good, wickedness is not something that replaces the goodness of a man; it is the staining, the darkening, the disfiguring of an innocence, a light and a beauty that remain. However *radical* evil may be, it cannot be as *primordial* as goodness."

(66) The Niebuhr (and Tillich) traditions here are developed in a revisionist manner in the several works of Langdon Gilkey: besides those works already cited, cf. Gilkey's forthcoming work on providence and eschatology. The various theologies of liberation, to be discussed in chapter ten, may also be cited as examples of this mode of

theological analysis, as may the developments and applications of Bernard Loner-gan's "intentionality-analysis" in an explicitly symbolic direction by the work of John Dunne and Michael Novak. For yet another formulation of this possibility, cf. William S. Johnson, *The Search for Transcendence* (New York: Harper & Row, 1974).

(67) This remains an assumption of the classical Aristotelian categories of act and potency.

(68) Cf. the discussion of limit-questions in chapter five for citations; cf. also, Schubert M. Ogden, "What Does It Mean to Affirm 'Jesus Christ is Lord?' " in *The Reality of God*, pp. 202–5; idem, "The Point of Christology," *Journal of Religion* 55, no. 3 (October, 1975); Van A. Harvey, *The Historian and the Believer*, pp. 246–91, esp. 258–65, 281–89.

(69) I understand this "sacramental" view of reality to be one of the most important and indeed constitutive characteristics of Catholic Christianity. In the midst of the vast literature in Catholic theology, for some clear examples of the centrality of a sacramental view for Catholic Christians, cf. Edward Schillebeeckx, *Christ: The Sacrament of the Encounter with God* (New York: Sheed and Ward, 1963); Karl Rahner, "Personal and Sacramental Piety," *Theological Investigations*, II, pp. 109–34; idem, *The Church and the Sacraments* (Herder: Freiburg, 1963). For a modern Anglo-Catholic retrieval of this vision, cf. Nathan A. Scott, Jr., "The Sacramental Vision," in *The Wild Prayer of Longing: Poetry and the Sacred* (New Haven: Yale University Press, 1971), pp. 43–76.

(70) This possibility (surely not one whose actualization is encouraged!) is standard Catholic teaching since Augustine's struggle with the Donatists; the issue is, of course, distinct from the issue of the need on the part of the recipient for faith (the *ex opere operato* discussion).

(71) The question of the "implied author" of Hemingway's fiction is an important hermeneutical question (cf. discussion in chapter four on interpretation theory); the *further* question of Hemingway's own life can, of course, become a question of real biographical interest: insofar as it does that life becomes another text, not the text behind the text of his writings.

(72) This is a familiar contemporary distinction: inter alia, cf. Paul Tillich, "The Meaning and Justification of Religious Symbols," in *Religious Experience and Truth: A Symposium*, ed. Sidney Hook (New York: New York University Press, 1961), pp. 3–12, as well as the several replies of Tillich's critics (ibid., pp. 12–93). Influential neo-Kantian formulations here include the works of Ernst Cassirer and Susanne K. Langer: inter alia, cf. Ernst Cassirer, *The Philosophy of Symbolic Forms*, 3 vols. (New Haven: Yale University Press, 1953, 1955, 1957); Susanne K. Langer, *Philosophy in a New Key* (New York: Penguin, 1948).

(73) As the fundamental theologian moves into the matter-of-fact questions of christology, he moves ever closer to the task of the dogmatic theologian. Still his task need not include the full set of christological questions present for the dogmatic theologian. In more traditional theological language, the fundamental theologian's task involves him in questions of the "work" more than the "person" of Christ: questions of "soteriology" as investigated from the viewpoint of the criteria for a

fundamental-theological statement. Although I recognize that the present observations (and criteria) have implications for the further questions of the "person" of Christ, such questions remain further questions. Although I am unconvinced by Wolfhart Pannenberg's criticism of the soteriological approach to christological questions (cf. his *Jesus—God and Man*, pp. 47–53), I share his conviction that Christological questions are best approached in the contemporary period by means of the typology "christologies from below to above" not "christologies from above to below" (ibid., pp. 33–37). It might be noted that Pannenberg's own major criticism of the dangers of the soteriological approach ("Has one really spoken there about Jesus himself at all?" ibid., p. 47) seems to involve the major assumption of contemporary christologies which this entire section is challenging, viz., that the only way to discuss the "fact" of Jesus is to discuss his own actualization of a possibility rather than the fact of Jesus—as the Christ—as the re-presentation of a possibility.

(74) For the historical and exegetical background for the titles "Messiah" and "Christos," cf. Reginald H. Fuller, *The Foundations of New Testament Christology* (New York: Scribner's, 1965), pp. 23–31 (Messiah) and 63–65 (Christos). I do not wish to imply here that Prof. Fuller would agree with the christological observations made here: for his own, cf. ibid., pp. 243–60. For a summary of relevant New Testament scholarship on the alternative presented in the text, cf. Schubert M. Ogden, *Christ Without Myth*, pp. 159–64.

(75) For summaries of the relevant exegetical discussions on this issue, cf. Günther Bornkamm, *Jesus of Nazareth* (New York: Harper & Row, 1960), pp. 169–79, 226–33; Hans Conzelmann, *Jesus* (Philadelphia: Fortress, 1973), pp. 36–51. This is not to deny that the question of Jesus' Messianic self-consciousness is not an important exegetical and historical question in reconstructing the words and deeds of the historical Jesus (cf. Bornkamm and Conzelmann for the summaries of the latter). It is to deny that a contemporary christology must await the results of that particular reconstruction. The "fact" which needs reconstruction in the alternative analysis of fact here is the meanings of the representative fact of Jesus as the Christ. For a response to the familiar Kierkegaardian charge that then Jesus becomes "merely a symbol of some timeless truth," cf. Van A. Harvey, *The Historian and the Believer*, pp. 285–89. For a distinct analysis of Jesus' consciousness, cf. Raymond E. Brown, *Jesus, God and Man* (Milwaukee: Bruce, 1967),pp. 39–107.

(76) For a contemporary expression of this tradition, cf. the following discussion of the "new quest."

(77) For these "psychologizing" tendencies, inter alia, cf. Friedrich Schleiermacher, *The Christian Faith* (Edinburgh: T. & T. Clark, 1928), prop. 94, pp. 385–89; Albrecht Ritschl, *The Christian Doctrine of Justification and Reconciliation* (Edinburgh: T. & T. Clark, 1902), prop. 48, esp. pp. 449–52; Paul Tillich, *Systematic Theology*, II, pp. 118–38; Karl Rahner, "Current Problems in Christology" in *Theological Investigations*, I, pp. 149–54; idem., "Theology of the Incarnation," *Theological Investigations*, IV, pp. 105–20.

(78) For an example, cf. Bernard Lonergan, "Christ as Subject: A Reply," in *Collection* (New York: Herder and Herder, 1967), pp. 164–98.

(79) Cf. the survey-analyses of this tradition by James M. Robinson, *A New Quest of the Historical Jesus*; James M. Robinson and John B. Cobb (eds.), *The New Her-*

meneutic (New York: Harper & Row, 1964); Paul J. Achtemeier, *An Introduction to the New Hermeneutic* (Philadelphia: Westminster, 1969).

(80) Cf. Robinson, *A New Quest of the Historical Jesus*, esp. pp. 87–125.

(81) Ibid., p. 85.

(82) Such a "new quest" is, of course, completely desirable as a strictly exegetical and historical task. The question of the text is whether it is needed for a contemporary theology in the manner suggested by James M. Robinson. For a criticism of Robinson's position on this and related issues, cf. Van A. Harvey and Schubert M. Ogden, "How New Is the 'New Quest' of the Historical Jesus?" in *The Historical Jesus and the Kerygmatic Christ: Essays on the New Quest of the Historical Jesus*, tr. and ed. by Carl E. Braaten and Roy A. Harrisville (Nashville: Abingden, 1964), pp. 197–242.

(83) The retrieval, for example, of the powerful claims to existential meaningfulness represented by Karl Rahner's christological writings could, in principle, be effected by employing the same criteria of relative existential adequacy to the re-presentative nature of the Rahnerian texts.

(84) A combination of these two methods provides the basis for the most important recent attempt at a modern christology in Wolfhart Pannenberg, *Jesus—God and Man*. It is no disparagement of this invaluable work of erudition and constructive originality to suggest that, whatever the other merits of Pannenberg's complex position here may be, the work (as suggested above) does not really address the alternative of representative fact and symbol. It may also be important to note again that I do not understand the comments on christology in this chapter to provide anything more than a reopening of the question of christology from the viewpoint of the present model of fundamental theology, not a resolution of the several further and crucial questions which a dogmatic would perforce involve. For some recent attempts at that larger enterprise, cf. David R. Griffin, *A Process Christology* (Philadelphia: Westminster, 1973); Peter C. Hodgson, *Jesus—Word and Presence: An Essay in Christology* (Philadelphia: Fortress, 1971); Piet Schoonenberg, *The Christ* (New York, Herder and Herder, 1971).

(85) For the general discussion, cf. the section on interpretation theory in chapter four; for the applications, cf. chapter six.

(86) Cf. Günther Bornkamm, *Jesus of Nazareth*; Norman Perrin, *Rediscovering The Teaching of Jesus* (New York: Harper & Row, 1967).

(87) For this and the following sections, cf. the summary and theological use of New Testament scholarship made by Van A. Harvey, *The Historian and the Believer*, pp. 271–75.

(88) For the best summary, cf. Günther Bornkamm, *Jesus of Nazareth*. This small work strikes me as all the more disclosive and, indeed, powerful for the quiet, almost underwritten way in which it unfolds the story of Jesus: for example, cf. the discussion (pp. 109–117) on "the commandment of love" in contrast to the kind of bloated sentimentality of too many sermons and books on Christian "love." The latter deserves Nietzsche's condemnation as "Platonism for the masses"; the former deserved but did not receive his admiration as a "transvaluation of all values."

(89) Ibid, pp. 100–9.

(90) Van A. Harvey, *The Historian and the Believer*, pp. 273–5.

(91) Ibid., pp. 273–4: "Are the Christs crucified while the Pilates die in their beds? What kind of world is it where this parable of a hanged man is thought to be the crucial one? Can the inscrutable last power who permits this to pass be called righteous? The cross does nothing more or less than recapitulate the whole content of Jesus' message and deeds" (p. 273).

(92) For a summary analysis of some of the theological interpretations of that belief, cf. Wolfhart Pannenberg, *Jesus—God and Man*, pp. 108–14; For Pannenberg's own position, ibid., pp. 53–108; For a formulation of the Bultmannian position, cf. Schubert M. Ogden, *Christ Without Myth*, pp. 83–88. For a major alternative formulation, cf. Willi Marxsen, *The Resurrection of Jesus of Nazareth* (Philistine: Fortress, 1968).

(93) Note how the christological meanings both recapitulate the meaning and truth of religious theism and redescribe them in a process of intensification which discloses concrete existential meaningfulness.

(94) In the sense of "true" as an appeal to one's own experience of the basic meaning of human existence as concretely lived, I find it impossible not to affirm its truth. In the further sense of rearticulating and redescribing (n. 93 above) the meaning and truth of the God-humanity relationship disclosed in religious theism, it meets criteria for truth used throughout this work. Perhaps the Heideggerian concept of truth as *aletheia* is particularly relevant to the former sense; the concept of truth employed in chapters four, seven, and eight is surely relevant to the latter. To speak of truth in this personal existential sense is also to speak of a *decisive* truth for one's life. For the fundamental theologian, to show that decisiveness—or, in the more classical terms, that "finality"—more historically would demand, I believe, a dialectical analysis of Christianity in relationship to the other world religions: a task which would demand a full-fledged use of history of religions in fundamental theology and would, in the final analysis, prove a theological task whose successful completion would require a complete Christian dogmatics (or, better, *Glaubenslehre* in Troeltsch's sense). For the first task, I am simply not sufficiently knowledgeable in history of religions to attempt more than formal remarks on method here, although I trust these remarks may serve to indicate my willingness to engage in the kind of collaborative effort that such a work would surely involve. For the second task, I am not in this work attempting to develop a model for a Christian dogmatics as distinct from a fundamental theology, or even to raise all the relevant christological issues from the viewpoint of fundamental theology.

(95) The addition of the parenthesis is important insofar as the claim that religious meaning can be received only in the context of correct thinking (whether historical scholarship or philosophical reflection) betrays both a profound intellectualistic misunderstanding of the reality of *faith* and an extraordinary lack of ordinary common sense. After one has studied exegesis, philosophy, and theology, does one really feel obliged to question the *faith* of, say, Francis of Assisi or one's parents as somehow radically inadequate because mythologically expressed? When informed (as I have been) that the alternative is "Gnosticism," one cannot but wonder what "gnosticism" is meant here: surely not the phenomena described by such scholars as Rob-

ert Grant and Hans Jonas. The Gnostics they describe, I believe, would be more than willing to write off St. Francis of Assisi or Dorothy Day—or practically anyone—as not in "true faith." Others—practically any major contemporary Christian theologian I can recall—would be, to put it gently, more wary.

(96) Cf. Schubert Ogden's correct appeal here to both scripture and Luther in "What Sense Does It Make to Affirm 'Jesus Christ is Lord'?" in *The Reality of God*, pp. 194–5.

(97) For a recent exegetical formulation of the Christian understanding of God as "Father," cf. Joachim Jeremias, "Abba," in *The Central Message of the New Testament* (New York: Scribner's, 1965); for a still powerful articulation of this central Christian insight, cf. F. D. Maurice, *Theological Essays* (New York: Harper, 1957), passim, esp. pp. 90–93.

(98) Cf. the Ogden essay cited in n. 96 above.

(99) That the Christian theological alternatives are not exhausted by either a "liberal" search for "timeless truths" and "mere symbols," or a neo-orthodox search for a non-metaphysical, "purely Christian" paradox may be taken as the material side of the formal dilemma posed in the discussion of chapter two on general theological models.

(100) For a succinct formulation of this from the viewpoint of a New Testament scholar, cf. Herbert Braun, "Der Sinn der neutestamentlichen Christologie," *Gesammelte Studien zum Neuen Testament und seiner Umwelt* (Tübingen: J. C. B. Mohr, 1962).

(101) This is, of course, by no means an exhaustive statement on the theological meaning of "church." It purports merely to be a statement from the viewpoint of fundamental theology in harmony with the position developed thus far. From the viewpoint of dogmatic theology, it is most in harmony with the "sacramental" or "re-presentative" model of church. On the latter application of "models" to church, cf. Avery Dulles, *Models of the Church* (New York: Doubleday, 1974). On the question of ecclesiology, I agree with the insistence of James M. Gustafson and Joseph A. Komonchak on the need for developing ecclesiology in relationship to social theory: cf. James M. Gustafson, *Treasure in Earthen Vessels: The Church as a Human Community* (New York: Harper & Row, 1961); Joseph A. Komonchak, "History and Social Theory in Ecclesiology" (to be published in Proceedings of Lonergan Workshop, Boston College, 1974, by Darton, Longman & Todd in 1975). As the next chapter will suggest at greater length, precisely the move to social theory is the methodological move needed to allow the revisionist model for fundamental theology to make some suggestions for a practical theology.

(102) This is not to suggest that there are not further questions either for fundamental or, especially, dogmatic theology: such further questions and answers as those posed by classical Chalcedonian christology or classical Trinitarian theology are especially pertinent here, as the still important revisionist dogmatic work of F. D. Maurice may serve to testify.

(103) For this interpretation of this famous Pauline passage, cf. Schubert M. Ogden, "Present Prospects for Empirical Theology," in *The Future of Empirical Theology*, pp. 73–6.

(104) In that sense, as a historical observation, it seems to me reasonably clear that the present work in fundamental theology is faithful to the Catholic theological tradition's understanding of the task of a "natural theology," even though the latter expression now seems a less than happy formulation for this task.

(105) The present account, for all its plea for symbol, remains a reflective theological account. The actual development of appropriately disclosive modern religious symbols is a task not for the theological interpreter but for the creative artist.

(106) In this sense, it seems to me that Bernard Lonergan's transformation-model for religious "conversion" as a "falling-in-love" and finding a new "horizon" of values is existentially meaningful: cf. Bernard Lonergan, *Method in Theology*, pp. 101–112. At this point also the spiritual tradition of "discernment of spirits" seems particularly pertinent.

(107) For some important cautionary remarks here, cf. n. 94 above.

Chapter 10

History, Theory, and *Praxis*

INTRODUCTORY SUMMARY

In one sense both the formal, methodological concerns of Part I of this work and the material, systematic concerns of Part II have already received their summary. For the basic meaning of the theological christocentrism advanced above is that a Christian fundamental theology informed by the revisionist model for contemporary reflection receives its appropriate summary, its adequate re-presentation, in christological language. If this reinterpretation of christology is at all accurate, then one may find there a re-presentative summary of the religious and theistic limit-meanings which the earlier analyses attempted to uncover in both our common experience and New Testament texts.

In another sense, of course, the reader has every right to expect a more systematic explication of how, for the author at least, the several components of this work may be said to form a whole. In general terms, that whole can be delineated as follows: after a brief analysis of the contemporary pluralist theological situation and of the models developed in response to that situation, I attempted to outline what model (and for what reasons) seemed most appropriate to the full dimensions of the contemporary task. Consequently, I attempted to spell out that revisionist model. Fundamentally, the model holds that contemporary fundamental theology[1] is best understood as philosophical reflection upon both the meanings disclosed in our common human experience and the meanings disclosed in the primary texts of the Christian tradition.[2] To possess more than methodological interest, these analyses must be applied at least to the fundamental questions of religious, theistic, and christological meanings.[3] Part II was an attempt to provide summary-analyses of some of the major positions in the contemporary pluralist situation which, either implicitly or explicitly, provide exemplifications of the kind of revisionist analysis proposed for these three questions. Hence, both a phenomenological analysis of the religious dimension of our common experience as both limit-to and limit-of that experience and a hermeneutical analysis of the explictly religious as limit-character of certain New Testament language merited closer investigation. Similarly, an explicitly metaphysical analysis of the limit-concepts available for the theistic referent of our common experience and of the God referred to by Christian texts demanded similar study. Finally, an analysis of the several meaningful facts of our actual situation and of the principal existential meanings of the factual—as re-presentative—limit-character of christological texts provided an opportunity both to summarize the earlier conclusions on religion and theism and to articulate the distinctly factual and disclosive character of christological language.

Those all too brief investigations of these central theological questions do not, of course, pretend to be a fully developed fundamental theology, much less a systematics. They do, however, strive to indicate how a clarification of the appropriate model for theological reflection may find some initial and tentative exemplification. *The* problem of the contemporary systematic theologian, as has often been remarked, is actually *to do* systematic theology. The major attempt of this book has been to propose a model which may perform some initial spadework for that larger enterprise and to interpret certain familiar instances of contemporary theologizing in what one hopes is the clarifying light of the model proposed. As I trust is clear from the text and footnotes, I have throughout Part II been heavily dependent on the work of analysts of several traditions. For the interpretation of their analyses, however, and especially for the reinterpretation of their work in the light of the revisionist model, I alone bear full responsibility.

If my analysis of that model and its applicability is at all correct, then the present pluralist situation in the disciplines of theology and religious studies need not be as dishearteningly confusing as it sometimes seems.[4] As far as I can see, *any* given constructive position depends for its evidence, its warrants, its backings, and its very structure of argumentation upon the basic model which explicitly or, as is more often the case, implicitly informs that position. At least five such models have been delineated and exemplified in this study. One model—the revisionist—has been advanced as more adequate for the common task of fundamental theology than any of the other four. If that claim holds, then a full systematic theology could and should be developed in relationship to that fundamental base. A properly systematic theology, to be sure, would need to apply and expand the model[5] not only in relation to those initial religious, theistic, and christological questions which this text addresses, but also in relation to the whole range of questions which Christian theology historically has addressed: ecclesiology, justification and sanctification, the trinitarian understanding of the Christian God, the Chalcedonian understanding of christology, etc. For anyone who accepts this model for doing theology, no one of the traditional Christian answers to these questions—or, for that matter, the questions themselves—can simply be assumed.[6] Rather all must be reinvestigated in the light of the set of criteria articulated in the model itself. In some cases, the symbols and doctrines may well find an appropriate contemporary reinterpretation by means of a hermeneutics of restoration. In still other cases, those symbols and doctrines may not bear the power of meaningfulness, meaning, or truth any longer—either to our common experience or to the central meanings disclosed by Christian texts and tradition. In these latter cases, those negative conclusions exemplified by various hermeneutics of suspicion upon Christian meanings should be honestly and candidly stated with a methodological and critical rigor appropriate to the seriousness of the subject matter.

The Christian theologian stands in service both to that community of inquiry exemplified but surely not exhausted by the contemporary academy and to that community of religious and moral discourse exemplified but surely not exhausted by his own church tradition. If that same theologian, as herein understood, is really to fulfill his service of critical reflection, he must start the inquiry without an assumption either for or against the meaning, meaningfulness, and truth of the symbol or doctrine under analysis.[7] It is unlikely that fundamentalists will welcome the intrusion of a revisionist theologian into their clear and distinct literalisms. Yet there are worse fates than the displeasure of the established powers. One such is the fate of those —in the churches and the academy alike—whose ideas of inquiry and integrity somehow stop short of demanding any critical and open-ended investigation of their own basic assumptions about the meaning of our common existence and the meaning of Christianity.

The basic proposal of this work, then, is the claim that the revisionist model for fundamental theology is more adequate for the contemporary task. If that claim is fallacious, the dialectic has still been advanced to the point where one more route at least has been found to prove a dead-end. My major assumption is that if the claims for this model are rejected, the rejection will come from evidence that I have erred in understanding our common experience or in understanding the meaning of the Christian symbols. If the rejection comes for those evidential reasons, the work will have fulfilled its proper purpose of attempting to encourage the discernment of both such sources of our common life.

Although this proposal is one for a contemporary fundamental theology and, by way of that discipline, for systematic theology itself, the proposal does not lack applicability to the other two major tasks for theology: historical theology and practical theology. In the former case, the applicability is relatively clear: insofar as the historical-hermeneutical method proposed is an appropriate one, its employment by historical theologians for their retrieval of past theological meanings may prove useful.[8] Moreover, insofar as historical theologians are also theologians, they may find the revisionist delineation of the criteria of contemporary theological meaning suggestive for the vexing problem of just which historical retrievals of past Christian meanings are especially appropriate for the present theological task.[9] For the historical theologian's principal task *qua* theologian is to decipher how and why past Christian meanings were meaningful and true for a particular cultural situation, and how and why such past meanings either are or are not meaningful and true today.[10] Whenever this latter task is attempted, the historical theologian is also a constructive theologian of *present* meaning. In a parallel fashion, since the constructive theologian of the revisionist kind is intrinsically committed to deciphering past Christian meanings, this mutual dependence seems altogether appropriate. Alas, the rarest phenomenon in our necessarily specialized age seems to be a contemporary constructive theologian who is also a historical and hermeneutical master of primary Christian texts. Indeed the exceptional character of such constructive and historical theological achievements as Rudolf Bultmann's only serves to clarify the general need for closer and more rigorous collaboration between fundamental, systematic, and historical theologians.

For theology's third classical task, practical theology,[11] the revisionist model may also prove helpful. Perhaps this is the place for a word on how that task may be understood in relation to the fundamental, systematic, and historical moments of theology. My assumption is that the fundamental and the systematic tasks of theology are principally concerned with the construction of the *present* meaning, meaningfulness, and truth of the Christian tradition. The historical theologian's major task is the reconstruction of *past* meaning for the present. The practical theologian's task, directly dependent upon the other two, is to project the *future* possibilities of meaning and truth on the basis of present constructive and past historical theological resources. Just as the historical theologian's principal aim is an adequately reconstructed *historia* and the fundamental and systematic theologian's principal attempts are to formulate an appropriately constructed contemporary *theoria,* so the practical theologian's task becomes the rigorous investigation of the possibilities of *praxis* which a reconstructed *historia* and a newly constructed *theoria* may allow.[12]

This understanding of the task of the practical theologian may now allow us to expand the context of contemporary theological pluralism to include an investigation of those political theologies of *praxis*—of hope, of liberation, even of revolution—which so strongly inform the present theological moment. The investigation of these important contemporary options, however, will prove to be a critical one: not merely negatively critical, but, one trusts, suggestive of how and why the revisionist model may aid in the resolution of some of the difficulties which present theologies of *praxis* find.

PRACTICAL THEOLOGY: The *Praxis* of a Revisionist Theory

It is important to note that this section on revisionist *praxis,* unlike the sections on revisionist theory for fundamental theology, has a merely anticipatory role. The actual fulfillment of that role would need the development

of a model for a Christian systematics as well as the further theoretical resources of a critical-philosophical social theory.[13] My limited aim here is not
to claim to do anything more than to indicate what possible light a revisionist fundamental theology might throw upon the pressing questions of a theology of *praxis*.

Since that claim remains in the language of promise, anticipation, and
possibility, it would be best to return to the present pluralist situation in
practical theology itself in order to examine critically the actual accomplishments and limitations of the reigning models for theological *praxis*. Such a
procedure of "clarification of a possibility through contrast with existing
actualities" seems necessary to maintain fidelity to the contemporary rich
pluralism of theologies and, at the same time, acceptable to those "eschatological" theologies whose own mode of analysis is a dialectical one favoring
the negation of present actuality in favor of a projected future possibility.

Commanding attention within the present pluralism, both the earlier and
still operative liberal model for theology and the more recent and probably
more influential neo-orthodox model informing most eschatological theologies seem to be the two principal models for practical theology. Certainly,
the orthodox model and the radical model have formulated practical
theologies as well;[14] however, the major discussion in contemporary theology, as in the culture generally, seems to be between "liberals" and "neo-
orthodox" radicals.[15] A brief analysis of their achievements is in order before proceeding to clarify the *praxis* possibilities of the revisionist model.

In their oft-renewed developments of "theologies of culture," culminating
in societal terms in the Social Gospel movement, the liberals undoubtedly
made real and enduring achievements for and in contemporary *praxis*.
Their commitment to the possibilities of rational analysis and responsible
individual and societal action freed them to reinterpret the Christian symbol-system in meaningful, as modern liberal, terms.[16] Through reinterpretations of the humanizing role of religion in Schleiermacher and his successors and through the wide-ranging developmental social reforms of the
Social Gospel movement, probably best exemplified in recent history by liberal American Christianity's role in the civil rights struggles of the 1960's,
the liberal record in practical theology continues to command real respect.
However, as the American culture at large throughout the climactic period
of the later 1960's began to discover the inability of liberal reasonableness
and social analysis to effect, on its own, the profound personal and social
transformations needed, the liberal model for theological and cultural activity seemed to find itself at the end of its resources. If the earlier analysis of
the limitations of the liberal model for constructive theology is accurate,
one need not find too surprising this *cul de sac* of the liberals in practical
theology. Indeed the major difficulty of the liberal theologian becomes yet
more clear in its practical consequences: his nearly complete commitment
to the modern Enlightenment view of humanity's rational possibilities pre-

vented him from either grasping theoretically or employing practically the profound and transformative Christian images of man's actual situation of sin and grace and, correlatively, the Christian image of a loving and just God whose acts are meant to transform that human situation beyond reasonableness and even beyond tragedy.[17]

The profound impact of Reinhold Niebuhr on the American scene or of Karl Barth in the European theological context can be understood even more clearly in its practical than in its theoretical forms.[18] The neo-orthodox model for theology, exemplified best in Niebuhr's own work, was able to retrieve a classical Christian image of humanity and God that resonated with profound possibilities for really filling the vacuum left by the collapse of liberal resources and the seeming loss of faith in the Enlightenment view of man's progressive, reasonable development. Nor is Niebuhr's work correctly interpreted as a merely conservative revival. Indeed, Reinhold Niebuhr possessed a well-nigh complete commitment to standard liberal causes of social justice, as well as a commitment to the central theoretical demand of liberal theology that Christian symbols and faith be directly related to our actual experience. Yet Niebuhr, unlike his liberal predecessors, was able to retrieve Christian symbols and faith in a neo-orthodox manner that brightly illuminated the actual situation of historical humanity and the transformative power of the central Christian symbols for and in that very situation.[19] Liberal commitment to rational social analysis and responsible personal and societal action was maintained; but neo-orthodox insistence upon the real transformative power of the Christian symbols in their full existential meaning challenged the modern Enlightenment view of humanity's actuality and possibility, as clearly as gospel Christianity challenged the classical Greek view of inherent human reasonableness.

It seems clear, however, that neither the liberal model for *praxis* nor the actualization of the neo-orthodox model proposed by Niebuhr command the central attention of most contemporary theologians of *praxis*. Rather those theologians, Catholic and Protestant alike, are more alert to the economic exploitation of the oppressed throughout the world and more aware —especially since Vietnam—of the real possibilities for evil, masked as either "mistake" or "realistic (i.e., Cold War) necessity," consequent upon either classical liberal policies of "development" or the classical neo-orthodox policies of "realistic" appraisals of power-politics. These contemporary "political" theologians of *praxis*—of whom Jürgen Moltmann, Johannes Metz, Carl Braaten, Rubem Alves, Richard Shaull, Juan Segundo, Gustavo Gutierrez, and Dorothee Soelle appear most representative—[20] seem, in most cases, to have transformed a neo-orthodox model for theology. Instead of challenging that model's basic adequacy, they have proposed new resources for actualizing the model in the present situation.

Central among such new resources seem to be two new possibilities, the one in the realm of theoretical clarification, the other in the realm of symbolic enrichment. The latter resource is surely the most obvious accomplishment of these new theologians of *praxis*. In fidelity to the classical neo-orthodox retrieval of the existential transformative power of Christian symbols, the recent theologians of *praxis* have managed to retrieve the societal and political, not merely existentialist-individualist, meanings inherent in the symbols of Judaism and Christianity.[21] Whether one notes the critique of Johannes Metz of his mentor, Karl Rahner, that "transcendental" theology too often results in an "individualism," or the critique of Jürgen Moltmann of his "existentialist" predecessors, especially Rudolf Bultmann,[22] one witnesses, above all, a retrieval of the Jewish and Christian eschatological symbols as symbols of societal, political, and religious liberation.

The impact and importance of this symbolic retrieval of the social and political character of Christian eschatological symbols becomes all the clearer when one notes the major theoretical resource joined to the retrieval itself. That new resource is, in fact, the rediscovery of and theological reinterpretation of the classical Hegelian-Marxist notion of *praxis*.[23] The earlier existentialist form of neo-orthodox retrieval found its principal theoretical forerunner in the radical authenticity of Søren Kierkegaard, "the individual" among the Hegelians, or in the continuance of that individualist tradition by Martin Heidegger.[24] On the contrary, this latter form of neo-orthodox retrieval finds its principal theoretical resource in the formulations of the task of *praxis* initiated by that other Hegelian, Karl Marx, and continued in the revisionist form of Marxism represented by Ernst Bloch.[25]

What seems to unite these diverse thinkers on a theoretical level is their common commitment to two fundamental Marxian axioms: the task of philosophy (here theology) is not to interpret the world but to change it; that task is best fulfilled when critical theory always informs, and is informed by, actual economic, social, and political practice. In short, the aim of all thought is *praxis*. Such *praxis*, of course, is not to be identified with practice. Rather *praxis* is correctly understood as the critical relationship between theory and practice whereby each is dialectically influenced and transformed by the other. The principal tool for such analysis is a dialectical method whereby one negates present actualizations of theory and practice in order to project future theoretical and practical possibilities.[26] Such possibilities, once actualized, may serve to negate the original negation, only to be negated in turn until the final end-point of a future, universal, personal and societal, complete transformation is accomplished: whether that future be viewed as a Utopian classless society without God or as the eschatological Kingdom of God.[27] The principal resources for such dialectical analyses of *praxis* may be found in analyses of both the economic infrastructures and the cultural super-structures of our societal lives[28] and in the retrieval of those symbolic representations of man's future possibilities disclosed in daydreams, Utopian visions, eschatological promises, and proleptic fulfillments.[29]

Whatever their other limitations, it seems clear that these eschatological theologies of *praxis* have provided an invaluable service to the task of practical theology. Not only have they de-individualized the focal point of theological meaning in favor of a contemporary model of social humanity; not only have they shown the radical dimensions of future, not merely present, possibilities disclosed by the limit-language of Christian eschatology;[30] but they have also explicitly introduced into the Christian theological context the enduring Marxian insights into the centrality of *praxis*, and the enriching possibilities of dialectical analyses of present economic, political, and cultural realities. For such achievements, the revisionist theologian, along with his liberal and neo-orthodox colleagues, can only express his gratitude and his "promise" to attempt to incorporate these achievements into a revisionist theology of *praxis*.[31]

Yet the revisionist theologian must hesitate to incorporate the neo-orthodox model which informs most of these eschatological theologies of *praxis*. The exact character of that critical hesitation must now be analyzed. That hesitation, as the social model informing the revisionist understanding of humanity and God alike makes clear, is not prompted by any call to return to individualism in theology.[32] That hesitation, made even clearer by the revisionist commitment to the need for religious symbols and for an analysis of the present and future possibilities which their limit-language discloses, is not due to any deliberate failure to appreciate the real accomplishments of this reinterpretation of the eschatological symbols.[33] Since the revisionist methodological commitment is to all modes of analysis which may at once illuminate our common experience and find formulation in terms of a critical philosophy,[34] the hesitation cannot be to that mode of philosophical analysis called dialectical and applied with such critical expertise to the infra-structural and super-structural factors constituting our common experience. Finally, the hesitation is not a disagreement with the central insight of this tradition that the aim of all *theoria* is *praxis*. In fact, the practical consequences of any fundamental and constructive theology bear the full weight of legitimate criteria for judging the adequacy of that theory.

The critical hesitation of the revisionist theologian in relationship to these contemporary eschatological theologies is, to formulate the matter in their own theoretical framework, that, in fact, these theologies are not faithful to the full demands of *praxis*. More specifically, if *praxis* as distinct from practice is always related to a critical theory applicable to all infra-structural and super-structural factors in human reality, then why is this critical theory so seldom applied to the very theological symbols which inform these eschatological theologies? [35] Perhaps the principal reason for this failure can be traced to the eschatological theologians' seeming refusal to challenge the neo-orthodox model of their immediate theological predecessors.[36] That model, as we saw, does not in fact permit a sufficiently critical analysis of such central Christian symbols as the classical theistic understanding of the Christian God and the classical exclusivist Christian claims for "special revelation" and christology.[37] Too readily satisfied with showing the existential meaningfulness of Christian symbols, the neo-orthodox theologians did not seem to allow for a critical investigation of the internal coherence (meaning) and truth of the traditional concepts employed by the Christian tradition in its self-understanding of such central symbols as revelation, God, and Christ. Whether the questions of revelation and christology be approached through the classical Catholic distinction of the "double-gratuity" of creation and redemption, as that tradition is brilliantly reinterpreted in the essentially neo-orthodox position of Karl Rahner; whether those same questions be resolved through a final appeal to a classically Protestant understanding of the exclusivist character of specifically Christian revelation, as in Rudolf Bultmann's attempt to distinguish "a possibility in principle" from a "possibility in fact," [38] the same neo-orthodox problem emerges. That problem, present most clearly in premature appeals to the "mystery" and "scandal" of specifically Christian revelation in the constructive theological positions of the neo-orthodox, reappears in *praxis*-terms in their practical theologies.

One cannot but ask with Marxist critics how a Christian commitment to a corporate *praxis* is finally intelligible if, even after demythologizing the "super-natural" world as not some world other than the world we actually live in, Christians continue to believe in the omnipotent, all-knowing, and unrelated God of classical theism and, at the same time, in an exclusivist understanding of revelation and christology which threatens the ultimate value and meaning of that basic secular faith shared by all those committed to the contemporary struggle for liberation.[39] It seems entirely appropriate to insist that if God is real, *we* as finite cannot fully understand his reality. Yet it continues to seem entirely inappropriate to employ this truism to bolster concepts of God and of Christian revelation which are neither internally coherent, nor able to illuminate our own ineluctable commitment to the ultimate meaningfulness of every struggle against oppression and for social justice and agapic love.

Such largely conceptual, constructive difficulties seem to worry the eschatological theologians of *praxis* as little as they worried their neo-orthodox existentialist predecessors.[40] For that reason, one must interpret their model for theology as an essentially neo-orthodox one. Yet how they can continue to retain that model, given their own prior commitment to the full implications of *praxis*, remains a puzzle. Why cannot that critical commitment, so admirably articulated in the critical interpretations of the social and political realities of our common experience, also be employed to interpret critically the possible conceptual incoherencies of traditional Christian symbols? Until and unless that task is attempted,[41] it seems unlikely that the eschatological theologians can provide an adequate understanding of contemporary Christian *praxis*.

A further clue to this difficulty may be found in the work of the eschatological theologians' favored conversation partner, Ernst Bloch. One need not disparage the ground-breaking work of Bloch as represented by his singular ability to analyze the existential meaningfulness of all symbolic expressions of man's future possibilities in daydreams, Utopian visions, fantasies, and the eschatological language and apocalyptic movements of Jewish and Christian history. Still one may well agree with the criticism of Bloch's fellow Marxist in the tradition of critical social theory, Jürgen Habermas, that Bloch is best described as a Marxist Romantic.[42] More exactly, Bloch's work on *praxis* does demonstrate the power of eschatological and Utopian symbols to negate present oppression and to disclose alternative and more humanly authentic societal possibilities. But Bloch's work, to my knowledge at least, does not demonstrate the kind of critical analysis of infra-structural and super-structural realities which can, in fact, be found in either the other major form of Marxian critical social theory exemplified in the work of Theodor Adorno, Max Horkheimer, and Jürgen Habermas or in the implications for critical social analysis exemplified in the American situation by the liberating influence of John Dewey or Charles Sanders Peirce.[43]

The central demand for the continuing refinement of genuinely critical theory and for its universal applicability to all experience and all symbol-systems is the chief distinguishing characteristic of both the contemporary revisionist model for fundamental theology and the "revisionist" model for critical social theory exemplified in the work of the Frankfurt School.[44] Yet precisely this demand for critical *theory*, and especially for its application to the theoretical meaning of the Christian symbols, seems as lacking in the eschatological theologians of *praxis* as it was in their more individualist and existentialist neo-orthodox predecessors.

More positively stated, the revisionist model for a practical theology, in consistency with its application in constructive theology, would attempt to continue the real achievements of these new neo-orthodox theologies of *praxis* while negating their lack of critical-theoretical rigor. That revisionist attempt, to be sure, remains here merely anticipatory.[45] As the brief reference to the Frankfurt School suggests, a revisionist theology of *praxis* would need at least one further mode of theoretical analysis to supplement and complete the earlier modes of analysis proper to constructive theology. That other necessary mode of analysis can perhaps be best described as a critical social theory. The key, of course, is the word "critical." For the revisionist theologian, that word would imply at least the following factors: strictly empirical analyses of our actual economic, political, cultural, and social situations (i.e., the kind of analyses probably best represented by the empirical character of the best of American social analyses rather than in the more theoretical and unfortunately too seldom empirical analyses of the Frankfurt School itself); rigorous ethical analyses of the possibilities and limitations of the various infra-structural and super-structural components of our social reality; critical retrievals, if possible, or critical inventions, if necessary, of various symbol-systems in accordance with their ability both to negate the oppressive forces actually operative in the situation, and to project those images of social humanity to which the authentic human being can commit himself or herself.[46]

These demands can, in fact, be summarized for the Christian theologian under the same rubric seen throughout this work. A revisionist practical theology would take the form of philosophical reflection upon the meanings of our common human experience and upon the meanings of the Christian tradition. Such a practical theology would be conversant with earlier constructive articulations, and then raise explicitly the questions of *praxis* by means of interdisciplinary work with empirical sociologists, critical social theorists, and ethicians. In brief, the critical-*theoretical* aspect of the constructive model would need the expansion of scientifically authenticated empirical data, explicitly critical social analyses, and ethical analysis. The *hermeneutical* aspect would need the reinterpretation of the societal and projective (future) limit-possibilities disclosed by the Christian symbols.[47] Admittedly, this methodological suggestion is no more than a formal and anticipatory one. Yet the actuality of such diverse critical social ethics as those represented by the work of James Luther Adams, Gregory Baum, Daniel Callahan, Max Stackhouse, Johannes Metz, James Gustafson, and Gibson Winter promises that this formal suggestion may not be merely anticipatory.[48]

In the favored Hegelian language of the theologians of *praxis*, perhaps the revisionist model can provide an *Aufhebung* and not mere negation of the other dominant models for theology.[49] If so, there remains every good reason to hope that the solid achievements of the eschatological theologians of hope, like the accomplishments of their existentialist and neo-orthodox predecessors, could be incorporated into a viable and interdisciplinary method of practical theology. That latter method could develop a *praxis* which would be more adequate in exact relationship to its more rigorous employment of both empirical evidence and critical theory to investigate the meanings of the social and political dimensions of our common experience and the social and political meanings disclosed by a critical reinterpretation of the major Christian symbols. A critical reappropriation of the symbols of Christian eschatological liberation, once united to a critical reformulation of the symbols God, Christ, and revelation, might free the imagination of the politically committed Christian and non-Christian alike to find symbols representative of their struggle for full-scale liberation. That all critical theories need the complement of symbolic representations has

been argued in the preceding chapter. But the hope of a revisionist theology
is that the return to symbols and, through symbolic meaning, to *praxis* be
achieved through, not around, the most critical reflection upon those symbols. At that point, a post-critical or second naiveté towards the Christian
symbols present in Western culture might be a real possibility for the Christian and non-Christian alike.[50]

That critical reformulation, moreover, might allow for the development
of genuinely new symbols that could aid what Paolo Freire has called the
"conscientização" of the masses.[51] If genuinely critical, these symbols might
function in a manner destructive of the vestiges of that mythological religious vision which, too often in the past, has functioned as the "opium of
the masses." [52] That critical reformulation should, in principle, eventually
allow Christian theologians of *praxis* to find words that may render that call
to liberation so clear that, as Albert Camus remarked, "even the simplest
man can understand its meaning." Such stark primal language was once
employed in the parabolic limit-language of the New Testament. That language could again be employed with integrity if and when the long journey
through hard empirical evidence and critical thought—parallel to the Christian and the Marxist long journey through the institutions—clarifies its own
fundamental self-understanding. At that point, the authentic simplicity, not
simple-mindedness, of the kind of life, thought, and commitment proclaimed in the Christian gospel as the true destiny of every human being
might find root again; this time, in a humanity whose historical journey
seems to have reached the point where we must find what values we can all
unite to actualize lest we die, each clinging with ever-diminishing dignity to
his own mythologies, his own ideologies, his own god.

A practical theology in interdisciplinary conversation with empirical sociologists and economists, and informed by critical social theory would find
its *praxis* grounded in, yet authentically be a major and new stage of development upon, the *theoria* of a newly constructed revisionist fundamental
and systematic theology and an ever-freshly retrieved historical theology.
That type of practical theology, moreover, by the dynamism of the critical
exigencies to which it owes its constitution, should not fall heir to either the
unconscionable insensitivity to questions of social justice so characteristic
of fundamentalist church piety, or even to the more sophisticated "transcendental irresponsibility" which Reinhold Niebuhr charged to the record
of some of the more existentialist and individualist among the neo-orthodox
theologians. Nor should this understanding of theological *praxis* allow the
too easy temptations of the liberal to last: a model of the enlightened
human being's possibilities which masks a naive understanding of the actual power of reason in most lives; an uncanny inability to understand the
destructive forces at work in the well-intentioned persons and well-posi-
tioned structures of liberal power; a curious refusal to believe that those the
liberal calls the "under-developed" peoples and nations may actually have

something to teach the "developed" liberal élite—starting, perhaps, with the understanding of the liberal's own illusions about the purity of his motives or of the power-structures which allow and enforce his liberal attitudes.

Yet one continues to hope that such a revisionist theology, by its fidelity to the liberating possibilities inherent in that kind of critical analysis and responsible action which liberalism at its best fostered in the modern spirit, may not fall prey to other temptations. Retreats into individualism and symbolic vagueness are too ready and inviting; premature announcements of paradox, scandal, and mystery still echo loudly. There still can be heard those dark and foreboding proclamations of our need to be "realistic" about the use of power in our fallen and sinful situation which tarnished the record on *theoria* and *praxis* alike of some neo-orthodox theologies and existentialist philosophies of the very recent past. By that same commitment to critical theory and hermeneutical reinterpretation, the revisionist theologian of *praxis* may also be able to resist those siren calls to "revolution" sung by the more apocalyptic-minded among the eschatologists, but whose precise social, ethical, and political meaning is left as vague as the exact meaning of that eschatological God of the future who will somehow, someday, assure the "revolution's" success.

Such a revisionist theology of *praxis*, to be sure, cannot even be said to be "proleptically" present in this present formal analysis. Yet if the need is recognized—and the interdisciplinary resources for achieving it are admitted—then the central purpose of this merely anticipatory chapter will be fulfilled. That no single theologian can any longer hope to systematize fundamental, historical, systematic, and practical theology is now a truism. The full meaning and force of this truism was recently expressed in Bernard Lonergan's critical and eloquent call for a theological method expressive of the real possibilities for critical collaboration.[53] The central promise of the pluralistic theological situation which this work has attempted to document and to diagnose is, in Lonergan's own terms, its promise of a critical ongoing collaboration. Perhaps it is not too much to hope that, even if this diagnosis of a revisionist model for fundamental theology is found to be as wanting as the earlier orthodox, liberal, neo-orthodox, and radical models, the work will not have been in vain. If a better model for our very real shared needs for contemporary theological self-understanding is available, by all means let us all employ that alternative. But let us employ it if—and only if—it is more appropriate to the basic meanings to be found in both our common contemporary experience and in the Christian tradition. A critical collaboration which would demand less than that would be neither authentically critical nor truly collaborative. A theological pluralism which could rest content in the merely aesthetic pleasure of a pluralist world is unworthy of the commitment of the Christian theological traditions to the Word as bearer of meaning and truth for all humanity, or to the seriousness of the present crisis of meaning in our increasingly global community of inquiry. If this work can even allow us to see those fundamental needs more clearly and our own communal responsibility to attempt to resolve those needs, then this work will have served its central purpose.

Notes

(1) The primary task of fundamental theology might be expressed as the attempt to determine criteria for theological argument. Its task is closely linked to the traditional "apologetic" task of theology. Although not identical to the task of Christian dogmatic theology, the criteria advanced in fundamental theology should find a place in dogmatics as well. In the latter case, the need for a "confessional" position which incorporates methods for truly public discourse seems especially pertinent here. In the manner suggested by H. Richard Niebuhr's notion of a "confessional" position which is also "apologetic" in the positive sense, a revisionist dogmatic theology must find some way to interrelate critically both its public character and its explicit relationship to a particular religious tradition. In that sense, the present comments in practical theology may also be taken as some initial indications of the task of a Christian dogmatic theology. For some more specific and personal comments on what a contemporary Christian systematics related to the present fundamental theology might encompass, see my article "Theology as Public Discourse" in *The Christian Century* series on "New Trends in Religious Thought" (XCII:10 [March 19, 1975], pp. 280–84). As I mention in that article, I am painfully aware that, even if the present revisionist model for fundamental theology is a viable one, that model, of and by itself, may not be allowed to serve as an adequate model for a contemporary Christian systematics. On the other hand, I remain convinced that, whatever form the latter model may eventually take, it must be informed by the concerns and criteria of fundamental theology if it is to perform its proper function of informing public discourse and helping to transform public *praxis*.

(2) It bears repetition to note that, although the analyses of the present work are largely limited to an analysis of texts, the questions of the interpretation of symbols, events, and witnesses is also a part of the task of the interpretation of the Christian "fact" (or "tradition").

(3) The logical order of these questions, as noted in chapter four, is of considerable importance. The logical order of the questions for a dogmatics might well work in the opposite fashion: for example, an analysis of ecclesiological and christological meanings may lead to an investigation of what we earlier labelled such further theological questions as the "dialectical" character of Christian religious limit-language (for the doctrine of revelation) and the analogical character of Christian theistic limit-concepts. Such further dogmatic questions, one hopes, can be advanced without abandoning public criteria for analysis of the tradition.

(4) The two disciplines are not, of course, identical. Religious studies may legitimately confine its attention to questions of historical and hermeneutical meaning. Theology, we have suggested throughout this work, is explicitly committed to raising the questions of meaning, meaningfulness, and truth to explicit attention. This difference need not be articulated, as it sometimes is, by practitioners of "religious studies," as implying that theology's self-understanding must be confessional in the narrow sense: for an example of that judgment, cf. Ninian Smart, "Religion and

Theology," in *The Science of Religion and the Sociology of Knowledge: Some Methodological Questions* (Princeton: Princeton University Press, 1973), pp. 24–49, esp. the discussion of the Christian theologian or the "buddhologist" as a "spokesman," pp. 43–48.

(5) Cf. comments in n. 1 above.

(6) For an example here, cf. Paul Tillich, "The Valuation of the Christological Dogma," in *Systematic Theology*, II (Chicago: University of Chicago Press, 1957), 138–50; B. A. Gerrish, "Jesus, Myth, and History: Troeltsch's Stand in the 'Christ Myth' Debate," *Journal of Religion* 55 (1975), 13–36.

(7) That he needs some "pre-understanding" of the subject matter is clear (cf. discussions in chapters one and four); that such "pre-understanding" is equivalent to belief in specific doctrines leads to a misunderstanding of both the nature of "pre-understanding" as "pre-conceptual" and doctrine as conceptual. Furthermore, the latter position seems to render any real possibility of *Sach-Kritik* impossible, as the differing ways in which Rudolf Bultmann and Karl Rahner employ the Heideggerian understanding of the pre-understanding involved in "retrieval" of past meanings may serve to indicate.

(8) Recall the discussion in chapter four on the historian's role in reconstructing texts. In principle, this role becomes even more crucial for the reconstruction of the "events," "symbols," and "witnesses" (tradition) needed to allow the proper functioning of the hermeneutical role outlined in chapter four.

(9) In recent theology, Bultmann's "retrieval" of New Testament meanings via his existentialist reinterpretation of scriptural texts and Karl Rahner's transcendental "retrieval" of several major doctrines of the Roman Catholic tradition may serve as paradigmatic examples. Recall also how the recent eschatological theologies are concerned to retrieve such "lost" meanings as the political meanings of the scriptural tradition and the left-wing of the Reformation. A recent and penetrating example of the latter may be found in Jürgen Moltmann, *The Crucified God: The Cross of Christ as the Foundation and Criticism of Christian Theology* (London: SCM, 1974), esp. chapter eight.

(10) For an example here, cf. Bernard Lonergan's comment on the Roman Catholic Marian doctrines: "Perhaps I might suggest that human psychology and specifically the refinement of human feelings is the area to be explored in coming to understand the development of Marian doctrines," in *Method in Theology* (New York: Herder and Herder, 1972), p. 320.

(11) More specifically, the present discussion of practical theology is limited to fundamental theological concerns—especially here the incorporation of *praxis* and thereby both empirical studies and critical social theory into a revisionist model for practical theology. The full development of a practical theology would also need the development of a model for Christian dogmatics mentioned above (n. 1). In Bernard Lonergan's alternative terms, a pastoral theology not only has its own specific tasks but assumes research, interpretation, history, and dialectics, as well as foundational theology, doctrinal theology, and systematic theology (cf. *Method in Theology*, pp. 355–68). It may be helpful to note that, although this present work is deeply indebted to Lonergan's notions of method for theology, I do not wish to suggest that

he is committed to a revisionist model for theology. Indeed, in terms of his theological "content" (as distinct from his "method"), his own self-description seems to me entirely accurate, viz., ". . . a Roman Catholic with quite conservative views on religious and church doctrines" (ibid., p. 332).

(12) Cf. Schubert M. Ogden, "The Task of Theology," *Journal of Religion* 52 (1972), 22–40.

(13) Cf. the resources from the Frankfurt School listed in chapter one as a major example here. This resource seems more in harmony with the revisionist model than the more widely used (by American theologians) Berger-Luckmann model in Peter Berger and Thomas Luckmann, *The Social Construction of Reality: A Treatise in the Sociology of Knowledge* (Garden City: Doubleday, 1967). It is no disparagement of this important work to suggest that, however valuable its interpretation of the model of the social construction of reality clearly is, it seems to leave relatively unexamined the possibilities for a critical reflection upon any given social construction and thereby leaves the status-quo unchallenged. For a pointed critique of Berger-Luckmann here, cf. Trent Schroyer, *The Critique of Domination: The Origins and Development of Critical Theory* (New York: Braziller, 1974), pp. 267–8, n. 22. Behind this contemporary debate lie, of course, the classical Marx, Weber, and Mannheim discussions. Besides the resources in the Frankfurt School listed above, the following should be mentioned: Paul Breines (ed.), *Critical Interruptions* (New York: Herder and Herder, 1970); Norman Birnbaum, *Toward A Critical Sociology* (New York: Oxford University Press, 1971); Jürgen Habermas and Niklas Luhmann, *Theorie der Gesellschaft oder Sozialtechnologie: Theorie Diskussion* (Frankfurt: Suhrkamp, 1971); Jürgen Habermas, *Zur Logik der Sozialwissenschaft* (Frankfurt: Suhrkamp, 1970); Herbert Marcuse, *Reason and Revolution: Hegel and the Rise of Social Theory* (Boston: Beacon, 1941); Max Horkheimer, *Eclipse of Reason* (New York: Seabury, 1974); Theodor Adorno, *Negative Dialectics* (New York: Seabury, 1974); Justus George Lawler (ed.), *Continuum* 8 (1970). I am indebted to my friends Prof. Matthew Lamb (Marquette) and Prof. Frederick Lawrence (Boston College) for my introduction to the works of this important school of critical social theory. Besides the works of Lamb and Lawrence cited in chapter four, cf. also Matthew Lamb, "History, Method and Theology: A Dialectical Comparison of Wilhelm Dilthey's Critique of Historical Reason and Bernard Lonergan's Meta-Methodology" (unpublished doctoral dissertation, University of Münster, 1974), esp. pp. 540–712, for an invaluable survey of references to these issues in relationship to theology. My own use of these resources, as this chapter manifests, is a highly limited, indeed, here a merely formal one: to suggest its methodological importance for theology of a revisionist *praxis*. I hope, in the future, to be able to address the issue in more substantive terms.

(14) The papal social encyclicals may serve as an excellent example of the first possibility, as may several modern Catholic formulations of the importance of *orthopraxis* in relationship to *orthodoxy*. Among the radical theologians, cf. Thomas J. J. Altizer, *The Descent into Hell* (New York: Lippincott, 1970), esp. pp. 52–58.

(15) In American culture, these possibilities may perhaps be symbolized by the kind of liberalism represented by *The New York Times, Harper's, Saturday Review, Time, Newsweek, The New Republic*, etc., and by the kind of secular neo-orthodoxy represented by *Commentary*, and the often secular neo-orthodox radicalism of *The New York Review of Books*. In theology, for an example of a discussion between several

liberal and neo-orthodox radicals (along with some revisionists), cf. the important collection, *Hope and the Future of Man*, ed. Ewert H. Cousins (Philadelphia: Fortress, 1972).

(16) An example would be the liberals' enduring analysis of the social character of the transmission of sin classically presented in Walter Rauschenbusch, *A Theology for the Social Gospel* (New York: Macmillan, 1918), esp. pp. 65–69.

(17) Inter alia, cf. Reinhold Niebuhr's early work, *Beyond Tragedy* (New York: Scribner's, 1937).

(18) For several analyses of the enduring impact of Reinhold Niebuhr's work, cf. the essays by Langdon Gilkey, Martin Marty, and Roger Shinn in the October, 1974, special "Niebuhr" issue of the *Journal of Religion*; on Barth's impact, cf. Wilhelm Marquardt, *Theologie und Sozialisms: Das Beispiel Karl Barths* (München, 1972).

(19) For the classical systematic expression of this Niebuhrian position, cf. *The Nature and Destiny of Man*, 2 vols. (New York: Scribner's, 1941–1943).

(20) Besides the works of Metz and Moltmann cited elsewhere, cf., inter alia, Carl E. Braaten, *The Future of God: The Revolutionary Dynamics of Hope* (New York: Harper & Row, 1969); Rubem Alves, *Theology of Human Hope* (Washington: Corpus, 1968); Gustavo Gutierrez, *A Theology of Liberation* (Maryknoll, N.Y.: Orbis, 1973); Richard Shaull and Carl Oglesby, *Containment and Change* (New York: Macmillan, 1967); Dorothee Soelle, *Political Theology* (Philadelphia: Fortress, 1974); Juan Luis Segundo, "Liberation: Faith and Ideology," in *Mensaje* (July, 1972); Jürgen Moltmann, *Religion, Revolution and the Future* (New York: Scribner's, 1969). I regret that the present context does not allow me to make more than largely formal remarks on the important and positive constructive suggestions of these diverse thinkers: cf. n. 15 above for the principal conversation-partners and expressed "hope" for future work in this area. For examples of the kind of analysis which this tradition renders available in relationship to the socio-economic-political background of various theologies, cf. M. Xhaufflaire and K. Derksen, *Les deux visages de la théologie de la secularisation* (Tournai, 1970), and M. Xhaufflaire, *La Théologie Politique: Introduction á la théologie politique de J.B. Metz* (Paris: 1972).

(21) The most influential example of this probably remains Jürgen Moltmann, *The Theology of Hope: On the Ground and the Implications of a Christian Eschatology* (New York: Harper & Row, 1967), esp. pp. 37–139; In the United States the most eloquent proponent of this tradition is Carl E. Braaten: cf. his *The Future of God*.

(22) Cf. references in chapter two, n. 60; cf. also Dorothee Soelle, *Political Theology*, esp. pp. 1–71.

(23) Cf. esp. the concise summary-analysis of the influence of Hegel's notion here on the Marxian, existentialist, and American empirical traditions in Richard J. Bernstein, *Praxis and Action: Contemporary Philosophies of Human Activity* (Philadelphia: University of Pennsylvania Press, 1971), pp. 1–230; for the historical background in Western philosophy, cf. Nicholas Lobkowicz, *Theory and Practice: History of a Concept from Aristotle to Marx* (Notre Dame: University of Notre Dame Press, 1967); for the analytical tradition, cf. Bernstein, *Praxis and Action*, pp. 231–304, and Glenn Langford, *Human Action* (New York: Doubleday Anchor, 1971).

(24) As indicated before, the American social ethician Gibson Winter is presently developing Heidegger's categories in the direction of a *social* ethics in the sense of a new "ethos": cf. Gibson Winter, "Human Science and Ethics in a Creative Society," in *Cultural Hermeneutics* (1973), pp. 145–77.

(25) For examples of Bloch's work, cf. *Man on His Own* (New York: Herder and Herder, 1970); Bloch's major work, parts of which are translated in the Herder and Herder series, may be found in Ernst Bloch, *Das Prinzip Höffnung* (Frankfurt: Sur-kamp Verlage, 1959). For the critical use of Bloch by the eschatological theologians, cf. Jürgen Moltmann, "Hope and Confidence: A Conversation with Ernst Bloch," in *Religion, Revolution and the Future*, pp. 148–77; Wolfhart Pannenberg, "The God of Hope," in *Basic Questions in Theology* II (Philadelphia: Fortress, 1971), 234–49; Johann Baptist Metz, "Gott vor uns. Statt eines theologischen Arguments," in *Ernst Bloch zu ehren* (Frankfurt, 1965), pp. 227–41.

(26) For the various developments of this method among the Frankfurt thinkers, cf. Martin Jay, *The Dialectical Imagination* (Boston: Little, Brown, 1973). Two major examples of this tradition are now available in English: Theodor W. Adorno's *Negative Dialectics*, and Max Horkheimer and Theodor W. Adorno, *Dialectic of Enlightenment* (New York: Herder and Herder, 1972).

(27) Cf. the discussions between Bloch and the theologians (n. 25 above) to be found in *Ernst Bloch zu ehren*; also Roger Garaudy, *From Anathema to Dialogue* (New York: Herder and Herder, 1966).

(28) The insistence of the Frankfurt School to examine cultural "super-structural" elements over against "orthodox" Marxian analyses of "infra-structural" (economic) factors almost exclusively is documented in Martin Jay, *The Dialectical Imagination*, esp. pp. 173–219. The works of Erich Fromm and Herbert Marcuse are probably the best known examples of this tradition in the English-speaking world. The recent and important work of the American Marxist historian, Eugene D. Genovese, on the role that the "super-structural" factor of religion played in the remarkable survival of enslaved American Blacks may be read as the kind of high-level analysis available here: cf. Eugene D. Genovese, *Roll, Jordan, Roll: The World the Slaves Made* (New York: Pantheon, 1975).

(29) Cf. the powerful and imaginative analysis of these realities in Ernst Bloch, *Das Prinzip Höffnung*, with the exception of the category of "proleptic fulfillment" which is Wolfhart Pannenberg's (cf. esp. *Jesus—God and Man*, pp. 53–66).

(30) Inter alia, cf. Jürgen Moltmann, "What is 'New' in Christianity: The Category *Novum* in Christian Theology," in *Religion, Revolution and the Future*, pp. 3–19; Carl E. Braaten "The Significance of the Future: An Eschatological Perspective," in *Hope and the Future of Man*, pp. 40–55.

(31) This may prove especially true of the theologies of *praxis* emanating not from North American and European but from Latin American sources: the achievements of Gutierrez and Segundo are especially noteworthy here. I wish to express my thanks to Arturo Gaete, S.J., of the Catholic University at Santiago, Chile, for his aid in helping to initiate my knowledge of these important and new theological possibilities.

(32) A major philosophical point of the process tradition employed in chapter eight, after all, is the demand for a social understanding of all reality: inter alia, cf. Charles Hartshorne, *Reality as Social Process* (Boston: Beacon, 1953). The *praxis* possibilities of some aspects of this tradition are discussed in Bernstein, *Praxis and Action*, pp. 165–230.

(33) Cf. chapter five on limit-language and the criticisms of the inadequacies on the symbolic level of the process theologies in chapter eight.

(34) It is perhaps noteworthy that Karl-Otto Appel and Jürgen Habermas have reopened the transcendental questions in the context of critical social theory: cf. Karl-Otto Appel, *Die Transformation der Philosophie* (Frankfurt, 1973); Jürgen Habermas, *Theorie der Gesellschaft oder Sozialtechnologie*, pp. 142–91. For one important study of this tradition and its relationship to theological concerns, cf. Matthew L. Lamb, "Methodology, Metascience and Political Theology" (to be published in Proceedings of Lonergan Workshop, Boston College, 1974, by Darton, Longman & Todd). I am also indebted here to the work of Dennis McCann who is presently engaged in a study of Reinhold Niebuhr's theology as critically interpreted from the viewpoint of this tradition.

(35) It is interesting to note, for example, that Gustavo Gutierrez in *A Theology of Liberation* applies critical reflection on *praxis* (pp. 6–21) with convincing power to the concept of "development" in favor of the concept of "liberation" (pp. 21–43), but does not apply that same method to any of the major Christian doctrines which inform his important work.

(36) This seems true of the important book by Robert W. Jenson, *The Knowledge of Things Hoped For: The Sense of Theological Discourse* (New York: Oxford University Press, 1969); for example, cf. pp. 232–33.

(37) A major exception here is Wolfhart Pannenberg who, with his own form of a revisionist eschatological theology, seems to me clearly to break with a neo-orthodox mode and enter into a revision of such central doctrines as the doctrine of God, revelation, and christology. Besides the work of Pannenberg already cited, cf. John B. Cobb, Jr., and James M. Robinson (eds.), *Theology As History* (New York: Harper & Row, 1967).

(38) For Rahner's position here, cf. "Concerning the Relationship between Nature and Grace," in *Theological Investigations,* I, pp. 347–82, and "Nature and Grace," in *Theological Investigations,* IV, pp. 165–88; for Bultmann, cf. the relevant texts cited and criticized in Schubert M. Ogden, *Christ Without Myth*, pp. 111–26.

(39) For summary-analyses of the Marxist critiques, cf. the essays in *Is God Dead?* Concilium 16 (New York: Paulist, 1966) by Gaston Fessard (pp. 7–25), Jürgen Moltmann (pp. 25–41), and Irving Fetscher (pp. 131–57).

(40) Jürgen Moltmann's dogmatic theology seems especially pertinent here. In either his earlier *The Theology of Hope* or his recent *The Crucified God* one may find both incisive criticisms of the existentialism of his neo-orthodox predecessors and disclosive analyses of the existential-as-politically-transformative power of the eschatological symbols while the same kind of neo-orthodox mode of paradoxical critique seems to continue. Carl E. Braaten, on the other hand, seems often open to

these constructive difficulties (cf. his comments on John Cobb in *The Future of God*, pp. 171-2, n. 2), and sometimes seems purely neo-orthodox (cf. his "The Significance of the Future: An Eschatological Perspective," op. cit., esp. pp. 49-54). For an example of the seeming inability of a neo-orthodox theologian of *praxis* to understand the very problematic of revisionist theological work, cf. Frederick Herzog's review of John Cobb's *Liberal Christianity at the Crossroads* in *Theology Today* 31 (1974), 164-5. For Herzog's own suggestive work, cf. *Liberation Theology* (New York: Seabury, 1972).

(41) Besides Pannenberg, the recent work of Johann Baptist Metz and Marcel Xhaufflaire seems to me clearly indicative of positions beyond neo-orthodoxy and involved in revisionist theologies. Besides the works already cited, cf. Matthew Lamb's interpretation of Metz's political theology, "Les présuppositions méthodologiques de la théologie politique," in M. Xhaufflaire (ed.), *La Pratique de la théologie politique* (Tournai, 1974). In the Latin American context, the work of Hugo Assman and Juan Luis Segundo seem indicative of this kind of direction in a manner which the work of Gustavo Gutierrez may not be (cf. n. 35 above): cf. esp. Hugo Assman, *Oppresion-Liberacion: Desafio a Los Cristianos* (Montevideo: Tierra Nueva, 1971)—I am dependent here on the interpretation of Mr. Joseph Holland (Center for Concern) on the nature of Assman's work.

(42) Cf. Jürgen Habermas, "Ernst Bloch—A Marxist Romantic," in *Salmagundi* 10 (1970), 311-25. I understand Habermas' critical but basically positive analysis of Bloch's work here to be a secular parallel to what I hope is the critical, but basically positive, appraisal of the theologies of *praxis* outlined in this chapter.

(43) That this latter tradition still provides liberating possibilities seems to me to be the case; for arguments to this effect, cf. Richard J. Bernstein, *Praxis and Action*, pp. 165-230, esp. 226-29; Jürgen Habermas, *Knowledge and Human Interests* (Boston: Beacon, 1971), esp. pp. 121-39, for a critical analysis of Peirce's work; for an analysis of the developments in American sociology with an argument for what might be labelled "liberating" possibilities, cf. Alvin W. Gouldner, *The Coming Crisis of Western Sociology* (New York: Avon, 1970), esp. pp. 373-410 and 481-513.

(44) It bears repetition to note that either the present formulation of *a* revisionist application (chapters five to nine) or the present appeal to the Frankfurt School are not meant to be exclusive examples of revisionist possibilities. For example, it seems to me that, although Gregory Baum's comments on what might be called the "revisionist" pastoral importance of Andrew Greeley's theological position in *The New Agenda* (Garden City: Doubleday, 1974) are entirely correct (ibid., "Foreword" by Gregory Baum, pp. 11-35), it would be incorrect to describe Greeley's political outlook as "somewhat conservative" (p. 21). The latter seems clearly liberal in the sense of articulating an American politics of liberal coalition. Furthermore, the kind of survey-research which American sociologists have perfected seems not only still appropriate but necessary. Indeed, one cannot but wish that such social theorists as the Frankfurt School might pay more attention to such needs, in a manner similar to Bernard Lonergan's recent plea for theologians of liberation to work in an interdisciplinary fashion with economists, and with James Gustafson's insistence that one not move from theology to politics without explicit sophisticated ethical reflection. My own conviction remains that only genuinely interdisciplinary work among empirical sociologists and economists (for providing the crucial data needed), critical social theorists, ethicians, and revisionist *praxis*-theologians (for providing heuristic

models for critical-*praxis* transformation) will allow for the eventual development of an adequate model for a revisionist theology of *praxis*. For example, although I do not share Andrew Greeley's mostly negative specific judgments of the Latin American theologians of liberation and the Frankfurt School theorists, I do share the major conviction which seems to inform his critique: the need for relating hard empirical data to what I would call heuristic models for critical social theory or theological symbols of liberation. At the same time, the authentically transformative possibilities for a Christian *ethos* provided by the Latin American theologians of liberation and the authentic refinements accorded critical theory in relationship to *praxis* by the Frankfurt theorists (especially Habermas) seem to me to be major resources for any contemporary collaborative attempt at a theology of *praxis*.

(45) This is important to recall insofar as the present comments are largely formal, in terms of methodological needs rather than of substantive proposals.

(46) The principal need here again seems clearly to be for a mode of inter-disciplinary collaboration between survey-researchers, social scientists, ethicians, philosophers, and theologians. Perhaps the German experiment at Bielefeld will prove illustrative here. I fear that anyone attempting to perform all these tasks on his own is either the most startling genius to appear since Leibniz or seriously deluded.

(47) It should be noted that the same methodological rule on the need for a hermeneutical collaboration of the limit-situations of the religious dimension of our common experience and the limit-language of the Christian religious tradition cited in chapters four–six would be applicable to theological discussions of *praxis*.

(48) Besides the works already cited, cf. Daniel Callahan's essays and editorial contributions to *The Hastings Center Studies: Institute of Society, Ethics and the Life Sciences*; Gibson Winter, *Elements for A Social Ethic* (New York: Macmillan, 1968); and the sections and references in Catholic social ethics in the invaluable annual review of moral theology by Richard J. McCormick in *Theological Studies*; for excellent examples of the Catholic social-ethical tradition at work, cf. the essays by J. Bryan Hehir and Peter Henriot in *Theological Studies* 35 (1974), pp. 47–70, 71–82, respectively; as well as Gregory Baum's use of Weber and Durkheim in "The Survival of the Sacred," *The Persistence of Religion*, Concilium 81, pp. 11–23.

(49) To continue to use that theological language, the present chapter does not claim to provide "fulfillment" here, but only hope and promise!

(50) An example of this possibility at work may prove illustrative here: the American Catholic Church intends to note the bicentennial of the United States by employing the resources of both the American political tradition and the Catholic social-ethical tradition to speak to the questions of American social justice in a manner that might allow for post-critical naiveté towards the disclosive symbolic and conceptual power of both traditions.

(51) Cf. Paulo Freire, inter alia, *Pedagogy of the Oppressed* (New York: Herder and Herder, 1972); for an analysis of Freire's work, cf. "Illiteracy and the Development of Self-Awareness in the Thought of Paulo Freire," by Rogério de Almeida Cunha in *The Crisis of Religious Language*, Concilium 85, pp. 114–27.

(52) For the classical Marxist texts here, cf. *Marx and Engels: On Religion* (Mos-

cow: Progress, 1972), esp. pp. 62–5 (the "Theses on Feuerbach"), and pp. 78–80 *(The Communist Manifesto)*. For a review of the history of the Marxist critique on religion, cf. the article by Irving Fetscher in *Is God Dead?* Concilium 16, pp. 131–57.

(53) Bernard Lonergan, *Method in Theology*, p. xi.

Index of Persons

Index of Subjects